From Housewife to Heretic

From Housewife to Heretic

SONIA JOHNSON

ANCHOR BOOKS
ANCHOR PRESS/DOUBLEDAY
GARDEN CITY, NEW YORK
1983

Anchor Books edition: 1983

Library of Congress Cataloging in Publication Data
Johnson, Sonia.
From Housewife to Heretic.
1. Johnson, Sonia. 2. Mormons—United States—
Biography. 3. Feminists—United States—Biography.
4. Sex discrimination against women—Law and
legislation—United States. I. Title.
BX8695.J65A34 1983   289.3′3 [B]
ISBN 0-385-17494-2 (pbk.)
Library of Congress Catalog Card Number 80-2964

*In love and gratitude
to the innumerable women in this country
whose dedicated labor for women's rights
never makes headlines*

Contents

8   *From Housewife to Heretic*

Author's Note

SHORTLY AFTER the excommunication I was in Boise, Idaho, as the speaker at an ERA rally, and did several short TV interviews. At the end of one of these, the young cameraman came up to me with a puzzled expression on his face. "But you're just a mom!" he said with great disappointment. I suppose I was the first heretic he had ever seen, and he had hoped for something more than "just a mom." I smiled and said to myself, "You know, Sonia, you've come a long way from housewife to heretic, and in a very short time."

That's the story I'm going to tell.

The only thing that makes my story different from the stories of most other women is the formal trial and expulsion. What happened to me spiritually has happened, is happening, and will continue to happen to women all over the world by the millions.

My story is every woman's story.

Acknowledgments

My special thanks to Susan Grode, my lawyer, personal counselor and friend, who told me I *must* write this book and assured me I could. And to my editor, Loretta Barrett, who believed in me and the book from the very beginning and, with great skill and caring, guided me through to its completion.

To my children—Eric, Kari, Marc, and Noel—for understanding and support beyond their years.

To Arlene Wood, Hazel Rigby, and Cari Beauchamp who stood lovingly at my side when I needed them most.

And to my mother, Ida Harris, who taught me to love truth and through whose life I came to hate injustice.

Acknowledgments

My special thanks to Susan Cameron and Ray, an person number one, and to all who told me if this world, his book and answer, the guide and many other. Finally, thank you. The believed in me and we both may the very beginning and, with great skill and the could time through the important ...

To my sister Rita, whose care under the deep care and ...

To Angus Wood, Hazel Kirby, and Cal, his mouth of who worth his father in the ...

And to my author Michelle, who hung ...
through ...

From Housewife to Heretic

Chapter 1

The Play's the Thing

December 5, 1979

". . . the decision of this court is that you are excommunicated from the Church of Jesus Christ
of Latter-day Saints. I must remind you that all
privileges of membership are hereby denied by
this action . . . I strongly encourage you to
repent. . . ."

REPENT OF WHAT, I wonder now. Of being happier than I have ever
been in my life? Because as I look up from my typewriter at the
snowy woods outside my window in the Virginia winter of 1979, I realize that I never *have* been happier.

Angry, too, of course. Angry that women must wage such long and
desperate battle for dignity against such immense odds. Yes angry,
very angry at that. But not sad anymore. I wake now to days rich
with purpose and the most deeply satisfying work I have ever done
or can imagine doing. In my favorite version of the future, this is the
work I do uninterruptedly until I die, this work for women, whom I
love. Now, all day long I go about it serene at the core of myself, perpetually delighted by the unfolding miracle of myself which is only
the everyday miracle of being human, humble before the extraordinary good luck of being alive at this time and in this place. Because I see the best of myself in all humankind, I am buoyed by
hope. And full of faith, especially in women.

Against yesterday's somber backdrop, today's well-being seems all
the more luminous and wonderful. There was a time not long ago

when I could not even imagine feeling such happiness as I feel now. A dark time when I thought my heart would ache forever.

I remember the exact moment the light first failed. And as we do with moments of crisis (where were *you* when John Kennedy was shot?), I recall every detail with a preternatural clarity: the very black night, blackness almost thick enough to extinguish the headlights; the *thwack thwack* of the windshield wipers, the sizzle of the tires on the wet pavement; the mingled odor of damp car, freshly shampooed hair and showered bodies, shaving lotion, perfume; Rick's face appearing whitely now and then in the approaching lights of other cars then fading back to dimness . . . all the sensory data of that moment are so totally accessible today that remembering has the power to break my heart all over again.

So now that I must write it all down, I find I can hardly bear to think of it. A year later, remembering can plunge me back so completely into that moment that it is impossible to get enough distance to deal with it myself, let alone to tell it properly to anyone else. In fact, I wonder how in the world I am going to tell it at all. Through tears, that much is certain.

I can at least give the story line.

We were on our way to a play in Washington, D.C., that rainy October night, my husband of twenty years and I, driving along on Route 7 past the little white shack with the sign on it announcing: "Steamed Crabs—Enter." (We had laughed at that sign ever since Rick had once suggested putting up another next to it cautioning: "All Others—Keep Out!") I had my hand on his gas-pedal knee, enjoying the rhythm of his muscles tightening and relaxing as he lifted his foot off the gas or stepped on the brake.

It was Halloween. Time for a little trickery.

We hadn't been talking much, but I had been thinking, thinking and feeling good about Rick and me. He had recently returned from six months in Liberia. During his absence we had both thought a lot about the dynamics of marriage in general and ours in particular, and he had come back with some practical suggestions for improvement. Not that ours was a bad marriage—in fact, I had always regarded it as one of the best I knew. But it was twenty years old, and like many others its age it was in the humdrums, the ho-hums, becalmed in the doldrums. It had, in short, become boring.

But there had been more than boredom to threaten it over the years. There had been several very rough patches along the way which at the time we had not been at all sure we would weather. All along, one of my major complaints was his absence from home, and even worse, his absence when he *was* home. For long stretches I felt as if I had not seen him for weeks, though his body might have been around a good deal of that time. His method of facing difficulty was withdrawal, which seemed a personal affront to me, and did not make him the most approachable parent in the world, either.

Heaven knows, he also had much to tolerate from me. But he is no confronter, and often kept his criticism or hurt from me for months, sometimes for years, so that I did not have the information I needed along the way to change things.

Rick seems to have begun life with sealed lips. He recounts a boyhood story of quietly, laboriously saving up a hundred dollars from his paper route when he was only a kid—ten or twelve years old—to buy a motorbike. When he came home with the new machine, his astonished parents, who had been kept in darkest ignorance of the stash, were positive he had stolen it. He had a difficult time convincing them he had been saving money for well over a year without their knowing it. "Kids can't keep secrets like that," they insisted. They did not know their Dickie.

I was never good at secrets, though, so I did not understand how to deal with this aspect of him. Always wanting things open between us, even if it meant discomfort, I never kept anything from him very long. All I had done wrong I had confessed to him and thoroughly repented of, in the church-prescribed way, years before. I always assumed that he was dealing with me with equal candor. And I refused to entertain for very long any suspicion that he might not be. I knew Rick. He was a good man.

While he was in Liberia thinking it all over for six months, he had decided, he informed me when he returned, that it was the institution of marriage itself that was the chief villain in our case, or at least the institution as it has been traditionally conceived in our culture. He concluded that our society's concept of marriage carries with it countless stereotypical expectations which leave couples with so little emotional room to maneuver that relationships strangle in their own web of role restrictions. Perhaps, he suggested tentatively one day—and went on to elaborate upon more fluently in the days to come—we would have an easier time establishing new ways of relat-

ing to each other if we were not so bound by conventional husband–wife, head–subordinate, breadwinner–nurturer, independent–dependent dichotomies. What did I think of getting a secret
divorce, one that only we knew about, to see whether being free of
those artificial restraints made any difference in our ability to change
the pattern—get out of the rut—of our life together?

Like Vietnam, it occurs to me now: destroy it to save it.

The idea of divorce, real or imaginary, frightened me, and I told
him so. Divorce meant life without Rick in it, and life without Rick
in it was inconceivable. He admitted that divorce frightened him
also, but assured me that the divorce would not be "real" in an emotional or practical sense, just philosophically; that he loved me and
would still be as committed to our relationship as ever—growing ever
more so—and that our deciding to stay and work together even when
we both secretly knew we were not legally bound to do so anymore
would prove, and strengthen, our love for each other.

I finally agreed to this "fake" divorce, partly because he was very
tender and very persuasive, but partly also because the health of our
marriage had always been solely my province—a heavy responsibility
that for a long time I had deeply resented bearing alone. I was
delighted and relieved to see him interested enough at last to carry
his share. Let me not to the true minding of marriage admit im-
pediment, thought I to myself.

In fact, he had taken the initiative in other, smaller, ways since he
had come home. For one thing, he had moved into his own bedroom
so, he explained, our sleeping together would be a deliberate choice,
not just a habit. We had been apart for six months at that time and
were both accustomed to sleeping alone, so I did not object, though
I felt a pang of rejection. But I reminded myself that he was doing it
for us, and that I should feel glad that he was consciously directing
his attention to a partnership we had both always expected to last
not just a lifetime but forever.

As time went on, I remember thinking he must care about us a
great deal to be spending so much time doing research in the library
about such things as property settlements and out-of-country divorces, to be paying a lawyer for consultation (to say that Rick is pe-
nurious is to indulge in flagrant understatement), to be so actively
and persistently taking charge of our marriage remodeling. And I was
confident of the outcome. With both of us now taking marital mat-

ters in hand, how could we fail? I had great faith in the Rick–Sonia team. So far, we had not failed at anything we had set our combined wills to.

Two days before the ride in the rain, I had signed the "fake" divorce before a notary, after seeing in Rick's face only reassurance, only benign good will.

(Anyone with any perception reading this will have difficulty believing that I couldn't see what was coming. I was totally blind, absolutely, besottedly trusting.)

Thinking about all this, I told Rick as we rode along in the rain how glad I was that we had decided not to bring our houseguest with us to the play and that we were alone. "We're going to have to try to spend more time together now that we're doing radical surgery on our marriage," I said.

Then, in a quiet, uninflected voice, he said the unthinkable thing: "I'm tired of working on our marriage. I don't care about it anymore. I meant that divorce to be real."

Now I have come to the part that I do not even know how to talk about. What can I say that would begin to convey the anguish of being betrayed by the man who for twenty years had been my best and dearest friend? I can only state a fact: for months after Rick's treachery, I ached from head to foot as if I had contracted a particularly virulent strain of flu. (Of course, a second betrayal, which was even then preparing to lunge at me from the wings, was to add its own unique dimension.)

While I drowned in pain, we drove on to the play. Looking back, I marvel at the absurdity of following through with our social schedule as if the earth were still solid, not shifting and breaking apart beneath my feet. Perhaps my failure to suggest the reasonable course of turning around and going home reveals more clearly than words the depth of my shock. As we do at such times, I turned on my automatic pilot and went through the motions of normalcy on the outside, so that I could concentrate all my powers on surviving the near-mortal wound inside.

So, absurdly enough, we went to the play, and I learned another thing or two about human nature. Although I wept unceasingly throughout—tears soaking my sweater and eyes swelling up like Mr. Magoo—and because of my emotional disarray might be expected not to remember anything at all about the play, in fact I remember it well. Which reminds me of the old sick joke: "But aside from that, Mrs. Lincoln, how did you like the play?" Mary Lincoln and I both lost our husbands violently around curtain time. Perhaps she liked the play. I know I did, strange to say, and can see it now in color and detail—*Teibele and her Demon*—on my mind's stage from start to finish.

And Sonia wrestling with hers, down front in the audience.

When, several days later, I was able to tell my friend Hazel what had happened, she was incredulous.* Never for one second would she have trusted her husband in such a situation, but then she had never really succumbed, as I had, to the ideal-Mormon-woman stereotype. She had somehow always managed to keep a healthy hold on reality; she hadn't bought the myths.

"This isn't the image I have of you, Sonia," she reproved me. "I can't believe you would be so naïve. I remember you as a graduate student at the University of Minnesota: independent, ambitious, successful, associating as an equal with men and women in your department who were neither naïve nor stupid. I'm shocked that you would allow yourself to be so easily duped. You *must* have realized that it might be a real divorce to him, that he might try to make that preposterous property settlement stick. How could you have trusted him so? Surely you must have wanted to be divorced or you would never have signed that paper."

Well, consciously at least, I did not want a divorce, and I did trust, and if my friends had not been very firm with me, I would have let Rick walk all over me with that preposterous property settlement—because he told me in his customary wiser-than-thou voice that it was a marvelously fair and just document, and I had always so *believed* him and expected him to watch out for my welfare that I could not understand at first that it was *him* against *me* and that he would take me for all he could. It was a real awakening, an ugly jolt, but good for me. His being so thoroughly a cad finally released me from him as nothing else could ever have done.

It was still raining when we came out of the play and began the long drive home to Virginia. In the dark, we took the wrong turning and found ourselves at 11 P.M. in Washington, D.C., coming down

---

* We had met Hazel Davis Rigby and her husband, Ron, when we were all members of the same group of young married couples in the Minneapolis Second Ward.

Constitution Avenue toward Roosevelt Bridge. As we headed into the intersection at the corner of Seventeenth and Constitution, a car from our left ran the red light. Rick didn't see it, but hit the brakes when I screamed. Too late. We slammed into its back fender, spun completely around, and found when we were able to assess the damage that, though no one was hurt in either car, ours was demolished beyond repair. The police found a cab driver who would take us clear out to our house—if his wife could come along to keep him company.

Accidents like that are no accident, rather dramatizations of inner violence.

We were both very shaken. My teeth were chattering and I noticed disinterestedly that though I was not cold, I was shivering. In the back seat of the cab on the way home to Virginia, Rick held me in his arms across his lap, as we had sat thousands of times in our life together, and with my face pressed against his shoulder I went on with the serious business of grieving and remembering—remembering from the first, mourning for it all.

Chapter 2

The Man Who Didn't Rock Ferris-wheel Seats

SUMMER SCHOOL at Utah State University, 1958. The first day I attended my psychology course, Rick walked in about ten minutes late: tall, slightly built, very thin, very dark, very intense, in a black knit shirt with white perspiration rings around the armholes, a crew cut and sunglasses. I recognized him from an education class we'd both taken the year before, and from seeing him around campus. In a predominantly Mormon campus population, he stood out as one of the "wild gentile Easterners." He was from Wisconsin—"back East" —and traveled with what I regarded as a fast crowd, including actual Jews from New York! (Utah is perhaps the only place in the world where Jews are gentiles. To Mormons, all non-Mormons are "gentiles.") And because I firmly intended to marry a Mormon, preferably a returned missionary, I hadn't given Richard Johnson a second glance.

The class, which met on the top floor of Old Main (the hottest spot in Cache Valley that summer), had about a dozen members. One of the major objectives of the professor was to have us all administer several different types of tests, score them, interpret them, and then write up the results as if we were actually school psychologists. So though we spent lots of time harassing our friends and families into letting us test them, other members of the class were nearest and fairest game.

When I arrived at the testing lab one day to do some work and found the door locked, I remembered that the geology museum next door was always nearly empty and had large tables. So I went in and there, sitting at the table nearest the door, was Rick. Our faces lit up as each recognized the other as a member of the class, and therefore a prime candidate for testing.

It was the first time we'd ever spoken to each other. I sat down across the table from him and we began. By the time we finished that day, we felt very amicable. Having scored nearly identically on the psychological inventories and extraordinarily close on the IQ measures and interest tests, we were both thinking, "Anyone so much like me can't be *all* bad!"

We continued to test each other through June, feeling only friendly toward each other. But on July 3, when we agreed to meet in the lab again the next day, we both sensed that matters were escalating to an altogether different kind of session. From a window of Old Main the next morning, I watched Rick drive up. He had sunglasses on and was wearing his black knit shirt. (He had two shirts at that time; the other was a red knit, also with white perspiration rings.) Instead of working, he invited me for a ride in the chartreuse Ford convertible he so proudly called Bucephalus. So off we went on the brightest blue day, through Blacksmith Fork Canyon across into Logan Canyon.

The road was nearly impassable in those days, and Bucephalus's tires were old, but we still must have set some kind of a record that day—three blowouts! Finally abandoning Bu and making our way down the canyon in the back of a truck on which we'd hitched a ride, Rick taught me, "I've got sixpence, jolly jolly sixpence." We roared, "There's a long, long trail awinding," "Tell me why," and "Shine on harvest moon" to the granite walls and swift river of the canyon and to passing motorists all the way down into town, where we bought another tire, borrowed a cab (from Dean Allen, from whom Rick earned board and room by keeping the cab radios in repair), and rushed back up to rescue Bu.

For a first date, it wasn't exactly run-of-the-mill.

Neither was the second, which intrigued me as most boys I knew had extremely limited ideas of things to do with girls. Rick called for me on a tandem bike and we pedaled over to Hyrum Dam, a journey of about six hilly miles. As soon as we'd found a nice spot on the beach of the reservoir, Rick actually began laying out the lunch. I wasn't surprised—I was flabbergasted! No *Mormon* boy I knew would invite a girl on a picnic and *bring the lunch himself!* It was always assumed that if a young man deigned to lend you his company, it behooved you to show proper gratitude by bringing the food. But since Rick hadn't mentioned it, and since I've hated preparing food since birth (probably because I could see eighty or ninety years of it stretching ahead of me without intermission), I hadn't. *My* presence, I had thought, would have to be enough for *him*.

Well, he'd not only prepared a lunch, but had made a special beet sauce for our ham sandwiches from a magazine recipe. Imagine! He wasn't just sitting around waiting for me to impress him; *he* wanted to impress *me!* I was entranced, and very touched. Little things mean a lot to the oppressed!

I have a picture in my mind from that day, as sharp and clear as the best photograph: Rick, wearing a snug black-and-white checkered swimming suit, standing on a small bluff, poised against the summer sky, lean, his legs as spare as those of the long-distance runner he was. He had his arms over his head, balancing on his toes, and then, with an imperceptible push, he dove almost splashless into the water.

Oh dear, dark boy. There was such promise of happiness balanced there. But your mama never rocked you when you were a baby, you say, and your daddy died when you were seventeen. And all the rest of us can never make it up to you.

"Come into the water," he called, swimming back to the beach.

"Promise not to duck or splash me, and I will," I called back. I was serious about that, but I didn't expect him to believe it. I'd made the same request, in seriousness, of dozens of boys and young men in my life. Without exception they had interpreted it as a flirtatious request to be ducked and splashed. And so although they'd laughingly promise, as soon as I'd jump in, they'd promptly duck and splash me. It was miserable and ruined my pleasure in swimming, and also hurt my feelings. But I tried to be a good sport and play by the rules—I wouldn't let on.

Of course Rick promised he wouldn't duck or splash, and of course I jumped in not believing him for a moment, ready to defend myself from a strong hand pushing me under or crashing water in my face as soon as I broke the surface, but miracle of miracles, he didn't live down to my expectations. In all our times together in the lakes and oceans and swimming pools of the world over the next twenty-one years, he never ducked or splashed me. It is a rare and wonderful experience, when you're female, to be taken seriously.

The bicycle-built-for-two afternoon still held surprises for me. We'd hiked such a long way around the dam to get to our secluded spot on the beach that by the time we were ready to head home, we were looking for shortcuts back to the bike. So rather than walking around, we swam across an inlet, holding our clothes out of the water with one hand. I'd put my sunglasses—brand-new and the first real pair I'd ever owned—on top of my clothes, and in the middle of the inlet they slid off. Down into the deep silt at the bottom.

As a rule I get over things quickly, and by the time we reached the other side I'd already resigned myself to the loss. But for a moment there in the water I'd been dismayed, and Rick had seen.

That was Saturday. As usual, on Sunday I went to church several times. On Monday, Rick came late to class as usual and sat at the end of my row. A few minutes later, I noticed something being passed along the row toward me. Then the person next to me handed me my sunglasses, the ones that should have been on the bottom of Hyrum Dam. After class, the story came out: while I was in church, Rick had gone back to the dam with his Aqualung and dived until he'd found them.

What about a guy like that! I felt cherished.

Today as I write this, it is July 25, 1980. Yesterday was Pioneer Day in Utah, the day Utahns commemorate the 1847 entrance of the first Mormon pioneers into the valley of the great Salt Lake. Yesterday, the biggest parade of the year took place in Salt Lake and Mormons for ERA from five states handed out white helium-filled balloons with "ERA YES" written across them in dark green letters, while overhead a plane towed a banner proclaiming, "In your heart you know Sonia's right!"

But twenty-two years ago on July 24, Rick and I went to the Pioneer Day celebration in Hyrum, Utah, arriving at the carnival just at dusk, that mysterious time I've always loved. The Ferris wheel glowed yellow against the mauve sky, and the tinny music of all the rides mixed together in that blur of sound that has an edge of sadness to it, as if it is already only memory.

As we wandered among the concessions, all the elements of carnival blended together to work their familiar magic in my heart: the smells of kicked-up dust, popcorn, and sweat, the surreal music, the incandescent curve of the Ferris wheel rising above it all. And through and over everything, the sweet sense of Mormon triumph.

It was too much for me. I wanted to hold it all to myself some-how, to see it all at once. "Let's go on the Ferris wheel!" I cried, and then quickly added as we turned in that direction, "but please be careful about rocking the seat, because I'm afraid of Ferris wheels. When I was a little girl, I lived only a few blocks from the fair grounds in Preston, Idaho, where the carnivals always set up. One night a seat broke loose as the wheel was turning, and spilled three people down into the machine. I've never forgotten the horror stories that circulated for weeks after that incident, and although I love Ferris wheels, whenever I'm on one I'm in terror that the seat will break loose and send *me* smashing down through the yellow-lighted girders."

By this time, we were being locked into the seat and I was re-counting to myself how many times I'd asked fellows not to rock the seat. How many times I'd told them that it really frightened me and would spoil my pleasure in the ride. And how every time they had as-sumed that it was part of my "helpless female" line, a hint for them to do that very thing so I could squeal prettily and cling to them. Maybe they enjoyed frightening me, or maybe it made them feel strong and powerful. Whatever the case, they *always* rocked the seat.

Never was there a more perfect night to ride the Ferris wheel than on the twenty-fourth of July, 1958. It was about 9 P.M.—early enough that the valley still held a little of the day's light, like a bowl, with the sky darkening into a glorious purple at the edges. And all alone, pure and steady in the west, the evening star brightening.

Down into the noise and dust we swooped, and up again into the cool canyon air. Then there were the stops to empty and refill the seats, and finally the grand moment when the machinery lurched to a stop and we found ourselves on the very top of the wheel, on the very top of the world, the seat swinging gently.

I waited. Gradually, the swinging stopped and we were still. I looked out at the lights below, the black shapes of the mountains be-yond, and the spunky little stars beginning to take over the sky, all through a blur of tears. Turning my head away from Rick and blink-ing hard and fast to keep the tears from falling, I marveled at how moved I was that he sat there so quietly, as if he weren't breathing.

At the time I couldn't understand the intensity of my reaction to such a little thing, though for an instant—and it was a feminist seed that would blossom twenty years later—I realized how little attention anyone had ever given to my wishes. I didn't know then that this is the natural condition of women in the world. I only knew that my heart swelled painfully and I began to cry because Richard Johnson, the stormy-looking "Easterner" from Wisconsin, sat still at the top of the Ferris wheel on Pioneer Day.

We kissed for the first time a week or so later, the loveliest kiss of my life: gentle, soft, urgent, and only one. Later that night, when I tiptoed into the bedroom I shared that summer with my friend Janice Baer, she was still awake. "You're going to marry that guy," she prophesied. "Don't be ridiculous," I said; "he's not even a member of the church." "Just remember that I said so," she yawned as she turned out the light.

By October he had seen the missionaries and was ready to join the Mormon church. In November, he was baptized and we thought of marrying in December, but besides my wanting a temple marriage—one in which we would be married for eternity as well as for our lifetimes, and which would not be possible until he had been a member of the church for at least a year—we weren't getting along well all of the time.

The main problem, it seemed to me, was that he wouldn't talk about the things that upset him, or let me talk about those that upset me. When the going got tough, he would simply leave. One night, as we were sitting on the floor in front of the stereo in my parents' living room, supposedly listening to music but actually quarreling—heaven knows about what—he suddenly got up and walked out the front door. At the window, my hands clenched at my sides, I watched him get into his car and drive away. Then I shouted after him (though, of course, he couldn't hear it), "That's the last time you walk out on me, Rick Johnson!"

Famous last words.

The next morning, shaking with anger, I took an armful of signs over to the house where he shared a room with another fellow and hung them up all over the place. The signs announced that I was through with him, and that this was Act 5, Scene 5—there wouldn't be any more acts or any more scenes with him.

But I loved him, and my anger wore off quickly.

Late that night, I took one of the marathon walks that characterized my adolescence and early adulthood. Dressed in my warmest clothes, I walked through empty streets piled with frozen snow, down to the railroad station, and then south to what we called the West Fields. My boots crunched noisily in the winter stillness. Though I hadn't encountered a single car, still I waited until the West Fields road to begin my business in earnest.

My business was prayer. As I walked, I prayed aloud, my heart seeking my Father in Heaven, pleading, pleading with him for Rick Johnson, telling him how much I wanted him, trying to force heaven to deliver him to me.

I had walked, my cheeks blistered with freezing tears, to the end of the road, when suddenly, in a rush of understanding, I stopped in the middle of the moonlit snow. Standing quite still, I stopped pleading and made the most important discovery of my young womanhood (which, unfortunately, I was not able to hold onto and am just now having to make again in my maturity). "Father," I prayed, "I give him up, gladly, if I shouldn't have him. Forgive me for telling you what to do. I don't have to have him to live. I can bear it."

And I knew I could. The discovery made me feel suddenly strong and sure. I knew that with or without Rick Johnson, I could go on with my life.

Having let go of Rick, I turned around and walked home, whole and calm. Mourning, but able to bear it. Grieving, but not incapacitated.

To understand how extraordinary this feeling was, it is necessary to understand that *I was a perfectly conditioned patriarchal woman.* By that, I mean I was well integrated into a society that believes that women are made to please men. A society that believes that a woman needs the acceptance of a certain caliber of man in order to prove that she is worthy, that she is legitimate, a "real woman." And I had never questioned it. I had always accepted the concept that I needed a man to "complete" me. I believed I could only exist through the name and eyes of a member of the superior, the acceptable-in-themselves, male race. As a woman, I had to have a man front for me in society, a man to lean on, to depend on for my definition of myself. And by remaining single past what was considered the norm in Mormon culture, I was already proving that I was psychologically warped and emotionally grotesque—in short, an unacceptable specimen.

At twenty-two I was a profoundly dependent woman, looking for some man (not just *any* man—despite my desperation, I was still discriminating) to fasten this dependency upon—someone to take responsibility for my life, the life, I had been taught, that I could not handle adequately myself.

None of this, of course, was conscious.

But that one bitter cold night I walked home in peace, at least temporarily. I was through storming heaven, through trying to force God. I would face what came and give up the manipulation, the continual lobbying of heaven that I'd learned from my mother. I had courage, at least momentarily.

A few nights later, I found a poem Rick had put on the driver's seat of our old gray Studebaker. In it he begged my forgiveness. The last lines read:

> *But I know that my biggest fault*
> *was just the loss of you.*

And so Rick and I tried again, both full of tumultuous feelings and having a tumultuous courtship. By spring, it was off again and we were both dating others.

At the beginning of spring quarter, I moved into a one-room apartment in a private home across from the Institute of Religion on campus. The year before, when I was a senior, I'd moved from my parents' home downtown up to a dorm and had since tried several other living arrangements, which were adequate but not nearly as heavenly as this little apartment. Rick had found it originally, but I'd talked him out of it—the view over Cache Valley was stunning and a little brook splashed beneath the window—and he'd gone instead to board with my parents down on Center Street. Years later he revealed to me his bitterness, still intact after more than a decade, at my having taken that apartment from him, though he'd said nothing at the time. I asked him why he hadn't spoken up then, why he'd saved it for so long and nurtured it so. He replied that it was just his usual "passive aggressiveness."

This kind of refusal to let me see his real face stood in the way of understanding throughout our married lives. Did it mean he thought

I wasn't strong enough to deal with his anger or his hurt, that I should be protected? Or did it mean he wasn't strong enough for the confrontation, and was protecting himself? (It's my feeling now that men's "protection" of women is typically a protection of their own economic and emotional selves.)

By June, however, we were sweethearts again, and I hoped he'd give me an engagement ring for graduation. Many of my friends were expecting to get them. Instead, he bought me a Rose Marie Reid swimming suit (the implied intimacy of which shocked his mother when she came out for his graduation).

So there I was, twenty-three years old, a college graduate with one year of graduate work, and no engagement ring. I felt a mounting desperation which humiliated me, and which I swore I wouldn't reveal. But how to contain myself? How to keep from telling Rick, or confiding to my friends, that I was in the grip of an incredible, seemingly unconquerable panic?*

One afternoon I saw the solution: an ad on the bulletin board in the union building for camp counselors in Massachusetts. Snatching it off the board, I zipped home and called the number. They'd be happy to have me, they said, but couldn't pay my way East. I vowed to get there somehow.

Two days later, Rick, puzzled and hurt, put me on the train. How could I have made him understand, when I scarcely did myself? Besides, those were definitely the days when rule number one was to keep your courting cards tight against your chest. We couldn't trust each other because male-female relationships were conventionally dishonest and exploitative, and we were children of our time. How could I have explained to him how it felt to be a Mormon woman

---

* When I was twenty-one, a year before Rick came on the scene, I'd felt desperate and shaken enough about being a senior in college and still not engaged that I'd decided to consult a counselor. This man promptly compounded my confusion and hurt by seducing me—a "good Mormon" seduction: everything but actual intercourse, since Mormons promise in the temple to have intercourse only with their legal spouses. (Seducing female patients has long been as much a sport of Mormon male psychotherapists and others in the "helping professions" as it is among non-Mormons.) Nothing more damaging has ever happened to me.

Then, shortly after I met Rick, the head of the English department propositioned me. He said he would make it easy for me to get my master's degree if I'd be his "friend." When I told him my fiancé wouldn't like that, he immediately backed off, respecting the property rights of another man.

Why I ever trusted men is quite beyond me.

my age and not even engaged, to say nothing of married, without terrifying him? Causing him to believe, erroneously, that I wanted to marry *him* only because I wanted to marry *someone*. How could I help him understand the terror of old maidhood that patriarchal culture instills in girls and women—a fate worse than death—and all it implied about non-entry into real life?

Though other young women seemed to glide effortlessly into marriage, most only seemed to. Many felt very alone and unacceptably different, because, like me, they'd rather have died than reveal their panic to anyone. It was a nightmare, but a shameful one. In private, I knelt for hours in prayer beseeching God not to let me fail in this one great above-all-else-necessary-for-life achievement.

Looking back, it's miraculous that our marriage was as stable as it was for as long as it was, considering that I went into it in the fifties, a time when everybody put such enormous and unnatural weight upon marriage as an institution, straining as I did to make it the be-all and end-all my culture teaches it should be. Nothing can stand up forever under such expectations.

I also realize now how much pressure I put on Rick to be a certain way, because as a husband he represented me, *was* me. If only I'd begun living my own life twenty years sooner, I could have left him free to be himself. But by the time I was ready to do so, the unnatural posture of so many years had taken its toll. Marriages of 1950 vintage were pressure cookers. It's hardly surprising that many of them exploded or burned out. And that some of those marriages are not only still intact, but happy speaks highly of the capacity of human beings to change and adapt.

So, full of my shameful secret, I went to Massachusetts and persuaded the camp director to take me on as a counselor—even though I couldn't do the Australian crawl worth a darn—just because I'd come so far on my own.

The camp, on a lovely clean lake surrounded by wooded hills, was all a camp in the Berkshires should be, though there were evidences that it wasn't going to stay that way long. I was put in charge of a cabinful of fourteen-year-old Jewish girls, mostly from New York, who were excitingly different from western, Mormon girls: outwardly tough (which made their vulnerability more poignant), sophisticated, rich, foul of mouth, truly funny, and very perceptive. They sensed immediately that I was made of more naïve stuff, and were thus obliged to initiate me.

It wasn't as if I hadn't learned something in my twenty-three years about toughness. I'd had a trial by fire the year before, doing my student teaching in English with juniors at Logan High School. The first day I appeared in class, the teacher got up from her desk, handed me a book, said "Good luck!" and then disappeared. (I never saw her again that term.) So I stood there, before a class of about thirty-five boys and six girls, totally unprepared—and they knew it. Immediately a blizzard of paper airplanes sprang up, huge, hulking fullbacks began leaping from desk to desk, spitballs spattered on the windows, and everyone generally went berserk.

Though I was well prepared academically after the first day, berserk went on for several days. The class had quickly developed a taste for running amok and there I was, small, soft-spoken, and only a few years older than they. How sadistically they capitalized upon all those points! One day I escaped into the hall, closed the door behind me (I was terrified that the principal or other teachers would hear the bedlam, see the airplanes and spitballs) and, weeping, prayed as hard as I've ever prayed for help. I'd been praying almost nonstop since the first airplane took off a few days before, but at that point I was at the end of my rope.

Funny, I don't recall how I did it, but before long we were working together, those kids and I, liking it and liking each other. As I should have suspected, they were a wonderfully creative bunch, and the experience of channeling that creativity from paper airplanes and spitballs into short stories and poems was one of the happiest of my teaching life. Thousands of students later, I still remember that bunch clearly, and with love. They taught me all I've ever needed to know about class management, and about the potential creativity of everyone, including hulking fullbacks.

Nearly two years later, the girls at the camp, screaming with delight and derision, locked me in the cabin toilet. Recognizing the politics of the occasion immediately, I fought down the little leap of apprehension in my stomach by examining the tiny room, detail by detail. At first glance, it seemed to contain only a toilet and toilet-paper bar. A second glance revealed a small screen-covered vent near the ceiling.

Quietly I climbed onto the toilet tank, on tiptoe reached the vent, wrenched off the screen and, holding onto the small ledge of the now-open vent, began to pull myself up, my rubber-soled tennis shoes climbing the wall. My shoulders squeezed through with only minor bruises and when my bottom finally popped like a cork through the vent to freedom, I let out a silent whoopee. Dropping to the ground, hunched over so no one could see me through the windows, I sneaked around to the front door where I straightened up, began whistling offhandedly, and strolled into the cabin as if nothing had happened.

This feat was regarded as evidence of supernatural powers, and from that time on I wasn't just the country bumpkin who didn't know "card games that even *babies* know" (poker). I had won respect and awe from my sophisticated younger sisters, and felt that young Mormon womanhood had been vindicated.

Like all other college graduates planning to teach, I'd been interviewed that spring by recruiters from various school systems around the country. One week into camp I received a contract from a secondary school in Oregon to be a part-time English teacher and part-time librarian. I sat holding it, thinking.

I knew I wasn't beautiful—regardless of what Rick said. Being Mormon, twenty-three years old, intelligent, and well-educated narrowed the range of young men who would be interested in marrying me, and vice versa. Although I'd dated a good many men during my college years, almost all of them returned missionaries, I'd met very few who were interesting enough to marry. I may have been desperate, but I was also fussy.

And I was not the sort of woman who appealed most to Mormon men, though I'd done my best to hide it from them. Rick was the only male I'd known for a long time who was intellectually alive enough and nonsexist enough not to bore me to death. (Sexism was such a non-concept then, I didn't comprehend for years that one of the most important reasons he wasn't sexist was that *he hadn't been reared Mormon.*) He didn't, for instance, regale me for hours with reminiscences of his boyhood rock collection—though, now that I think of it, he did tell me dozens more of his boyhood experiences than I told him of my girlhood ones. So far, no man I've ever met has been interested in my life as a child.

So it is rather strange and amazing how many men have assumed over the years that I am profoundly moved by their stories about themselves, often before I've even had a chance to know them well enough to care personally about them at all. It's as if men think that women automatically find men's life stories or daily experiences spellbinding. I've cautioned my sons that though society—and young women—may give them this egocentric message, it's simply not true.

Extrapolating from past experience how long it would take me to find someone again as compatible as Rick, especially in a non-university environment, and thinking of the letter I'd just received from him addressed to "Sweetest Soni Lu" telling me that his life had been "a vacuous empty unfilled disgusting mess since you left," I put aside my pride and, with the teaching contract in hand, called him long distance.

He was at radio station KVNU in Logan, where he worked nights as engineer. After I told him about the contract, I put the problem to him bluntly: "If I come home instead of going to Oregon, will you marry me?" I didn't consider this a proposal. He had very formally, and quaintly, proposed to me one freezing December night in the car out in front of the co-op house on campus where I lived, and I'd said yes. So, I told myself, this was merely reaffirming that contract. He could have said no. But he didn't. "Yes," he said, happily. "Come home!"

Years later, in the throes of our divorce, he once accused me of "forcing" him to marry me. I understand now that this is standard operating procedure for men who have treated their wives badly—a projection of guilt, a justification of sleazy behavior. But even then I was only hurt for a moment, because I had reread the letters he wrote to me the summer we were married:

"Two hrs after your call: Dearest of darlings, was it delightful, tremendi, great, sweet, wunnerful, terrific to hear your voice! I have been toying with the idea of calling you ever since you got on the train, and it struck me that you were escaping the awful clutches of marriage with me. Ah hah, but this time you shan't get away without promising to love, honor, and obey from then on. . . . I took the liberty of telling your mother the news that we are making plans for this permanent type marriage thing, OK? I love you with whole heart and soul and miss you terribly—can't stand it without you."

But I was also receiving other, very different, letters from the home front that summer. Mother, fine as she is, cannot resist passing along the latest rumor to concerned parties, because she *believes* rumors and they worry her; she wants matters cleared up. She can't imagine anyone making up such things, and of course they don't. They just see what they want to see, even if it doesn't exist.

I grew up in a community constantly abuzz with rumors, which is typical of any small town, though rumors in small Mormon towns, where drinking is nearly as shocking as adultery, have their own unique flavor. Reports had it that in my absence Rick was having a very high old time indeed, and Mom thought I ought to beware, ought to come home.

So one day I pushed the aging despot who owned the camp too far and he fired me, without pay. With what little money I had left, I got to Milwaukee to Rick's family. There his mother, in the course of telling my fortune, predicted that Rick and I would marry—which was comforting after all the rumors of previous weeks. She lent me forty dollars to take the train home.

After getting off the train in Brigham City, I sat on my suitcase by the side of the road feeling ecstatic to be back in my own country. The day was all gold sunshine and blue sky, and still as only insect-less Utah can be. Breathing in the sagebrush tang, the clean, thin canyon air, and looking out for miles and miles across the valley—all aspects of the West I'd missed in the claustrophobic woods of the East—I felt on the brink of something momentous. "The next day will decide my life," I thought with a dramatic shiver. Would I find the rumors true? Would I have to give Rick up—again?

Mom and Dad picked me up and we drove back through Sardine Canyon to Logan. I went straight to Rick's apartment. He wasn't home. At KVNU, an old friend of ours from college gleefully related all the evidence of Rick's moral decline. During the rest of that doleful afternoon, I heard dozens of rumors from as many mouths. No one could wait to tell me the bad news. When I learned that he was in Yellowstone with two women friends I nearly despaired, but remained determined to let him speak for himself when he returned.

That night I stayed in his apartment, waiting, praying he'd tell me the truth and that I'd know it. I'd begun fasting the day I arrived because I wanted all the help from heaven I could get, and I believed, as I'd been taught by my parents and church leaders, that fasting intensified the effectiveness of prayer. My mother was always a great faster. (Rick turned out to be one, too.) When he hadn't returned by noon I gave up and went home, but checking back at his apartment a few hours later, I found Bucephalus parked out in front.

Heart pounding with mixed delight and fear, I took the stairs three at a time. Hearing sounds of splashing from the bathroom, I knocked on the door. In a few minutes he appeared in his bathrobe all warm and moist and delectable. But I stayed firm. Were any of the rumors true? "No." I believed him. Right there and then we planned to be married five weeks from that day—the day after he finished summer school.

Although Rick hadn't been a member of the church for quite a full year, my parents, who had high connections in the church, were able to get permission for us to be married in the temple. We went for our temple interviews—only members who have proved themselves faithful can enter that most sacred of all Mormon edifices—received our temple "recommends," and began the arduous business of preparing for the wedding.

But then something began to bother me. I couldn't put my finger on what it was, so I began to pray more and more often, until I was praying nearly all the time in my heart. What was wrong? Why didn't I feel peaceful? I'd done all I was required to do. Rick and I had managed to control our sexual urges—if only just. Again and again I went over everything in my life that might account for that uneasy feeling, and found nothing.

Finally one day after I'd been on my knees in my room for a long time wrestling with this feeling of urgency to *correct* something, I realized with a shock that I was seemingly being cautioned not to take Rick to the temple. I couldn't believe it, and instantly dismissed it. But praying harder and trying harder to leave my mind open only brought that same message more firmly to my soul. Finally, I gave in and accepted it.

Downstairs, I did one of the hardest things I've ever had to do. I announced to my horror-stricken parents that I'd been inspired not to go to the temple at this time, but to change our plans and prepare to have the wedding somewhere else, perhaps at home.

They both became nearly hysterical, Mom weeping, Dad stomping and shouting around. "The Holy Ghost would never tell you not to marry in the temple," they insisted. "You are receiving direction from the Evil One."

"Mom, Dad," I explained painfully, "for a week now, something has been very wrong. I've prayed and fasted and prayed some more, trying to understand what it is, but have become increasingly disturbed and uneasy. When I finally accepted the feeling I had that I must not take Rick to the temple yet, I became peaceful at once. I can only follow this feeling, as you and the church have always taught me."

I knew what they were not saying. The question in both their minds was, What will the neighbors think? The three of us knew what they'd think, and understood the speculation that would go on behind our backs. They'd think I was pregnant, or that Rick and I were morally unfit to enter the temple. It was simply not acceptable in certain strata of the church—my family's strata because of Dad's job as seminary teacher for the church, Mother's church positions, the strictly orthodox backgrounds of both their families as far into the Mormon past as we could see—not to be married in the temple. It bespoke unrighteousness, or apostasy, or both. It was also considered low-class.

My heart ached for my parents. They deserved the reward of having the neighbors see their children follow in the acceptable paths, the paths of righteousness. It hurt deeply not to be able to give them this moment of victory and honor.

Being the decent parents they were, however, they resigned themselves to my decision, both certain I was dead wrong, and went forward bravely with a whole new blueprint, morally and socially unpalatable as it was to them.

Rick, however, accepted my decision without question. He always had faith in my judgment, and he hadn't been a Mormon or lived among Mormons long enough to understand the social implications of what I proposed. I didn't enlighten him on the issue, either, figuring it was just as well for him not to realize, as we stood in our receiving line, that many of those smiling and shaking our hands were wondering how "far along" I was, or speculating about the nature of our wrongdoing.

We were married by Bishop Heber Sharp, one of our psychology professors, on August 21, 1959, in front of the picture window in my parents' house. When he got to the "you may now kiss the bride" part, Rick, much to my surprise and embarrassment, and to the delight of our assembled close friends and families, gave me a long, impassioned kiss.

We spent our first night together before a fire in a cabin in Logan Canyon. Trained from birth that I was to please men, looking back now I deem it a miracle that I was still a virgin that night, though I was that only by great good luck, not superior self-control. Many Mormon girls and those from other religiously fundamentalist homes didn't manage the double message—"please men but be chaste"— nearly as luckily. And I believe the situation is still as grave as it was in my youth. Perhaps more so.*

After the requisite sexual performance on our wedding night, I lay awake wondering, as I'm sure millions of women have wondered before me, "Is this *all?*" All those years of fighting almost overpowering sexual urges, thinking what total bliss it would be when I could just let go and have at it, and *this* was *it*? Fortunately, over the years we improved upon our initial adventure, but the long years of thinking of myself as a commodity to be used and of my sexuality as the trap of evil for men, as well as the long years of Rick's macho socialization, kept us from fullest happiness. Not just in a sexual, but in an everyday, moment-to-moment sense. Alas for the oppressed. Alas for the unwitting oppressor.

Rick went back to school that fall to finish his M.A., and I did what I'd been conditioned by Mormon culture to do—went to work to "put him through." The trouble was, he didn't need putting through and he didn't want this sacrifice from me. He remembered our test scores and my scholarly bent, and felt uncomfortable continuing his education while I worked as an assistant bookkeeper at a canning factory. But I was determined to be the ideal Mormon wife, to follow the stereotype blindly whether it fit or not.

Our disagreement on this created serious tension in the first months of our life together. One night when he was working late at KVNU, we had a ferocious quarrel over the phone about it. Afterward, about midnight, I fell asleep fully dressed, expecting him home any minute. When I awoke at 4 A.M. to an empty bed, I tore out of the house, down past the tabernacle, and down Center Street to my

* For instance, in Utah where nearly three quarters of the population is Mormon, 70 percent of teen brides in 1978 were pregnant when they married, and 40 percent of Utah's brides were teens. Not surprisingly, the teenage suicide rate in that state for young women in 1978 was double the national average and rising. So though the rhetoric prohibited sexual license, the belief of both men and women that women were made solely as objects of pleasure and for service to men produced incredible conflict. Catch 22's are potent inciters of suicide.

parents' house, which in those pre-paranoid days was never locked. Sneaking in, I lifted the car keys gently from the blue dish on the mantel, sneaked out again, started up the Studebaker, and pulled out onto Center Street. To my horror, I found that the car had no brakes, but I figured there'd be little traffic and few police, so I drove slowly through all the blinking red lights down Main Street and out to the radio station. As I turned into the drive to the station, pondering wildly how I was going to stop, a huge dump of furnace ashes loomed before me. With a sigh of relief, I drove calmly into it and came to a stop.

The muffled crash woke Rick, who'd been sleeping on a cot by the window. He opened the window, I crawled in, and we made up. We were so easily hurt, both of us.

In February Rick finished his master's degree and, taking my fifteen-year-old brother Mark, we went to western Samoa to teach for the church. Rick taught math, I taught English, and Mark—whom we affectionately called "Pubert" because he was in the throes of adolescence—was in both our classes. Among the many notes and letters from Rick to me is this little one that I've saved:

"Sister Johnson, would you please admit P. Harris, my brother in Christ and my brother-in-law to class a matter of 645 seconds late. Thanks, hate-mate. I'll be in to report in a few minutes. Hus."

Some days I'd walk into class and find my Samoan students, who could scarcely read English, staring blankly at a poem like this on the board:

> As *slummer flues the hipplecourse,*
> *and glies the rupple glate,*
> *Nihl and temmy applerun,*
> *Sloshmoor the balden tate.*
> *Wot hie the glammer glipper gosh?*
> *Once throudly palsied he—*
> *Begot a speckled hoppenoosh*
> *Benigh a golden three.*

It was fun living with Rick.

The high moment of our Samoan experience occurred one night as we were driving home from church on our scooter past the harbor, where spiny palm branches were etched across a huge tropical moon.

We stopped because it seemed irreverent to go by without paying homage to that loveliness, stereotyped though it was. Rick turned to me, and to the accompaniment of softly slapping waves announced, "I want to go home so I can take you to the temple. I can't *wait* to get you there!"

So when we returned to the States, we went to the temple to be married for eternity, eighteen months after we'd been married for life. As we knelt across the altar from each other and Rick put my ring on my finger for the second time, I was astonished to see that his eyes were shiny with tears. I am always surprised when people love me.

Years later, he told me casually one day, "It's a good thing we didn't go to the temple when we were first married. I wasn't ready for it. I'd have left the church."

Rick immediately went back to school again, this time in Minneapolis at the University of Minnesota, and began working on his Ph.D. in educational psychology. Still not having learned my lesson, still determined to follow the pattern I'd been conditioned to believe was the only right one for young Mormon wives, I went to work in the neurology department of the university hospital.

But Rick wouldn't stand for it this time, and this time I was a pushover. He easily persuaded me to quit and to register full-time for graduate classes in the English department. I can't express how much I loved it. I couldn't get enough of it. The next quarter I applied for and won a teaching assistantship, and met Karl, another teaching assistant and a faithful Mormon with a wife and five children. Over the next couple of years he taught me what it meant to be a "liberal" in the church. At the time, I thought he was very brave and daring. I would never have believed that someday I was going to find Mormon liberals as conventionally and disappointingly fearful as their conservative fellows.

Karl was distraught about the problem of black men being denied the priesthood—an issue that burned in the church for about twenty years—and begged me to pray that the leaders would change the policy, that they'd have a revelation. So I joined the throngs of Mormons praying for the end of racism in the Mormon church, and there *was* a change in policy, fifteen years of anguished prayers later.

If I could find Karl today, I'd plead with him to pray for a revelation about women. But he probably already is doing just that.

After a year at Minnesota, I decided it was time to have a baby. I think I really did want a baby. After all, I'd been conditioned to believe that if I didn't have babies, I wasn't worth much. Having children was what women were made for. That and being helpmeets to men were our only excuse for existing. But I also think I did not dare be too successful. A baby would be an excuse not to have to get the master's degree I was coming so close to.

Since then, I've met dozens of Mormon women—and I'm sure it's true of others—who quit college to get married just short of finishing, or who in similar ways made sure never to provide themselves with evidence that they shouldn't be the second-class citizens, the servants of their husbands and children, which the church and society encouraged them to be because it was their God-ordained duty and destiny. If they never proved to themselves that they were capable, talented people, then they would have less frustration performing in roles that required them to be, in many important ways, both incapable and untalented. If these women never raised their expectations of life, never expected to have the excitement and feel the power of developing and using their minds and skills, then they would never feel thwarted and miserable. Only, it didn't turn out that way for most of them.

I believe I was also afraid to have to prove myself in the big world. It was easier to remain a child, immature, protected. And, too, I hadn't been gearing myself up all my life for coping in the "man's world" as boys had been. It seemed foreign to my thinking. I wasn't psychologically ready for it.

This was never any more conscious to me than it is to most women, but I know I experienced these feelings. I remember them. I was afraid of success because I knew it would make demands of me that I was not at all confident I could meet. If I got a master's degree, I would be required to do something with it, and I might fail. Or I might find that I preferred doing something out in the world to being a sanctified housewife, and that would displease God (meaning the men, who, the church assured us, spoke for God).

Fear of facing the world on my own, the infantile longing to retreat to a little house in the suburbs and never have to try my wings and turn into an adult, fear of not finding my role satisfying after worldly success, fear of success, fear of failure, fear of adulthood and its responsibilities, fear of God's wrath, fear, fear, fear.

So we had Eric, whom I loved from the moment of conception, although from that moment I was miserably nauseated for five months. Teaching two freshman English classes, studying German, taking a full course load on top of constant nausea—it was all just too much. I dropped some classes, which ruined my chances of getting my degree there; Rick was already looking for his first post-Ph.D. teaching position and it would likely turn up far from the University of Minnesota.

On the night of July 10, 1963, I was talking to Rick on the phone. He had gone back to Utah to teach summer school at Utah State, and I'd stayed behind in Minnesota to have the baby at the university clinic. As I stood there in the bedroom of our mobile home with his voice in my ear, the membrane broke and amniotic fluid gushed hotly down my legs. "It's coming, Rick!" I cried. "I'm on my way," he promised. Shirley Wallace, a Mormon friend who lived near in another trailer (and who would be in the same hospital having her third baby a week later), drove me to the hospital that night.

There I began an agonizing thirty-six-hour labor, during which it's possible I might have died if Rick hadn't arrived and forced someone to come and look at me. "Oh," they said. "How long do you say she's been in labor?" "Thirty-six hours!" he bellowed. So they checked me, realized I'd never go into the final stages on my own, and gave me some intravenous chemical to make up for my lack. I realized with shock that if I'd lived a generation or two earlier, I'd have died in childbirth. That experience was also the first time, but not the last, that I was made aware of the immense indifference of many who attend women in hospitals.

That Rick had dropped the phone and sped to Minneapolis to be with me was very gratifying. But he could never bear to wait, and as the labor dragged on and on he became annoyed not just at the doctors, but at me for having prompted him to come so soon, as if I should have been able to foresee my thirty-six-hour-long performance. On top of the postpartum blues, which struck me down while I was still in the hospital and subsequently tortured me for weeks, guilt was subtly created in me because of his unnecessarily long wait in Minneapolis, when he should have been finishing up his class at Utah State.

As I look back, I realize that women have always been manipulated by guilt. Men are socialized to deal with women this way, and we women are socialized to accept the guilt they lay on us.

After having been pummeled half to death in the preposterously and unnecessarily long labor, which it seemed nobody cared about except Rick and me, Eric was finally born. A wizened little old man. (I called him "Oldie" for a long time.) Because of his rocky horror of a birth, he was a colicky, restless baby for the first few months. As I slogged about in a fog of fatigue and postpartum depression, I found myself wondering why I had to bear this burden so alone.

From the first, Rick was never very interested in parenting and consequently never did much of it. This disappointed me, but I accepted it as The Way Things Are.* My friend Hazel reminds me of the day, a week or so after Eric's birth, that I called her in tears. My breasts were infected, I had a temperature of 104, and Eric, not being able to nurse, was even more colicky and cross than usual. I'd reached the limits of my endurance. Could she please come over and take Eric home with her for a little while so I could rest? She sped over, to find Rick studying in the kitchen, seemingly oblivious to any problem, and me, dizzy with fever and fatigue, determinedly bathing Eric in the kitchen sink so he'd be fresh for her to take. She remembers being shocked and angry at Rick and thinking to herself, "It's rough for me," (she was having extreme difficulty adjusting to the Mormon wife role) "but Sonia's got it worse."

In those first few months of motherhood, before I succeeded in stifling such "unnatural" thoughts, I wondered guiltily whether it was possible that I'd been deceived about motherhood's being the totally fulfilling activity the church and society assured me it was. It didn't take me long to learn that this was indeed a myth for a good many women, if not for most.

That didn't mean I didn't love my baby and find aspects of being a mother delightful. Though I chafed at the full-timeness of it and at Rick's nonparticipation, I found Eric endlessly entrancing. I adored nursing him and would keep him at the breast for hours (de-

---

* And apparently it's The Way Things Still Are. In the New York *Times* of January 23, 1981, an article by Mirra Komarovsky entitled "College Women and Careers" carries this quote from a male senior at an Ivy League college: "I would not want to marry a woman whose only goal is to become a housewife . . . I want an independent girl, one who has her own interests and diversions. However, when we both agree to have children, *my wife must be the one to raise them.*" (Italics mine.)

spite the warnings in the books), because while he nursed I could read and he wouldn't fuss—both highly desirable. Those cozy hours with him in my arms and a good book on my knees were delicious and nourishing to me. A reprieve, for a moment, from striving. I felt like Mother Earth. And Eric soon changed from a thin, colicky infant into a chubby, gorgeous child, pleased with himself and the world.

Rick finished his Ph.D., accepted a teaching position at Rutgers University in New Jersey, bought an old truck, and pulled the mobile home with Eric and me in it to New Brunswick. I thought I should be ready now to settle down and be a wife and mother, but I was already seriously bored, and Rick was still uncomfortable.

"Why don't you finish your degree?" he suggested. "After all, you're so close." I didn't need any more encouragement, but checking with the English department I found that none of my master's credits transferred toward their M.A. "I'll have to do it all over again in their department," I reported to Rick disconsolately, "and I can't bear to begin all over again."

"Well," he suggested, "why not see how many credits you can transfer to the Education department?"

All of them, as it turned out. So I went back to school, and in a year had finished both my course work and master's thesis, carrying Eric on my hip as I went about collecting data from local high schools and doing my library research. Before he was one, he'd spent more time in more libraries than most college students spend in a year.

"Now," Rick said after I had my degree, "go get your doctorate."

I became pregnant with Kari sometime during my doctoral course work, and again suffered miserably from nausea. One morning in my philosophy of education course, having taken two anti-nausea pills instead of one, I suddenly felt sickeningly faint. As soon as I got outside the classroom door, I did faint. When I came to on the hall floor, I dragged myself into the lavatory, and gratefully fainted again, there on the dirty floor; I didn't care how dirty it was. I just wanted to lose consciousness in some semblance of privacy. So I did, on and off for over an hour—wake up, faint again. When I finally got home, I was so frightened by the experience that I threw the anti-nausea pills down the toilet. At least when I vomited I was conscious.

That next summer Rick led a group of students to Italy to stay with Italian families while I, eight months pregnant, took Eric home to Utah to finish writing my dissertation. The night of June 24 at about ten o'clock I wrote, with infinite relief, the last word, and stood up to stretch and exult. Just as I did, I had a contraction, the first. Labor had begun. I smiled to myself at the appropriateness of it. I had just given birth to my dissertation and tomorrow would give birth to (I hoped) my daughter.

I'd wanted a girl this time, having done my duty and produced a male as was proper for the first child and for which I'd been properly grateful. So I was euphoric when that huge stomach turned out to be Kari. She was, and has continued to be, all I could hope for in a daughter. But when I became a feminist she became even more dear to me, more precious. I felt as if I were seeing her for the first time, as indeed I was. Until I could regard myself as valuable and lovable as a person, I had difficulty regarding anything female as valuable, though I was not aware of this and would have denied it if I'd been asked. Until I discovered how much I admired and loved the woman in me, I did not admire it or love it properly in myself or anyone else, even my daughter. I had viewed her as only an extension of me, and who was I? Rick's wife, the kids' mother, a housewife—not a person with value in her own right outside the family. Always a role. Not Sonia first; not Sonia ever, until I was forty-two.

I am indebted to the women's movement for truly giving me my daughter.

Marc, my third child, was the easiest of the three, probably because I was learning to relax and enjoy. And he *was* enjoyable. Every night when I'd tuck him in bed I'd nuzzle him and say, "Markie, you're my boy!" In a few minutes his little two-year-old head would appear around the living-room door and with infinite lovingness he'd say, "Mommy, you're my boy!"

I became pregnant with him when we lived in northern California, just when I finally got a teaching job. It was only a night-school class, but getting it was no small feat in the Palo Alto area where people with Ph.D.'s were washing dishes and sweeping floors. I went to every class so sick I thought I'd die, thanking my lucky stars that I had the class to go to since it took my mind off my churning middle a little. I remember the exact day the nausea disappeared. On Thanksgiving Day, 1967, I awoke to a nausea-free world. I felt jubilant, but all day I was still inwardly wary, waiting for signs that I was rejoicing too soon. We went to the park to eat our Thanksgiving dinner, and afterward I lay on the grass in the sun, feeling unspeakably blissful. I wanted to live forever.

But darker clouds than morning sickness were already growing across the sun. "The problem," as we called it, was the first and most destructive. Rick was suffering severe anxiety attacks with increasing frequency, and each one left him exhausted and uncertain. Sometimes they would assault him at work, and for several seconds, maybe as long as half a minute, he would be in the grip of such fear of dissolution that he not only missed what was being said to him, but could hardly keep others from noticing how he trembled and perspired. We rarely talked about "the problem" because he thought discussing it encouraged renewed bouts.

He first confided in me about it during his second year of teaching at Stanford, when Marc was a baby. I succeeded in getting him to talk to a psychologist friend of ours about it, which did no good whatever and only made Rick feel exposed and weak. (I think he has since judged all psychotherapists by that grossly incompetent friend of ours.) There were good times when he was relatively free of his affliction, and then there were bad times when the attacks threatened him several times a day and through the night.

As women do, I somehow felt responsible—or, at the very least, felt that if I could be better or nicer or different in some significant way, these attacks would stop—even while I knew intellectually that it wasn't my problem at all. For years Rick could never correlate his anxiety attacks with the state of our relationship or consistently with much of anything. They seemed to come and go with a logic inscrutable to us. They caused him to be withdrawn lots of the time, mentally absent when he was physically present. I remember feeling very lonely and estranged from him during those times. I expressed it once in a short poem:

> DREAM
> *Being married to you is*
> *stopping the elevator at every floor*
> *floor after floor*
> *and calling your name*
> *down each corridor.*
> *Calling your name,*

then calling and crying.
Then not calling.
Then not crying.

It was during that grim second year at Stanford that I began to suffer an overwhelming fatigue. While Rick was secretly battling his nemesis—which meant spending most of his time on computer programs to keep from thinking about anything that might spark another attack—I was stuck at home with three small children and only the church for an outlet. I'd find myself lying down on my bed "for just a minute" at noon and fighting my way up out of slumber as if I were resurrecting at three in the afternoon. Then the panic: were my children all right? Bruised with guilt and as tired as if I hadn't slept for weeks, I dragged around my house fighting that nap, only at last to give in to another marathon unconsciousness and wake with my heart pounding in dread at what might have happened to the children while I slept.

I thought I was just depressed and feeling more bored than I'd ever felt in my life. I knew that depression makes women tired, gives us headaches, backaches, makes us eat too much. Perhaps I hadn't yet seen this syndrome labeled "housewives' disease," but I knew it existed, I'd seen it in other women, and I thought that was what was the matter with me. I needed to get out into the world more, I told myself, needed to find another class to teach. But nothing was harder then than finding a class to teach in Palo Alto, and Rick was gone most of the time and when he was home he was lost in computer strategies.

The only bright spots in that year were the Palo Alto second-ward women I came to know and love better than any other group of Mormon women anywhere; my friend Ellen Robson and her retinue of bright, witty, warm young Mormons; and the little house with the gorgeous Japanese garden we were renting in Barron Park. But though I adored the women at church, the lessons of the women's auxiliary and the Relief Society were still gauged for dull normals and, though pleasant, could hardly offer the kind of intellectual stimulation I so fiercely craved that year. (If I could have foreseen the unimaginably wretched fare we would be offered a dozen years later in Relief Society, I'd probably have gone into a catatonic trance.)

I believe that all the frustrations and inchoate longings and boredom of that time, and the guilt at not being perfectly happy doing what the men of the church taught should make a woman perfectly happy—being a full-time wife and mother—all this negative energy turned inward, combined into a potent weapon, and attacked me. Ten years later I wrote about the war I waged against myself:

ARTHRITIS

One May morning when I was thirty-three
I woke and knew the enemy at once.
Like wounded birds my hands lay
beside me where they had fallen
in the dark battle lost while I still slept.

Hot lids clamped over furious eyes,
I watched my seething hands
break to bits and mend crazily
grotesque
as if glimpsed through riffled water;
like dying drying leaves
my hands, my young hands
don't take my hands!

A decade calmer, I note their slender
straightness appreciatively
as if they were someone else's
borrowed for a time.
For in the margins of my life
the future has scrawled
graffiti
about my hands,
my baobab hands.

The morning I woke up to find both hands stiff, hot, and throbbing, the thought that leaped to my mind was: rheumatoid arthritis. And the terror of that twisting, crippling pain washed over my whole body in waves of hot nausea. I tried to calm myself by taking in the very commonplaceness of the room: Rick sleeping on his stomach beside me, the birds spilling their early morning secrets out over the garden, the sun splashing happily through the cracks at the sides of the window shades. But it was no use. Life, I was certain, would never be the same. I saw myself in a wheelchair, unable to lift my babies, unable to love my husband, unable to play the piano, to turn the pages of a book, locked in a lifelong contest with pain. How could I have taken the healthy world so for granted?—my walking, typing, being able to do everything so easily and so heedlessly.

We were just a week or so away from leaving for Malawi, a small country in south central Africa. When it had become apparent that Rick would not be offered another contract at Stanford, he was ready to go overseas again at once. As far as I was concerned, anything was better than the emotional, spiritual, and intellectual limbo I'd been in all year in Palo Alto.

So when I woke with arthritis that morning, I knew I had to get to a specialist quickly; two weeks and we'd be far away from good medical aid for several years. I called the clinic and, because it was an emergency, got to see a doctor whom, his nurse assured me, I was extraordinarily fortunate to be able to see since he was the "best rheumatologist in the U. S." By the time I got to him I was aching in my elbows, knees, ankles, and feet, as well as in my wrists and hands. And I was near despair. Hospital personnel X-rayed, took blood samples, and gave me a sad lesson in how to treat my hands with hot wax to keep them mobile.

When we returned to learn the results a few days later, the "best rheumatologist in the U. S." looked grave. At that look, my heart turned into a sieve and all the hope drained out of it. "It's serious, very serious," he told us as he led us down the hall to look at the X rays. "See those wristbones?" he tapped them with his baton. "This disease has been progressing for a long time. The bones here are almost hollow." He sang this requiem over all the rest of my poor joints, and then said, "Arthritis is a degenerative disease. That means it gets progressively worse." Maybe he saw the fear spring into my eyes because he quickly added, "There *are* periods when it seems almost to disappear, though these alternate with periods when it is very bad indeed. That's what makes people with arthritis so vulnerable to quacks: if a person has a normal brief remission, she attributes it to whatever crazy cure she has just tried rather than to the nature of the disease."

There didn't seem to be much he or anyone else could do. "Take as many as fifteen aspirins a day. Aspirin is by far the most effective drug for arthritis yet discovered. And don't do any hard work, work that strains your hands, like wringing diapers. We call arthritis the tired disease. You'll need lots of sleep. Take two one-hour naps a day, one in the morning, one in the afternoon, and get nine or ten hours of sleep at night." Dully I remembered my nine-month history of deathlike slumbers and knew I'd been ill, not just lazy. It wasn't much comfort.

It took me years to figure out that I may very well have given myself arthritis to punish myself for not being happy doing God's will. That I'd turned my body into a battlefield for my emotions.

At the time, I thought nothing worse could possibly happen to me. I had three young children to rear. I was a young woman. Life seemed over before it had begun. I was desperate for reassurance, for comfort, for support. But Rick seemed as distant as ever, untouched somehow, sorry of course, and concerned, but seemingly without any idea of the vise of fear I was being crushed in. As I look back now, seeing myself in that little house facing Rick, an interesting notion comes to my mind. I think if I were there now I'd shout, "What does it take to get you to pay attention to me?"

One evening during that time we had an appointment to go to dinner at the home of a couple whom Rick was trying to reactivate in the church. He was always being assigned as home teacher to inactive members—difficult cases—because he handled them well. Our appointment was at six. At 6:15, when Rick hadn't come home, I called the woman and told her we'd be a little late. At 6:45 I called, trying to control the anger and humiliation in my voice, and told her how sorry I was that he hadn't yet appeared, and that I would simply have to ask her not to expect us that night.

When I hung up the phone, I was seething. How many hundreds of times had I waited like this, only to have him appear sometimes hours late. "How many hours of my life have I spent being demeaned like this?" I asked myself as I tore around the house, putting some clothes in a bag, getting together some bedding, finding some money. I had some vague notion of sleeping in someone's driveway in my car. At least this time when he came home, he wouldn't find me there waiting for him.

Just as I rushed out the front door, he came in the back (I'd waited so the kids wouldn't be alone). I spent that night in a nearby motel awake and in mute dread of the undying fire in my bones, and angry and hurt at being left alone emotionally to face it.

The next morning when I returned we were both repentant. I'd made an appointment with the bishop the day before to have him "administer" to me on Sunday (anoint my head with oil, lay his hands on my head, and pray that I'd be healed). I'd asked him to do it instead of Rick, perhaps to punish Rick for not caring, to hurt him, because Rick would ordinarily have been the one I asked to bless me. But I felt that even the bishop, who hardly knew me, cared more than my husband.

But that Saturday morning when we made up, I asked him to fast with me in preparation for the blessing, and he readily agreed. I also called my family in Utah and solicited their fasting and prayers in my behalf. Then as I fasted, I made deals with the Lord constantly in preparation for Sunday: "If I can only be allowed to rear these children—that's all I ask. Just let me keep my hands long enough to get them out into the world."

Aside from the deal making, I prayed and fasted as hard as I ever have in my life. I knew God was there and I knew healing was possible. There are in my family dozens of what we call "faith-promoting incidents" about healings, several in my own lifetime. My Uncle Ben had laid his pudgy old hands on the head of my seven-year-old nephew, Brad, when Brad was so full of nephritis he had swollen to twice his size, and commanded him to get well. And he had. Rapidly and forever. It was a miracle, the doctors whispered. "But of course," said my Uncle Ben calmly.

Miracles were a part of life. I believed in them and I intended with prayer and fasting to wrest one from the bosom of heaven.

When we and the bishop and his counselors gathered in the bishop's office the next evening after sacrament meeting for the blessing, Rick and I had been fasting for nearly two days. Bishop Taylor suggested that we all kneel first for prayer, and he called on Rick to pray. I don't remember the words of the prayer, but I remember how moving they were, how full of sincere and earnest pleading for my health, how full of love. I was convinced that I had underestimated his feelings for me, and I began to cry. And wished again that somehow he could let me know more often how he felt.

His prayer was like rain on my parched heart. The bishop's blessing was anticlimactical, though I'm sure it sufficed. Rick had really done the blessing. Oh Rick, I cried in my heart, why couldn't you let go of your pain and love me like that all the time? I would be so responsive.

Now when I tell you that, although I have never been free of indications that all is not perfectly sound in my joints, I am hardly ever conscious of having arthritis and am no longer terrified of the physical future, I expect that to be regarded as some kind of miracle.

A couple of years ago I decided to see a rheumatologist here in Virginia, since I hadn't consulted one for ten years, just to make sure all was really as well as it felt. Rick and I went together to hear the results of the consultation. The doctor hung the X rays of my hands up against his lighted screen, took out his pointer, and dropped these words onto a suspense stretched so tight they bounced. "Perfect! No signs of disease or of there ever having been disease." Ditto elbows, knees, ankles, feet. Tears of gratitude filled my eyes. Looking quickly at Rick, I saw that he too was blinking to keep tears from falling. He reached over and gripped my hand hard. It was a miracle, and we both knew it. For days I sent grateful thoughts heavenward, and silent paeans of praise.

Four years after the blessing, when we were in Korea, I had a wonderful, albeit perplexing, experience connected with our last child, Noel. It happened one day when I went to pick up Marc at school. On the way over in the car I'd been praying aloud in thanksgiving. It was a glorious spring day, we were so blessed in our family that I went around knocking on wood, and I was very happy. Odd, looking back on it now, that some of the happiest stretches of my twenty years with Rick were times when, I discovered later, he was most miserable. (Could there be some message in this, I wonder?) Living in Korea was perhaps the happiest time of my married life. I was teaching a class for the University of Maryland on the army post, and the gospel doctrine class in the serviceman's branch of the church. At home were two Korean women who had joined the church through our encouragement and who took excellent care of us. They did all the cooking and kept our house beautifully polished, from the lovely hardwood floors to the great windows where, from twelve stories up, you could see the Han River over the roofs of apartment buildings. I was freed from the bondage of housework to be able to have a full life of my own outside the house. I had time to spend with the children, to study and prepare my class materials, to write poetry, practice the piano, to make new friends and cultivate them. My every wish was someone's command. It did me good; I flourished. I shamelessly basked in it as it poured down upon me like sunlight. Ah, how well it helped me understand men:

How good, how very good it is to have a wife!

That particular afternoon, I parked the car and started up the path to the school. Along the path were great beds of iris in riotous bloom; the odor and color nearly made me dizzy. In fact, I felt suddenly as if I were standing just a little off the ground, surrounded by light, and I heard my own voice clearly in my head say to me, "I want to have a baby." Gradually the sensation of being full of light faded, my feet were prosaically on the ground, and there I was, on a gorgeous sunshiny day, in the midst of the flowers, knowing that what I had just heard myself say was true—I did want a baby though I hadn't known it until then. In fact, I had thought I really did not want another child, because I knew Rick didn't.

I gave birth to Noel Harris nine months and two weeks later in Seremban, Malaysia.

But I remained puzzled by that experience, not understanding why I had heard my own voice. I could have understood if I had heard another voice commanding me. That would clearly have been inspiration and direction from God, delivered perhaps by my guardian angel—but the voice had been mine. I simply couldn't resolve this. So occasionally I'd bring it up in prayer and ask that I be able to understand, because up until then, that day among the iris was the most wonderful spiritual experience of my life.

Four years later I heard my own voice again, and finally understood. But much had to happen first.

When I was seven months pregnant with Noel, we sold nearly all we had and left Korea for Malaysia, where we planned to live on the beach for an indefinite period of time. I wrote to Hazel:

"We're finally here! But then I don't suppose you know how long we've been planning this escape from the madding crowd. Years. Rick, like so many other great men (I tell him) has been very much influenced by Thoreau; keeps *Walden* by his bedside and goes about pronouncing from it, with gestures. The idea that most interests him is T's insistence on nonmaterialistic values. This Rick interprets as not working eight hours a day (or at all, for that matter) at a job he doesn't particularly like just to make a living—if he doesn't have to keep us from imminent starvation. Says he's interested in living, not in making one, and doesn't want to waste any more of his life, at least not in the same old way—a sort of occupational menopause (he's entering the critical forties, which is significant here, I think). So we're taking a year's leave of absence to think things over, to try to become more contemplative and less "busy" and, as the jargon has it, get in touch with ourselves. Just hope we haven't left this until we're too sot in our ways. But it's fun trying anyway, and Rick's relishing his leisure and freedom."

But I wasn't enjoying mine. What I didn't want any more of was unstructured time. I'd just had the best teaching experience of my life in Korea, and I wanted nothing more than to go on with it forever. Now, suddenly, here I was on the beach of the Strait of Malacca, with only the children between me and total uselessness—again. I missed my Korean "wives" desperately; I missed my work. I wrote some inconsequential poetry to while away the time.

Early one morning in February of 1974, we rushed off again to the hospital with amniotic fluid gushing stickily into a thick towel between my legs. And this time we took all the kids, not wanting to leave them out there alone in the house on the beach.

The hospital in Seremban was like nothing I'd seen since we'd left Samoa years before. Bloodstained bandages hung drying in the sun over railings, and washing hung out everywhere. Because the hospital didn't provide gowns or clothes for newborn infants or patients, you had to bring your own, wash them in the sink of your room, and hang them over your balcony. I hadn't brought clothes for the baby or for me, thinking Rick would bring them when he came to take us home.

The expensive first-class air-conditioned labor room was already occupied—another "rich foreigner," no doubt. So they put me up on one of a long row of rubber-sheeted tables in a large room with open louvered windows, through which the families of the women lying in labor peered in at us all. It was stiflingly hot, as it always is in Malaysia, but the heat seemed intensified in that room. All the other women had brought cloths with them to put over their bare bottoms as they lay and panted silently in a row. I took off my trousers before the interested eyes at the window, got up on the table with only my blouse on, and wondered if I had to go through the whole procedure with my bottom totally exposed to the world.

At the feet of our tables, doctors, nurses, cleaning men and women, and assistants of all sorts marched constantly by in armies. What are they all *doing* in here, I wondered frantically, as they passed my bare bottom impassively. Why don't they get them out of here? Why can't we have any privacy? I hollered in my mind. A balloon of panic began to inflate in my stomach.

At especially trying times in our lives, we need the reassurance of familiarity. We need the comfort of knowing exactly what is going on, what is going to happen. We need the security of the commonplace.

Nothing could have been less commonplace or less familiar to me than being in that room with a dozen women in all stages of labor— each a different color and culture, and *none of them making so much as a whimper*, though I could tell that many were in very advanced labor. And with everyone looking through the windows by my head and walking casually through the room at my feet, and me half naked, and grotesque. The woman who had brought me in had gone, and I didn't know whether anyone in that room could even speak English. My heart drummed with fear.

I don't remember how she found me, but a midwife who could speak English did appear, to my sobbing relief, found something to cover me with, and listened to my almost hysterical explanation of how I wouldn't go into serious labor without chemical help. And how afraid I was of having my baby on this bare table with all this audience and just that sling of cloth with the paper towels in the bottom to lay it in afterward.

Nothing seemed properly serious.

Just then, as I was beginning to get hold of myself, someone casually dropped a naked, bloody, mucus-covered baby into *my* sling, and I realized that without any fuss and without a sound, the tiny Indian woman on my right had just given birth. I nearly fainted.

I knew *I* was going to scream bloody murder. During my first labor, I had tried to remain circumspect and not cause any embarrassment or difficulty for anyone. But I gave that up with the second when I found that yelling helped a lot. By the time Marc came along, I'd stopped caring altogether what people thought. It hurt like hell, and I screamed like a banshee, which seemed appropriate and which comforted me.

I didn't want to scare everyone in the quiet birthing room and all the spectators to death, but I knew myself, and I knew I wasn't going to be masochistically silent about this for any reason. Besides, I think some of the women in that room were bringing their babies themselves, without help except for cutting the cord, and I was a pampered American. I wanted attention. I was afraid *not* to have attention. I didn't want to do it myself, and I didn't know how.

So I pleaded with the midwife until she promised to stay near me. She monitored every contraction with a little megaphone pressed against my belly to hear the baby's heart. But I was beginning to need to scream, and there was that audience at the window, and all those ladylike birthing mothers. What would they think of American women after I got through the upcoming performance?

Rick came in when I'd just begun to give up on any remaining-silent possibility, and announced that the woman in the first-class delivery room was nearly finished. "Tell her to hurry, for heaven's sake!" I hissed illogically through clenched jaws. The thought of a private place to scream seemed like the ultimate luxury. And a doctor! "Is the doctor going to be there?" I gasped. "Oh yes," the midwife assured me.

But by the time the room was ready for me, I was in full tearing final labor, screaming for help and sobbing that I was going to die, and as soon as the doctor walked into the delivery room, I demanded the local anesthetic he'd promised me the week before in his office. He acted as though he didn't hear me. "Do it!" I shrieked. "You promised!" Ignoring me, he went calmly about his business, and soon Noly came bursting through my pelvic channel, and I had, willy-nilly, without wishing to, without knowing how to, experienced natural childbirth. I'm sure I didn't breathe right once.

In the letter to Hazel from Malaysia, I wrote:

"Three and a half weeks ago, the world's longest pregnancy (subjectively speaking) came to a satisfactory conclusion, and three weeks early, too (some children know how to get on the right side of their parents from a very early age). So instead of being born on March 6 as the shamans predicted, our third son and fourth child, Noel

Harris, was born on February 14 at the gov't hospital in nearby
Seremban. Rick was in at the kill (and I hardly speak euphemis-
tically; it was a 'natural' childbirth much against my wishes; but then
who listens to a woman in labor? It's as if she weren't in her right
mind, presuming she had a mind, or not present at all) and nearly
fainted with delight when Noel didn't turn out to be mentally
deficient, or twins, or—as he'd secretly feared—both. (I was nearly
thirty-nine by the time Noel was born; that's why he worried so.)"

From this letter I can see that my feminism was also pushing to be
born.

Poor Noly, my love child. No clothes for him, no diapers, no anything. They wrapped him in paper towels and Rick shot off to the
village, to return with only a terrycloth bath towel and some paper
diapers. The three kids outside were sunburned and tired. But now,
with Noel, we finally had our family together—all there were going
to be of us—for five more years.

We gave up the living-on-the-beach experiment and moved back
to Palo Alto the next September, in time for the kids to start school.
It was there, in a quiet house with my Noly playing near my feet,
that I began to write poetry in earnest. Not because I write good poetry, but because I was beating so loudly against the walls of my co-
coon that I had to do something to quiet myself. As I look at those
poems now, it is almost as if I knew I was on the brink of something,
just about to discover a new world. There is almost a recognition
that this was a pause before the bursting of the chrysalis:

> INTERLUDE
> *Another auburn day*
> *blue and candid of gaze.*
>
> *My bright baby, splashed*
> *like a sundrop near my feet,*
> *casts spells with*
> *dust mote mirrors.*
>
> *Surface and depth*
> *in momentary truce*
> *pause—still as deer*
> *hunted into thickets.*

RISK

Dull as old silver
I dream I could gleam again if challenge buffed me,
if I were jostled and scuffed by the crowd,
if ideas milled, stormed, bumped about
in my head and irresistibly spilled out,
polishing my tongue and hands.

But the lusterless days I pin one by one
to the faded year
may be evidence that burnishing will bare
only glitter, not flame;
or under the tarnish, not shining silver
but corrosion.

Dare I chance it?

I dreamed freedom dreams, and didn't understand them, so I put them into written form:

DREAM IN ALLEGORY

I stand on the windy foothills
cold in shin-high mud
burdened, misshapen with bundles
and trembling with weariness.
As I turn to tackle the mountainside
the skin of the packages grows slippery
and I juggle them frantically.
One drops.
Bending to pick it up, I drop another
and both are soon lost in the ooze.
I relinquish them since I must,
stinging with fear of vague but
bitter consequences and
determined to hold tighter.

At a bend in the trail, I crumple upon a rock
to rest,
and try to see where I have been
but the valley churns and growls with freezing mist.

Later, checking my parcels,
I discover with a hot lash of horror
that more are missing, probably left at the rock.
Miserably I stumble on, certain
that if I go back, I will die at that turning.

A bright plateau above promises rest and warmth
and I climb faster, in my eagerness
dropping several more packages
until when I burst out onto the sunny ledge
my hands hold only one small box.
There in the crystal breeze and ringing silence
I open it and see that from the first
I need to have carried only this.
I must reach the top with it
but it is light
and easy to carry.

In many ways for me, those were good years, full years, and satisfying at least in the sense that I was fulfilling the expectations of my Mormon culture. But I was always dimly aware of a gnawing sense of something lacking, which I could keep at bay and not allow to overwhelm me into depression by finding a class to teach, joining a poetry workshop, teaching in church—finding something to do. But the nagging never stopped.

I thought it was just the human condition: after all, no one is ever fully satisfied; thought that that urgent, nagging voice was what kept us from stagnating. But since I don't hear that voice anymore, I have to believe that what was constantly nagging me was myself pleading to be let out, Sonia trying to make herself heard above the imperative voices of the patriarchy. It took me forty-two years to become depressed and angry enough to outshout my enculturation.

Chapter 3

Blood Ties

MOTHER SAYS THE doctor let her hemorrhage all through the night I was born. The pool of blood that splashed around her hips on the rubber sheet until morning is symbolic to me of the life she, and her mothers before her, have bled away for others—making vampires of their husbands and children and leaving their own inner selves anemic and ravaged.

Dad first saw her in the summer of 1923, galloping bareback over the Idaho plains in men's overalls, her hair whipping behind her. Because there were so few sons and so many daughters in the Howell family, Mom helped with the outdoor farm work. The labor was often so heavy and so almost impossibly hard that it made the small, slender girl weep as she did it. Despite that, Mom still preferred it to the work of the women in the house: the endless cooking and scrubbing, sewing, soapmaking, preserving. Just washing clothes was a superhuman feat, boiling water over an outdoor fire and stirring and wringing and hanging and ironing—a two-day chore that had to be done every week by all the women of the house.

Her mother, short and plump and silent, was the first one up in the morning to build the fire, put the bread in to bake, and prepare the huge breakfast, and the last one to bed at night. Mom says her mother was always tired and didn't talk much, but confided to her once that she only wanted to live to get her children grown and then to die. She got her wish. Mom's father, whom Mom idolized, lived through two more wives after her mother died.

Mom filed all this away in her unconscious.

Late one summer night, three years ago, in the kitchen of my house in Virginia where womanhood finally found and claimed me, for the first time my mother looked squarely at what it had meant in her life to be female. On the farm in Woodruff, she confided, the men came in from their work at dark, ate supper, sat around and talked a little, perhaps, and then went off to bed, while the women, who had been up in the morning before the men, wearily washed the dishes (without soap, so the water could be fed to the pigs) and got to bed an hour or two later. I asked her what she thought of her near-perfect father for behaving this way. Her eyes filled with tears and she whispered, "It wasn't fair."

Since that night she has regained some of her defenses against recognizing the blatant injustices of such a system, so when I've reminded her of what she told me that night, she's insisted that she hadn't remembered correctly, and that her father often had helped with the dishes and had not gone to bed leaving the womenfolk still hard at work. But I remember that night in my kitchen and the terrible things that were dawning upon both of us, and I know she remembers what was required of her as a girl. After a bonebreaking day in the fields, she was to drag her exhausted body and her screaming muscles about the kitchen to help the women with the supper and the washing up while the men were allowed—even expected and encouraged—to rest. And despite going to bed two hours later than the men, she had to arise earlier than they did the next morning to begin it all over again. There was no rest for the women—only endless drudgery until the children were reared, and then death.

No, it wasn't fair, Mama. You were right. It wasn't fair.

Why? I asked myself for days after our night in the kitchen. Why was my mother born with superior intelligence and extraordinary gifts as an organizer, an administrator, a financier, and an artist if she was not meant by her creator to use those gifts fully?

And why has she turned into a timid, frustrated woman?

Because she was allowed—forget any rhetoric to the contrary, I really mean *allowed*—only her family as an outlet?

The family is a very narrow sphere. It is cruel to bottle up immense talents there. It isn't fair, Mama, what happened to you. Listen to those echoes: not fair, not fair—not kind, not decent, not loving, *not fair!* Where is that girl who galloped bareback across the Idaho plains with her hair flying? That she is lost, that her gifts were ignored and spurned and pounded out of her is a cause for grief to those of us who know and love her. But multiply her life by the billions, and try to keep from howling with rage and despair at the impoverishment that women's bondage has wreaked upon the human family!

My mother's childhood took place before cars or radio struck rural Idaho, when families had to make their own entertainment if they were going to have any. Deeply believing, deeply Mormon, her family's idea of a good time was to sit around after supper—often hordes of them, including married children with children of their own who were living there temporarily, and friends stopping overnight on their way to somewhere—and tell "faith-promoting" stories, stories full of wonderful, scary, supernatural stuff. Everyone had stories to tell of miraculous healings. Everyone had seen, expected to see, or knew someone who had seen spirits, or had had glimpses beyond the veil. The recounting of these experiences not only entertained and comforted everyone, but reaffirmed their faith. Truly there was life after death, we would see our loved ones again, they did still care for us—were, perhaps, looking after us, seeing and hearing us even now. The veil between the living and dead, between God and his children on earth, was very thin and might become completely transparent at any moment.

Years later I, in turn, listened spellbound to those same stories. Mom's sister, my Aunt Ruby, had had a young son die horribly from tetanus. That he had been in agony when he died troubled Ruby's heart continually, and though she prayed and time passed, she could not be reconciled to his death. She grieved constantly and prayed that she might know "of a certainty" that he was all right.

As the story went, Ruby, who was ward chorister in Woodruff, was at the meetinghouse one afternoon practicing, facing the front door. Suddenly the door opened and a strange young man walked up the aisle toward her. As he drew nearer, Ruby, transfixed, recognized him as her son, who had died as a much younger boy. He took her hand gently and assured her that he was happy and busy where he was, and that she needn't worry about him any longer.

I loved that story as a child, because in the end Aunt Ruby wasn't sad anymore.

Uncle Ben, Ruby's husband, was a renegade Mormon in his youth and in their early married years generally dismayed his family and community. Apparently he also dismayed heaven, because, as Uncle Ben told it, one night when he was seriously ill his long-dead father appeared at his bedside and commanded him to get up and follow him. Together they stepped into an elevator which rose and then opened to let them off in a place that was so glorious it was always beyond Ben's descriptive powers. There, he recognized many of his deceased friends and family members, all peacefully going about their business. And in the midst of them stood one being whose beauty and majesty outshone the others as the sun outshines the stars.

Ben was particularly drawn to the wonderful being and longed to stay among these people, but his father guided him firmly back onto the elevator. This time it descended, and when it stopped again and the doors opened, Ben knew at once that he did not want to get off in this other world that spread before him. When he protested, his father, with mournful mien, explained that it was this place, not the first, that Ben's life had merited.

Appalled, Ben pleaded to be allowed to have another chance and not have to die in a state of unworthiness. He promised that if his life was spared this one time, he would repent and sin no more. Miraculously, his wish was granted, and Uncle Ben kept his side of the bargain for the rest of his life. It became a gentle family joke (we all loved Uncle Ben) that as a self-righteous old man, he often excused some fault in himself with a solemn "After all, I'm just human like the rest of you!"

I often heard Mom tell about the time her father, who had left his family in Idaho while he served a mission for the church in the South, had a dream in which he saw his sons hauling logs over the river in winter. As he watched, a huge log rolled off the load, crushing and killing one of the men. Grandpa knew even while he was dreaming that he was not really dreaming, but was being allowed to witness an actual event. He wrote to his family, mourning the loss of his son, weeks before word of it reached him from home.

The hand of God was seen in all such experiences, and in most incidents of everyday life as well.

This is the world my mother gave me to grow up in—a warm, secure world in which the living and dead were on speaking terms, and where heaven and its powerful inhabitants were intimately involved in human affairs and perpetually on call.

But such talk of miracles, which used to be daily fare in Mormon homes, is discouraged by the church today and is in danger of becoming extinct. We are told that we must base our beliefs not on miracles, but on scripture and on the words of our leaders, which are considered of equal weight.

I believe that this restriction, this mandate for us to rely more upon our leaders for spiritual direction and less upon our own personal relationship with deity, stems from a desire in the hearts of the leaders to gain ever more control over our lives. This trend is evident in many fundamentalist churches across the country, not just in the Mormon church, though the Mormon church provides a model for studying such "New Right" phenomena. A prophet, a pope, or a TV minister is a superstar who denies us, as ordinary church members, the right to the gifts of the spirit. Because spiritual gifts are individual and personal, they strengthen and embolden us. Centralizing these gifts in a charismatic leader, instead, empowers him and the institution he heads. By effectually cutting our individual spiritual life-lines to heaven, church leaders make us dependent upon them for word from God. This is spiritual oppression.

At Brigham Young University in October 1980, a Mormon General Authority told seminary teachers and their wives that true believers do not go ahead of their leaders. When my mother relayed this to me, I was instantly reminded of the story of Anna and the King of Siam, in which everyone had to keep his or her head lower than the king's on pain of death. The King-of-Siam syndrome functions powerfully in the Mormon church today. No one dares have spiritual experiences that might seem to be *more* than those the prophet is having (we are assured that he is having them, but we receive no details, which keeps us even more fearful of "out-holying" him). No one dares seek an experience which might appear to put him or her more in touch with heaven than the prophet is on any issue under the sun, or more in tune with the Holy Ghost. Many exceptionally spiritual members of the church have thus put themselves on hold, lying flat on their spiritual stomachs with their cheeks pressed against the ground (and some have no doubt had to take to the trenches) to avoid raising their spiritual heads above those of the leaders of the church. There they lie, waiting for the day they can look up without fear of finding themselves towering above the General Authorities.

This is one of the reasons there was such relief and joy in the church when the stricture against black males holding the priesthood was lifted several years ago. Thousands of members of the church had had personal confirmation of the Lord's will in the matter of racial prejudice some twenty years before the leaders received it, but lay cramped and chafing on their stomachs until the leaders got the message. When President Kimball was asked when a like revelation would come concerning women, he replied, "Never."

When I was a child, the spiritual and supernatural had not been fenced off "for General Authorities only," and I was as much at home there as in the tangible world. Later in my life, when I went to live in Africa, I felt immediate sympathy for the once-colonized Africans. They lived with a kind of dualism I understood well: on the one hand, their ancient unfragmented world in which the lines between the living and dead were blurred and where mystery and the supernatural were natural, and on the other, European rationalism. I understood it because I, too, had lived with a split consciousness for much of my life: credulous, faithful in my Mormon world, interpreting all natural phenomena in a personal or supernatural way, and critical, skeptical, objective as an educated twentieth-century citizen of the greatest technological state in the history of the world.

The February night in 1936 when the doctor nearly let my mother bleed to death after my birth, Mom and Dad had driven the nearly snow-blocked roads to the small town hospital in Malad, Idaho. At that time, they were living in Washakie, a Shoshone Indian reservation just over the state line in Utah. They were schoolteachers there, grateful to the Lord to be working for the government during the depression, teaching and feeding the "Lamanites," as Indians are called by Mormons. Dad was collecting Shoshone Indian legends for his master's thesis, while Mom did most of the teaching as well as preparing the daily lunch the school was required by law to give the Indian youngsters. Two children had already preceded me into the family: Joyce, aged nine, and Paul, four.

Shortly after I was born we moved to Ferron, Utah, where I spent the first three years of my life. I remember little about that period except for two things: I learned to walk on the top of the round dining-room table, and one day when I answered a knock at the door, a stranger with a mustache grabbed me up in his arms and kissed me. It was my father, returning from a mission to Minnesota. In the three months he had been gone, I had forgotten him.

Those early years seem as if they happened in twilight. Perhaps the house was a dark house. Perhaps it was the feeling inside the house that was dark. My parents were not very happily married, which might account for there never being an excess of warmth or joy in our home, though to be fair, our life as a family was pleasant enough and often happy.

My real memories begin in Preston, Idaho, where we moved next and lived until I was twelve. Dad taught seminary in Preston, and my mother—always the ambitious and risk-taking one—found and bought a house for us after a couple of years of unsatisfactory renting. It was from that house that I went off to school and discovered the miracle called reading.

I will never forget the power and excitement I felt as I began to realize that marks on a piece of paper could speak to me. Learning to decipher those marks and to receive the communication was the most transcendent experience of my young life; reading has remained one of my greatest pleasures.

Like many children, I was a longing and often lonely child. I don't mean that I was unhappy or that I didn't have many friends, but that I sensed early in life the truth that we are all ultimately alone, even in the midst of others. That our uniqueness, which is our greatest glory, is also our greatest burden.

My own longing and need produced rich and various fantasies. Because of them (and because I'm descended from a line of tall-tale tellers on my father's side), for several years I told a continuing story to a group of girls I walked home from school with—each day a new episode, rather like a soap opera. A wandering minstrel, I, beginning my lifelong love affair with words.

My private fantasies became my way of dealing with the atrocities of the Second World War, which was raging during my formative years. Making myself small and inconspicuous so I wouldn't be shooed away, I listened to the grown-ups talk for hours about the savage brutality of the Nazis: their prison camps, the extermination of the Jews, the experimental operations that rumor said were being performed on helpless prisoners without anesthetics. Sometimes one of the adults would look up and see me crouching quietly nearby in large-eyed horror, and hiss to the others, "Shhhhhh. Not in front of the children!" But the conversation would lag for only a moment; soon they would forget me and take up their speculation where they'd left off.

My dreams after these sessions were chilling.

Over the radio I heard the voices of Hitler, Roosevelt, Churchill. The newsreels at the picture show were full of goose-stepping Nazis, tanks, bombs, and death. My young mind was continually wounded by visions of mutilation, starvation, and deprivation of all kinds— bombs shattering cities, bodies, whole countries. It was too big, too hideous for me.

So to deal with it, I turned to a fantasy in which I was transformed into a young man named Jack. Jack went about in the midst of catastrophes and *did* something about them.* He rescued people from the boxcars where they were packed and suffocating on the way to the extermination camps, carried children to safety from burning buildings and found loving arms for them and food and clean, soft beds. I imagined myself, as Jack, sneaking boxes of food in to starving prisoners.

After a while, though, I began occasionally to notice something frightening about Jack's behavior in the face of cruelty. The first time it happened, I was imagining myself as Jack about to rescue a woman from an experimental operation, when I noticed that I wanted not to rescue her, but to *watch.* I had become so excited by the strong sexual overtones that I could not resist watching the mutilation instead of stopping it as I had planned. To watch was repellent and pleasurable at the same time. I would sometimes realize that I was enjoying being not only the observer, but the victim and the perpetrator all at once.

It was deeply guilt-provoking. I was only a little girl, and this knowledge of myself was too terrible, too huge, too complex for me to understand and to forgive. I thought I must be an evil person and that if anyone ever guessed what I was really like, they would detest me. Surely I was the only person who had ever had such feelings, such fantasies. I'd never heard so much as a reference to such things at home or at church or in school. I was so frightened and haunted by them that it took several years of deliberate and fierce exertion of will for me to force them out of my life. In the process, however, I believe I may have damaged my fantasy-producing equipment, be-

---

* That I had to become male in order to *act* is a grim commentary on my view, already formed at this early age, of myself as female and on my idea of femaleness in general. I have never been aware, except in those early daydreams, of wishing to be male. Perhaps I was only being realistic—not wishing to be a man, but wishing to be able to do what men do: act.

cause since that time my fantasies have been few and sketchy. Feeling guilty and isolated in my sin, I successfully strangled my fantasy life by the time I was twelve, and in doing so harmed my spirit.

Though in a way I gave in to it, another part of me resisted the idea that I was evil. Before I was midway into first grade, I had begun to try to read the books in the public library, which rapidly became a haven for me, as well as a laboratory in which I searched eagerly for information about the feelings, longings, and deepest impulses of other human beings. I was searching for answers about myself. I was resisting the conclusion that I thought and felt the way I did because I was a bad person. I longed to discover that other people were like me, and I wanted to know how they dealt with their personal complexities and contradictions.

The people I knew best—those in my Mormon community—weren't telling. On fast and testimony Sundays (the first Sunday of every month, when everyone fasts for twenty-four hours and gives the money they would have used for food to a fund for the poor), if someone wishes to stand and say what's on their mind, they may. At those meetings, people customarily present their most righteous, most acceptable selves for their neighbors' viewing. It is a meeting from which many people are likely to go away feeling more alienated than ever from themselves, more determined to keep the real self from detection, even from themselves, and more convinced, deep down, that nearly everyone else is living closer to the Lord and is more worthy than they. Fast and testimony meeting is a perfect method of keeping social control of members of the church, by encouraging them to reaffirm their orthodoxy and squelch any nagging doubts—much like communist "self-criticism" sessions.

That was not enough for me. Perhaps the people in books would say how they really felt, would disregard public opinion and expose themselves to me.

Most of all, over the years, I wanted to know about sex—what it was all about, why it was bothering me, and whether it was bothering other people. No one ever spoke of it in my family. When I began to menstruate in the summer between fifth and sixth grades, I hadn't a clue about it, but I wasn't frightened; just curious. My mother, out weeding the garden, told me very little after I came running to her waving my stained panties, except how to cut up cloths to string one between my legs and attach it to another pinned around my waist; how, when they were saturated, to put them to soak in cold water overnight and then wash and hang them out the next day to be used again—all surreptitiously, so no one else in the family would know. I think now, what was there to be ashamed about? But at the time, I simply accepted it as fact that menstruation was the shameful thing it was generally considered.

Now, I wish that my mother and I had announced it triumphantly to the whole family, and that Dad, instead of dying of mortification as he would have (he was almost morbidly prudish), would have been openly delighted and demonstrably proud. I wish we had had a celebration in honor of my becoming a woman.

If men menstruated, this *is* how it would be.

Instead, all during the sixth grade I felt like a freak—taller than anyone else in my class, my breasts hard ugly lumps on my front, my dresses all too short, and my knees bony. I was the only girl in my class who still wore braids; as I recall—although it can't have been true—all the other girls had short blond curls.

When I changed my menstrual rag in the lavatory, I'd stand on the rim of the toilet so no one could possibly discover my secret from underneath the door. I felt old and disillusioned every time I passed the Kotex dispenser where, just the carefree year before, my innocent friend and I were sure little dolls were inside awaiting the drop of our nickels.

The best thing that happened to me in my first twelve years was that I learned to read; the worst was that I began to be haunted by the complexities of my human nature and by the nature of sexist society.

My friend Wendy Strachan whom I met and loved at once when we both taught at the University of Malawi, asked my mother not long ago to tell her about my childhood. All Mom could think of was that I was a happy child, that I skipped or danced wherever I went, could carry tunes before I could talk, was graceful and bright, friendly, and much beloved by teachers and other children at school and church.

But by the time we moved to Logan, Utah, in the summer of 1948 when I was twelve, I was no longer cheerful or good-natured. True, I'd just about squelched my disturbing fantasies, but I was nevertheless becoming progressively more puzzled and perplexed about myself. No one told me about hormones and adolescence, though all adults must surely have known. But especially no one told me about sexism, because no one knew what it was or how it permeated every thought, every action, every feeling of our lives. So I thought I was the only one in the world whose feelings were in a constant state of quake and eruption. I felt as if something were deeply awry and, as females are taught to do, assumed that something must be deeply awry within *me*. It never occurred to me to look outside myself and into my society to find the place to lay much of the blame for my confusion and hurt. Like so many females before me, I took the blame tenderly into my own heart and nurtured it there. For thirty more years I let it gnaw at my self-confidence, and now I can only marvel that I was as happy as I was during the half of my life that I sheltered my deadliest enemy in my bosom.

Soon after we moved to Logan, I became organist for the junior Sunday school in the Logan First Ward* and kept that position for years. After playing for the opening exercises, instead of going to my class to hear the lesson, I'd often walk the short block over to the canal that ran alongside Logan High and Woodruff Elementary School, stand on the little bridge under the huge old poplars, and watch the water slide clear over the brown rocks. I'd stand there and pray aloud and weep and strain to find the reason for my restlessness, my persistent feelings of hopelessness. And often I'd cry, not because I was miserable but because whenever I was alone in that lovely flickering light, or stood still long enough in the fields west of town where I often walked, I became conscious of an irresistible longing for something, a massive overwhelming desire to expand and break out of my skin and soar. I'd stretch up my arms and close my eyes— and remain quite solidly earthbound.

I often interpreted this as sexual desire, because my culture allowed me no other legitimate desire—only the desire for wife- and motherhood, both sexual in nature and both determined by the sex I was born. And I began to accept the indoctrination that I could only be happy, only soar and finally be free, if some good man chose to marry me. I was in the world to serve a sexual function. I was a sexual being—no more, no less. To keep my husband happy and to bear his children was enough.

I could do this, I knew. Then why this ache? Why these years of

* A Mormon ward is roughly equivalent to a parish in other churches.

weeping on the bridge during Sunday school, these endless nights of walking in the fields, my face and shirt soggy with salt and dew? What did I *want*? I didn't know, but oh how I wanted, wanted, *wanted* it!

All my human desires, all my human passion and talent and complexity became simplified and focused on the narrow, self-negating, self-destructive goal of finding a man. I thought the frustration I felt was that I could not be fully sexual with any young man until I married. Perhaps some of it was. Now, though, I believe it was mostly that I could not be fully me with myself or anyone. If society and the church had their way, I could only be *sexual* me, all the days of my life; and I was so very much more.

There are two ways to look at sex: as the sex that people *do* and as the sex that people *are*. In my earlier years, no one mentioned sex much except in the first sense and always in the pejorative: "Don't ever 'play nasty' again!" (when a little girl friend and I were caught with our pants down playing doctor in the vegetable garden). Sex in that context—the kind people do—seemed very much centered around where babies came from. While we still lived in Preston, my younger cousin, Cheryl Baugh, came from Logan to visit and, as we walked along one day, confided to my quivering antennae that her mother had told her a startling new bit of information: *babies are just sort of grunted out.*

"Like a bowel movement?" I asked, incredulous.

"I suppose so," she shrugged.

We pondered that imponderable all the way to town, an imponderable highly conducive to associating birth with bad smells, slime, dirt, and shame.

Something was sick about a society which fulsomely extolled motherhood but wouldn't even tell young women what aperture of their bodies babies issued from, as if we had no right to understand our own various orifices. It was as if somehow our bodies, and especially our sexual organs, didn't ultimately belong to us at all, and that if we thought about them or touched them, we were trespassing upon someone else's property. Which, of course, is patriarchy's clear message to women. From the moment we're born female, our bodies belong to that faceless male who will one day marry us.

Men's bodies belong to themselves from the moment they are born male.

But sex of the second sort—the sex I *am*—is the sex that so hurt-fully dominated my life. The fact that I was female was supposed to define me utterly, to explain everything about me. Biology was des-tiny, which helps me understand now my overriding concern with sex in my youth. I knew instinctively that it was at the heart of my dis-ease, but I thought it was sex of the variety that people *do*. True, that variety *did* trouble me, but only because it was all bound up with the whole problem of being female. The message from society, doubly underlined by the church—that since I was female I was only suited for wife- and motherhood and that that would be enough for me if I were a *real* woman—made everything about my present and future sex-related, sex-based.

No wonder that as I grew older, I grew more troubled. No wonder I mourned on that bridge, no wonder I walked hundreds of praying miles into the fields and mountains during my girlhood. How could I become reconciled to having only one aspect of my multifaceted na-ture allowed me? How could I give up, how could I repudiate, all in me that had nothing to do with sex, with wifehood and mother-hood? But I couldn't even ask that question then. I could only pray, and pray, and plead with heaven to lead me aright and to forgive my evil nature that struggled so against God's will.

The reality, of course, which I surely knew in the depths of my soul, was that I was only *incidentally* female, that it should not be the overriding fact of my existence, and if it was, then it was a perver-sion. That I was a human being was and should have seemed the central defining fact of my life. After all, my eyes saw what human—not just female—eyes see; my brain registered the ideas human—not only female—brains register; my heart felt the longings of all human hearts, not just female hearts. And my physical systems—circulatory, digestive, regulatory, nervous; all but my reproductive system—were simply *Homo sapiens*.

I was being methodically reduced by my society to mere ovaries, womb, and vagina. Even taken all together, those parts make a very small, very limited, very stunted, and very partial woman.

No wonder I was miserable.

Sex is a topic so fraught with anxiety in the Mormon church that it is no surprise that countless distortions have arisen around it. My first overtly rebellious act in the church came about because of a lec-

ture on chastity given the young women in the Logan First Ward in
the early 1950s when I was about fifteen. Chastity night was held
once a year and, as I recall, was invariably dreadful. Later, as an
adult and president of the young women's organization, I remembered my own youth and did what little I could to make chastity
nights times of useful discussion. But this particular night took the
all-time atrocity award.

About twenty girls, some with their mothers, were gathered to listen to a woman we had heard marvelous things about for the preceding few weeks. She was the wife of a high official of the church in
our area, and she herself worked in the temple. Either one of these
qualifications was impeccable, but together they were formidable.
Therefore we could be assured that she would speak with the spirit
of the Lord and that all she would say would be inspired, hence true.

She was indeed lovely to look at, slender, dressed in white, her
every hair starched in place in true 1950s fashion (as Mormon
women in Utah still wear theirs), and a pleasure to listen to as she
spoke with the gentle, beautifully modulated Mormon-woman voice.
In front of her on the table, in a white bud vase, stood a single white
rose, a pure, virgin rose. As she spoke about the evils of necking and
petting and referred vaguely to other acts of physical intimacy between males and females, she tore off the rose petals one by one,
crushing them between her thumb and forefinger and dropping
them, bruised and wrinkled, onto the table. Hypnotized, I watched
those ruined petals fall, one by one, each striking shame to my soul
as I remembered the kisses and embraces and occasional hot fum-
blings at bodices and crotches I had indulged in at one time or another (and felt certain many of the other girls in the room had as
well).

Then, by way of finale, she staged a major performance by trying
to pick up the brown petals and fit them back onto the stem. Impossible, of course. Triumphantly she announced, "You are just like this
rose. If you sully your body by allowing boys to touch it in forbidden
ways, you can never be whole or beautiful or pure again, just as the
petals of this rose can never be pure and white again. No good man
will ever want to marry you."

This declaration shocked me out of my trance of self-hatred and
self-condemnation. She might be the wife of a local dignitary of the
church, she might be a temple worker, I might be only fifteen years

old, but I knew the gospel of Jesus Christ and I knew she was dead wrong. I was always surprised to find that adults, especially adults whom everyone looked up to, were often wrong. Now as an adult I wonder why I was ever surprised.

I went from that meeting out into the cool night air and took one of my very long walks around the west end of Logan, letting the fresh air help clear away the doctrinal murk of the rose performance. As I walked I pondered what I had seen and heard. After going over it all in detail and all I had been taught in my home and in church and had read in the scriptures, I decided that despite her lofty qualifications she was, as I had initially supposed, flat-out heretical. Satisfied with my conclusions and how I had reached them, I went home to bed.

The next Sunday was fast and testimony meeting. I sat in the alto section of the choir facing the congregation. It is hard for me to believe now how naïve I was that day; I had no idea that when I rose and said what I had to say it was going to upset anybody. I believed that because it was true, others only had to have it pointed out to them to agree. So I rose and told the congregation that day that a temple worker had come and preached false doctrine to us young women. I described her performance and attacked her conclusion on the basis that Christ had taught repentance as a method of becoming totally whole and pure and beautiful again: though your sins be scarlet, they shall be white as snow.

I don't remember being or sounding angry, though probably I was undiplomatic. But I had certainly been shortsighted not to anticipate the results of disagreeing with adults, especially the temple worker, and repudiating her white rose.

When I sat down, the president of the young women's organization, who had been responsible for the chastity night program, stood up. In tearful frenzy, trembling at my lack of gratitude, she castigated me for my insensitivity to the spirit which the temple worker's speech had showered upon our youthful heads. She personally, and she was sure everyone else in attendance at the white rose ceremony would agree, could testify that she had been spiritually lifted—just about off her feet—and here I had to spoil it all by being contentious!

Others followed her, denouncing me in less direct ways (Mormons know a hundred ways to show disapproval without frontal attack. I know; I've been the object of them all), but doing their best, all of them, to reestablish in the meeting a firm core of orthodoxy by opposing the aberrant. Each had to make clear to others and to themselves that *they*, at least, were sound in the faith.

When the meeting was over and my best friend turned to me and said, "Why did you have to do that?" I was stunned. Couldn't she see why I had had to do that? *Someone* had to do it, didn't they? Could we leave all those young women thinking there was no hope for them if they weren't perfect? Errors with such serious consequences, I was convinced, had to be corrected.

My parents had been in the audience. At home Dad scolded me and worried, as usual, about what others would think of *him*—a seminary teacher who couldn't train his daughter not to behave in such a distressingly and essentially un-Mormon confrontive manner. Escaping into the bathroom, I locked the door and sat down on the toilet seat to think it all over. Mom knocked gently and asked to be let in. She comforted me as well as she could, though she also cared far too much about public opinion (perhaps as much a small-town as Mormon trait, though Mormon small towns are doubly rigid). She knew that what I had said was right. And though I dismayed her, she cared as much about me as about her own reputation. This has always been the difference between her and my father.

My father's response to my peccadilloes was always the same. I brought public shame upon him briefly again when I was eighteen. A man from our ward was hauled bodily off the podium at stake conference one Sunday for preaching polygamy. Now, though polygamy is still believed by church members to be an eternal principle (God is polygamous), one that all righteous souls will practice in the hereafter, and though it was once regarded as the ultimate sign of righteousness in Mormondom, and though Mormon men still anticipate having many female bodies at their disposal in the hereafter (which strikes me now as a very Eastern and hedonistic view of heaven), it is now heretical and excommunicable to practice polygamy on this earth. Preaching it at such a formal, orthodox gathering cut the man off at once from the good will of the Latter-day Saints. He became an instant social disaster, a pariah.

Watching from the balcony, I was as horrified as the next Mormon when he waved his Doctrine and Covenants—the Mormon scripture that contains the revelation from God to Joseph Smith establishing polygamy—and announced that the leaders of the church had apostatized from The Principle.

His name was John and I knew him slightly. He'd walked me home from church once or twice and preached polygamy to me, so I'd already known his views on the subject and hated them. After the session in which he performed so electrically, I bumped into him outside the front doors of the tabernacle.

"John," said I, "you shouldn't have done that. People are half dead with shock." As we talked, we walked down the street toward home—together, in full view of the entire stake (the Mormon equivalent of diocese).

When I got home Dad was fit to be tied, or, as folks said where Mom grew up, he was "having a fit and falling in it."

"You know what people will think, Sonia," he raved. "Birds of a feather flock together!"

"You can call my feathers anything, Dad, but polygamous they most certainly are *not!*"

And so on. Again I had heaped shame on my father's head, but it was short-lived. Everyone soon saw that I had no intention of becoming one of John's wives—I wouldn't have wished to be his only one—and when he later left Logan he went somewhere and, rumor had it, married much.

Remembering those days in detail, I wonder now whether Mother was perhaps proud of me, if only a little and fearfully. Probably not.

Looking back, I recognize that what most outraged me about the temple worker's rose drama and about polygamy was the sexism, the blatant sexism. I had, of course, no way even to organize myself to think about sexism; it was a non-concept. But I know that its manifestations invariably outraged me. And confused me, because I could not, as the phrase goes today, get a handle on it.

Another incident happened at about this time in my life that completed my evolution into a lifelong foe of the double standard. I remember hearing Elder Mark E. Peterson, one of the most revered of the church's twelve apostles, speak about chastity in the venerable and lovely old Logan Tabernacle where all stake conferences were held when I was young. One example he gave has not lost its putrescent luster over the thirty intervening years: "Girls, every time you let a boy kiss you, it's like someone licking butter off a piece of bread. What man is going to want a piece of bread with all the butter licked off?"

The implications behind this are legion and obvious, and I must get on with my story. But briefly, I felt, though I could not understand it clearly then, that this denied female sexuality entirely. It denied that girls kiss boys, too. It said that they were sexually passive—objects that males act upon. The buttered bread theory also implied that boys never had their butter licked off, no matter how many females they kissed. They can kiss and neck and pet their heads off and still have their butter intact, but are well within their self-righteous rights to go around checking suspiciously for *girls'* butter. But most of all, what this said to me was that *men* are not roses, they are not pieces of buttered bread. They are not objects, they are human beings. Only women are things—roses and bread.* Never in the church do we hear men referred to by analogies that make them objects or anything less than fully human. Women, like objects, are presumed to have been created for men's use. We don't use people; we use things. Men are the consumers of women.

The double standard is the basis of the patriarchal order: men have privileges that women do not have, only one of which is that they never lose their chastity—never get their butter licked off. Chastity is not a concept that relates to men. No woman would refuse to marry a man who was no longer a virgin. It is a concept men impose upon women, not upon each other.

Several years ago, in a sacrament meeting in the Sterling Park Ward in Virginia, a young woman who attended Brigham Young University and was home for the summer was speaking. (Mormons do not have a paid clergy; members do all speaking and administration at the local level.) She told about going out with a young man at BYU whom she came to like very much, and apparently the feeling was mutual. One night after he had taken her to visit his family,

---

* Tellingly, at hearings on the Human Life Amendment in the early summer of 1981 in Washington, D.C., women were never referred to as women, but as "space capsules" and "tape recorders," and other "things." Objectifying women in this way distances men from the emotional consequences of what they are proposing, from the human suffering they would have to take into account if they were to think of women as having feelings and desires and capacities like their own. So they strip women—and their other enemies—of any human qualities in order to justify committing atrocities against them. You can deprive, torture, rape, and kill people without regret if they are just "cunts"—or "Japs" or "Gooks" —and not women and men, not your sisters and brothers.

which seemed a hopeful sign, he drove to the local parking spot and parked. She was dismayed and panicky, because she knew she had only two options. On the one hand, she could allow some lovemaking, which might make him think she was "easy" and therefore not a nice girl, not the sort of girl he would want to marry. On the other hand, she could insist that they leave, and risk humiliating him and, therefore, losing him. The classic double bind. I believe she said an urgent silent prayer at this point—I certainly would have if I'd been of her mind—and then said to him, quietly and oh so gently so as not to offend, "Do you think Jesus Christ would approve of this?"

Silently he started up the car and took her home. For the next few days she lived in a state of agonized apprehension. Then, thank God, he called, and as they drove around town he told her how much he respected her for doing what she had done, and confided that if she had "let" him, he never would have gone out with her again.

She ended her speech in church by saying how thankful she was that the church had made her the kind of girl who could keep the affections of this kind of boy.

In the audience, not yet fully a feminist but a foe of the double standard in its most obvious forms since my rose-and-butter days, I was appalled at her recital. And even more appalled at her blindness to what she was actually saying. How could she still think highly of a boy who would park and neck with *her* but despise her for necking with *him*? If she had not totally accepted the double standard entrenched in the church, she would have sent that clod scampering for his life, instead of being humbly grateful that he still liked her. Humble, nonsense! Grateful, fiddlesticks! She is worth a dozen of him! I hope she never settles for any man who does not take equal responsibility for the decency and goodness of their relationship. Because any man who is willing to let the woman he claims to love bear the terrible weight of responsibility and guilt for any sexual misdemeanors loves a suspiciously unloving love.

Soon after I was excommunicated, I received a letter from a Mormon woman that said: "My awakening occurred twenty years ago at the end of a pristine (in my view) date with a young Mormon man who brought me to my door, called me a Jezebel, and castigated me for the lustful thoughts I had aroused in him. He ordered me in his best patriarchal voice to enter my home, fall on my knees, and pray for forgiveness for the sins I had made him long to commit. A few

days later when the shock wore off, I began a long process of analyzing the church's attitude toward women . . ."

In the Mormon church, the subject of sex is so unspeakably
fraught that leaders in dealing with it often cannot bring themselves
even to say the word "sex," let alone the names of the sexual organs.
In a little pamphlet entitled "To Young Men Only," Boyd K.
Packer, one of the twelve apostles of the church, speaks of the male
sexual organ as "the little factory" throughout, admonishing boys
not to tamper with it. The word "masturbation" does not occur
once.

(I suspect that what this little pamphlet really accomplishes is to
insult young men with the word "little," and that the emphasis on
the sin of masturbation does not teach Mormon males not to mas-
turbate, but to lie about it.)

When to speak the names of the acts of sex or the sexual parts of
the body is so powerfully taboo, it is little wonder there are so many
sexual cripples in the church. God gave us our glorious bodies. It is
as foolish and as unclean to be excessively prudish about them, to
treat them as if they were shameful pits of iniquity, as it is to abuse
them. Bodies are scientific facts, not to be feared, but to be respected; not to be made dirty by endless insinuation and circumlocu-
tion and adolescent hush-hush, but to be dealt with in honesty, with
integrity, as they deserve.

I was the middle child of five, and in my particular family that was
the best possible position to have been born into. My sister Joyce
was too much older for me to have known her well. I did know she
was having difficulties in her life, but I was too young to understand
them. Now I believe that one of her main problems was the same as
mine: she was born female to parents who, like most people of their
time, did not value femaleness. I lay my sister's considerable suffering
at the door of the sexism in American culture and, intensified as it is,
in Mormon culture. Today Joyce is a humorous, kind, and gentle
person, and unjoyful. My heart aches with the intimations of what
she could have become if she had not been pounded and battered by
her culture into being merely female.

I knew my older brother, Paul, better when I was a child because
he was nearer my age, and he figures more prominently in my story
now because he is the only one of my siblings who personally made

strong efforts to get me excommunicated from the church—for my own good, of course. While he was not unnaturally cruel as a child, neither was he particularly kind, and until this, never took much interest in my life. I do not believe he ever liked me much then, so I feel no great loss that he does not like me now. Like the leaders of the church, however, he has vowed that he "loves" me.

Late one night in the summer of 1978, Paul called us from Utah. When I answered the phone, he harshly commanded, "Get me the patriarch of the family!" I was so shocked at his ferocity that I sprang to get Rick, and listened intently to his side of the conversation. His side was continually interrupted by the diatribe on the other end, but he finally managed to say that he was neither my father nor my boss, and I was a free agent and could do as I wished.

When he hung up, I asked, "What was *that* all about?" He shrugged and said, "Oh, Paul's hysterical about you and the ERA. He ordered me to be the head of the house and forbid you to be involved with it." (At that time, the extent of my ERA activity had been marching in two parades with Rick and the kids.) As just this one incident demonstrates, Paul believes that men have the God-given right to govern women. He accuses our mother of being responsible for all I've done by providing me with a poor example: she had, he tells her severely, "worn the pants in the family." I notice, however, that Paul is participating eagerly enough in the inheritance that Mother amassed for her children by uncommon diligence, skill, and wisdom, and by wearing the pants.

Two boys were born after me, Michael seven years later and Mark nine. They were too young to have much effect on my life until they were teenagers. It was then that I began to be angry at the system into which I had been born. The boys were never required to help with chores around the house, a fact I found bitterly unfair. But my mother was only doing what she had seen done. Those were the days when we still ironed, and though she and I would iron as many as two dozen shirts at a sitting (or standing), it would never have occurred to anyone that my brothers should have been ironing their own shirts, pressing their own suits, picking up their dirty clothes and washing them, to say nothing of ironing Mom's and my blouses, pressing *our* skirts, picking up *our* dirty clothes and laundering them. Those who airily maintain that women are not the servant class of the world either had the very good fortune not to come from families with a power distribution like mine—which I think were the rule, not the exception—or are simply still not aware.

My mother misunderstood the scripture, and the church helped her in this: "He who would be first among you, let him be the servant of all." She did not realize then, although I think she does now (theoretically if not practically), that her being our servant made my father and brothers monsters of selfishness and immaturity, and that none of us is grateful for her sacrifice, since it damaged both her and us. Her sacrifice, in fact, seems self-indulgent: it was easier to do it herself than to have the gumption to counter the prevalent theory of male supremacy in the home and see to it that everyone did his share because this is the way life is. Mom should have had a life of her own, separate from us, so she couldn't have waited on us hand and foot and so we would have had to respect her as an individual person with rights of her own—rights to freedom from drudgery—as we regarded ourselves. She caused us to think of women as negligible, because, somehow, when someone is eager to be a doormat, those around them always seem equally eager to oblige by becoming foot wipers. Which is devastating for doormats and foot wipers alike.

It was not just "lack of gumption" that kept Mom subservient in our home, however; serving us was her way of compensating for Dad's impatience with us. She admitted this to me when I was a teenager.

My father. What can I say? He is an old man, and has been humiliated before his friends by my excommunication. He was never able to love anyone very deeply, a fact I understood early in my life. As I look at every member of my family, I see how all of us have been at the mercy of the accidents of birth. Dad became the person he is from growing up in his parents' home, where he was not adequately loved or respected. Who was to blame—his parents? Who failed Bob and Sylvia before they failed my father in their turn? How far back should we go to look for the culprit who sowed the first seeds of unhappiness by not honoring and hallowing all young and old human spirit and flesh?

My father was a bookish child in an anti-intellectual small western frontier town, and he was ridiculed for it. He loved to read in a society that considered reading for pleasure sissified. He was a sensitive child, and his father tweaked his ears hard when he made mistakes in arithmetic. He had a younger brother whom his parents adored and who could do no wrong, whereas *he* somehow could do no right. Little wonder that he came to marriage with wounds that never healed and could not be healed, and lumps of scar tissue on his psyche that had twisted his perceptions of himself and the world all out of shape.

But, like Mom, he is unable to find fault with his parents. His enculturation, however, tells him it is all right to blame his wife for his failures, so he does. "I would have been great," he scolds my mother, "if you'd stood behind me and supported me like Velda did Devere (Dad's much-adored younger brother)!"

I weep for all of us in that family, and yet it was as good a family as most I know. I weep for all people in all families because we are all still so hurtful to one another, even the best and happiest. There is always much to overcome. My own children are having to come to terms with the legacies Rick and I left them. May they have God's blessing in it.

My parents both believed mightily in God. They also both firmly believed that Joseph Smith had seen a vision in a grove near Palmyra, New York, in the early nineteenth century and had consequently established Christ's church, in its original purity again, upon the earth. Because of Smith's vision, my mother's father came across the plains with his family when he was three years old, and my father's grandfather, who was one of the first members baptized in England, emigrated to be with the Saints. Mormonism is almost part of their genetic makeup; it is in their very blood and is confirmed in each beat of their hearts. To some of us they passed this intact. To me, for instance. Joyce, having done all that is required of her, goes to church and finds solace there. Paul uses it to justify and bolster his intolerance. Mike, who believed deeply for many years, has in the past few years found much amiss with the doctrines and the general day-to-day operation of the immense and hierarchical corporation that is Mormonism. Mark, the last in line, was less impressed with it all than the rest of us until recently, but was never any less righteous. He was always slow to judge others, and as quick to believe the best as Paul is to believe the worst. Dad is afraid not to conform; fear has always been behind his orthodoxy. Love as well as fear are behind Mother's, but she is not totally blind to the discrepancy between the rhetoric of the church about women and women's actual position in the church and society.

And I, of course, have become a child of the devil, a heretic. But I am jumping ahead of my story.

My parents were well educated by secular standards as well as thoroughly trained in the teachings of the church. If the church had awarded Ph.D.s for knowledge of its doctrines and for living them, both would have earned them *magna cum laude*. When Dad was not at work teaching religion classes for the church, which he did for thirty years, he was reading. Most of what he read was church-related, often the scriptures, which he knows thoroughly. He was an inveterate information sharer, and would read especially provocative passages to anyone who was handy, following us around, saying excitedly, "Listen to this!" We had family prayer morning and evening— or at least Mom tried to get us there—and once a month we got together for family night before the weekly family home evening program was put into effect. Every month two men came from the church to give us some gospel message and to make sure all was well with us, and two women from the Relief Society made a call on Mama. In the meantime, we all attended church for about four hours every Sunday—priesthood meeting early in the morning for the men, then Sunday school for everyone. In the evening we went back for sacrament meeting, sometimes attending choir practice earlier or an informal "fireside" gathering afterward. During the week there were auxiliary classes for women, teenagers, and children, organized and taught for the most part by women, except for the advanced scouting program. And there were frequent and wonderful parties.

Our lives were absorbed by this activity, centered around the church. The church *was* our lives. Life without the church was unthinkable. At every meeting, every social function, the concepts of the religion were in some way clarified, the purpose being to strengthen the resolve of the Saints to follow them. From a very early age, I was so resolved.

As I grew older, married, and lived in many different wards and branches of the church, I realized that my religious training at home far surpassed that of most Mormons, partly because discussion of religion was going on in one way or another much of the time, and partly because I had a philosophical bent and searched it out myself with interest and enthusiasm.

My father was the student of religion, my mother the mystical participant in it. My father read, my mother prayed. She took as a command the scriptural admonition to pray always, and went about much of the time in a state of grace. I used to feel as if I was interrupting something whenever I wanted to speak to her, and I was. Her belief in and love of God were nearly palpable, and as much a part of her as her gentle manner and iron core.

Perhaps because his earthly father had been unloving and tyrannical toward him, my father's view of God was punitive and harsh, a view the Old Testament and the Book of Mormon were right in there doing their part to corroborate. My mother thought her father had been perfect. When he died I suspect she simply transported him to the heavens as God and took up her old relationship with him. But perhaps I'm wrong. She confided to me not long ago that, in opposition to the dictates of the church, she has always thought of Jesus Christ when she prayed, not God the Father. This little rebelliousness shocked me. But then, as I told my bishop in one of his probing sessions, if he could see into the hearts of the members of his ward, he would probably find it necessary to excommunicate at least half of them.

In 1968, nearly twenty years after the temple worker sadistically mauled her rose and planted a seed of feminism deep in my brain, the bishop of the Palo Alto second ward, Henry D. Taylor, Jr., watered and cultivated it by reading from the pulpit a priesthood directive sent out by the first presidency of the church prohibiting women from leading the congregation in prayer in the sacrament meetings of the church from that time forward.

Sitting in the audience with baby Marc on my lap, I was stunned. My first reaction, shared by every Mormon woman I ever discussed this directive with, was "What have we done wrong? What have women done to deserve this?" assuming, as it is the custom of good church members to assume, that if the leaders had done this, then it must be the will of God, and therefore that women had somehow displeased him.

But close behind this reaction came a clear, crisp knowledge: this was *not* the way God behaved in his relationship with his children. The teachings of the scriptures said that before God punishes anyone, he warns them. Many of the stories in scripture revolve around God's warnings for people to repent so he won't have to punish them. And only after many warnings and no repentings does he finally and reluctantly punish them. I knew in that second instant after hearing the directive that this policy was not from God, because *women had not been warned*. And in that moment, I saw that the men of the church had arbitrarily taken away from women rights and privileges that are ours from our Heavenly Parents and that are therefore inviolable. I also realized that we are without recourse because we are without a voice in the policy making of the church.

After the meeting, I went to talk to Bishop Taylor, whom I respected and liked. He couldn't explain it to me, and seemed dismayed at it too. He was a decent man, and I believe he knew in his heart that this was foul play. But like the rest of us, he was willing to go along with it because it only concerned women.

Several years later, still troubled by the implications of this policy, I approached one of those bishops who look right through women as if they don't exist. He didn't even hear me. Very young, very pompous, very smug, he assured me that if the leaders had done it, God had wanted it done. That was that. He was not at all dismayed; he even showed me in the Bishop's Handbook the passage specifying that only holders of the priesthood could offer prayers in sacrament service, and told me the reason probably was that men, being holders of the priesthood, needed more practice being in the public eye, needed to be accorded more important duties so they would "feel good about themselves," needed to learn how to perform public duties. In the classically patriarchal sexist mode he elaborated upon this theme. Women are more spiritual and righteous than men; therefore, men *need* to give prayers more than women do to teach them to be better persons.

I asked him when God had begun punishing people for being more righteous? I told him that had not seemed to me to be God's way. But if it were, it certainly behooved women to be as backsliding as men so we, too, could be allowed to have the privileges and responsibilities in the church that made for growth.

His answer was that since women were able to have babies, men should have everything else. I'm sure he did not realize that he was outlining for me how the patriarchy justifies male rule, and how it punishes women for being the bearers of children by effectively cutting them off from all other growth opportunities.

I have since been accosted by enraged Mormon women who have asked cuttingly, "Why is it so important to you to give prayers in public? You must really need attention!" How do they think men would react if suddenly they were not allowed to lead the congregation in prayer in any meeting in which women were in attendance? Would they think the men just wanted attention if they protested? No, because men are humans and have rights and authority. It is natural for them to wish to pray and speak and preside. I know many men who have wished to become bishops more than anything in the world and have finally made it. No one suggested that it was because they wanted adulation, recognition, attention, power. When we're talking about men, we attribute noble motives: they wish to serve God.

Well, I, too, have always wished to serve God, and praying is serving God, a right all mortals have, and should have equally. But as women we have been taught to distrust any motive in ourselves or other women that is strong and brave and demanding of justice. We have been taught it by the patriarchy, whose purposes it serves to have us meek, passive, submissive, and distrustful of one another as females. In this way, male leaders keep us from joining with one another against a system which oppresses us, which belittles and trivializes us.

During the next ten years, I sat in anguish through every sacrament-meeting prayer. That we women had had that right so dishonorably stolen from us never stopped hurting until, at the end of that decade, I had the rare good fortune to be influential in putting matters straight again.

During this same decade, 1968 to 1978, leaders of the church also put into effect a system of administration called the "priesthood correlation program," which effectively stripped the women's auxiliary of autonomy and made women subject in all things administrative and budgetary to the men of the church. In this action, the men almost overstepped themselves and woke the women up. And though most women were so deeply unconscious that they merely muttered a little in their sleep, some proved they had not yet been totally robotized. Their cries of rage and pain echoed all through the church. Even my gentle, church-adoring mama regarded it with astonishing clear-sightedness as the treachery it most assuredly was. And though Mormon women can rationalize this fall from trusted adulthood into permission-asking childhood, I have heard more upright Mormon women complain about this usurpation of power than about any other action of church leaders in my lifetime—until the advent of the Equal Rights Amendment. Many women who would not dream of criticizing church leaders on any other matter under the sun cannot prevent themselves from complaining bitterly about this power play.

Somewhere, not much beneath the surface of my own awareness, anger at the treatment of women in the church was coming to a rolling boil.

Then in Palo Alto, where we had returned from Malaysia in 1974, Rick began to chafe at his job; he was also finding other women attractive, he told me, and this worried him. So he found a job we could do together: going about the country for the U. S. Office of Education, teaching educators how to evaluate their Title I projects. We bought a motor home, put all the kids in it, and set off for the next year. Twenty-one bicentennial states, hundreds of hours of teaching our own children and of feelings of severe strain on our marriage later, we came to Virginia. On Kari's eleventh birthday, June 25, 1976, we bought the house in which the seeds of feminism, planted long ago in Logan and watered and cultivated along the way by various repressive church programs and edicts, finally sprouted.

Hello Virginia, Sterling Park Ward, ERA, feminism, and the new world!

Chapter 4

The Bursting of the File

IT ALL BEGAN unsensationally enough. It all began with Hazel.

A year after we left Palo Alto, we abandoned our motor home for the first house we ever owned, a big red brick beauty in the Virginia woods. The first time we went through it, we got lost. Hallways, room after room, doors—it was a large, complicated affair that I loved at first sight. The dimensions, the light, the enormous open, windowed space convinced me of the psychological effects of architecture. The house was the perfect set on which to stage my private feminist drama, which was one of spiritual expansion and of ever-increasing light and spaciousness. I feel now as I walk about this house as if my inner and outer environments are finally in harmony.

Soon after we bought the house, I called Hazel. From Minnesota, where we had all been graduate students together and all very active in the church, she and Ron had moved to Alexandria, Virginia. While Rick and I had moved all around the globe, we had kept in sporadic touch. But I hadn't actually talked to Hazel for fifteen years, and when I hung up the phone from that first conversation I turned to Rick and said, puzzled, "Something has happened to Hazel. She sounds shocking!"

What had happened to me was that I had just spoken to my first feminist, an experience that has been known to fill even the stoutest hearts with alarm. Perhaps the reason I had not encountered a feminist until ten years into the women's movement and forty-two years into my life was that I was a Mormon—which provides substantial protection from reality. Also, I had spent so much of the pre-

ceding twelve years out of the country in places where the concept of
women's rights is still light-years from dawning. Even though we had
lived a year or two in the United States between these adventures
abroad, so that I knew there was something called the "women's
movement" going on in this country, I really didn't have any idea
what it was all about. I didn't feel hostile toward it; I just wasn't interested. Because one thing was clear: *I* didn't need it. I was having a
very good life, doing exactly what I wanted to do; I was happy, and I
mistakenly thought that only unhappy women were interested in
women's rights. Even after I began calling myself a feminist, I continued to be surprised that the feminists I was meeting were such
well-balanced, warm, good-natured women. Which taught and continues to teach me that being actively engaged in a noble cause is
healthy for the soul.

When she hung up the phone from talking to me that first time,
Hazel must have turned to Ron and said, "Nothing's happened to
Sonia. In fifteen years!" I know I was an anachronism but things *had*
happened, and I was ripe for Hazel.

Hazel. Tall and elegant, tough, analytical, candid, loving, loyal.
And feminist to the core. She discovered her political activist bent in
the civil rights movement of the sixties—no easy position for Mormons then—and accurately assessed the women's movement as its
logical extension.

The women's movement was for everyone, she said, even happy
women like me. Several months later she introduced me to Mormon
feminist friends of hers, one of whom recommended that I stick my
toe into the life-changing waters of feminism by reading a little book
called *I'm Running Away from Home, But I'm Not Allowed to
Cross the Street*. From that primer, I advanced to weep and storm
my way through *The Female Eunuch*, loving Germaine Greer's dash-
ing and brilliant outrage, thinking with admiration, "Now, here's a
real woman!" I agonized through the first chapter of Kate Millett's
Sexual Politics (since that time I have wholeheartedly detested
Henry Miller and Norman Mailer), but was in over my head in the
second chapter and laid it aside for a while.

Rick, who kept our copy of *The Female Eunuch* on top of the toilet so he could read a little every day, suffered the sort of shock and
guilt only men can when their eyes are opened to sexism, and to
their own unwitting part in the systematic oppression of women.

The natural tendency is to feel responsible for all the atrocities per-petrated upon females by the patriarchal system, and initially Rick felt that. Equally as natural is to react against such unreason by de-nying any part in the system at all, and he tried to do that too. One night he came into our bedroom with the book in his hand. Leaning against the doorframe he said, "Everything she says in this book is true. She's right; I know that. But I keep thinking of you. You've had a good life, Sonia. How does all this pertain to you?"

I had to agree that I'd had a good life, better than that of any woman I knew. "But think for a minute back to when we were first married," I said to him, "and think what both our lives have been since. Now ask yourself this question: If we were twenty-five again and just married, would you change places with me, not for just a day or a year, but *forever?*"

I've often read in books how faces "pale." Actually, faces "green," and go taut around the nose. At least that's what Rick's did. For a moment he just stood looking stunned. Then he came over to where I was sitting on the bed, knelt down between my knees, put his arms around my waist and his face in my lap, and wept.

"I had no idea. Please forgive me, Soni. I really didn't know. I'm so very, very sorry. Can you ever forgive me?"

He had looked into his experience and had not shied away from what he saw, had not romanticized and falsified it. Though he did not keep that vision very long, at that moment he was an honest and courageous man. Despite all that has happened since, I will re-member that there was once in him an uncommon sensitivity and decency.

In those winter months of 1976, as Rick and I began our feminist reading, I felt only sadness. I was not yet in touch with the serious anger that had built up in me over my lifetime. The full emotional realization of it, the full fury, lay unplumbed for several more months. I still felt no need to act, no need to change the world. Like most Mormon and other traditional women, I had not yet learned to dare to feel angry at men and their institutions, preferring to turn my anger inward and let it eat away at my well-being instead. It was less frightening to be depressed than to be angry at men.

To be angry at men was to be angry at God.

I was beginning where many begin with feminism—grappling in-tellectually with the fact of the systematic, millennia-old degradation of females. I turned page after page in feminist books, nodding my head in violent agreement, shouting aloud to whomever, "Hey, listen to this. It's so hideously true! This is the way it *is!*" marveling, as I read about incidents in other women's lives, how I'd experienced similar things myself and had not *seen.* How could I have been so blind?

But I didn't really understand the revolutionary implications of what I was reading and of what was beginning to happen to me. Ideas and insights were crashing about in my head, but their yeasty meaning hadn't penetrated my bones, weren't yet swimming in my blood, beating with my heart. I was intellectually engaged, but the business of re-creating myself had barely begun.

Ironically, but naturally enough, it was the church that catapulted me into the appropriate state of anger. And it took the church to force me to transmute that anger into the energy necessary to go forth and fight to right the ancient wrongs.

Over the coming months, as the church cooperated so fully in my transformation, I began to mine and unleash years of pent-up rage upon Rick. Knowing very well that he had not invented sexism, knowing that he was a product of his culture, knowing that he was trying to understand, to be patient, and best of all, to change his own attitudes and behavior—for which I loved him more than ever— still, to me he represented the destructiveness of male supremacy to females, and every new insight into the incredible maiming done to women would fill me with such pain and wrath that rays of my rage would pierce him many times a day.

He had, of course, not been guiltless of dozens of varieties of sexism on a personal level in his relationship with me. Over the years he had made me feel incompetent and not very bright hundreds of times. I had so little self-confidence, I always assumed that he knew what he was talking about and that therefore I did not. While seeming to be eminently just and fair, he condescended mightily and knew very well how to put me down hard. Though somewhere I believe I always knew he bluffed a lot, perhaps I refused to face the fact that in subtle but devastating ways he bullied and belittled me, because I needed to believe in his superiority, too. After all, I'd sacrificed a great deal to be allowed to become part of him. I could not let myself see that I had put all my eggs into one less-than-perfect basket.

In defense against my anger, he resisted feeling personally responsible for women's oppression, including mine. (We both knew that for the most part he had been an unwitting accomplice in the past. But that was *then*. *Now* I couldn't bear it anymore.) But if he expressed his anger at being made to bear what he felt was an unfair measure of the blame, he felt guiltier than ever, so in true Rick fashion, he kept his anger to himself most of the time—a defense that proved ultimately disastrous. Feminism, a simple ideology of equality, is not easy to live. We have no models.

By spring I had come to the end of my capacity to repress my anger and to continue to dodge the issue. One afternoon I sat on the basement stairs and wondered why I felt so depressed. We had a lovely house, I had a part-time editing job (which I didn't enjoy much, but I could do it at home and it left plenty of time for the children and church work); the house was clean, supper was ready to go into the oven, and I had several free hours before everyone came home. Ordinarily all this, plus the fact that we were all well and our lives were going smoothly, should have given me a feeling of contentment. But there I was, swamped with despair and praying aloud, "Why, Father, why do I feel so *awful?* What's wrong with me?"

Just a few days before, on May 3, I'd written a letter to my parents:

"I don't know whether I asked you to offer prayers that I would get the teaching job at the state university in the fall. The classes would be in the evening when Rick's home and would be the salvation of my soul, as I feel now. I am so enormously and thoroughly bored and so much needing to do what I love to do and do so well. I feel certain that can't be offensive to the Lord, and hope you'll join us in asking him for that boon if it would be right for me and the family. When we first moved here, I told Heavenly Father not to worry about me for a while but to get my husband and children established and happy first and I would help with that and not ask for more—for a while. It seems to me that those things have about been accomplished and that—this may sound selfish—it's my turn now. I am really unhappy when my mind is not stimulated and employed, and when I have to rely on church associations for all my fulfillment and stimulation. It makes me dissatisfied with the church. But I don't think the church should have to bear that burden, since the Lord has allowed me to prepare myself to find fulfillment in secular ways as well. Has not only allowed me, but seemed to encourage and bless me so that I could."

Sitting there on the stairs, I wondered briefly whether my malaise might really be what I'd thought when I wrote that letter: that I was bored. So I prayed about it. Was this it? But I knew without asking that lack of mental exercise alone could never cause the kind of despair I was struggling against. I prayed on and on, aloud, as is my wont when I'm alone, but the deadly, leaden feeling refused to budge. And then I remembered a talk I'd heard in church the Sunday before, which suggested that since we don't always understand ourselves well enough to know what we should pray for, we should ask God.

So I did. And no sooner had I done so than I surprised myself by saying, still in vocal prayer: "Father, I know there's something I've been trying to avoid knowing for a very long time—probably all my life—because I've been too afraid to face it, afraid of what it might do to my life and family, afraid I couldn't handle it, that it might overwhelm me and maybe even drive me insane. But I have become so unhappy by not dealing with it, that doing so could not make me any more miserable. So no matter what it is, I am ready to know it. I want to know it. I must know it!"

Immediately, I heard my own voice in my mind say clearly, "Patriarchy is a sham."

Long afterward I was delighted to read in Gail Sheehy's *Passages* that many people, as they begin to understand themselves during mid-life, hear their own voices inside their heads. Probably not often, though I can only speak for myself, having heard it only twice in my life. And according to Sheehy, it is a good sign, a sign of having broken through our socialization and faced what we are, not what we should be or what we wish we were or what others think we are, but what we honest-to-goodness are. What we honest-to-goodness think.

I was a person who had unconsciously known for a very long time that something was wrong with patriarchy, but because my entire culture, to say nothing of my church, was based upon it almost as a given, I hadn't had the courage to face what I knew. And I had never before been close to a context in which I could have understood it even if I had faced it. I had finally become miserable enough that I was willing to risk viewing the evidence I had accumulated from which I had deduced the error of male supremacy. Since the evidences against the divinity of patriarchy are legion, it is no wonder I had a hard time hiding it from myself.

But it is also small wonder I had avoided it for forty-two years. For several minutes it plunged me headlong into a pit of whirling, heart-smashing fear. In the Mormon church, patriarchy is sacred; it is held to be the principle of organization by which a male God created and governs the world through other males like himself. It is the masculine glue that holds the world together. I had been taught this all my life, and had had it reinforced one hundredfold in the temple, that most sacred Mormon structure in which the divinity of patriarchy—of maleness—is the basic message.

Though the terrible, incapacitating fear vanished quickly, the pain of intense conflict remained for years.

I marvel now at myself, that despite the shock and confusion of that moment I did not doubt that what I had told myself was true. My voice in my mind had rung with perfect conviction. The person who had spoken those words in that way knew whereof she spoke.

About a year and a half later, in a letter to friends I described the conclusions I drew from that experience:

"The next few months were very difficult. I had to feel my way along, carefully and painfully. I asked to be given truth as I could stand it, line upon line, precept upon precept, and often felt it had been given before I could stand it. I asked to be able to know what to do with this new information, how to integrate it, how to bear it, how to figure out what it meant in my own life. My husband also prayed and thought and studied, and together we began to move through the wild dark forest of error that has grown up over thousands of years about women. And as we did, I realized why I had heard my own voice and not someone else's—not God's, not my guardian angel's, but my own true voice.

"*I* was the authority about my life, about what being female meant to my existence. *I* was the one who could speak with understanding and truth about myself. My life was *my* responsibility, my salvation was *my* reason for being on the earth. . . . This experience gave me a whole different view of authority. I listen now to the content, not to the prestige of the person who speaks. When it is about women, it must agree with my perceptions of myself and other women, my experience and the experience of women I know intimately and love. Women are the only experts on women."

At the time I sat on the steps and accepted the truth from myself, I hadn't read yet—or if I had, it hadn't registered—what feminists and the women's movement had to say about patriarchy. I did not know yet that I was just one of the millions of women the world over receiving the same message. I did not know then that the Holy Spirit was resting upon all the women of the earth, urging us to come forth out of the long night of patriarchy into the morning of equality. I was euphoric when, many months later, I finally began to understand this.

A few afternoons after the incident on the stairs, as I was lying on the bed in the guest bedroom over the garage pondering all this, I noticed that something seemed to be issuing from me and gathering in a cloud in the corner under the skylight. I sat up on the bed and, pointing at the accumulating grayness, addressed it with surprised recognition: "I know what you are! You are what has troubled me all my life. The problem is that I was born female!"

At this, the cloud spiraled up into the corner and disappeared through the ceiling. And I felt as if I had just made the most profound discovery of my life.

But patriarchy and the problem of being born female were still two separate pieces of a puzzle whose outlines were frustratingly vague in my mind. Because I did not understand what patriarchy really was, I had not yet seen the connection between them. In fact, I did not even understand clearly yet what sexism was. But something I did know: the awakening was upon me in earnest.

During this time, I conducted a very informal poetry writing workshop once a week for a small group of women in my ward. Each time we met we would bring what we had written during the week to read and discuss. Now as I read the poems I wrote then, I remember how I despaired of being understood by those women I loved; I also see my struggle to emerge from my warm dream world, my half-asleep world, into the biting cold clarity and challenge of reality. The poems are mediocre at best but, like a journal, reveal my thinking and feeling at the time:

> *In ten years I will be fifty-two.*
> *Still a dilettante?*
> *Still dependent, childish?*
> *Where is the way out,*

the exit from this small room?
I've been claustrophobic for
half a life.
Open the door, Lord,
and let me out.

I developed a raging intolerance for sermons by men for and about women, so much so that I could hardly bear to sit in the same room. But since I could not just walk out and leave the organ untended, I wrote during such speeches to drown out the nonsense that was issuing from the pulpit:

POWER PLAY IN CHURCH

Here I am again, pouring out
to avoid being poured into, singing
to drown out the cacophony.
It's the "God's will for women" theme again
as decided and decreed by some man again
(a particularly virulent form
of hypocrisy in human males).
It is difficult to pour out, however,
as fast as he pours in
which hardly seems fair
since he is after all tampering with my life
not me with his.
Believe me, if it were vice versa,
if I were insisting that God intended

nay, commanded
all men to be farmers because Adam
was a tiller of the soil
and any who resisted were in league
with you-know-who to destroy the family,
the nation, civilization—
If I were extolling the exquisite joys
of shoveling hog manure in subzero weather
and taking out endless mortgages
in withering heat
and from my spectator's seat

(light-years from such a fate myself)
pontificating that in these tasks

alone
lay the righteous and complete fulfillment
of men's true natures,
hosts of embattled non-farmers would find
a quick way not only to shut me up
but to lock me up
permanently.

Ah he's almost finished, dazzled by his own
magnanimity and noble condescension, awash
with zeal, unassailably righteous
and immensely comfortable
like a nineteenth-century missionary to darkest Africa.

It might smudge his shining smug to learn
that despite his dishonorable intentions
I won—I wrote louder than he talked,
and for the love I bear myself
I'll live louder than he talks
And I'll win.
Amen.

Once a month, all the women of the Mormon church all over the world have a lesson in Relief Society, the women's auxiliary, called "cultural refinement." I taught this lesson up until the time of my excommunication, always with great enjoyment despite the lesson manual. The women in my ward were so intelligent and insightful that I was perpetually frustrated with the insipid, doctrinaire, over-simplified, romanticized class materials sent out from church head-quarters for my lesson, and furious that this and the other courses of the Relief Society came masquerading as university course equiva-lents, which couldn't be further from the truth. I suspect matters are not much different in women's courses in other fundamentalist churches across the land. Women of the churches deserve better than to have their intelligence and their abilities so grossly underes-timated and so determinedly ignored. Becoming angry in earnest at the discrepancy between how bright and talented we are and how stupid so many of us think we are, and understanding how our undervaluation by church leaders reinforces—if not directly causes—our low opinion of ourselves, I was not always able to keep my evolving feminist voice out of the lessons.

I am not significantly different from other women. If I had known the truth about women's condition all along, deep inside myself, then all women must know. But having accepted the patriarchal myth that they cannot survive in this world without male protection and approval, they struggle, as I did, to keep the knowledge of their oppression from their own consciousness. In Relief Society when I spoke in my feminist voice—my real voice—I think I made my sisters' studied non-awareness more difficult to maintain, and threatened to wake them up and make them take responsibility, be fully adult and independent humans. I know many of them deeply doubt that they are capable of this; they are the ones my voice disturbed the most. They did not want to hear it. I don't blame them; neither did I for forty-two years. In true nonconfrontive authoritarian Mormon fashion, they took their complaints to the bishop. Not one of them ever spoke to me about this to my face.

Sitting in the midst of the women of my ward, I often thought back to an afternoon nine years before in Palo Alto. A Mormon friend and I, in talking about some poems we had written, had drifted naturally into a discussion of the feelings that had led up to them. Mona Jo was a therapist, and perhaps because she saw me hedging, pulled out a technique guaranteed to shake my complacency.

"Who are you?" she asked. I was flustered at this shift from friend to therapist, but I answered, "I'm Rick's wife." "Who are you?" she asked again. "I'm Eric, Kari, and Marc's mother." "Who are you?" she demanded the third time. To my surprise and dismay, I began to cry. "Who are you?" she persisted. "I don't know, I don't know!" I sobbed.

I didn't know. I didn't even know how thoroughly I didn't know, and I didn't want to find out. Perplexed and frightened by the implications of my outburst and determined not to think about them, I tucked the whole episode away. But I didn't forget it.

Every woman should have a friend who cares enough about her to force her, relentlessly, to face that question, one who will not let her sneak under, over, or around it. I have been tempted to ask it in Relief Society, but have never felt sure I could deal with the consequences.

I miss teaching Relief Society because I miss my Mormon sisters. But we could not talk to one another now, the men have so successfully divided us.

But of all things in the church, I miss most playing the organ. I'd been trained as a pianist, not an organist, and needed lots of practice not to treat the organ as a piano when, about a year after we had moved to Virginia, I was first called as ward organist. So I'd go over to the church early in the mornings two or three times a week to practice. I felt very much at home there. That quiet building, as inelegant as it is, represented the church, its teachings, Mormon culture and tradition—all that was at the core of my existence and around which my life revolved. That I was Mormon was my first and most significant identification. Mormon first, human being second, American, wife, mother—everything else sprang from that firm center.

As I acquired enough proficiency at the organ so that my attention was not wholly absorbed by technique, I spent more and more practice time praying: playing and praying. My performance was not improved by my loud sniffles or the tears dripping off my nose or the tear-slippery keys, but the purity and grace of the music simultaneously hurt and healed a heart already aching with the prescience that all this, which was so precious, could not stay the same. "Cast Thy Burden Upon the Lord" . . . "My Faith in Thee Is Sure" . . . "My Heart Is Filled with Longing" . . . My heart *was* filled with longing—a fierce, tearing longing, for what I didn't know. During those practice sessions I cast that burden upon the Lord, and though I left no wiser, I left comforted and refreshed.

Then, on Sunday afternoons—I'll never forget the long, low rays of the sun at that time of day or the twilight settling gently down outside the bright, friendly room—with intense pleasure I accompanied the congregation in the hymns that were so familiar to me and as much a part of my natural environment as the sounds of crickets or rain. Now, when I hear them, infrequently and from a growing distance, I feel as if I've become partially deaf. I miss them, but in a way that hearing them cannot relieve. I shall never hear them again as I did for more than forty years, with the feeling of community warm and deep in my bones. (Months after the excommunication, the only thing that could make me cry while appearing on a TV show was talking about playing the organ in church and realizing that I'd never do it again.)

Not that the hymns are great music by any standards, or even good music. Several are outright ludicrous and half a dozen are musical catastrophes. But they are the music of the Mormons, the songs of "Zion," of my people.

A bonus in sitting on the stand was being able to watch the audience. I'd look out into the faces of those people I had come to know so well, watch them hug their kids or spank their bottoms and take them out into the hall to cry, or fall asleep, or yawn, or cuddle one another surreptitiously, and I liked them. I liked them a lot. Even those I knew had come to dislike me because of my ERA activity, and who spoke unkindly and often falsely about me behind my back, seemed dear as I watched them in the midst of their families, being human, growing old, having troubles, getting along. They seemed more than they were, like representatives of humankind—touching, lovable, invincible, archetypal. I couldn't seem to get enough of looking at them, wondering about them, remembering this and that conversation or event. I memorized them. I remember and miss every face.

Yesterday, when I was looking for a picture of this house for the realtor, I found instead pictures taken at a Relief Society Christmas party here, and there were the faces. They looked out at me from a different world, centuries removed, unreal, but they had the power still to melt my heart. At that party the estrangement had already begun. That picture is a reminder of what I was beginning to confront internally, while externally I was laughing and waving my hand in some game we were playing: the bittersweet knowledge that cake cannot be had and eaten, too. By December 1977, I had begun to eat my cake.

Not long after we settled in Virginia, which was—and at the time of this writing still is—a very, very unratified state, I began hearing about the Equal Rights Amendment. The place I heard about it was church, and everything I heard was bad.

This disturbed me. Not because I cared about the ERA—I didn't even know what it was for a long while—but because I found that hearing politics being discussed so much in our most sacred church services interfered with my feelings of reverence and worship. It was disorienting to me for sacrament meeting to change suddenly, right in the middle, from a religious meeting to a precinct meeting. And, too, I liked the *name* of the amendment. I couldn't help feeling uneasy that the church was opposing something with a name as beautiful as the *Equal Rights* Amendment.

At that time, the church was also resisting racial equality by continuing its refusal to allow black males entry to the priesthood. Hazel had told me with disgust how church members in Alexandria had fought tooth and nail against integration of Alexandria schools. I had been troubled for a very long time about the race issue, ever since I had known Karl at the University of Minnesota, but I had been quietly troubled, with firm faith that everything would work out as it should. But this was different. Women were the issue, and I was a woman. This time we were talking about *me!* Without knowing much about the ERA, I felt directly implicated and involved. And the church would not let me forget, but kept the issue before my eyes, forcing my attention back to it week after week.

I would like to have forgotten about it, frankly, because in being driven by the church's vehemence to study, and growing more and more positive about it the more I studied, I was also growing more and more miserable: guilty about not being able to agree with the Brethren (as we call the leaders of the church) and seriously perplexed about why they had taken another such obvious anti-human-rights stand. I had never been in any serious opposition to the church's policies or doctrines, and I wanted nothing more than to preserve that record to the end of my life. And to teach my children to do likewise.

But instead of lessening, the political excitement, talk, and activity in the church only intensified over the next year or so, until I was in serious emotional distress about the issue. So I was pleased when, in the spring of 1977, it was announced one night in church that after sacrament meeting the next Sunday evening, our stake president (roughly equivalent to a Catholic bishop) was coming to our ward to explain the church's opposition to the ERA. I didn't know this stake president—he was new—but I was impressed by his credentials. Not just that he was a local church authority, which always impressed me in those days, but that he had, some years before, been the Project Director of the Army's Jet Propulsion Laboratory for the manned exploration to the moon!

I was still so naïve, I thought that meant something about his intellect.

So I rushed home and called Hazel and Ron, who were also suffering about the church's anti-ERA stance. "You people have to come out to my ward next Sunday night," I commanded. "The Project Director for the manned exploration to the moon is going to be there to explain why the church is against the Equal Rights Amendment. *Finally* we're going to hear something intelligent on the other side of this issue!"

That was before I knew that there *wasn't* anything intelligent on the other side.

The next Sunday night when the Project Director got up to speak, nine of us pro-ERA Mormons (in a group of twenty or thirty of the other kind) sat hoping that he would help us understand why our church, the Church of Jesus Christ, had taken what seemed to us such an *un*-Christlike stand. But he wasn't halfway through his first sentence before he had murdered that hope.

He had not, he informed us, prepared anything to say that night. And while he was on his way to the church, he had begun to get a little nervous about this ("I should think *so!*" I whispered to Rick). In the midst of his growing alarm, he suddenly remembered someone's telling him there was an article about the ERA in the latest *Pageant* magazine ("That woman's magazine," he called it, which did little to halt my plummeting estimation of the Army's Jet Propulsion Lab since *Pageant*, now deservedly defunct, was a C-grade *Reader's Digest*). So when a 7–11 store miraculously appeared on the horizon, he had dashed in, bought a *Pageant* and, while we were having our opening song and prayer, read that article. Now, he announced triumphantly, he was ready to talk to us about the ERA.

This confession, which he seemed to regard as charming, dumbfounded me, and a fury like none I'd ever felt before anywhere for anyone—to say nothing of in church and for a church official—began to boil up inside me. On my recommendation my friends had driven an hour to get to this meeting. In our small pro-ERA group alone, there were three doctorates and three master's degrees, and *Pageant!* Really! *Pageant* magazine. Such an insult, and not only to us. It was a slur on the mind of every person in that room, none of whom was feebleminded.

Looking incredulously at the bland, empty, smiling face of the

Project Director, I knew the answer to the biblical question: "Which of you, if your child asked for bread, would give her a stone?" The answer was, "My church leaders." We had come hungering and thirsting for help, for a reason to believe that the leaders of our church were inspired, for a reason not to have to become renegades. We had come asking for thoughtful answers, for good sense, for concern, for comfort. And he had given us a stone. We had brought him our pain and our longing to believe, and he had given us *Pageant*.

In all our asking of church leaders since, the women and men of the church who by the thousands are troubled by the church's anti-female activity have systematically been given stones.

As I watched him I realized that if he had been speaking on an issue that affected *his* civil rights—*men's* human rights—he would have prepared very thoroughly indeed. But like all other leaders of the church with whom I have spoken or whose words I have read or heard since, he obviously considered women's issues so trivial, so peripheral, that he did not feel any need to inform himself about them before going forth to teach and work against them. Women's problems do not need to be taken seriously. Women must continue to put their needs and desires last for the sake of the kingdom, which belongs to and benefits men. Women's pain does not matter as long as the institution prospers. In his infinite ignorance and insensitivity and lack of love, the Project Director of the manned exploration to the moon stood before us as a true representative of the leaders of our church. It was a heart-stopping revelation. I began to be in serious spiritual pain.

But it accomplished good things. It helped me begin to free myself from the bonds of Mormon leader worship. Since then, leaders in the church have had to prove themselves worthy of my respect before I give it; I no longer automatically bestow it upon them because of their positions, as I did for the first, incredibly naïve forty-two years of my life.

And few, very few—almost none—have proved to deserve it.

How can I have any respect for them? Men who can not accept that women are anything but child bearers and caretakers, who refuse to see women as full, competent, strong human beings who do not need to be told by men what is best for them but who know this themselves, being fully offspring and heirs of God in every sense men are—these men have not grown to maturity; they are emotional and spiritual adolescents. We may like them, as we do children, but we cannot respect them, because they are *not* children. And we certainly cannot trust them.

Then the Project Director made his second critical mistake with me: he read the short and beautiful text of the Equal Rights Amendment: *Equality under the law shall not be denied or abridged by the United States or by any state on account of sex.* Although Hazel and I had often talked about it, and although I had felt very positive toward it despite my lifetime desire not to oppose the opinions of church leaders, when he read those words in that hostile room that night, they took hold of my heart like a great warm fist and have not let go for one single second, waking or sleeping, since.

I don't claim to understand the dynamics of that. Perhaps it was like being born again.* All I know is that every time I hear someone describe the born-again experience, I am reminded of the night of the Project Director.

Then, after he had converted me heart and soul to the Equal Rights Amendment, the Project Director began to read the letter from the first presidency of the church explaining their opposition. It was then that I had an experience of a sort I had been teaching college students about for years, but had never experienced personally, or known anyone else who had. I'd even begun to think only characters in books had epiphanies—but I was wrong, because I had one that night, and I don't recommend it as a way to come into the women's movement. Far better to move slowly, if you can, an inch at a time, getting used to it, as you would to very cold, very invigorating water.

I say an epiphany because it was a profoundly enlightening and spiritual experience, but I don't think there was anything supernatural about it. I can explain it best by analogy.

All day and all night, as long as we are sentient beings, each of us is bombarded constantly by stimuli, countless bits of information that register upon us though we deal consciously with only a few. In

---

* I saved a church bulletin from that time, on which I had written:

> Is it possible that
> first birth
> was this stunning?
> I wake and feel the fell of
> womanhood.

fact, we have to be very selective about which and how many we acknowledge or we would soon be overwhelmed. So we select from this immense smorgasbord of continually accumulating data only those bits we need to appear sane and reasonable to our friends, and we file the other bits away for future reference or for oblivion. But though we consciously deal with only a minute portion of the incoming data, the experts tell us that we never lose any of it. So what we have in effect, each of us, is miles and miles of underground corridors full of filing cabinets in which we busily file away mountains of data every day.

Somewhere in these endless subterranean storage cabinets, women have a unique file entitled "What it means to be female in a male world," and from the moment we are born female and a voice says, "It's a girl," we begin dropping pieces of data into it. For some women, this file is readily accessible; they can look into it whenever they wish, and it often offers its contents to them spontaneously. For still others, this file opens only infrequently and is so threatening that it is quickly closed, though the owner knows and remembers what she has glimpsed there. There are all degrees of awareness and willingness to cope with this file until at the other end of the continuum are women like the woman I was, traditional women, deeply male-oriented and patriarchal in our view of the world and ourselves. Our file is buried deep, deep under all the others, and our defenses against its contents intruding themselves upon us of a sudden are inordinately powerful. We, more than other women, fear the knowledge that file contains, so much so that even when we are forced to look, we deny what we have seen, we distort the data to make it fit the myth patriarchy teaches women to live, and we thrust the file deeper, down into the bottom corridor and underneath stacks of files we never open. No matter. This subterfuge does not fool our unconscious sorter. Data about being female under male rule still drops at an alarming rate into that file, and the file grows fuller and fuller—there is so much data!—until the seams begin to crack. We reinforce them frantically (perhaps by fighting the ERA). Finally, however, no matter how strong that file—and patriarchal women have almost bionic files—there comes along the one piece of data that breaks it wide open.

Not everyone responds identically to the bursting of the file. Women who have no faith in themselves, who are totally dependent upon approval of both patriarchal men and women—as is classically the case in fundamentalist church settings—and whose feelings of self-worth have been almost totally crushed, these women must still deny what their now open file tells them is the truth. But in order to deny now, in the very face of the truth, they must distort reality so much that they become ill: emotionally, physically, and morally. Not facing their file data is the way to self-destruction, which women choose more or less deliberately rather than face the implications. Depressed women, women with psychogenic illnesses—backaches, headaches, chronic fatigue—these women are still acceptable to their institutions. Even insane women are more acceptable than free women.

The woman who faces the contents of her file chooses the way to health, inner strength, and peace. This woman—and she is multiplying until one day she will fill the earth—is a threat to patriarchy because she has faced and accepted the great secret whose discovery is taboo: *women are oppressed and have been since the dawn of recorded history*. This is the knowledge women hide from themselves in that file, and would often rather die, or at least live miserable half-lives, than know. Because to know is to be in danger of having to do something about it, of having to *be*, and patriarchy trains women to believe that they cannot *be* except through men and male institutions; only through patriarchy. That is the great deception, which keeps women enthralled.

That night, when the Project Director read the letter from the first presidency, my forty-two-year-old file, which had been absolutely bulging before, had just been stretched to the breaking point by that very large piece of data called *Pageant*. The seams, repeatedly and desperately mended, glued, and clamped, were trembling under that strain when two more little bits of data fluttered from his lips, finally breaking the file's back. In a tremendous psychic explosion my defense gave way, and there it all lay before me.

The miraculous part of an epiphany is that when the file bursts, and all the file data flood into the conscious mind, they are perfectly organized; they present one with conclusions. I knew instantly what the women's movement was all about; I knew it in my very bones. It hit me like a ten-ton truck. I knew where women were in this society and where they had been for thousands of years, despite the rhetoric to the contrary, and I thought I would die of knowing. It was the largest lump of pain I had ever been handed at one time, and I found myself concentrating during the remainder of that meeting simply on surviving it. Hazel says that (and this is bizarre behavior in a Mormon meeting) I was shaking my head back and forth and saying in a loud voice, to the great consternation of everyone else in the room, "Oh no! Oh no!"

That is probably the moment my estrangement from members of my congregation began, for I was oblivious to them. Finally I was faced with all I had kept from myself for forty-two years. Before that night, I had thought I knew a good deal on the subject of being a woman, but I had only begun to prepare myself to know. I had discovered my true feelings about patriarchy, I had found that being female was the central conundrum of my life—as it is for all females in patriarchal cultures—and I had read the writings of the great women leaders of our time. But until that night, feminism with all its implications and reverberations had never struck my soul. Everything had been encompassed in my head. Intellectualizing had kept me from making many necessary connections. Until ideas touch the quick of emotions, they are only facts; they may be hurtful facts, but they can never be cataclysmic; they can never revolutionize our lives.

I did not want to stop loving the church. Despite everything, I meant to hold on, I meant to endure to the end.

And so it was not until that night, in full view of the Sterling Park Ward, that I came together, heart and mind. I began to be born—not a woman, but a human being. A painful, beautiful birth.

When I reveal the two little pieces of data that caused my file to explode, you may be disappointed and wonder how two such small things could have done such a great deed, but you must remember the state of my file—how very bulging it was, how cracking and straining at the seams, how trembling with the pressure of its contents: how *ready* I was to know.

The first presidency's letter, which the Project Director read, began with a reminder of how the men of the church have always loved us. Although I had heard that rhetoric for forty-two years, until that night I had refused to hear how condescending, how patronizing that language is. I realized that the women of the church would never write a letter to the men telling them how much we loved them. We simply are not in a position to—what?—*matronize?*—

them like that. Women are the condescended to. We are the patronized.

The letter went on to say how Mormon women have always been held in an exalted position. I can explain best what I knew this meant by describing a banner I saw the next July as, one hundred thousand strong, we marched in Washington, D.C., for an extension of the time limit for ratification of the ERA. The banner stretched most of the way across Constitution Avenue, and was all white except for a big deep hole painted right in the center. Down in the bottom of the hole were painted two little pedestals and on the pedestals were painted two little bitty women. Way up on ground level you could see the big heavy boots of the men walking around in the real world. And down in the hole, one little woman has turned to the other and is saying, "I'm getting tired of this exalted position!"

As Hazel says, "What you learned that night, Sonia, is that pedestals are the pits!"

Later, in reading Mary Daly's *Gyn/ecology*, I found to my delight that she had named and discussed at length the "pedestals-are-the-pits" syndrome. Since Adam first named the beasts and Eve, men have had a monopoly on naming, both objects and experiences. But because they were men and functioning in a patriarchal tradition, which holds that only men's experiences are central and valuable, naturally they only named men's experiences.

This succeeded in including and unifying men while excluding women from the men's group and separating them from one another as well. Not having their own experiences defined and named, to be accessible for discussion with one another, kept women from "bonding" in the way men were able to. It is difficult to talk about a feeling that has no name; it is difficult even to feel it in any but an inchoate way. You just can't put your finger on it. Which is why Betty Friedan so insightfully called the unhappiness of women in the suburbs of the fifties "the problem that has no name," and then proceeded to name it—the feminine mystique—so women could conceptualize it and unite around it.

Today, many feminist theorists are fulfilling an essential and invaluable function by providing women with language that describes our basic feelings and experiences and that can therefore unite us. Mary Daly does this in naming the pedestals-are-the-pits syndrome "patriarchal reversal." As I understand it, this theory says that as the rhetoric about women in a patriarchal institution or society escalates, as it becomes fuller of praise, more lush and purple, more elevated, more *exalted*—women are copartners with God; women are more pure and holy than men; women are more than equal: they are superior; women have never had it so good! As this rhetoric becomes more and more elevated on the one hand, on the other, in the real world where women actually experience their lives, the lid of oppression is *descending* at the same rate that the rhetoric is *ascending*. The language is a deliberate attempt to distract women from noticing what is really happening to them in their lives. It is a deliberate attempt to manipulate our perceptions so we will believe what it benefits men to have us believe. Because men are regarded as the authorities in this world (notice any TV ad) and set themselves up as the authorities on women as far back as we can see, women take their self-serving rhetoric at face value and *are* distracted from noticing the truth about their own and other women's experience. Despite oceans of evidence to the contrary, they persist in believing that all is well, has never been better for women, *because men say so.*

We are living in a time of extreme patriarchal reversal. All around us today we hear that women have never had it so good, that things are constantly getting better for them. But why, if this is true, is it that the gap between what men and women earn for doing the same work widens every year? Women made 61¢ for men's dollar in the mid-sixties; it has now fallen to 59¢. Why, if things have never been better, is it that there are fewer women in tenured positions in universities today than in the 1930s and 1940s? Why is it that women with university degrees make less than men with eighth-grade educations? Why is it that of the 28 million people living in poverty in this country, 24 million are women and children? (By the year 2000, if the trend continues—which it will without the ERA—100 percent of the Americans living in poverty in this country will be women and children.* Why is it, if things are so good for women and we really are men's equals or even superiors, that the United Nations reported that though women do two thirds of the world's work (put in two thirds of the working hours), they make—what? Two thirds? One half? How about one fourth, or even one fifth? No,

* Washington *Post*, October 19, 1980.

women make *one tenth* of the world's money, and own—not two thirds, not even one tenth, not even one fiftieth, but *one hundredth* of the world's property.

These are not the statistics of oppression. They are the statistics of slavery. Women are the dispossessed of the earth.

The tremendous oppression-resisting value to women of the concept of patriarchal reversal cannot be overestimated. Mary Daly has, in effect, given us a thermometer with which to gauge the intensity of the continually renewed efforts to oppress us. She has alerted us to listen to the rhetoric about women in our churches, in our political parties, in our government agencies, in all the institutions of our culture and to know that the more we are praised, the more we are assured that we have never been happier or better-off—the higher the mercury rises, that is—then the more we are being distracted from our true condition and from the fact that any rights and privileges we may have are perilously endangered, and the more we must beware.

Nowhere is this more true than in the Mormon church, which in fact provides a classic and impeccable example of patriarchal reversal, as I realized that night listening to the Project Director.

That night in April, 1977, when I finally allowed myself to see through their rhetoric to the pervasive and profound sexism of the leaders of my church, I was such a mass of emotions when I left that meeting that I am surprised I didn't atomize on the spot, that I couldn't be seen for miles. I felt betrayed, because I had been betrayed, because all women have been betrayed. And I felt ashamed and humiliated that I, who should have known better, had been so easily duped for so long. Humiliation makes one angry, and I felt a fury that I had never dreamed possible. But most of all I felt an incredible sorrow. Sorrow for the lives women have lived for as long as we have record, sorrow for my grandmothers' lives, my mother's, my own. I thought I couldn't bear the pain for fifteen more minutes, let alone for the next forty years, of knowing what it has meant all these centuries to be female.

On the way home I turned to Rick and said, finally, what I had been resisting saying for a long time. "I am a feminist. In fact, I am a *radical* feminist!" I didn't even know what that meant, but I knew that radical meant "at the root" and I knew that at the very roots of my soul I had been changed, that I would never be the same, nor would I wish to be. I knew what women have to know, I felt what women have to feel, to become fully human.

Feminist. The word felt lovely, true, and delicious on my lips. Since then, I have never been ashamed or reluctant to say it. Thank God I finally and truly became one!

Not long afterward, I wrote to a Mormon woman in Maine who was distressed about my position: "I'm a feminist to the core and will be until I die . . . fiercely, passionately, reverently, and totally committed to justice for my sisters on this earth. I feel, frankly, as if I had been born in this time because I have always felt this way—even in the preexistence. This is the right time for me. I feel as if I have come home."

When Rick and I reached home that night, I was ready to explode with emotion, and needing to, and no longer afraid to. If I was going to live, I had to. And soon. So I made sure Rick and the kids were safely in bed on one side of the house and I went over to the room above the garage, locked myself in, and let God have it.

I told him what I thought of a supreme being who had made women so full, so rich, so talented and intelligent, so eager for experience and so able to profit by it, and then put us in a little box, clamped the lid on tight and said, "Now stay there, honey!" I told him that was the most vicious, the ugliest, and ultimately the most evil thing that had ever been done, and that if I could get hold of him I would kill him.

I know this is shocking. But I was coming to grips with the ugliest, most insidious and damaging aspect of my enculturation. In our patriarchal world, we are all taught—whether we like to think we are or not—that God, being male, values maleness much more than he values femaleness, that God and men are in an Old Boys' Club together, with God as president, where they have special understandings, figurative secret handshakes, passwords. God will stand behind the men, he will uphold them in all they do because he and they, being men and having frequent, very male, very important, business dealings, know what they know, a large part of which is that women must be made to understand that females are forever outside their charmed circle, forever consigned to the fringes of opportunity and power. Forever second-best, and a poor second at that. I had been taught as we all have, not in so many words but nonetheless forcefully, that in order to propitiate God, women must propitiate men. After all, God won't like us if we don't please those nearest his heart, if we don't treat his cronies well.

Believing such unutterably hurtful nonsense, which is the foundation of patriarchy, no wonder I was furious. No wonder I considered God villainous and treacherous in the extreme. Since such a God is eminently hateful, my hatred and rejection of him, though perhaps shocking, was perfectly appropriate. One of my first signs of health was my beginning to make appropriate responses.

For two solid hours I raged at him at the top of my lungs, screaming and sobbing. I think you must understand that this was quite unlike my usual parlance with God. I have a naturally quiet voice and am not given to raising it in anger, to say nothing of screaming. In addition, I grew up in a family where God was much respected (by my father) and much loved (by my mother). Despite what Nancy Friday says, *I* always wanted to be just like my mother, and because her most salient characteristic was her deep faith, from my earliest years I had tried to establish the same close, loving relationship with heaven that she had. I saw what comfort and strength she found in prayer, and though I did not understand then why she needed it, that it is one of women's only possible recourses in misogynist society, I determined to have it also. And so, despite the serious handicap of envisioning God as the Old Testament tyrant, which is the way he is portrayed in Mormon scripture and worshipped in the church, I had come to love and trust him because I loved and trusted my mother. And I had also read the scriptures, and knew that people who did not respect God got zapped. There is a lot of zapping in the Old Testament (and in the Book of Mormon). I respected that kind of power.

But that night I didn't care if I *did* get zapped. I figured I didn't have anything to lose—that I *had* been zapped, that all women have been zapped; and I even felt that it might be a relief to be hit by a bolt of something, because what was I going to do with this horrendous stuff out of my file? It hurt so much I didn't know how I was going to live from one moment to the next. How was I going to go from day to day knowing what I knew, seeing so clearly? I didn't know how long a person could feel so much pain and keep from dying, and I wasn't sure I wanted to find out. But nothing happened except that my frenzy continued and my horror spilled out into the night.

The only frustration I felt through the whole wild scene was that my vocabulary was not potent enough for the job. I had led such a sheltered existence that I just did not have the appropriate verbal ammunition; when the best you can do is, "You rotten old rascal!" or "You son of a gun!" it leaves a lot to be desired. But I made up in volume what I lacked in vocabulary, and fought God with all the might of my accumulated pain and rage and sorrow.

When my vocal cords and lungs finally gave out and I found myself reduced to an exhausted perspiration-and-tear-soaked heap, I discovered to my amazement that I felt wonderful—absolutely euphoric. I even got the fanciful impression that up in heaven there was general jubilation at my coming of age, that my friends there were saying to me, "Well, Sonia, it took you long enough! Forty-two years and you're just figuring it out! We thought you never would. But we don't mean to scold. Congratulations on coming around at last. And now don't waste any more time. Get busy and do something for women!"

I would, I silently promised, but first I had to do something for myself. Because I thought of myself foremost as a religious person, for the next few months I concentrated on coming to terms with heaven, on making some weighty decisions about God. First I decided to continue to believe in the existence of a supreme being, because I wanted to. That is all any of us does—chooses to believe or not to believe. I chose to believe.

But I could no longer choose to believe in the God of the Old Testament, which is the God of the Mormons: very patriarchal (male hierarchical), very firm and easily angered; loving perhaps, but more stern than smiling, more just than merciful, more stern and punitive than loving—as witness the model the leaders were following in excommunicating me. A very exacting God, one with little respect for individual differences (though presumably he made us all so wonderfully various); a God who cares a great deal about being worshipped (a trait we find repugnant in human beings) and is immensely interested in how one worships him, whether or not one gets out of bed to pray on the floor, or (reprehensibly) kneels up in bed under the warm covers.

To that God, the one I had loved and worshipped all my days, I wrote at that time:

I do fear thee, Lord
Finally and with a fear blind
as faith
foremost in all this fearful creation
now I fear the Lord truly.

The once trusty earth slips
sways, crumbles underfoot,
gnawed, consumed, torn all away,
and in the widening pit
I do not see his face.

Once I trusted wholly
in the justice, the good
of God;
that his and mine met
and married in pivotal places,
that mine was his
bequeathed me.

But I can no longer trust,
and therefore fear him
with a fear fiercer than faith,
famished for his face obliterated
by the anguish
of the question scrawled across it:
Lord, why madest thou woman?

If the God we worship in many of our churches (the Mormons do not have a corner on either sexism or a tyrant God) moved in next door to us, we would not like him. He would be a bigot to begin (and to end) with—selfish, arrogant, and unforgiving. Also pompous and full of himself. I decided to rid heaven of that being. *My* heaven.

To keep God and to learn to trust again, that was the first requisite of my revolution. To do that, I had to establish first that he was not sexist—which is a good deal easier said than done. Patriarchy's concept of woman as servant and man as master had been bred into my very genes and chromosomes. My mind told me this was nonsense, but hearts are where revolutions take place, and bringing myself to believe what I knew was like trying to change my genetic makeup, my DNA structure.

The more I thought and prayed about it, the more sanguine I felt. I said no—intellectually—to God's sexism. Gradually, stroke by stroke I redrew deity, piece by piece I reorganized heaven, because I wanted neither to give them up nor to fight against them. I had been in close communication with them all my life, and I had found comfort there. My prayers had at least put me in touch with the best in myself, they had kept my mind open, they had caused me to desire to be more than seemed possible. My concourse with heaven and its ruler had been good for me. I determined to continue it—if possible.

If, that is, God were not sexist.

In the middle of all this, the president of the church announced in early summer that black men would be allowed to hold the priesthood. Rick and I, like most Mormons, were jubilant. But late that night, the significance to women of this event began to seep into my consciousness—and hurt. I wrote to God again:

BLACKS TODAY, WOMEN TOMORROW

An end to the silent sorrow of sex
sown deep in the psyche like birthache
an end to archaic animal answers—
size, strength, the dark bloody womb.
An end to mere practical uses of women,
a desire in others to be useful
to them.

A new kingdom, please, God,
for this humble offering
of hearts and bodies—female and broken,
feared and despised.
An end, please, God,
to the silent sorrow of sex.

When I have a problem, everybody in the family has it, too. My method has always been to work things through verbally, which means I talk about it with everybody close to me—interminably. "Talk" is too mild for how I worry subjects. Better is that I "hash things out," as Mom says. So my husband and children were always deeply, albeit involuntarily, involved in my philosophical struggles, and the effort to know God is the most basic, most important of philosophical struggles. Rick, having read most of the feminist literature I had read, and having witnessed the Project Director and other atrocities with his own eyes, was primed for these discussions and was himself forced to grope toward some more acceptable view of God than the Old Testament monstrosity, quintessentially sexist, we had so taken for granted until now. He was also, I believe, truly concerned about me. He saw that this question was of such moment to me that I could not leave it for two seconds at a time, and he wanted for both our sakes to help in its resolution.

At the height of this intense spiritual search, he went to a professional conference for a few days and told me this story when he returned:

Not being able to concentrate on the convention speeches because of his immersion in the problem of the nature of God—it was of the utmost importance that God not be like church leaders on matters pertaining to our sexual nature or we were all doomed—he stayed in his room for the whole three days, fasting and praying. Rick was always good at both fasting and praying. As he knelt praying one afternoon, he had an ineffable experience that is going to have to remain ineffable. He could barely explain it to me, but the gist of it was that he felt surrounded by love, in the midst of which he sensed clearly that God was neither male nor female as we understand these terms, but beyond our weak sexual definitions—something much more wonderful and desirable. In addition, his recognition that God was not only totally nonsexist but in fact *anti*-sexist was complete. When he came home, he put his arms around me and said, "Soni, this much I know. God is *not* like the leaders of the church in understanding of sex and sex roles. I felt surely and strongly that the ideas on earth about this today are totally man-made. God puts no one in boxes. We have nothing to fear from God."

My mind had known it all along, of course; it is only reasonable, loving, and just. I had been having my own experiences, my own new ideas and feelings, and Rick's testimony gave me confidence in them.

In the days that had followed the night of the Project Director, I had made several critical discoveries, one of which was that I was not going to be zapped.* At least not by God. I began to understand that God is not going to punish women for thinking, for questioning, for seeing through the myths that bind us, for being angry about what so richly deserves our anger, for going forth boldly to fight against the injustices that have been visited upon us so casually and so cruelly for so long. I began to understand that women are, in fact, going to be blessed and strengthened and comforted for this. I began to understand that we are going to be made joyful.

I say "began to understand" these things because this knowledge came and went, it would not stay put. It took several more profoundly revolutionizing experiences to make this truth firmly mine and to help me stop feeling automatically that when I displeased the men of the church I also displeased God. Forty-two years of habit were hard to break.

Also soon after that fateful night, I made the totally un-unique discovery one day that men had made God in their own image to keep control of women. Why then could not women remake God in a way that would, instead of disenfranchising and dehumanizing half the human race, empower everyone, make everyone whole?

It was clearly time for women to desegregate the club and reorganize heaven.

Thinking about this, I remembered Mother in Heaven, the divine being to whom Mormon doctrine attests (and who was put there, appropriately enough, by a female prophet—probably when the men were away at some Old Boys' meeting). Remembered, sought her, and found her. And loved her. Oh, how I loved and continue to love

---

* Nowadays women in my audience sometimes insist, "Well, I never felt that I was going to be zapped." And I can only answer that I know for a certainty that out there in the New Right, as we call it, out there where the moral majority lives, where the Mormons and other fundamentalist religionists keep patriarchy sacred on their altars, women *do* fear that they will be zapped. I know because I have been there. This is their strongest, most motivating fear. If they are not subservient, they will lose their husbands. If they are not subservient, men won't love them. If men don't love them, God won't love them. Everything will go wrong in their lives if they lose the support of men, which means losing the support of God and of their society. (Divorced women, widows, single women—all have no real place in religions of this kind and are perpetually in conflict about their worthiness to be allowed to live without a male overseer. Immense pressure is put upon them to complete their incompleteness by finding a man. The pressure is cruel and in the end absurd. Women can live very well, very happily, very healthily, and very usefully quite on their own. As I'm finding out to my great satisfaction.)

her! As I gradually reinstated her in her rightful position in my new heaven as equal in power and glory to Father—not in subordination, as the churchmen so wishfully think (and won't they be surprised!) —I began to feel a wholeness and a personal power that transcended any happiness I had ever known. With Mother on her throne as a model for me in heaven, I felt wonderful. I felt wonderful knowing that femaleness is as divine, as desirable, as powerful as maleness. "No wonder men have felt so great for so long!" I marveled. "No wonder they have loved having a male God!" It felt marvelous to be able to identify with God. I felt like Boadicea, deeply and contentedly strong. Nothing seemed impossible. I was eager for experience, open to everything.

With Mother and Father in Heaven loving me and wanting me to come forth and really *be*—with a cheering section like that, how could I not cry out, "Come on, life! I'm ready for you. I'll take you on bare-handed!"

Life takes you at your word, I found. Grappling with it bare-handed is all I thought it would be, and more. Looking back, I wouldn't give up a second of it, and I look forward with calm and cheerful anticipation to all the battles that lie ahead. I am a warrior in the time of women warriors; the longing for justice is the sword I carry, the love of womankind my shield.

Chapter 5

Uppity Before the Senate Subcommittee

In July of 1978, the year after I was converted heart and soul to the Equal Rights Amendment, we marched, one hundred thousand of us, for an extension of time to ratify it, seven years having proved too little time for such a revolutionary concept as legal equality to be properly understood by the country. Knowing that time limits imposed by Congress upon amendments are arbitrarily chosen and not constitutionally mandated, we felt confident that an extension would not violate our basic American document. On the hottest day of that summer, about twenty of us marched under the Mormons for ERA banner—and no one who ever saw that banner ever forgot it. As the New York *Times* joked shortly after my excommunication, "Mormons for ERA? Isn't that a little like astronauts for a flat earth?" We were a contradiction in terms, and people did double takes, shook their heads disbelievingly. "Can I trust my eyes?" one woman gasped. Another took me by the shoulder and whispered in my ear, "You're not really Mormons, are you? You can tell me. I won't tell anyone."

So what happened next was hardly surprising. When the extension bill passed the U. S. House of Representatives and went over to the Senate, Senator Birch Bayh, who has paid a high price for being such a good friend to women, asked his staff to get a religious panel together, because he was going to hold hearings about the extension and about the ERA in the Senate Subcommittee on Constitutional Rights, which he chaired.

People must have groaned, "Another hearing on the ERA! Fifty-five years this has been coming before Congress and we have to hear about it *again?*" And Senator Bayh might very well have replied that we do have to keep reminding people that Americans who love God, who love their families, who love their country and their flag, and who love justice, also love the Equal Rights Amendment. We have to keep reminding people that the majority of good and decent Americans find the amendment in harmony with their deepest religious and patriotic convictions. He was right to hold hearings that would emphasize this again, because, despite our proving it repeatedly, the opposition, having so little genuine content to their opposition, continues to rely on personal attacks. One of their major tactics continues to be to portray ERA supporters as godless perverts who let the flag touch the ground and who never write to their aged and venerable parents.

As conspicuous as our banner had been, it is not surprising that someone on Senator Bayh's staff remembered it and decided to find one of us Mormon "astronauts" to take part in the hearing. It is, however, ironic that I was the one they called. At the time I was only a baby feminist, about three and a half months old. Of the four Mormon women who eventually became the founding mothers of Mormons for ERA, I was the only one who was not employed at the time, and who never had been a career woman. Not only were Hazel and her friends Maida Withers and Teddie Wood all married and with children, they were feminists of long standing and career women as well. I was the only full-time wife and mother of the four, and for that reason had not joined the others for a vacation they were taking at the beach that July. I love the irony that, because I was the one at home doing my wifely, motherly duties, I was the one who got the telephone call that turned my feet forever into a different path.

I am about to relate a typical Mormon story, the kind I grew up on. But first let me put you in the spirit of things by relating a particularly well-known example of this genre. It concerns an early Mormon dignitary who parked his covered wagon under a big tree one night and went inside it to sleep with his wife and children. In the middle of the night, and for no apparent reason, he awoke in the throes of a powerful impulse to get up and move the wagon. This seemed absurd so he turned over and tried to go back to sleep, but the feeling soon grew so intense that he leaped up to obey. No sooner had he moved the wagon than a violent storm sprang up and lightning felled the big old tree right across the spot where the wagon had so recently stood. Mormons always give the credit for such miracles to God, and to the man's living in harmony with God's laws. Having always been a very orthodox Mormon, I have always been strongly inclined to such interpretations myself.

My contribution to this genre happened one afternoon toward the end of July. I wasn't home, but Rick and the kids were, all out working in the yard. Suddenly Rick, who was mowing the lawn with our very noisy old electric mower, got the feeling that he should go into the house. Urgently. Since this did not make sense to him, he continued mowing, but the impulse grew so irresistible that he dropped the mower, took the steps three at a time, and dashed into the kitchen.

The phone was ringing. He picked it up, and the voice on the other end said, "Oh, I'm so glad you answered the phone. I was about to hang up and try someone else. Is this Sonia Johnson's home?" She left a message: Senator Bayh's office wanted a Mormon for ERA for a religious panel to testify for extension the next Friday morning. Since it was then nearly five o'clock on Friday, Rick said he would have me call her back on Monday. When she hung up, he stood there with the phone in his hand, pondering what he had seen while they were talking.

Looking at the bulletin board behind the phone area without really seeing it, as we do when we talk on the phone, he seemed suddenly to be looking *into* it. Later, as he was relating this incident to me, he said, "Our lives for the next few years passed quickly before me, so quickly the only sure impression I was left with was that everything had changed dramatically. I knew that with that phone call, some great change was coming in our lives."

We had been planning to leave for Utah by car the next morning, but decided to wait until Monday to give me time to make a careful decision about the hearing. In case I should decide not to participate, we could then all drive out together. That weekend I called Hazel and the others at the beach and among us we decided that I should be the one to testify. Rick sighed. "I knew you had to do it when I answered the phone," he said. "There was no sense waiting for your decision. I should have set out for Utah with the kids just as we planned and arranged for you to fly out after the hearing."

I looked at his forty-four-year-old face and remembered the

twenty-seven-year-old Rick face that had turned up in Folwell Hall on the University of Minnesota campus during a violent rainstorm, and was waiting outside the door of my class when I came out. We had planned to meet in the parking lot to go home by scooter as usual, but the professor had kept my group very late. It had begun to rain and I knew Rick did not know where I was on that vast campus. I was afraid he would wait out by the scooter in the rain and get soaked and angry. Worrying wildly, I tried to decide whether I dared walk out of the class, but it was a seminar and there were only a half dozen of us. When one sixth of the class leaves, it is hardly inconspicuous. "Rick, I'm coming. Please don't wait in the rain!" I thought, again and again.

And when I came out, there he was at the door. "I heard you telling me the professor was holding you late," he explained, "and telling me not to go out to the parking lot. So I just followed your voice until I found you."

During the early years of our marriage such experiences were commonplace.

Early Monday morning, after Rick and the children left for Utah, I called and accepted the assignment to testify. The house was very still. I began to notice my heart beating. Generally my heart beats along without any recognition, but it was beating so hard I could see my blouse jump. "As if I were frightened," I smiled to myself, bemused. But when I thought the word "frightened," my heart gave a fearful leap. "Good grief! What is this? I can't be frightened. There's nothing to be afraid of."

But as the hours went by, the fear intensified. I would find myself turning quickly to check what was behind me as I walked through the house. "Paranoid!" I would try to laugh, but I did not stop doing it. I did not feel like eating. My breathing seemed irregular. Worst of all, I could not sleep. As soon as I would doze off, some vague dream, some half image as of a gun at my head about to go off or a knife in my ribs would shock me rigidly upright with my pulse sounding in my ears like feet pounding down an empty street, my whole body shaking with terror and slippery with perspiration.

Since the first flickerings of this inexplicable fear, I had tried to pray about it. I would, of course, have prayed about the hearing anyway, fear or no. Prayer was an important part of what I did to make sure that large and small projects were successful. I prayed before every class I ever taught, and during preparation for them. I prayed every Sunday before I played the organ and much of the time during —praying and playing music go naturally together for me. I prayed every night and believed in praying every morning, though I often forgot but made up for it during the day, praying informally as I went about my work. So it was unthinkable not to pray long and hard about the testimony I was writing, since it was crucial to get it just right.

But I found that when I knelt, I could not collect my thoughts. I could not form a coherent beginning-middle-ending prayer. So I finally just opened up my mind to heaven and cried mentally, "Help me. Help me." All day I went about sending up SOS's.

And all day I felt foolish for being so afraid. "It's only a five-minute testimony, and you *read* it," I reminded myself. I was accustomed to teaching mature university students. Why was I so afraid of this? I was ashamed of my fear, and tried to rid myself of it by ridiculing myself, calling myself a boob and a ninny. To no avail.

By Wednesday, I had finished writing the testimony except for the last paragraph. The rest of it consisted largely of quotations from my great Mormon foremothers of the late nineteenth century, who not only fought for suffrage but who with all their souls wanted equal rights under the law as well. Their early magazine, the *Woman's Exponent*, is full of rhetoric about women's rights that today's Mormon women would find shockingly radical, and for which, if they were to utter or write it, they would be looked upon with grave suspicion. Our foremothers in the church, though many were polygamist wives (an interesting contradiction) were far more liberated than their granddaughters and great granddaughters. They would be right at home with the Gloria Steinems, the Eleanor Smeals, and even the Sonia Johnsons. They would be as at home with us as they were with Susan B. Anthony and Alice Paul. In fact, I think they *are* at home with us.

Whatever the case, they are venerable women, our Mormon mothers—real saints. And coming from them, the ideas in my testimony had the force of their known piety and of their honored position in the present-day church. After all, *I*, Sonia Johnson, was not saying it. Emmeline B. Wells was. *I* wasn't saying it, Lucinda Dalton was. How could anyone fault *them*? Of course, I intended it as more than a protection for me, though it certainly was meant to function as that too. I wanted to remind the church of the humanitarian and liberal roots it was repudiating by opposing women's rights in this century. I wanted to remind Mormon women, my sisters, of what strength and courage and conviction our mothers had about the necessity of the liberation of women, and pose the unasked question: "What, then, has happened to *us*? What has made us so much less interested in women's condition, so much more afraid to speak our minds, so unlike the women of our not-so-distant past? Come sisters, let us remember them. Let us read their words and echo them in our own hearts and lives."

That is a lot to ask of one five-minute speech to which both members and leaders of the church were bound to be instantly hostile, and it did not entirely succeed. It was, however, a pronounced success in another, unforeseeable, way.

When I had nearly finished the writing of the testimony, I felt a great desire to end it well, so I decided to try once more to offer up a bona fide, honest-to-goodness prayer, a coherent prayer, one in which I explained lucidly, did not just send up inchoate SOS's. I knelt by the couch in my library, shut my eyes, and said simply, "Dear parents, help me." Hearing a rustling, I opened my eyes, and there around the three sides of the room, with their heads about six inches from the ceiling, stood a throng of women in old-fashioned dress. Not like a photograph or a tableau, but moving slightly.

I knew at once who they were. They were the women whose words I had been reading all week with gratitude and love—my foremothers. They did not speak to me so that my ears heard their voices, but I heard their message clearly and ringingly in my mind: "Don't be afraid. This work has to be done. It is hard, but it is our work too, and we are helping you all we can. Have courage. Know we are with you. And don't be afraid."

I felt surrounded and lifted up by loving arms. Nothing like that had ever happened to me before. I am not a visionary person or the least bit psychic, and have always regretted having no noticeable gifts in those directions. Others around me may be sensing that something out of the ordinary is about to happen, while I remain oblivious. I am always the last to suspect and the last to know.

There must be a dozen ways to explain this phenomenon. My Mormon background encouraged me to think of these women in dun, tan, and brown dresses as real personages of the spirit, actually there. And that is the way I basically still do think, being basically still Mormon in many ways. But when confronted by those who do not believe in the reality of spirit bodies or of anything mystical, I am willing to entertain any reasonable explanation that leaves the feelings of love and support and necessity intact. Perhaps, as I offered to a particularly unbelieving friend of mine, perhaps these marvelous women, and all the extraordinarily courageous and farseeing women of the past who have cared deeply about other women—which is extraordinary in itself in a patriarchal culture—perhaps all their caring, all their suffering and sacrifice, all their long years of labor for women's happiness, all the passion behind all the bonebreaking work, perhaps all that simply does not disappear off the earth with their physical bodies. Perhaps it does not simply dissipate into the atmosphere and drift away into space and become lost, but instead accumulates here upon this world where it was engendered in pain and love and where it is always so desperately needed. And perhaps sometimes when we are especially in tune with it, especially sensitive to it and in need of it, we flip some spiritual switch and *voilà!* there it is, accessible to us, waiting to encourage and lift us, to hearten and embolden us. Perhaps we know about this storehouse somewhere in our deeply unaware selves, and when we most need it, give it to ourselves as a gift.

Whatever it is and however it happens, I learned later that I was not alone in having experienced it. A week after the Senate hearing, I told this story to Jan Tyler in Salt Lake and she said, "I've seen those women, too, Sonia. One day in 1974, during the heat of the Utah Legislature's debate over the ERA—in fact, the Monday after the church published its first anti-ERA statement in the *Deseret News*—I gave a pro-ERA speech to the wives of Utah legislators at the Utah Historical Society. Many of my friends warned me beforehand not to give the talk. I was teaching at Brigham Young University at the time and it could very well cost me my job to go against church leaders. (As it happened, the president of the university *did* call me in, as did Elder Gordon Hinckley.)

"I stayed up all night checking my sources, most of which were the writings of our great feminist Mormon foremothers, and examining my heart. Feeling that my information was correct and clearly more necessary to impart now even than before, I decided to give the speech.

"As I was speaking, I looked out and saw women in old-fashioned dresses standing all around the sides of the room. Like you, I knew who they were, and I also felt their love and encouragement.

"The legislators' wives there that day knew I was doing a danger-ous thing by going through with the speech, and afterwards many crowded around me, glad I had done it but concerned about me, and distressed about the church's new anti-ERA posture. I turned to one among them I knew was pro-ERA and said, 'There were other women besides us present here today.' She replied, 'I know. I felt them.' I was not the only one who received the definite sense of connection, the affirmation of our unity of purpose with the women of the past."

Nearly a year and a half later, two months after the excommu-nication, I told this story to some sympathetic Utahns at Marilee Latta's home one night in Salt Lake City, and as I was telling it, Marilee turned to Jan and said, "Isn't it surprising how many of us have had that same experience!"

And, of course, not only Mormons have had it. Although it is not part of my usual speech, I have told this story at least half a dozen times to non-Mormon groups. Every time but once, a woman has come up to me afterward and said excitedly that she has had the same experience, and that she interpreted the women to be her suffragist foremothers. All of us have felt the same affirmation of the dignity of women. We have felt the sure knowledge that we are in the tradition of our foremothers, carrying on the work they only lived to begin, and that they would be with us if they were here—that they *are* in fact with us now in some mysterious but very real way.

When I rose from my knees that afternoon, I was not afraid anymore. The dread and recurring panic were gone, and I have never felt them since. I went directly to my desk and wrote the final para-graph: "We [Mormons for ERA] believe that what our early sisters would have wanted, what they would be working for if they were here today, what constitutes the whole loaf with which they would be contented, is ratification of the Equal Rights Amendment."

I did not just believe it; I knew it.

For a long time I wondered about the terrific fear I felt those few days alone in my house writing that testimony. Months later, in a conversation with Alison Cheek, one of the eleven Episcopal women ordained in Philadelphia in 1974, I mentioned it. "I still don't understand it, Alison," I admitted. "But it was very real and very powerful. I thought I was going to be killed."

"I've had a similar experience," she told me (one of the wonders of the women's movement is that we are all telling each other our stories; we are not isolated any more), "and I think I know what it's all about." She went on to give this explanation. There are, even in our sophisticated, technologically advanced cultures, deep-seated taboos. Taboos regulate matters of life and death. The difference between our taboos and those of more "primitive" people is perhaps that theirs are more conscious, often overtly codified into law. They are openly discussed and warned about. In societies of this sort, persons who have broken taboos have been known to lie down under a tree and die, knowing that, having broken a life-governing rule, life is not possible.

Much of life in our culture is also taboo-regulated, but our chief taboos are no longer conscious. They do not appear as themselves in our laws, and for the most part are not spoken of directly. But when we break them, or even think of breaking them, our unconscious knowledge that we are violating sacred rules causes us to feel as if our lives are threatened, as if we may not be allowed to live. Since we cannot tell where this panic comes from, it appears irrational, ridiculous; we are ashamed of ourselves, castigate ourselves for our weakness, think we may be having a nervous breakdown.

Women in a patriarchy are governed by many taboos, the king of which is that life will cease to be possible if we go against our male leaders, if we refuse to follow male authority. Tradition is male authority. Convention is male authority. Men have, for thousands of years now, told women what it is possible for them to be, to do, to think, to say, to wear, and still keep men's approval—still be allowed by men to live. And when women have refused to do, to think, to say, to be, only what male tradition and authority allow, they have found it difficult, often impossible, to survive. Women remember, in their very bones and blood, the burning times of the Middle Ages, when, according to Mary Daly, nine million women were burned alive at the stake because they were perceived by *churchmen* not to be living within the bounds male authority had set for them. And because men have been politically—and thus economically—in power, women have always been quite right to fear for their lives. Even now, those of us in the women's movement live in peril, a truth which is profoundly sensed by the fearful women of the New Right, and which prevents their joining us.

Alison told me about being on the train heading toward the first service in which she, as a priest, would celebrate the Eucharist. She became so overwhelmed at the immensity of her rebellion that she froze with fear. "For an hour or so on that train I could not move my limbs," she confided in her rich Australian speech. "We are breaking taboos, my dear," she continued, smiling.

She is right, of course. But those of us who are must have love and patience and understanding for those of our sisters who are still "frozen with fear" of the consequences of listening to their own hearts and voices instead of to the voices of men. I remember very clearly how it felt to be one of them. And I shall never forget the days I spent in terror for my life as I planned to speak out against the authorities of my church, finally trusting myself and my relationship with God, finally trusting that I, as a daughter of deity, could be right against the millennia-old patriarchal order.

I am grateful to my foremothers for lifting me over that chasm onto the firm ground of my own integrity and conviction, which is the only firm ground any of us has.

The Friday morning of the hearing I was an hour early getting to the District of Columbia, so I found a place to park, curled up in the back seat with our "Mormons for ERA" banner, and went to sleep. When I entered the building an hour later the long, gracefully winding stairs to the chamber were already double-lined with waiting people, a good many of them anti-ERA Mormons who met my homemade "Mormon for ERA" button with hostile eyes. I shivered at the unaccustomed coldness which was to become the customary Mormon response to me, and climbed to the head of the line to be with the other members of the panel. There, to my immense relief, Hazel and Ron joined me. They had driven all night from the beach to be there with me—Hazel has never let me down—and we all went in together. Senator Bayh came up to me on the front row, shook my hand, laughed at my button and said "I'd like to get a picture of *that!*" "Go right ahead," I said, and smiled back.

Through the entire experience, from the time I walked into the room until I walked out again, Birch Bayh treated me with extraordinary gentleness and concern. I am sure he could see how inexperienced I was in such matters, how naïve and vulnerable. Grateful for his kindness and good humor, I wrote to thank him a day or so later: "Dear Senator Bayh, until yesterday the idea of cloning seemed bizarre and undesirable. But after watching you in the hearings, I have decided to nominate you for the first man to be cloned—quickly, and by the hundreds of thousands. If this sounds like a love letter, it's because it is. Gratefully, Sonia Johnson, A Mormon for the ERA."

By the time the hearing was ready to begin, the room was overflowing; people were standing around all sides of the room. There were probably about 325 people in attendance. Senator Orrin G. Hatch, one of the subcommittee members, made his entrance to the packed house flanked by two young male assistants. Senator Bayh's assistants were both young women.

Our panel was scheduled first, so we immediately took our seats at the table facing the subcommittee and the press. Senator Bayh cautioned the audience not to applaud or otherwise interrupt the proceedings.

The first woman to read her testimony was Joan Martin, a black Presbyterian minister from New York representing the National Council of Churches and the Religious Committee for the ERA. She had immense dignity and presence, and was splendid under interrogation. Also intimidating, to me. When she finished, the next participant, Judith Hertz, representing the National Federation of Temple Sisterhoods, read her fine testimony.

During both these testimonies, I was trembling so that without looking directly at it, I could see my skirt dancing across my knees. But when my turn came, I suddenly felt very calm and strong. I could feel Hazel behind me supporting my every word, and I could feel the other Mormon women wishing I would make a fool of myself. It was eerily quiet in the room as I read, my voice sounding enormous in the stillness.

When I finished, the audience—at least what must have been much of it—exploded in applause so loud and so sudden that I almost leaped off my chair. For the briefest, most absurd instant, I thought I had been shot.

Senator Bayh, grinning from ear to ear, rapped on the table for silence and reminded the audience that applause was not permitted. "Now the other side will have to be given a chance to applaud [and he did give it to them later]. Please let us not get into a cheering section about this matter, as we have too little time. Hold your applause, if you will." Turning, he welcomed the last participant.

When the last testimony was read, the committee members prepared to ask us questions, and my heart started knocking about in my chest again. But I prayed for calm, and felt better immediately.

Senator Bayh, being the chairman, led off. When he came to me he asked, "Ms. Johnson, what percentage of the people within the Mormon church share your views, do you believe? Has there been a study of that or any scientific effort to check that out?"

"No," I answered, "there has been no scientific effort or study. We know of many people like ourselves. We hear from them daily, but we have done no polls."

Then he asked with concern whether or not I would find myself in trouble with the church because of my position on the ERA. I told him I hoped not. "So do I," he replied. Senator Hatch quickly leaned over and said, "Oh, I'm sure she won't!"

After Senator Bayh and the panel had clearly established that there is no connection between the ERA and abortion rights—since men cannot have abortions and the ERA only applies to laws that pertain to both sexes—it was Senator Hatch's turn to interrogate us. Sitting rigidly erect as if in a back brace, his posture presumably symbolic of his moral rectitude, "fairness"* was what he wanted to talk about, and he clearly did not want to hear what we had to say about it. After he had spoken to William Callahan, the Catholic priest who told Hatch's deaf ears that anyone who really cared about fairness would certainly be alarmed that many state legislatures had not even allowed the ERA to be brought to a vote, he turned and asked me what my viewpoint was on this: did I believe it was basically fair to allow extension and not permit recision? I replied, "I believe you are asking a rhetorical question and do not want to hear the answer." We got nowhere with that issue for the next few minutes, but the exchange was not fruitless, because when he addressed me, I had another of those innumerable insights we have every day after our "feminist awakening," all of which are grisly.

When Senator Hatch spoke to me, his voice changed. He put on

---

* One of Senator Hatch's major objections to the ERA, he says, is that it tampers with the Constitution, so I was agog when I read in the Washington *Post* of December 1, 1980, of his proposal of a constitutional amendment to curtail affirmative action programs for minorities and women.

his churchman's voice for me—unctuous, condescending; I was not alone in hearing it. Several people asked me afterward whether I had noticed. Indeed I had, and had said to myself incredulously at the time, "For heaven's sake, Sonia. Do you mean to say that men in the church have been speaking to you like that for forty-two years and *you've never noticed it?*" It is incredible how we blind and deafen ourselves so we will not see the truth of how men really feel about us and really treat us. I suppose the only reason I heard it that day was that such a tone was wildly inappropriate in the marble chambers of the Senate Office Building, so out of place that even I, whose ears had become inured to that insufferably patronizing tone from hearing it since birth, was shocked into awareness. This was not church, he was not my spiritual superior in this room, and he was not supposed to be functioning as if he were—that is, as if he were a Mormon male. But he forgot himself and related to me as pompously and arrogantly as he must have related to women in the church all his life, this style came to him with such ease and naturalness.

Though I have heard the churchman's voice in every Mormon service I have attended since the day Orrin Hatch unstopped my ears, I have heard it in many other churches as well, and realize that Mormon men have a corner neither on pomposity nor on the voice that conveys it. The churchman's voice is a nearly universal speech defect among religious males.

While the revelation of the churchman's voice was maddening, it also gave me unique power. The senator became a known quantity. I understood at once with whom I had to deal, and that recognition calmed and sharpened me. Hatch, on the other hand, being the sort of patriarchal male who tends to view women as so much alike that one approach will work for all, prepared to assert in his usually successful ways his innate male superiority.

This faulty judgment always gives women the upper hand when dealing with patriarchs, because such men usually have not developed alternative strategies, and are left defenseless and foolish when their stereotypes fail them—as they are increasingly failing them.

"Mrs. Johnson," he intoned down his shiny Boy Scout nose, "you must admit that nearly one hundred percent of Mormon women oppose the Equal Rights Amendment." (Here's where Bayh allowed the Relief Society sisters from Hatch's ward and stake to applaud and stamp.)

When the tumult subsided, I replied, "Oh my goodness, I don't have to admit that. It simply isn't true."

When one has just spoken in one's churchman's voice, one does not expect to be answered back like that and Hatch, chagrined, began his serious work of intimidation and humiliation. Ironically, however, the harder he worked, the more ruffled he himself became and the calmer I felt. We began to have a delightfully brisk dialogue —at least, I enjoyed it:

Hatch: I notice in your letter to the legislature that you had twenty women listed.

Johnson: There were not just women on that list. . . . The point here is that numbers of adherents have never proved an issue true or false. You yourself belong to a church of only three million members which purports to be the only true church in the world. That is a pretty precarious position. I am accustomed to being one of few and right.

Hatch: I notice you are very self-confident that you are right and everybody else is wrong. I would have to admit that the majority can be wrong, but on the other hand I have also seen the minority wrong many times. You may well be wrong here, as confident as you are.

Johnson: You may very well be wrong, as confident as you are.

Hatch: That is true, and I am very confident. As a matter of fact, I am very confident that I am right.

Johnson: And so am I.

During this interchange, Hatch began to show signs of ego wear. Repeatedly pulling at his tie, tugging at his sleeves, leaning across the table as if he were preparing to spring at me, he had fended off pleas from his aides who knelt at either side of him (imagine taking oneself so seriously as to have an aide kneeling at one's either side!), and paid no heed to a note from Senator Bayh who was becoming progressively more alarmed as the Utah senator's control visibly and swiftly disintegrated.

Finally, the struggling senator lost his composure altogether. It was wonderful. I wish everyone who has worked long hours and years for human rights for women could have been there to see it.

He began innocuously enough. You couldn't have foreseen that he was about to found Mormons for ERA on a national scale. In my journal, I have it recorded like this:

"It's implied by your testimony that you're more intelligent than other Mormon women, and that if they were all as intelligent as you, they would all support the Equal Rights Amendment." And then he banged his fist on the table in angry emphasis and shouted, "Now that's an insult to my wife!"

The audience inhaled as one. Ahhhhhhh! And everyone woke up, including reporters from the Associated Press and United Press International who had been snoozing over in the corner during the boring religious stuff. Suddenly they were all over the place, thrusting microphones under our noses, switching on tape recorders, carrying TV cameras out of the marble walls, and next day, all across the country, newspapers carried articles with titles such as: "Mormon Senator and Mormon Woman Spar"; "Utah Senator and Mormon Woman Clash at Hearings on ERA." My favorite was: "Mormon Family Feud on Senate Floor." Oh, those newspaper reporters!

As I wrote to an angry Mormon man in Salt Lake a few weeks later: ". . . Several Mormon men, also anti, who work on the Hill came and told me that Hatch had behaved very badly, had obviously tried to intimidate me, and that he deserved to have it backfire on him. Despite what the papers say—and surely you know about media distortions—I did not lose my temper. Hatch did, and badly. . . . More than anything, I wished *not* to damage the church, and fasted and prayed for days while I wrote the testimony (as did all my friends and family), and was fasting during the hearing. I believe the Lord means for us to have freedom of opinion and speech, for both sides of issues to be expressed so that people can choose."

I told the Hatch story to a reporter from *People* magazine after the excommunication. *People* published a very condensed version of it, and Hatch objected in a letter to the editor that the reporter had not checked his facts. The magazine editors asked the writer to check the story out, and this is what he sent back to them:

"It's hard to believe that Hatch would want to challenge Sonia Johnson's account of their meeting at the Senate ERA-extension hearing, August 4, 1978. According to three eye-witnesses and the transcript of the proceedings, Sonia's version and our reporting were right on target. By all accounts, Hatch fumed at Johnson through much of her testimony and blew up several times during the question-and-answer period that followed.

"The transcript of the proceedings—which can be amended by Senators after the hearings—retains some of the acrimony of the debate. After one exchange, when Johnson and Hatch were arguing over the extent of Mormon opposition to the ERA, committee chairman Birch Bayh had to step in as referee.

"Cheryl Arvidson, the UPI reporter who covered the proceedings, maintains that Hatch 'did explode' in the hearing room. In a phone conversation on Friday, she recalled, Hatch just jumped down her throat. He basically said, 'You don't speak for everybody,' and went off on this tirade. It went back and forth and there was a pretty heated exchange.

"'I don't particularly remember his foaming at the mouth any more than he does in normal situations,' continued Arvidson, who has covered Congress for six years. 'He has a somewhat intemperate nature at hearings. Since I've been up here at the Senate, I've seen only two instances of him really jumping on a witness. And that was one of them. He was very much on edge.'

"Father William Callahan, a Catholic priest who testified with Johnson at the hearings, also confirms her account of the incident. 'It was a semi-shouting match,' remembers Callahan, 'and Hatch entered into that fully. It definitely wasn't a situation of lofty senatorial posture. There was enough emotion that everybody was perspiring during the exchange.

"'As to Hatch being restrained, well, nobody came out and grabbed him by the arms and dragged him off. But I remember someone there reaching out and saying, "cool it." Certainly, Birch Bayh intervened to cut it off, I think, on two occasions.'"

When I walked out of the hearing room into the foyer, the anti-ERA Mormon women surrounded me at once. All the while my religious convictions were hotly on trial there in the rotunda among my Mormon sisters, I could see Hazel and a group of women off to one side talking to Hatch, and since I was not being allowed to say much anyway—every woman wanting to bear similar testimony to me of my wrongheadedness and of her rightheadedness in the eyes of God, and several asking me in great anger how I could call myself a member of the church when I was so obviously following Satan (the first of countless times I was to hear that the reason I am perceived as handling myself well in difficult situations is because Satan is helping me)—I remember wishing mightily that I were with Hazel hearing what was going on over there with Hatch, wishing I didn't have to participate in fruitless comparisons of my unrighteousness with my sisters' righteousness. Being attacked by one's family is not a pleasant experience, but fortunately it is one that has become less painful with time and repeated—almost identical—performances. The first time, though, was very hard and very frustrating.

From the outset, I have known it is fruitless to try to convince members of my church of the correctness of the Equal Rights Amendment, fruitless because Mormons who are anti-ERA are anti-ERA not because of the demerits of the amendment, but primarily because the president of the church—who, good members believe, is a prophet as Moses and Isaiah were—has taken a very firm anti-ERA stance. And though Mormons are repulsed by the word "infallible," its being such a papist concept, they nevertheless believe that God will not allow the prophet and president of the Mormon church to make a mistake. They therefore believe in the infallibility of the prophet, while strongly denying belief in infallibility. It is all very compartmentalized, this thinking; all very morally and intellectually dishonest.

Teddie sent my testimony, with an accompanying affidavit from Hazel, to all the General Authorities of the church. In her statement, Hazel recounted how the Mormon anti-ERA women who besieged me afterward felt I should not have made "it" a Mormon issue, and how I replied that the *church* had made it a Mormon issue by choosing to publish their opposition widely, in the Congressional Record, for example. She tells how these women were also offended that the anti position on ratification and extension was not heard, and that I responded that the church's negative position was well known, but that this was the first time, to my knowledge, that anyone had publicly enunciated a Mormon proponent position. "Though these women were undaunted in their opposition to her remarks," writes Hazel, "they did acknowledge the 'sweet spirit' with which she delivered her testimony."

She pointed out the divide-and-conquer tactics of the patriarchy: "Mr. Hatch also made an attempt to place Sonia in debate with other Mormon women as to their intellectual capacity. There was nothing in her testimony or in her prepared text that would even allude to such an endeavor as he described. I have known Sonia for many years and have had frequent opportunity to hear her witness to the psychological, intellectual, and spiritual strengths of Mormon women."

She ended her statement thus: "As Sonia gave testimony before the subcommittee, I joined with her and many of those present in celebrating the power and joy of womanhood expressed by our Mormon ancestors in their efforts for equal rights. I am grateful that Sonia had the desire, the spirituality, the willingness to prepare the text, and the courage to deliver it in her name to such an open and august forum. What it did for my psyche to be present and hear it is worth mentioning. I feel her testimony has opened the way for others of us to express our desire for the divine right of choice and space to exercise our righteous individuality."

We received many responses to my testimony. Perhaps the image of greatest terror crawled from the psyche of Hartman Rector, one of the General Authorities of the church: "In order to attempt to get the male somewhere near even, the Heavenly Father gave him the Priesthood or directing authority for the Church and home. Without this bequeath, the male would be so far below the female in power and influence that there would be little or no purpose for his existence in fact [*sic*] would probably be eaten by the female as is the case with the black widow Spider."

We refer affectionately to this as "the Spider letter," gratified that male fear of being "eaten up" by women is so openly expressed in it. It is not often that the naked terror of the patriarchs at the prospect of losing control of women is so starkly exposed.

The Rigbys and I stood in an ERA demonstration in front of the Senate Office Building after it was all over, and Hazel told me what had been happening with Senator Hatch in the rotunda while my sisters were reestablishing their orthodoxy. Apparently, Ellie Smeal and a group of ERA supporters had cornered Hatch and were questioning him about the church's ERA position and how much it influenced him (not at all, of course!). Hazel joined them just as Hatch was saying loudly to Ellie Smeal, "I'm *not* a Utah Mormon! I was raised in Pittsburgh, in the East, just like you!" With this, he turned and began to walk back toward the hearing room. The women, puzzled, turned to Hazel with her "Mormon for ERA" button and asked, "But he *is* a Mormon, isn't he?" "Senator Hatch," Hazel called after his retreating figure. "Come back here a moment. You left these women thinking you were not a Mormon. I'm sure you'd want them to know you are."

Hazel says it wasn't that he was trying to give the impression he wasn't Mormon, so much as that he wanted them to know he wasn't small-time, small-town—not a Utahn, but an intellectual, sophisticated Easterner like them. Later, when we visited his office, his office staff made it quite clear that they were also wary of his politics being associated too closely with those of Utah and the church. Hatch's trying to disassociate himself from a Utah or Mormon image incensed Hazel so much that she wrote a letter to the editor of the Salt Lake *Tribune* describing the incident and alerting Utahns to the fact that their senator publicly disavowed them when he was safely out of their sight in Washington.

I rode with Hazel and Ron back to the beach that night where we stayed up most of the night with Maida and Teddie going over the day. As soon as we got there, I called Rick at his mother's house in Milwaukee, told him briefly what had happened, and made plans to meet him and the kids the following Monday at the Salt Lake airport. It was good to hear his voice and to talk to the children. By this time I was very lonely for them. I also missed having Rick there to share this significant experience. I believe it was the first time he had not been with me, at least physically, at a critical juncture in my life. Perhaps it was an omen.

Next day, we found that the Washington *Post* and *Star* and both Baltimore papers had carried the story. What we did not know yet, though, was that hundreds of Mormons all over the country were reading it that day in their own local newspapers and determining to get in touch with us.

In typical Mormon fashion, the first thought I had as I read the paper was that it would misrepresent me to my ward. I wanted my friends in my congregation, my extended family, to understand what had happened better than the newspaper had explained it. So we dashed back to Alexandria to sleep at the Rigbys' that night, and in the morning I rushed out to Sterling to change my clothes and go to church.

Stuck in the door of my house when I got home was a long, frightened letter from Kris Barrett, one of my closest friends in the ward. Afraid for me to come to church, she told me what animosity there was against me, what terrible things people were saying, but that she loved me and was still my friend, though she was shaken by what I had done and clearly thought I was "misled."

I had been praying all the way from Alexandria that I would do what was right in the situation. Heaven knew whether it would be better for me not to attend church that day, and I would stick with heaven. So since the feeling that I should most certainly go did not abate the whole while, and Kris's letter only made me more determined, I leaped into a dress and sped to the church house.

When I arrived, another of my friends who was standing outside the door came up to me quickly, put her arm around my waist and walked me into the church. Fast and testimony meeting was just beginning. There were no seats in the back so I walked alone to the front on the other side—a long journey through stretched-tight emotions. I no sooner sat down than another friend, Patricia Kuehn, slipped in beside me, gripped my hand, and stared defiantly, her chin out, at the men on the stand as if to say, "If any of you try to hurt *her*, you'll have to deal with *me* first!" Dear friends. In my personal revolution, I finally became so radical that most of the women in my ward could no longer define me at all except in terms of sinfulness, could not forgive what they could not understand, and chose, in typical Mormon nonconfrontive fashion, simply not to deal with me at all. Which is just as well, I suppose. I found it increasingly painful, as I came more fully awake, to watch them sleeping through their lives in fear of what they would have to face if they opened their eyes. Not stupid women by any means—just afraid.

After we had sung and prayed and taken the sacrament, the bishop opened the testimony portion of the meeting by bearing his testimony. At the end of his remarks, he said, "If there is anyone here who thinks they may have offended me, I want them to know I'm not offended." I assumed that this was his way of trying to defuse the anger of the group, and at the same time to reassure me. I wondered fleetingly why he thought it was his approval I cared most about. Although I knew he was "in authority" in my congregation and would be the one I would have to answer to if ever I had to answer, I never, to the end, cared what he personally thought of me.

But I *did* care about the women and what they thought of me. They were the ones whose love I wanted to keep. I wanted them to understand that in finding my own way in a new direction, I was not putting them down. How could I? I had thought and acted exactly like them for forty-two years. I could not think disparagingly of them without devaluing myself; couldn't negate the value of their lives without negating the value of half my own. And I knew my life had had value. It had been a good life, in many ways.

It was the women I came to church for that day.

That day, when those who wanted to bear their testimonies were speaking from the podium, the hand microphone that was usually passed around by the young men was not in evidence anywhere. (Kari once asked whether she could pass it around and was told it was a "priesthood activity." Passing around the microphone?) A line was forming, people were sitting in the front row of the choir seats on the stand waiting their turns. About midway through the meeting, I walked up to the stand and sat down on the end of the piano bench to wait my turn. I had known since I saw the Washington papers the day before that I was going to have to do this, and had been praying that I would be able to express my feelings in a way that my ward family would understand and that would, at least a little, heal the wounds and restore them to me. If a final separation was inevitable, I did not know it, and did not want to know it. On that piano bench I was praying furiously for, more than anything, the right spirit in that room. I wanted us to have love and tolerance for one another, despite our increasingly insurmountable difference of opinion about women, the ERA, and what sorts of political action members could take who did not agree with the church's position.

When I finally stood before the congregation, the antagonism was almost palpable. But I had expected that, and I knew also that the hostility was mingled with curiosity, lingering feelings of friendliness, and just, perhaps, a touch of admiration. I began by telling them that I had not implied that I was more intelligent than other Mormon women, because I knew I was not. I reminded them that our not agreeing on this issue did not mean we could not love one another. I told them I knew that the principles Jesus taught would, if lived, lead to individual and universal peace. I ended by affirming that the Lord (I always spoke their language when I was with them so as not to shock and offend) has room in his large and loving heart for all of us, that he does not compare us with one another, that he does not take sides, but is *for* each of us on all our sides as we work to try to bring about justice.

When I sat down, the high councilman from my ward, an eccentric old gentleman who can get away with much because of his age and position, stood and said, "I want everyone here today to know that I tried to call Sister Johnson yesterday. I wanted to congratulate her on her courage, and tell her that I support her in her right to say what she believes. We each have the right to be wrong," and went on to stress—what else?—every Mormon's obligation to follow the prophet.

He succeeded in setting the tone for the rest of the group, giving them the permission they needed to feel and do what they wanted to do anyway. After the meeting, a great many of them came over to where I was sitting, shook my hand, hugged me, told me they loved and admired me even though they did not agree with me. Everyone assured me that what I had done had not changed their feelings about me and they supported me in my right to choose to speak out. One of the two "lady" missionaries in our ward at the time—Sister Weeks, a highly successful missionary—sat down by me on the bench, put her arm around my shoulders, and said, "You're a gutsy lady. I don't agree with you on the ERA, but I admire you." I said, "Speaking as one gutsy lady to another, right?" Because she *is* one. She converted more people to the church in her short stay than anyone before or after her, and did not get to baptize a single one of them because she was female. (In the Mormon church, almost every male has that right from the time he is sixteen.) I wonder how the "gentleman" missionaries would feel if they never got to baptize their converts but had to sit by and watch the women do it every time.

It had been a long time since I had seen the gospel of Jesus Christ practiced as I saw it that day. They did not judge me; they just loved me and let it go at that. Two women, however, before the whole group boldly declared themselves supporters of the Equal Rights Amendment. That was how much the issue had been defused. To everyone who would take one, I gave a copy of my subcommittee testimony so they could see for themselves exactly what I had said. And then the next day I flew off to Utah to join my family, and to face whatever might prove to have to be faced in the lion's den.

I was welcomed in Utah with a totally unexpected response. After a story about me appeared in the Salt Lake *Tribune,* dozens of people called in support, and by the time I left two weeks later, I had personally spoken with at least a hundred Mormons who were outraged at the church's stand and, relieved that something was being done at last, wanted to be in touch with us in Washington.

I am sure the volume of Hatch's mail doubled in the following weeks, because many who wrote to him sent copies of their letters to me. In the Salt Lake *Tribune* of August 19, ten Mormon women signed their names to this letter: "Sen. Orrin Hatch is wrong in assuming that only $\frac{1}{10}$th of 1 percent of Mormon women support ERA. The names listed below belong to a segment of Mormon women that are not afraid to sign their names in the support of the Equal Rights Amendment. We urge other LDS [Latter-day Saint] women who share our views to step forward and do the same." On September 9, eleven more did: ". . . Sonia Johnson's testimony before Hatch's committee on Aug. 4 eloquently voiced the sentiments of thousands of Mormon women who dare not speak in favor of ERA because they have been intimidated. We sincerely feel the ERA has been distorted and misrepresented by its opponents. We do not believe it threatens the family any more than women's suffrage did in 1920. Add our names to the growing list of women who are not afraid to speak out in its favor."

One Mormon woman warned Senator Hatch, "Be it known that there is a vast concourse of women in the church who share Mrs. Johnson's views. . . . A sea of smoldering women is a dangerous thing."

Although I have always heard from more pro-ERA Mormons than from the other sort, I must not give the impression that all Mormon response to this event was positive. Barbara Smith, president of the Relief Society of the church, wrote to assure me that the early Mormon women I quoted in my speech would never have opposed "the Brethren" in anything and that "it is a sad misrepresentation of their great testimonies to suggest" that they would. A man who had known me in Sterling Park Ward wrote me from the University of Utah: ". . . you cast yourself as the stereotype ERA advocate: frustrated, loud, and desperate. Most objectionable of all were your unconscionable attacks on Mormon leaders and insults to Mormon women. You are an intelligent woman. I'm sure your emotions are precluding you from exercising better judgment. I am only sorry that your emotions appear to have carried you to such extremes."

The typical male put-down. Women cannot be taken seriously because they are governed by emotion, not intellect. Their emotions just carry them away. Though he had only the newspaper account to go by, my friend quickly filled in the gaps with vicious sexist stereotypes: frustrated, loud, and desperate. In fact, it was Hatch, the male Republican senator from Utah, who was carried away by his emotions, who was frustrated, loud, and desperate, the very stereotype of the ERA advocate! Why is it that ERA advocates, none of whom I have *ever* known to fit this stereotype, simply cannot shake it?

Any woman who dares think, who dares act, who dares *be*, must be frustrated, loud, and desperate. Men who dare think and act and be are calm, dedicated, and courageous. This is the base-line sexism that permeates our culture, especially Mormon thought and action.

From a bishop in Cache Valley who knows my family: "Now Sonia [can you imagine my answering him with a letter that began "Now Cal"?], if you want to oppose the Prophet of God and lose your own soul, that is your privilege . . . but I hope that with faith and prayer you can see your way clear to fully support and sustain the Lord's anointed leaders before Satan has deceived you and bound you with chains of destruction and you lose not only your own exaltation but you lose your family and all you hold dear."

And from a Mormon woman in Salt Lake: "The Lord is at the head of the church guiding His prophet. He has promised He will never let His prophet lead us astray. However, that does not mean we must follow His prophet blindly . . ." Doesn't it?

This eagerness to obey a leader regardless is not just a Mormon peculiarity. The Mormon church is an excellent example of the authoritarian, hierarchical thinking that is prevalent in many churches today, notably those that make up the New Right. The spirit of religious totalitarianism is abroad in the world; it is in the very air we breathe today in this land. Everywhere are those who claim to have a corner on righteousness, on direct access to God: the Right-to-Lifers, the moral majority—all the holier-than-thous, all the one-and-only-right-way-ers. The bigots of the world are having a heyday. Sometimes it seems as if everyone is hungry for a "prophet," hungry enough to drink the purple cyanide Kool-Aid on command.

But even if the basic attitudes were not the same throughout the New Right, the fact that Mormons are now wielding national political power makes understanding of their notions of allegiance to prophetic authority, and their view of themselves as the chosen people, painfully relevant to every American.

While I was still in Utah, I picked up the newspaper one day and read, to my infinite satisfaction, that the president of the church had lifted the anti-prayer injunction from women. Apparently what happened was that my testimony before the Senate subcommittee—in which I quoted church leaders' affirmation of the "exalted role of woman in our society," and pointed out that they considered women too "exalted" to offer prayers in sacrament meetings—began circulating immediately and widely underground in Utah, alerting many Mormons for the first time that women had been officially cut off from such prayers for a long time. (Bishop Taylor in Palo Alto, it seems, had been more courageous than 99 percent of Mormon bishops who, though they dared not read the directive to their congregations, were only too willing to put it quietly into effect.) Most Mormon women, accustomed to having so few rights in the church, had not even noticed, and besides, not allowing women to pray in sacrament meeting had been well on its way to becoming standard practice in many localities of the church *before* the directive. What does *that* say about how men in the church protect women's rights? What it says to me is that if women do not actively stand up for their own rights in the church and elsewhere, men will be only too quick to take them away, one by one. Mormon women have been almost stripped of rights already; our great Mormon foremothers would not recognize their place in the church if they came back.

One woman in Provo, Utah, read the testimony and vowed that she would not sing in church until prayer privileges were restored, because "the song of the heart is a prayer unto God." Several faculty members at Brigham Young University were shocked into action and demanded an accounting from church headquarters. In the end, so much hue and cry was raised that President Kimball was forced to admit that the policy was not in accord with scripture and could not stand, asserting that women should be allowed to pray in any meeting they attended, both opening and closing prayers.

But where were the apologies? Where was the sensitivity to acknowledge how much this had hurt women, if not consciously, then unconsciously, for ten long years? The message had not been lost on women that female is not worthy of addressing deity in behalf of a congregation which is partly male. Not worthy, not worthy, not worthy . . . the message that knells soundlessly through all the church.

While I was still in Utah, I also learned that Utah Mormon Senator Jake Garn was still threatening to filibuster to keep the extension bill from coming to a vote during the Ninety-fifth Congress. It seemed to me only fitting—even necessary—that Mormons for ERA be the ones to stop him. For the church I had loved and represented all my life to go down in history as the institution that ultimately blockaded the road to justice for women was more than I could bear. The four of us founding mothers of Mormons for ERA recognized that Mormons are privy to special knowledge about one another which makes us more powerful enemies than outsiders can ever be, and we had tried hard to come up with some strategy that would stop the filibuster. To no avail.

But Gandhi's tactics of nonviolent resistance to injustice had been in my mind for a long time, and finally I suggested hesitantly that we fast on the Senate steps if Garn attempted to filibuster. Fasting is a very Mormon activity, and a good deal of what I wished to accomplish was to stress the Mormonness of the opposition to the ERA, to alert people to the power the church was wielding against women. I wanted an unpleasant spotlight on the bigotry and hypocrisy of a church that intoned that it "loved" women and kept them in an "exalted" position and then, hiding behind that smoke screen, fought to deny women inclusion in the Constitution of the United States. I hoped that adverse public opinion might eventually cause them to modify their behavior (as I still think it will someday; it is not always going to be popular to be anti-female any more than it was to be racist). Basically I already believed what I still believe, that church leaders must not be allowed to block women's rights with impunity, but must take the consequences of their stand. It must not be easy or pleasant for them to step on women's faces with their cleated boots.

The three other founding mothers of Mormons for ERA held full-time jobs and could not be expected to take part in such a fast as I proposed, and besides, they had reservations about the whole idea, and perhaps they were right. They thought people would think we were just crazy extremists and discount us.

But I kept hold of the idea because I thought it might work if we did it right. So knowing I was the only one who didn't have a job and who really liked the idea, and could even make much use of it, when I heard this threat again while I was at my parents' home in Logan I sent both Senators Garn and Hatch (with copies to the news media) the following telegram on August 18, 1978:

"Since you have announced your intention to filibuster when the ERA extension bill comes before the Senate, I am announcing my intention to begin fasting on the Capitol steps in Washington as soon as the filibuster begins—a genuine Mormon fast, without food or liquid—and to continue until you stop talking or I die."

If this seems a radical step at that point in my evolution, I can only offer as explanation that in breaking the taboo of publicly opposing the leaders of my church, I had broken through the last barrier to total commitment to women's rights. After that Senate subcommittee hearing, I was never seriously afraid again; my path was clear and straight before me. And trusting my instincts, I never looked back.

The experience of preparing and delivering that testimony made me what I had said I was months before, the night of the Project Director—a radical feminist. If it seems to have happened unbelievably quickly, I can only say, "That's the way it was." I do not claim to understand it fully. I just know that I was ready and fully prepared, at the time I sent that telegram, to give my life if necessary to help in the struggle for justice for women. I never questioned it or analyzed it, this feeling, this knowledge.

We know, because of a very unexpected leak in the Salt Lake City post office, from the sort of person one would not suspect of caring about women's rights, that telegrams began to fly back and forth between Salt Lake and Washington as soon as the senators got my telegram. Leaders of the church asking, in effect, who was this Sonia Johnson? What were the two good senators going to do? and suggesting that perhaps they had better not filibuster. And Garn and Hatch answering cockily that Sonia Johnson was nobody, that she had no following, and that of course they would go on with the filibuster.

What men don't realize is that you don't have to be somebody and you don't have to have a following to make a difference.

As soon as I got back to Virginia, I applied for a permit to stand on the front steps of the Capitol (one cannot get a permit for the Senate steps), and Mormons for ERA began planning our big family home evening program, to be held with all our members and all our children on the front steps on Monday night—or any night we happened to be on the Capitol steps. We had the permit for twenty-three hours a day, and I made plans to sleep across the street in the

Methodist building, so I wouldn't have to drive or have somebody take me back and forth every day. It was swelteringly hot, and we all worried about dehydration, but I said that would just hasten the end of the filibuster. I knew that the church could not afford to have one of its good members die in protest of its anti-woman position, and that the filibuster would end before I did. Then for several weeks—a month—I renewed that permit, kept in touch with what was going on in the Senate, and had everything in order—my family, my home, my spirit. Through it all, Rick and the children loved and encouraged me.

To my immense relief, however, Garn decided not to filibuster. I don't know why, and he would deny it violently, but I rather think that neither the church nor the Utah senators were willing to chance the sensational headlines: "Mormon Woman Dies of Mormon Senator's Prolixity." Because if you once decide to go into a situation like that, you have to decide to go in the whole way. How would it have looked if indeed I had fasted him silent? Weak of him, very weak indeed. If he decided to filibuster, he would have to decide I was bluffing and call my bluff. But what if I weren't? How would he look if he were willing to sacrifice a human life to stop a bill? Like a murderer, that's how. So, better not get into such a contest of wills in the first place; this woman may be serious.

He was wise not to, because I was serious. I would have defeated him, one way or another. In the end, Mormons for ERA defeated him anyway.

That he decided not to filibuster does not mean he decided not to do his darndest to keep the bill from passing. The second-best way to prevent its coming to a vote was to stall proceedings on the floor until time ran out, by forcing the Senate to follow every rule it had ever made, by arguing every point of order with precedent or traditionally disregarded procedural rule. By being first on the floor and last off, and by staying there all day every day, leaving a proxy in his place when he went to the toilet, and eating a sandwich for lunch without interrupting his vigil, he succeeded for weeks in keeping anyone from raising the issue of setting a date for consideration and discussion and vote on the extension bill. The National Organization for Women held an emergency rally of 2,000 desperate ERA supporters outside the Senate Office Building to organize a lobbying blitz and to come up with strategies to stop Garn. Senator Byrd, presiding over the Senate, was going quietly mad at the frustration of not being able to move business along in a Congress that had stopped dead in its tracks.

Anyone who says there is no God, or even such a thing as fate or destiny, is going to have trouble explaining what happened next. Mormons for ERA had been trying to get in to see Garn for a very long time. We wanted to tell him there were members of the church who not only supported extension and ERA and opposed him, but whose families—his constituents in Utah—were also disgusted with his taking orders from the church on U. S. Government business as we knew then, from our unexpected source, that both he and Hatch were doing. He consistently refused to see us until we threatened to tell the Utah press that he was so biased he would not even talk to those who held opposing opinions. At this, because he knew we *had* been getting Utah press, he finally told his staff to make an appointment for us—four o'clock on Wednesday September 27, 1978.

Although I missed that most remarkable conclave and will regret it forever, Hazel, Maida, Teddie, and Geraldine Glover, a friend of Maida's, told it to me as I have set it down here.

Hazel and Teddie arrived, and waited. Finally they requested that Garn's administrative assistant, Oliphant, notify Garn that they were there to keep their appointment. When Garn finally appeared, cross and harried, he seemed to have in mind merely to scold them for manipulating him into this visit, and then to run back to the floor.

The women had brought an old tricolor basketball as a gift for him, with mottoes penned on the white stripes: "Don't block our Equal Rights," and "Overtime is part of the game." Garn was always comparing women's human rights struggle with a basketball game (that's how significant it was to him):

"In simpler terms, the extension proposal is like a basketball game in which the team that is losing asks to extend the contest with the condition that only it can score—until it wins!"

Hazel and Teddie asked whether he would allow them to have their pictures taken presenting the ball to him. By the time Maida and Geraldine arrived, they were deep into ERA matters, neither Hazel nor Teddie allowing Garn to get by with anything. And I guess he tried everything. He read them an entire editorial about himself, one which outlined clearly how magnificent he was. Seeing that this hadn't softened his visitors, he tried another tack. It was so difficult being a senator. They had no idea. And he was newly married. The strain (sigh), the strain upon him was so very great. He got teary thinking of the sacrifices of senatorial life.

But Garn, like Hatch, is very unsophisticated about women, thinking we are all the Total Woman. Nothing could have left Hazel and Teddie colder and more disgusted than his "poor me" ploy. Did he think women were so stupid as to fall for that line? Apparently so. When Geraldine and Maida arrived, he was railing about how ERA advocates are pro-abortion, etc. At this, Geraldine started to cry. "I'm the mother of two children, and I have always wanted ten. How *can* you say I'm pro-abortion?"

Just exactly the right thing to do as it turned out, though she did it sincerely, not manipulatively. Garn was apologetic, as well he ought to have been.

All this took the better part of an hour, at the end of which an assistant rushed white-faced into the room: "Senator Garn, you'd better get back over to the floor *right away!*"

Even then, Garn was too involved to leave and had to try a little longer to convince the women he was a good guy. By the time he realized what was happening, forgot his ego and dashed over to the floor, it was too late. The extension bill was on the calendar of the United States Senate.

"You can't do this! I was speaking to some of my pro-ERA constituents!" Garn raged. But they could do it, of course, and what's more, they had.

So willy-nilly, without planning to, without even realizing what we were doing, Mormons for ERA accomplished what the entire bastion of pro-ERA forces had been plotting and scheming to do for weeks: we got Garn off the floor long enough for Byrd to put the bill on the calendar. The beautiful irony, the almost poetic justice of it all, is still splendidly satisfying to our Mormon souls.

Which simply proves that the movement needs Mormons for ERA.

Chapter 6

Astronauts
for a Flat Earth

As WE STEPPED into the house on our return from Utah that August the phone was ringing, and it has seldom stopped for very long since then. Mormons all over the country who had been suffering under the conviction that they were the only members of the church who supported the ERA (which says volumes about how little one dares communicate with others in the church on this issue) had read one of the wire stories about Hatch and me, had thought, with boundless relief, "Now there are *two* of us!" and had begun to try to contact me. When you stop to think how most of those who finally reached me had to call every single Johnson in the northern Virginia telephone directory* (and there are five pages of them before you get to R—my name was Richard in those days), you get some idea of how urgent the problem is in the church. I'd get calls at all times of the day and night, and typically a zombie-like voice would repeat what had come to sound like a recorded formula: "I'm looking for the Mormon woman who testified before the Senate subcommittee." "You've found her," I'd answer, and they'd say, "Oh, I can't believe it!" Some of them would start to cry, which goes to show what a trauma it was to call all those Johnsons. Johnsons are nice people but this is ridiculous.

I sometimes think of those who fainted from exhaustion in the G's, or lost hope in the M's, or died in the P's, and realize that we heard from only a tiny fraction of those who even set out on the

* Let that be a lesson to us women to get our own names in the phone books of the world.

quest, to say nothing of those who felt the way we did but did not try to call or write. Obviously, the first Mormons for ERA were the fittest of them all.

In a matter of three months, several hundred members of the church had, by hook or crook, found Mormons for ERA. Most of them were, or had been until recently, active members of the church, and because they still cared about it they were in acute pain. Those who had long since ceased to believe were not disturbed in the same way. Having suffered their disillusionments on other issues (notably the priesthood and blacks), though dismayed, they were not being pulled apart emotionally.

But for those who were, I set up an emergency first-aid phone service, and from my library staunched bleeding wounds, slapped on bandages, and called upon all the understanding and love that were in me to help ease the misery. They were crying, "I don't know what to do. I love the church; at least I *did* love it. And I *want* to love it. I don't want to lose what I had there. But I don't know how to hold onto it. It hurts so much to go to church nowadays that I can barely force myself." Many of them, because of the church's vehement anti-female ERA opposition, had been shaken into consciousness of the churchman's voice and could not *not* hear it all the time. Many were feeling battered half to death by male pronouns, by the pervasive maleness of Mormon worship. Having once recognized the basic anti-femaleness of patriarchal religion, they were stung by it again and again.

So many so deeply wounded women and men that I was sometimes nearly ready to despair. And all the while the church fathers maintained breezily that there was no problem!

Looking back, I am appalled by my arrogance at that time. I thought I knew what was best for all Mormons for ERA. I told all those hundreds of sufferers, "Don't leave the church; that's not the solution. The church has been good for us, it has made us what we are, and I don't think that's a minor accomplishment. We have a responsibility and an obligation to stay and help it through this moral crisis."

"Besides, it's *our* church. It belongs to us as much as to the men at its head. Our families, our ancestors, sacrificed for it, paid full tithes to it, worked without pay in it all their days, did everything they knew to make it strong and good, to make it grow and flourish.

And we have done the same in our time. We must not abandon it now in its hours of trial. It needs us. It deserves our loyalty and help."

And I would always end by saying something like, "If *I* can stay in the church, *you* can!"

Which just goes to show.

Adding the people who had contacted me when I was in Utah to those who called and wrote in the next few months, by January of 1979 we had more than 500 names of Mormons for ERA. (As I write this two years later, there are slightly twice this many on the mailing list.) One day the four of us—Hazel, Maida, Teddie, and I—looked around us and realized that we had become, whether we wanted to or not, a national organization. So we declared ourselves such, with me as president, because again, being a nearly full-time homemaker, I was the only one who had time to be president. We had never intended for matters to take this turn. We had been content to operate as the small guerrilla group we were—striking here, striking there, not having to run everything through a board. But because Hatch pounded his table and shouted at me, we became a national organization in spite of ourselves.

And we have always been grateful to him for this. We think it is the best thing he ever did, and I personally think it is the only good thing he ever did. I never miss an opportunity to thank him publicly for his contribution, however inadvertent, to equal rights for women.

We certainly were not the first group of Mormons for ERA in this country, but we seemed destined to be the ones to get most of the recognition, partly because of our location in the Washington, D.C., area. And we were certainly late on the general religious scene as religious feminists working within our church for change. Everywhere churchwomen have been having similar problems and experiences for well over a decade, all of us part of a religious revolution unparalleled in the written history of the world—the democratization of the most hierarchical social structure humankind has ever known.

As Mormons for ERA, we aligned ourselves first with the National Women's Party in January of 1979, giving them some new blood in exchange for some financial support, but we were really far too independent to function under anyone's wing, and a touch too unconventional for that venerable group—though Alice Paul would have smiled at that—and gradually left the nest and flew on our own strong wings.

Funny I should mention flying, because that has come to be one of Mormons for ERA's specialties. Our aeronautical career began as a consequence of not being listened to by the leaders of the church.

As a group and individually, we had been trying for a long time to get the president of the church to agree to meet with us, and had been repeatedly rebuffed. After I had accumulated a hundred or so pro-ERA Mormon letters heavy with pain and need, I wrote to him again, offering to bring them to him personally because I knew he needed to read them. I knew that since his mail was extensive he might not be able to read all of it, and therefore might have little idea of the extent of the anguish. I wanted to ask him outright whether he knew what was in the hearts of the women of the church. I wanted to ask him outright whether he had had a revelation from God on this subject, and if so, to plead with him to make his revelation or lack thereof public. But his male secretary, Francis Gibbons, my pen pal in the president's office, wrote back:

". . . President Kimball regrets that he will be unable to meet with you as suggested. He also asked me to say that he is conscious of the needs of the sisters of the church, and with the aid of the priesthood, and the Relief Society, and under the direction of the Lord, is endeavoring to fill these needs."

By doing *what*, I wondered, and why is he choosing not to listen to members? This seemed—and seems—to me a dangerous course. Any leaders ignore their constituents to their own peril.

On Freeman Reports, a TV news and talk show I did out of Atlanta in July 1980, a Mormon woman in the audience asked me why I thought the leaders of the church should have talked to *me?* Who was I, anyway?

Why *not* me? I asked. Who I was was a child of God. If Christ were on earth, I told her, I am sure I would have no trouble getting to see him. He did not agree to have family home evening only with the rich and famous. He did not shut himself away from the people and refuse to see those who opinions differed from his. He did not refuse to talk to all but the sycophants. He went about with prostitutes and tax collectors and the poor and the sick. Again and again, by refusing to talk to us the leaders of the church acted very unlike the man whose servants they declare themselves to be.

Many Catholic women in this country understand this situation and identify with our feelings. To say nothing of Episcopal women and women in scores of other churches.

Still, I could not bring myself to believe that President Kimball knew all I knew and was still doing nothing about it. I chose to believe that he was being so insensitive because he was uninformed.

In February 1980, two months after my excommunication, in a conversation with Gordon Hinckley and Neal Maxwell—both high-ranking officials of the church—I touched on this issue of insensitivity to women in the church. They turned the full force of their scorn—and of their bottomless ignorance about women—upon me and launched into what I call "the exalted woman rhetoric" of the church. Finally, as the grand slam of logic, intended to knock me over the brink once and for all into belief in the church's great love for women, Hinckley intoned, "You know that President Kimball has done more for women than any living man!"

"Such as what?" I asked quietly.

Taken completely by surprise—Hinckley is not accustomed to having to account for his information, to being challenged; he simply hands down such pomposities for the nodding, unquestioning acceptance of the obedient mass—he flushed, swiveled his chair completely around, picked at his tie, cleared his throat and, trying to maintain his confident authoritative tone, trying to disguise the dreadful, threadbare weakness of the anticlimax he was about to create, said, "He treats his wife so well."

At that, I should have left a large silence while this excrescence slowly dripped down the air between us and gathered in turgid blobs on his desk. In absolute silence I should have made him watch this disgusting mess congeal before his eyes. But afterthought being by definition always too late, instead I said, "A good many living men treat their wives well."

"Yes, yes, exactly, exactly!" he burbled triumphantly, as if he had actually scored a point.

Good grief!

These men need a good deal more intellectual sparring for exercise; they need the oil of controversy on their rusty mental hinges. Every angry woman in the church—and there are a hundred thousand of them—should challenge the leaders to a duel of wits. This goes for women in other churches, too. Right now it's an easy win, but it is to be hoped that men will sharpen up in time and begin to be worthy intellectual opponents for us.

One day, as Teddie was telling her boys about our frustration at not being able to get a message to the prophet, Dylan, her older son, said casually, "You should hire one of those planes like they have at the beach that pull advertising banners."

"Why not?" she thought. "Why not!" we echoed—and hired a plane in Salt Lake City to tow our first banner over the international assembly of Mormon patriarchs* on Temple Square that April, 1979.

The plane got off the ground late—it had been snowing but suddenly cleared up. Off it went, blithely, our brave little banner all alone in that hostile Mormon sky: "Mormons for ERA are everywhere!" Our spies on the ground were having a lovely time watching the men's reactions, the most common of which was—and still is, after we've flown several dozen times—to take one look, and then fasten their eyes steadfastly on the ground, refusing to look up again for the entire hour the little plane carries out its mission. (And never the ghost of a smile though the situation is, we think, wonderfully amusing. Mormons—and a good many other men—take themselves so very, very seriously that they make wonderful targets for teasing.) But in that one quick glance they steal, those on the ground get the message despite themselves, and although they do not look up again, they can hear the little plane dauntlessly putt-putting around and around and know the unpleasant piece of information is still sailing insouciantly along behind it.

I once described how the Brethren responded to our banner:

"A reporter phoned the public relations office of the church to ask how the Brethren were taking this little prank, and was told that they found it 'amusing.' Then the PR man suggested that the reporter put a cartoon in the next day's paper showing our plane flying over the

---

* Mormons have attacked me about this, insisting that the meeting is as much for women as for men, but I would advise them to look around next time and see who gets the reserved seats, who gets personally invited, who gets their way paid. The entire bottom section of the tabernacle is reserved for priesthood leaders and when women get in at all, they must sit in the balcony. If mothers are as revered in our church as the men insist, why isn't the bottom section reserved entirely for mothers, leaving the men to fend for themselves if any seats are left over? I'd like Mormons who insist that male supremacy isn't a problem in our church to take a good look at the stand. It is filled with men. How many women speak at conference, though they make up over half the population of the church? We know who is valued by behavior, not by words.

Angel Moroni atop the temple (as the actual newspaper photo had), but instead of his trumpet, this time picture Moroni brandishing a machine gun! One does not need to be a psychoanalyst to understand how 'amusing' the Brethren found our little prank."

We were out of their control, and that is what patriarchy is all about—control, primarily control of women. Our lighthearted thumbing of noses at the patriarchy reeked of disrespect. We were clearly not in awe of men whom four million people worship almost as deity itself, and over whom they consequently fawn. Which has not been good for any of them—the fawners or the fawnees. The fawnees have come to believe that they *are* more spiritual, more wonderful, wise and righteous than mere humans, and with such loss of perspective it is small wonder they cannot bear to be treated as ordinary political opponents. While they are not above playing political games in deadly earnest, they consider themselves above having to take the consequences. And both the fawners and fawnees are shocked that to some of us—because we refuse to accord these men the deference that they expect for their patriarchal office—these church officials are simply Gordon and Neal and Boyd. When I address them by their first names, it is devastating to them, accustomed as they are to the kind of deference one usually gives an idol. But women must learn not to be deferential. When high church officials fight us in the political arena, we are all equals. In politics, these are ordinary men who are using the church as a political lever to perpetuate patriarchy in the land. Patriarchy has been good to them. It has made them rich and, to a certain adoring segment, famous. And as Frederick Douglass knew, power concedes nothing without a struggle. We were—and are—determined to make them concede, and we welcome the struggle. In it we are discovering our own strength. As a California Mormon for ERA once wrote to me:

"In the end, the men of this nation and this church may wish they had handed us equality without a struggle. The struggle is making women strong. We will win our rights, and when we have won them, we will have learned from the struggle what we could have learned no other way: we will have learned for ourselves about power."

I am sure I am not the only feminist who is occasionally clear-sighted enough to be grateful to Phyllis Schlafly for making us have to fight so hard for the Equal Rights Amendment. Whether in the end this amendment is the way women will achieve legal equal-

ity or not, it is still true that the struggle over its ratification has provided the greatest political training ground for women in the history
of the world. And when this particular battle in the long war for
equality is over, there will be more women than men in this country
who understand how government works and how to get, keep, and
use power. Ironically, because of Phyllis—who does the men's work
of trying to keep *other women* in their place—women's sphere will
never again be exclusively, or maybe even primarily, the home. And I
mean women on both sides of the issue. The patriarchs (and this is
another of the lovely ironies with which the whole situation
abounds), in sending the women out to front for them in the ERA
lines, have lost control of them. If they think to call them all back in
now, or to continue to control them—as they assuredly do, perpetually underestimating women—they are about to sustain the shock of
their lives. Women of all political hues are initiated into the secrets
of power now and are loving it. Women on both sides of the ERA
battle share in that. We are women who know and understand the
importance of our presence in politics and intend to stay there.

Move over, gentlemen.

Like the guerrilla warriors we were, Mormons for ERA kept the
pressure on and the banners flying. In the fall of 1979, we hired
planes to announce in five-foot-high letters: "Mother in Heaven
Loves Mormons for ERA" over the Washington, D.C., area conference and the general conference of the church in Salt Lake City. The
four founding mothers of our little band had gotten together for a
couple of hours of hilarious sloganeering and "mother" had won. The
alternatives—"Patriarchy Is Malarky," for one—were wonderful, but
a bit too wild-eyed, we thought, and were reluctantly abandoned.
"Mother in Heaven" may have been more dignified in tone, but it
was easily the most revolutionary slogan we could have chosen,
striking as it does at the foundations of patriarchy. We knew that.
And we knew those foundations had to be struck at, again and again.
It felt good to have Mother in Heaven as an ally.

There is a good deal of irony in my having spent the next eighteen
months after the Senate hearing trying my best to keep others—and
myself—in the church, and being accused by church leaders and
members of trying to get people to *leave* it or to keep them from
joining it. Recently I found a letter I wrote in December 1978 to a

woman who was thinking of joining the church, but who was distressed by its position on women and the ERA:

". . . if you have chosen to join the church, you will find very great pressure brought to bear upon you to obey the Prophet's injunction to oppose the ERA actively, especially there in Georgia. I can tell you from my own and others' experience that this is a very alienating and painful experience . . . in the church, either way with the ERA is difficult and dangerous. . . . On the other hand, it is possible that when the issue is resolved, you will still wish to become a member and will join without having to be right-wing in your politics to be a good, comfortable member of the church. It is also possible that if you wait, you will lose interest and lose out on a very good thing indeed. In short, I see no easy way for a person who cares about women and their civil rights and also about the church. . . ."

I have no desire, and never have had, to fight against the specific doctrines of Mormonism, and I realize that patriarchy is fundamental to the social structure of the entire world, of every major church and government. I am as content to allow Mormons to believe what they wish as I am to allow Buddhists, Catholics, and Moslems such freedom. I was, and am, in political opposition only, and if the politics impinge upon the church's belief structure, that is not my doing. The leaders who have chosen to lead the church deeply into politics and in so doing have melded church and state—they are answerable for that.

Another ironic twist is that I was totally wrong when I avowed that the church belongs to the members as much as to the leaders. This simply is not true. But I can't express how thoroughly I once believed it was, which is one of the reasons I fought so long and hard against my excommunication. Didn't my love and service count for *anything?* I couldn't bear that it didn't. It seemed to negate my whole life—that I had, with my entire heart, loved and served seemed written off as if it meant nothing, had never been. I felt as if, in separating me from my history, the men of the church were destroying part of me.

But I learned the bitter lesson that, despite having given thousands of dollars and hours to its maintenance, any member can be ousted from the church at any time for any reason. The church belongs to its hierarchy, which is men in power. Those outside the hierarchy, and especially women, are at best only renters and at worst squatters in religious territory.

This truth is graphically expressed on occasion, as when one looks at a picture of the leaders of the church and sees row upon row of exclusively male faces. This is true on a local level, too. A year or so ago, the leaders in my ward decided it was time to build the long-awaited addition to our meetinghouse and invited the press to the groundbreaking. I was shamed by the picture that appeared in the paper, showing five or six men goofing around with a shovel. A reporter friend of mine, seeing the picture, called me and asked, "Aren't there any *women* in your church?" "Not that matter a lot," I answered. The picture told the whole story. Though half—or more—of the church population is female, the church belongs to the men; women are there only on sufferance. If we will be supportive and quiet and work hard and obey and never rock the boat, we can attend the meetings of the Old Boys' Club. But we can never belong.

By August 1978 when I testified before the subcommittee, the church had only succeeded in making me a feminist. And although the pain of being a woman in a church which was fighting women's rights was deepening every day, threatening to invade my whole life, I still thought I could be a good Mormon and a good feminist at the same time. It took many months, many instances of church leaders' behaving in unethical ways, repeated beatings of my unbelieving head against the solid rock of chauvinism, and an excommunication, to teach me the impossibility of that combination. I learned that either one is true to oneself as a woman and to other women out of the direct experience of being female, or one is loyal to patriarchy's idea of what a woman is, which comes out of men's direct experience of being male and benefiting from the devotion and unpaid labor of women.

But women cannot serve two masters at once who are urgently beaming antithetical orders, though I know many who are trying to do just that—compromising, adjusting, rationalizing, excusing, apologizing for the men and for men's system. I understand perfectly why they do this, having done it myself for years. But it is psychologically unhealthful and in the long run spiritually disastrous for both sexes. Either we believe in patriarchy—the rule of men over women—or we believe in equality. We cannot believe in both at once. Neither can we with impunity choose not to choose which one we believe in. To remain in indecision, and perhaps thus to have our cake and eat it too, erodes great chunks of our identity, along with great chunks of our integrity.

I know whereof I speak. For the seventeen years preceding my feminist awakening in 1978, during which I was consciously and otherwise excusing the inequities of patriarchy, I was living a sort of half life, in half light, a grayish, half-awake limbo of neither clouds nor sunlight, a gray, same numbness. Because I was not allowing myself to feel the pain of oppression, and was in fact actively denying it, I was unable to feel emotions on the other side of the continuum either. When I cut off the pain, I cut off the joy. As Mormons know, there must be opposition in all things.

I accomplished this great reductionist feat by lowering the threshold of my awareness, allowing very little stimuli into my consciousness for fear of inadvertently letting in the scary things. At the same time, I unconsciously dulled my perception of the stimuli I did choose so that I would not see clearly what I did not want to see, would not feel what I did not want to feel, would not have to face what I feared to face. Because I refused to feel and experience fully during that time, I could not remember things well. For many years I thought the problem was simply that I had a bad memory.

I remember, for instance, that my husband and mother would sit together recalling with gusto and excitement all we had seen and done in our few months in Europe on the way home from Nigeria. To my dismay I could remember hardly any of it, and what I did I remembered only dimly. That first seventeen years of my marriage lie like a flat gray canvas in my mind, with only the haziest hints of texture or color, becoming flatter and grayer as the years passed. I feel bereft of memories because I am bereft, as if I have had amnesia. But I do not mean to imply that I was miserable; I was contented.

So, having been a star somnambulist myself, I recognize that condition quickly in other women. My ward is full of women who are sleepwalking. The church is full of them—women strangling their feelings, flattening and graying everything down to a dull, automatic contentment bordering on endurance. Their choosing not to feel their oppression for what it is cuts them off from joy as well as pain.

A tragedy, of course; a terrible and shocking waste of life. Patriarchy demands inordinate sacrifice from women, far out of proportion to anything we could ever possibly gain from it.

Then feminism, like sunshine on growing things in spring, kissed me and woke me up. And the world I wakened to is no longer the flat, gray, featureless plain I knew for so long, but a richly textured landscape lavish with form, gorgeously and riotously colored. A new world on the frontiers of civilization. Every woman born to feminism feels like Keats's Cortez looking from that peak in Darien out across the immensity of the great Pacific. Feminism called upon me to have the courage to grow up, to discover and exercise my womanly strength, to be unafraid of pain—and the pain is immeasurable—knowing that fully experienced, it makes joy fully possible. If Mona Jo were to ask me today who I am, I would answer unhesitatingly, "I am Sonia—woman, human being, glad to be alive, loving every second of it. I was dead and am alive. I had wandered far from home and have at last found my way home again."

I have often been asked whether I recognized that feminism was a threat to the kind of life I had been living. Without consciously articulating it, I am sure I knew from the outset that feminism would change my life. I didn't know just how, but my instinct told me that I had infinitely more to gain than I had to lose. I never wished to retreat, even during the most painful times. Not once. The rewards always overshadowed whatever I had to forfeit in order to reverse the processes within me that had weakened me since childhood. The truth did make me free.* Becoming a feminist was like taking the tight bindings off my soul. Nothing could induce me to bind myself back up.

Feminism says, "Choose you this day whom you will serve." As for me and my house, we will serve humankind (which the Bible says is the way to serve God). By refusing to be oppressed, women rescue men from the evils of oppressing. By choosing to face and to feel the whole truth of our lives and to take our share of the responsibility for doing something about them, we regain our integrity and our health and become glad participants in the life of the planet.

But if, in favor of ourselves and humankind, we choose equality, as surely as night follows day we will find ourselves in danger of burning at the patriarchal stake. To preach equality is to preach overthrow of patriarchy. In a patriarchy, to preach equality is to preach

---

* The day I signed the "fake" divorce, Rick gave me—unbelievably enough—a poster of a rag doll going through a wringer, with this inscription on it: The truth will set you free but first it will make you miserable.

treason. To preach such a doctrine in a patriarchy is to preach the most powerful of all heresies.

Feminists are heretics, then, and traitors.

A heretic and a traitor in August 1978, I was nevertheless the most apolitical of all possible apoliticians, the most a-causist of all a-causists. I had been an adult in the early sixties when women and men who were willing to risk their lives for human liberty marched in Selma, in Montgomery, demonstrated and protested all over the country, and I was with them—in spirit. While I washed my dishes, or marked student papers or wrote my own, I wished the demonstrators well. They figured largely in my prayers. But it never occurred to me to join them. I loathed the Vietnam war and, safe at home, cheered the anti-war protesters on and prayed for the success of that movement. I love whales and porpoises and hate nukes. But until the ERA came along, I never dreamed of carrying a sign for or against anything. And if, when I closed the curtain of the voting booth and prepared to pull the little levers down, I knew the names and a little something about both major candidates for President of the United States, I figured I was on top of things politically.

Then in the fall of 1978, after the subcommittee hearing, I learned what lobbying was all about. Hours and days of lobbying later, I sat in the Senate gallery and watched the women of this country win an extra three years and three months for ratifying the Twenty-seventh Amendment to the Constitution. What a marvelous day that was! After celebrating with hundreds of delirious others in Dirkson Office Building across the street—where Ellie Smeal gave prominent mention to Mormons for ERA as one of the groups that had helped in the extension push—I treated my freshman composition class at George Mason University to a minor munch-out, and allowed no serious business, just rejoicing. They rejoiced because they did not have class. I rejoiced because equality had another chance in my lifetime.

By then, I think I thought I was a political creature. But I was still almost as innocent of serious political understanding and motivation as a child. If we had won the ERA then, I would have gone home and forgotten politics.

But in November 1978 the church, having only made me a radical feminist, proceeded to make me a political activist. Knowing how unpredisposed I was toward politics, perhaps you can understand better the intensity of a trauma that could catapult me from hardly any political awareness whatever to full-blown activism in a matter of days.

What happened was that the Mormon church organized against the ERA in Virginia.

Gordon Hinckley, one of the twelve apostles and head of the Special Affairs Committee, which is the political action arm of the church, instructed two regional representatives in the Washington, D.C., area, Julian Lowe and Don Ladd, to organize the Mormon women there into an anti-ERA lobbying coalition. Elder Lowe sent the message on down the hierarchical ladder to the bishops to have their Relief Society presidencies find two women from each ward to attend a special organizational meeting. The date and place of this meeting were announced just the night before so—as my Mormon friends in Las Vegas tell me, who watched the same thing happen there—pro-ERA people would not find out about it and picket, or cause a disturbance, or infiltrate.

But Mormons for ERA are everywhere and we were among the first to find out the place and time of that meeting—November 8, 1978, 8 P.M. at the Oakton stake center, where nearly fourteen months later my trial would be held. Hazel and Ron, incensed that our church buildings were being used for political purposes, as if every member who contributed to their construction and maintenance were in political as well as religious accord, called Elder Lowe: "If you hold anti-ERA meetings in the stake center and call people to attend, you must allow us to hold our meetings there, too, and invite members. These buildings belong as much to us as to our anti-ERA brothers and sisters."

"We have a perfect right to use our buildings in this, since the first presidency of the church has told us to oppose the ERA," Lowe told them (we were beginning to get the message about who owns the church). "But we will hold our meeting somewhere else rather than have dissension over it." And he proceeded to move the meeting to the home of our then stake president, the Project Director for the manned exploration to the moon. Mormons for ERA attended to find out firsthand what the church was up to, and a couple of us took tape recorders, thank goodness. Otherwise, no one would believe our account of what happened there that night.

Despite the fact that we were sitting with the other women in the stake president's home from 8 to 11 P.M., the robust rumor that we

were seen picketing the stake center that night took months to die—
perhaps isn't dead yet. Rumors have long half-lives.

Regional representative Lowe addressed the gathering first, telling
them that Gordon Hinckley had instructed him and Don Ladd to
organize "as has been done in other states, that the services of the
Sisters might be appropriately focused, and Brother Ladd and I decided to organize in the way the church has suggested." He announced that this new group, which originally called itself the Po-
tomac LDS Women's Coalition and later the Virginia LDS
Citizens' Coalition, was to be a coalition, as its name implied, and
work with other anti-ERA groups, and that it should submit a
budget which it was Brother Lowe's job to get funds to cover. And
then he said, "Let me say one more thing. I have been given counsel
in this. In other areas,* we have found that it is not so good for the
men to be vociferous. It works against the cause. Experience is that if
the Brethren are out beating the bushes it looks like, in the eyes of
some, that we are trying to *keep the women subservient* [his exact
words! If we let them talk long enough, they say it all] and it is far

---

* I am certain he is referring to the experience the church had all over the country with the state International Women's Year conferences, at which Mormon
men with megaphones, whistles, walkie-talkies and signs shepherded Mormon
women about, body and soul, telling them when to sit and when to stand, when
to come and when to go, what to say and when to say it and, especially, how to
vote on every single issue. This clear evidence of the total subservience of the
Mormon women to the men horrified non-Mormon participants and opened their
eyes to the condition of women in the church. It also opened a good many Mormon women's eyes. (Non-Mormon women who watched these Mormon demonstrations of male supremacy in their state conventions and at Houston later could
hardly believe that I, or the other Mormon women who refuse to be herded
about and have ceased to ask permission in the church, really exist.)

Having discovered that the animal-trainer posture harms the image of the
church (and wakes even Mormon women up!), church leaders have abandoned it
in favor of the more usual and subtle patriarchal stance—puppeteer. Now they
pull women's strings from the anonymity and safety of the arras. I watched with
recognition as Arab and Iranian women puppets performed (their masters never
far away) at the Copenhagen World Conference on Women in the summer of
1980, realizing afresh how absolutely basic and indispensable it is to patriarchy
that women be used to perpetuate their own oppression.

The Mormon church's political organization provided me with a blueprint—a
microcosm from which I was able to understand immediately the patriarchal
macrocosm. It is the same the world over: women doing the men's work of keeping women subservient, women renouncing their humanity at men's behest,
women relinquishing their will. (Like Mormon women in their relation to the
prophet, Iranian women would change their minds about "women's place" overnight if the Ayatollah changed his.)

from that. This is the exact opposite of what we are trying to do, but is always interpreted that way. Why don't I quit while I'm ahead."

In clearly meaning the opposite of what he was saying, Brother Lowe provided a fine example of patriarchal reversal. What he really meant when he said people wouldn't understand the men's true motivation in organizing the women against an amendment giving women a constitutional guarantee of justice under the law was, of course, that *everyone would understand perfectly* that here are men using women as tools of their own oppression again, as they have from time immemorial.

His inadvertent admission of Mormon women's subservience did not upset me; that's what I had learned in April at the feet of the Project Director. I even smiled grimly when Lowe realized in confusion what he was saying and tried without success to cover his tracks.

But a flame of anger leaped up in my breast as he asked those good faithful women, my sisters—who are *me*—to misrepresent the facts, not to tell that the men are behind the scenes pulling their strings. In short, to lie. And I subsequently *did* hear them lie about this, first in Virginia, then in one state after another, states in which Mormons for ERA knew exactly what was going on and relayed it to us. The magnitude of the moral crisis in this church cannot be overstated.

Brother Lowe ended his little introduction by encouraging everyone there to treat the dissenters among them (meaning us) with love.

Next, the coalition Chairman, a professional woman, trivialized the lives of women who do not work outside the home by exhorting them to sacrifice because there was so little time before the next Virginia legislative session: "We are going to have to decide that we can't make the handmade gifts we wanted to for Christmas."

Dapper little Bob Beers, Mormon political action coordinator in Virginia for Schlafly's Stop ERA, contributed this gem: "If you go to your state senator and say that he should be against the Equal Rights Amendment because the prophet is against it, you are going to get nowhere. That may be why we are against it, but when you are trying to convince a legislator to do something, you better talk his language, not yours."

Mormon women in every unratified state and in many others were instructed at meetings such as this to go back to their congregations and enlist ten more women, or even more, and their husbands, and to instruct each of the ten to get five more and their husbands, thus mobilizing an entire congregation.

There is not another ERA group in this country, pro or con, organized as tightly and thoroughly as the Mormon church, nor another organized group with such fabulous wealth to back it. According to a 1979 Associated Press story, the Mormon church brings in nearly four million dollars a day, and a *Fortune* magazine editor told us that the church is one of the twenty wealthiest corporations in this country. With such financial backing and such a ready-made, obedient constituency, it poses by far the greatest threat to equal rights for women in this country of any New Right group. It is the archenemy of the Equal Rights Amendment. It is the archenemy, therefore, of women. If all other opponents of women marched off into the ocean like lemmings and drowned—and let us linger a moment over this pleasant fantasy—the Mormon church could and would defeat the ERA single-handedly.

Besides the money and the person power, in no other group is there anything like the spiritual coercion used to enlist Mormons' support, as evidenced by the following excerpts from the transcript of Virginia's organizational meeting.

Chairman: "You have got to take this seriously as a calling [a formal, ritually sanctioned duty in the church]. When the call comes, you march with your forces."

From the floor a woman interrupted: "Are these women going to have a calling from their ward and be set apart [officially ordained to the position]?" The answer was no. The next question was, "Why not? Even church baby-sitters are called and set apart. Is this a calling or not?" And another, "I would hope there would be something official done. If this is a calling from the Lord and everyone knows it . . ."

Brother Lowe said he would talk to the stake presidents about it. Later, in a meeting at my ward, the Chairman announced that she had had hands laid on her head and been set apart with a priesthood calling.

Another comment from the floor: "There are good Latter-day Saint women who are for ERA. I really believe that from the pulpit we have no position saying that we must vote this way or that way. When you put them in the position of saying, 'These people are called and to maintain your status in the church, you *must*—' "

"That is not what we are saying," the Chairman reproved her. "What is being said is, women are being called because this is a moral issue. You are not being told you have to be for or against the ERA. But indeed if this is your stand . . . If you feel that you follow the prophet, then we know where you stand. So there is no question."

Stubbornly from the floor: "I think it should be made a calling and then people in the church could know for a surety what they did had the sanction of the church; it would reinforce the idea, certainly."

Chairman, exasperated: "When the prophet speaks, he speaks scripture. Right? He is the living voice of God on this earth. He has spoken."

Determined voice from the floor: "Officially setting apart would be a very good idea."

Harassed Chairman: "*I* have no question of where *I* should go. Without being set apart, I will do what is appropriate to do *because the prophet has asked me to do it.* I don't need any of the rest of that and I don't think any of the rest of us here do, either." Turning impatiently to Brother Lowe: "It would be nice if the priesthood* knew what was happening and helped us."

At about this point in the meeting, Teddie arose and introduced herself as a Mormon who supported the ERA: "I feel it is important to introduce myself since we will be meeting in Richmond and other places on opposing sides of this issue. I have been an active supporter of equal rights for the past ten years."

Chairman: "Well, I think you came a little late. We have already discussed the approach we're taking to this issue. We've decided we're doing it with love."

---

* I have been interested in the last few years to watch the transmogrification of the word and concept of "priesthood" in the Mormon church. When I was a young woman growing up in the church, we were taught that the priesthood was the power to act in the name of God, and referred to the men who had had this power bestowed upon them by ordination as "priesthood bearers" or "holders of the priesthood." Nowadays, however, even Mormon language is changing to reflect the last, desperate struggle of the patriarchy to maintain primacy. The priesthood is no longer a power men can wield. It *is* men. Men *are* the priesthood, more overtly underscoring the subtle but pervasive patriarchal philosophy that since God is male, male is god. Men and God's power—men and God—have become melded in Mormon thought and language: "We would like to thank the Aaronic priesthood for the reverent manner in which they administered and passed the sacrament today."

Undaunted by being told that the love part was over, Teddie went on to point out that church leaders have indicated that each member should make her own decision on this matter.

Chairman: "That was before the letter from the first presidency." And she repeated like a litany, "*When the prophet speaks, it is scripture.*"

The meeting closed with a singing of the hymn "I'll go where you want me to go, dear Lord."

But this was only the beginning. Matters rapidly grew worse. In subsequent meetings which we were not allowed to attend,* but about which we heard from a variety of sources, the women were instructed to say, when they were lobbying in Richmond (and in other state capitals) that they were acting as private, concerned citizens, not as an organized church group. Brother Lowe first sounded that note in Virginia at the November 8th meeting, and Mormons echo it all over the country. Clearly this rhetoric, intended to camouflage the church's deep involvement in politics, comes from Gordon Hinckley and his Special Affairs Committee in Salt Lake. Despite the extensive organizing of the church all over the nation, and despite the "spiritual blackmail" (as one Utah Mormon terms it) brought to bear upon members to be politically active against the ERA and other political-moral-legal issues (mostly women's), the church leaders continue to assure members that though they are organized by church officials in church buildings to go to their legislatures to lobby, often on buses arranged for by church leaders, bearing anti-ERA materials prepared, printed, and disseminated by the church, they are really not acting as church members at all, but as "citizens"; and such is the power of the authority of Mormon church leaders that members deny their own perceptions and believe that indeed they are *not*

---

* The Chairman herself ordered me out of the next one the following week. "Why is the church holding secret meetings?" I asked her as she edged me firmly toward the door. "This isn't secret, it's just private," she insisted. I replied that I was an active member of the church, and that if I could not attend a meeting my Mormon sisters were attending, and that if the proceedings were purposefully kept from me, I considered that not private, but secret. I thought then and have often thought since of the Mormon scriptures which warn against "secret combinations." As for Mormons for ERA, anyone who wishes may attend our meetings. We send our newsletter outlining our activities to the General Authorities of the church. We are tired of the immature, top-secret-spy-conspiracy-secret-handshake-password games men play.

organized by the church and *are* acting out of personal private conviction.

The incredible implications of moral leaders' requiring dishonesty from their followers only gradually sorted themselves out in my mind. At first I was astonished and disbelieving; as evidence mounted, I was horrified. Then a mixture of grief and anger at what was happening to my church overwhelmed me. How dared they do this to my church! How dared they do this to my sisters!

And there was something else, something still not clear to me but connected to the Old Boys' Club rule that it is all right to lie to women. Something to do with its also being all right to use women deceitfully against themselves and others for one's own purposes since they are meant to be used by men. Something about how it doesn't matter if you instruct women to lie since women, not being fully responsible adults, don't really count.

My outrage was matched by that of the other founding mothers, and we called upon Julian Lowe at his home on the evening of November 15, the day I had been kicked out of the second coalition meeting. Looking back, I almost pity him. Nothing could have been more intimidating than facing, alone, Hazel Rigby, Maida Withers, and Sonia Johnson in their white-hot, albeit controlled, fury (perhaps it is just as well that Teddie had to miss this one; Julian would not have survived all four of us).

He did indeed manifest all the signs of extremity: squirmed and shifted in his chair, put his head in his hands, and even wrung his hands, ran his hands distractedly through his hair, stammered continually, cleared his throat, and became paler and paler of visage until, when we rose to go, he was positively haggard.

During the course of that confrontation, we asked him whether the church's stand against the Equal Rights Amendment was based on direct revelation of the sort that was presumably received about blacks and the priesthood. He answered no.

We asked how he could justify sending to the legislature women saying they were simply concerned Virginia housewives, when in fact they had been called to full-time missionary callings in the church, and had been organized and trained by the church to carry out its work. Didn't this seem deceitful? Didn't he think such tactics would reflect poorly, if not disastrously, upon the church?

We pointed out to him that on the organizational chart of the

Virginia LDS Citizens' Coalition, the line of authority is traced back an exceedingly short way—Beers does not even appear, nor does either Lowe or Ladd. "You said in the meeting last week that you were acting under the direction of Gordon Hinckley. Church headquarters has stated several times that nothing is being organized under their auspices. You don't seem to agree. Which of you is telling the truth?"

"The church has officially stated several times that it is not involved with Phyllis Schlafly or the John Birch Society. But in the packet handed out at the meeting, both organizations were well represented among the materials. Is this with Hinckley's knowledge?"

"Where does the money for the budget come from? Who financed the kits each woman received?"

We urged him to be aboveboard about the whole thing, to send out a press release right away announcing the formation of the coalition and informing the public that it was a church-sponsored, church-organized, church-financed, and church-directed political action committee. "Tell the citizens of Virginia who you are and what you're doing," we pleaded, "so our sisters won't have to lie."

But uneasy as he most definitely was, I suppose he simply could not entertain the possibility that a few women with no authority at all could possibly have a more correct perspective than his superiors —all men, after all, and all *authorities*. Like most men who have been successful in climbing the hierarchical ladder in the church, he is an authoritarian man whose loyalty is to human leaders, rather than to abstract principle. So deeply does he trust those above him to follow principle themselves that he apparently feels no need to make any differentiation between men and principle. Obedience and loyalty are *his* principles.

Hazel asked him that night whether he would do anything the church leaders told him to do, even if it were against his principles. He answered that he could not imagine the leaders' ever going so far that he would not do what they asked him to.

It was that night, from Lowe's lips, that we first heard of the Special Affairs Committee of the church, which Gordon Hinckley heads and which is currently the most active and powerful arm of the Mormon church, directing action against women's bills all across the country and anti-ERA campaigns in every unratified state.

At the organizational meeting, an announcement had been made that Gordon Hinckley and Phyllis Schlafly were coming out to appear at a special ERA rally on November eighteenth. We asked Lowe whether the place for that rally had been decided upon. Squirming about in his chair, he told us that that meeting had been canceled. We asked him again before we left if he was sure there wasn't going to be a meeting on the eighteenth. He was sure.

On Tuesday or Wednesday of the next week Mormons for ERA turned out, along with the bishop of my ward, Jeff Willis, and his wife Judy, and the coalition Chairman and vice chairman and members of the Mormon anti-ERA board, to an ERA debate between Bob Beers and Barbara Weiss, a community activist and homemaker, at the Thomas Jefferson Library in Falls Church, Virginia. The room was packed with Mormons as well as others—mostly women. The Willises and the Chairman stood against one wall, and Hazel, Ron, Ruby and John Bailey—early members of Mormons for ERA—and I stood against the other. During the question and answer period at the end of the debate, Bob's little coterie of Mormon cheerleaders, never betraying that they knew him, asked him obviously rehearsed questions. Every time he did well, they lovingly applauded. Finally, Hazel could not bear it any longer. At one point during the debate, Beers had said he had originally supported the amendment but had later changed his mind. So she asked loudly and clearly, "Brother Beers, did your change of heart have anything to do with the Mormon church's pronouncement in 1976 against the ERA?"

Up until this time, the fact that the room was laden with Mormonkind had not been apparent to the unsuspecting gentiles among us. They had no idea Beers was Mormon, either. I watched as all at once this realization dawned, along with the understanding of the applause for Beers and the phony questions. At Hazel's question, there was a hostile stir among the Mormons in the audience, and Brother Beers became rattled. Everything had been going well for him. Wrapped in clouds of safe warm female adoration, he had not been prepared for Hazel's icy exposure. But he managed to say no, he had taken his anti position before the church had taken its (which is what they all say).

After it was over, the Mormon antis who knew Hazel came marching right over to set her straight. I stood and listened. Ron walked over to Jeff—they had been on some presidency together in some ward at one time—and asked him what he was doing there. Jeff answered he was there to lend support to the "ladies." Library assistants were trying to get us out so they could lock up, so we were all crowded together near the door when the Chairman and Jeff, suddenly face to face with Hazel, told her how sorry they were for her, having her attitude and all, and the Chairman defended poor Bob— how unethical, what a blow below the belt, that question of Hazel's had been; how small to put Brother Beers on the spot about his religion when he was up there defending a position. "You did that on purpose!" she accused. "Of course," Hazel replied calmly. "I wanted everyone there to know that the Mormon church is getting into politics."

"Well, it wasn't fair for you to do that," the Chairman unaccountably persisted. I say unaccountably because the whole church coalition was there in force. Why she thought we should keep that fact secret is beyond me.

"Lots of things in this world aren't fair," Hazel answered her, "not the least of which is what is happening to you women. I understand from Elder Lowe that you are *not* going to be called to your coalition positions, that there will be no formal settings apart, that you are going to have to give up your church positions and are not going to be allowed to use church buildings for your meetings. Church leaders, having called you, are not going to back you up."

The Chairman drew herself up to her considerable size: "A meeting was held last Saturday [the eighteenth], and Gordon B. Hinckley himself was there."

Another of the coalition officers, having overheard Hazel, pushed in: "What you said about not calling us or setting us apart, that's not true at all. Just last Saturday, we *were* called to our positions officially and they *did* set us apart and laid their hands on our heads. And Elder Hinckley was right there in the room!"

"That makes it even worse," Hazel shot back, "because President Lowe told us just the other night there was *not* going to be a meeting, that this was definitely *not* going to happen, and that Gordon Hinckley was definitely *not* going to come out here!"

A little over a year later, when Jan Tyler and I confronted Gordon Hinckley in Salt Lake City, he denied having been in Virginia at that time or having anything at all to do with the organization of the Virginia LDS Citizens' Coalition. I asked him who was lying, the women in my region and President Lowe or him? He skirted the question. So I asked him again: "Who's lying, you or Julian Lowe?" From that meeting I discovered one of the unwritten rules of the Old Boys' Club: It is all right to lie to women; lying to women is like lying to idiots and other mental defectives. Necessary, expected, and totally excusable.

At our meeting with Julian Lowe at his home, when we urged him to keep the church honest by informing Virginians of its political organization and activities, he let us know that the church was not going to make this activity public through press releases or in any other manner. It was at that point that we told him, portentously as it turned out, "President Lowe, if you don't tell, we will."

And we did. During the Virginia legislative session of 1979 we saw to it that articles exposing the manner in which the church was organized and what it was doing appeared in Washington, D.C., and northern Virginia papers. Reporters noted that the coalition was raising funds that were being laundered through a Maryland bank account under the name of FACT: Families Are Concerned Today, that the church structure was sending members by bus to the state capitol to lobby,* and was in the process of distributing 150,000

---

* Everywhere Mormons insist, "But we're not using church funds!" But what does it mean to use church funds? How are church funds defined? If they are defined as funds gathered by the church to further church purposes, then church funds were—and are—indeed being used to fight the ERA all across the country. If you are a Mormon and your bishop appears on your doorstep—as bishops, stake presidents, high councilmen, Relief Society presidents, and even regional representatives did and are doing all over Mormondom—and tells you in desperate tones that church leaders fear that the liberal candidate who supports the ERA will win unless "our group" can raise more money, and will you please, please contribute all you can, are you likely to see him as a "private citizen," just old Jeff from down the block? Of course not. You're going to see him as the bishop of your ward, your ecclesiastical leader, whom you have voted to sustain and support. You know that the anti-ERA organization for which he is collecting money was organized through the church and is church sponsored; you have likely been through the temple and promised to give everything to the church if required; you believe that the president of the church, who has encouraged all members to fight actively against the ERA, is a prophet of God. So you give money, not because you're a concerned citizen, but *because you're a Mormon.* You're a concerned Mormon first and only second—and a very distant second—a concerned citizen. As Richard Chapple was quoted as saying to a high-ranking church official about this issue in the Miami *Herald* of April 20, 1980: "You can take off your tie. You can put on a sports shirt. You can work in the garden and even get your

anti-ERA brochures door-to-door—all in the guise of "private citizens." Finally, in March 1979, shortly after the session ended, we alerted the press to the fact that the coalition, though spending much more than the one hundred dollars which would require them to register as a lobbying group, had in fact failed so to register. The coalition was subsequently investigated by the state and forced to register.

The press pictured us as a sort of truth squad, set on forcing our church, through the use of public pressure, to come out onto the battleground and fight a fair and honest fight. What the church was doing was legal in most—though not all—instances; churches have a right to take political positions and to work actively toward political goals as long as they abide by very stringent rules, one of which is never contributing money to candidates' campaigns—a rule they broke most grievously in Florida. But though it is being legal for the most part, the church is being unethical in that it obeys the letter but not the spirit and true meaning of the law.

In choosing to use every single legal loophole presented to them, they succeed in an elaborate deceit. Think for a moment about January 15, 1980, when the Missouri Citizens' Council (the church's front group in that state) bused about 2,000 members to Jefferson City to lobby against the ERA. Imagine yourself one of those Mis-

hands dirty, but I cannot divest myself from seeing you as my spiritual leader." And as Charlotte Robinson, a Florida Mormon, said in the same issue: "I don't even know what he was running for. I contributed because our church wanted us to support this man."

Everywhere the story about busing people to legislatures is that the church doesn't, because it doesn't *pay* for the buses. Women are required to pay their fares as they board. True, women often pay their fares as they board. But church members, selected by bishops or stake presidents or Relief Society presidents, arrange for those buses, reserve them, organize telephone brigades from the wards to call all ward members and get them to the church houses to board them. And members perceive the church as busing them. Because, of course, it does.

In the spring of 1980 the church published a very slick, very expensive anti-ERA pamphlet which turned up in every single media office I ever visited or which communicated with me by phone. This one single propaganda blitz must have cost the church millions of dollars—maybe as much as a day's income! The church pays expenses for church leaders and PR people to fly all over the country speaking against the ERA. These are just a fraction of the political activities requiring funding. The pretense that church funds are not being spent on their anti-ERA campaign is utter nonsense. Every Mormon who supports equal rights for women should, as a matter of conscience, refuse to pay tithing to the church until the church stops its fight against women.

souri legislators, so ignorant about Mormons you think they all live in Utah and have a dozen wives. As you watch this mob surge through the legislative offices, you think in astonishment, "Wow, look at this huge grass-roots movement that's sprung up! Why, everybody in Missouri must be anti-ERA!" Your experience tells you that for every person who actually turns up to lobby, there are 1,500 to 2,000 others who feel the same way but who didn't get to Jeff City today: couldn't find a baby-sitter, lost the car keys, took the wrong exit, woke up with the flu. You think, seeing so many actual bodies, that though the majority of folk in your state supported the ERA in the last poll, opinion must have swung violently around. You are deceived into thinking this group must represent the majority of people in your state, when, in truth, they are Mormons and represent a tiny minority of people, people for whom the ERA is not even the basic issue; a tiny minority of people for whom obeying the prophet of God in Salt Lake City, Utah, is the reason they are in your office today.

And a tiny minority who, if the prophet changed his mind about the ERA tonight, would change their minds by morning.

I am convinced that one reason—besides negative public opinion—that the church keeps its organizations secret and its lobbying identity hidden is to do just this: exaggerate the size of the anti-ERA sentiment, wildly exaggerate it, to other citizens and legislators. And I am convinced that it is as unethical and dishonest a practice as it is a shrewd and calculated political strategy.

Like termites, the Mormons are silently and secretly eating away the beams of the house of justice women are struggling to build. When the house falls in—in Arizona, in Nevada, in Florida, North Carolina, South Carolina, Georgia, Missouri—everyone wails, "What happened?" Mormons for ERA are now on hand to announce, "You've got Mormons!"

In Virginia, we understood their strategy at once and were appalled at the callous skewing of honor it necessitated at all levels of the church, from top to bottom. They and other opponents of the ERA were always crying, "Fairness! Fairness!" and all the while we knew the church itself wasn't playing fair. It isn't fair for the proponents of the ERA to have to fight an invisible enemy. We succeeded in our determination to make the Mormons visible, as they so richly deserved to be.

Because I was the only one who had the time—being again the only full-time homemaker of the group—between sink and stove I called and talked to the press that winter, so my name was the one that appeared most frequently in the articles outlining covert Mormon anti-ERA activity. Because I was a homemaker and at home most of the day, I had the time to get evidence together and take it down to the Secretary of the Commonwealth proving that the coalition did indeed need to register as a lobbyist. The articles connected with the discovery of its failure to register and the consequent state investigation and forced registration were particularly humiliating to church members. Humiliation makes people angry, and since my name figured prominently in that story, members of the church in my area became very angry at me, which was like being angry at the messenger that brings the bad news. I do not suppose it occurred to many of them that the sure way to stop Mormons for ERA from exposing Mormon activity was for the church's political organization to surface, become legitimate, and thus deprive us of exposable material. Odd how it became more of an evil to point out the church's dishonesty than for the church to be dishonest in the first place. If church leaders and members did not want us to tell what they were doing, if they did not think it was honorable, why were they doing it? And if they thought it *was* honorable, why did they so dislike our telling it?*

During and after the church's Virginia campaign, we heard from outraged Mormons in other parts of the country: "It's happening here, too! It's happening here just like in Virginia!" "Tell your

---

* At one point in the early months of 1979, when Mormons for ERA got together a great sheaf of evidence convicting the church of covert and deceitful organizing and lobbying in Virginia, Maida called Jack Anderson's office in Washington, D.C., to offer the story to him first. Jack Anderson, intrepid Mormon investigative reporter. One of Anderson's staff members was very interested and asked Maida to send him everything we had; he would see that Jack looked it over, he promised, and would let us know what Jack thought of it.

Maida duly sent him a large packet of information and waited for the response. Several weeks went by. Finally, she called him again. Yes, he said, he had received the material and had put it on Jack's desk as he had promised her he would.

Well?

Well, Jack had handed it back to him a few days later. "This is a good story," he admitted. "But I wouldn't touch it with a ten-foot pole!"

Being afraid of losing status in the Old Boys' Club seriously undermines integrity. As a friend of mine said when I related this incident to her, "Jack will take on the Sicilian Mafia, but he won't touch the Mormon Mafia."

press," we urged them. "Put public pressure on the Mormons to be honest." "I can't," they cried. "I'm the bishop's wife!" or, "I'm the bishop!" or, "It would kill my parents," or, "I have two sons on missions [or at BYU]; what would it do to them?" In short, for one reason or another, fear squatted like a dank toad in many Mormon hearts.

Eventually, however, after I had gone personally to several states to talk to the press in place of local Mormons who stood to lose employment or be otherwise harassed by their Mormon community, and after I had been misquoted in enough newspapers to get myself excommunicated, other members of the church *did* arise in many states and take over the responsibility of informing citizens of the state and the country of the threat to women's—and therefore to human—rights posed by the Mormon church.

And many of us in many states wrote to legislators, informing them of Mormon lobbying strategy and registering our dismay. In a letter I wrote to Senator DuVal in Virginia, I explained in greater detail how the Mormon men were motivating the women: "Mormon men of high standing often attend the meetings to urge the women on. Certainly the most potent and persuasive tool they are using to convince these women to work against their own civil rights, other than the charge that they must follow the Prophet or be damned, is a nineteenth-century prophecy which has become a tradition in the church. It is generally believed by church members that in the last days (which these are) the Constitution of the U.S. will 'hang by a thread' and the Elders of Israel (Mormon men holding the priesthood) will save it. Mormons therefore believe it is their divine right and destiny to become leaders in the government of this country."

I went on to say: "I am repelled and appalled at the manner in which these men are using and manipulating the women—to say nothing of deceiving them and asking them to be deceptive in turn. Although I am still a member in good standing in the church, and although I love the doctrines, I feel increasingly alienated from the reactionary leadership. Such ideas as I have outlined above chill me to the bone. I do not believe human beings are basically evil and must be controlled by those who know better; I do not believe any one group has all the answers and all the righteousness and that all others are untrustworthy. In short, I do not fear democracy."

Rick wrote a letter to Virginia legislators describing what was going on in Virginia and ending thus: "I deplore this covert activity in my church and its conspiratorial tone. I deplore the exploitation of religious commitment for political purposes. I fear such invasion of the will. Such practice does not seem in harmony with the gospel of Jesus Christ. From the depths of my personal conscience, I urge you to help bring the ERA to the floor for a vote, and to vote that civil rights for women be guaranteed by the Constitution of the United States."

Along with this letter, Rick sent excerpts of a talk given by Charles Dahlquist, a member of the Oakton stake presidency, in the Sterling Park Ward chapel on December 14, 1978, that exemplify the sort of pressure put upon members of the church to follow the prophet. In this speech, Brother Dahlquist also makes clear that the stake presidency helped "call" the sisters who were to head the coalition, "set them apart" and gave them a special priesthood blessing in doing so. ("Setting apart" is done by the laying on of hands by male leaders.)

". . . With that introduction, I turn now to my topic which can be summed up in just four words. Those four words: *The prophet has spoken.* . . . Now, it is important to understand that today, as in past years, the Lord is revealing his will and his word through his living Prophet to all, and particularly to the members of the church. . . . What the First Presidency say as a presidency is what the Lord would say if he were here in person. This is the rock foundation of Mormonism. If it ever ceases to be the fact, this will be an apostate church. So I say again that what the presidency says as a presidency is what the Lord would say if he were here and it is scripture. . . . It's my testimony that the only safety in this life lies in following the words of the living Prophet. . . . As a stake presidency, we encourage you to listen carefully tonight and to sustain the First Presidency and the stake presidency in actively opposing the ratification of the Equal Rights Amendment. Let us not proceed blindly. But as President Tanner once said, 'Given a choice, I would rather proceed blindly following the Prophet than proceed on my own with little knowledge. . . . It is my personal experience that whatever we do, we must stand behind the Prophet.'"

Thirty-five minutes of pounding into the minds and souls of Mormons that they had better not dare make their own decisions!

Brother Dahlquist was enraged that Rick should have sent his sacred words out into the hostile sectarian world, and wrote and told
him so, scathingly. I loved Rick's reply: "Dear Brother Dahlquist:
All you have to do to keep me from disseminating your appalling
public statements is to stop making them. Sincerely."

How well I remember the night our good brother gave that spiritually coercive talk in our ward. The bishopric was all there on the
stand, with the Chairman of the coalition, Bob Beers, and Brother
Dahlquist. The bishop opened the meeting in solemn tones, and seeing Rick and me on the front row with our tape recorder and camera, recognized that "there are some who will want to record but we
will ask you to refrain. It is not the custom." Rick flipped on the recorder at this point with a loud click. "It is not the custom for political meetings to be held in our chapels, either," I retorted under my
breath to the bishop. We sang, "We are all enlisted," had our
prayer, then Brother Dahlquist enlivened us first by comparing God
with the man in the moon and then by ramming home obedience,
obedience, obedience. The Chairman followed, but I soon realized I
had heard her speech before, so I signaled Rick and we walked out.

Out in the foyer, the woman who is our ward's "key coordinator"
for the coalition had prepared stacks of brochures—"Equality Yes,
ERA No"—with maps of the neighborhood on which sections had
been outlined in red. When the people left the meeting, they were
to take their bundles and walk the district, distributing pamphlets
door to door. We were just preparing to leave when I heard Bob
Beers's voice. The story the coalition was telling reporters was that it
was not a church organization and was not using church buildings;
somehow I associated Bob most with the telling of that tale. So I
turned quickly to Rick, "Take a picture, quick, of Bob there in our
chapel, so we can prove that the coalition uses our buildings and that
Bob himself, as a leader in the coalition, goes about speaking in
them!" The doors into the chapel were shut, but each had a long
narrow window down its center. As Rick held his camera up to one
of these windows and began to focus, our valiant key coordinator
rushed over and stuck a brochure between his camera lens and the
window. He simply backed away and took a quick picture through
the other window. Which turned out splendidly, by the way.

No sooner had he moved back from the door than it swung open
to emit two members of the bishopric—both furious to the point of

near speechlessness: Lou Hampton and Lorin Jensen. Lou's face was twitching so fascinatingly that I could hardly listen to what he was saying, and actually don't remember much of the conversation except that Lorin hissed, "How can you call yourselves members of the church? You're not as far as I'm concerned!"

As amazing as Lou's twitch was, the most amazing part of the whole evening turned out to be the folklore that rapidly grew up around it. By that weekend the rumor had fastened itself securely to the obese body of Mormon myth about "apostates" that Rick and I had physically attacked the key coordinator there in the foyer. One of the aspects of folklore that puzzles me, since I am no expert, is how the three other people besides us in that foyer—key coordinator, her husband, and her friend—can *all three* have verified that something actually happened that did not ever come close to happening. Because all three must have verified it and, I think, must have *believed* it. It is a cause for wonderment.

I wore my "Another Mormon for ERA" button to church in those days, one button to counter the bosomfuls of "Equality Yes, ERA No" buttons there. Those "Equality Yes, ERA No" buttons turned up at the legislature that year. I know, because I was there with my "Another Mormon" button to counter hundreds of them in the corridors of the Legislative Office Building in Richmond. Often, I would follow their turn with some delegate or senator, and as I did, I gradually began to discover that the Mormon women of Virginia, with those "Equality Yes, ERA No" buttons on their breasts, were lobbying against every single women's bill before the legislature that year, bills that had been in the making for years and were considered so good that surrounding states were plagiarizing them.

The Mormons say they don't want the ERA because it would release men from having to pay alimony (any woman who thinks the majority of divorced men pay alimony these days has either never been divorced or lives in fantasyland), yet they helped defeat a bill which would have made it possible for officials of Virginia to cross state lines to apprehend those men who were dodging alimony and child support and make them pay. Mormons say they don't want the ERA because it would remove "protections" from housewives. Yet they lobbied against a bill that would have given the housewife's work in the home monetary value at the time of property settlement in divorce. There is a good deal of hypocrisy and double-talk out there in the ERA opposition, as there has to be. The opponents of the ERA, whether they know it or not, are working in every case for what is good for *men*, not what is good for women. But they believe the men when the men tell them it's for their own good. They are so very, very fast asleep. . . .*

The hypocrisy behind those bebuttoned bosoms was not lost on legislators, either. One of them, in being interviewed by a reporter (who later told me the story), said, "I told those women, 'How can you lobby against these bills wearing those buttons? These bills were designed by women legislators and lawyers to protect women's rights in this state.' I couldn't believe it. That's what I call hypocrisy!"

All four of our women's bills in Virginia, as well as the ERA, were killed that year by women who vowed that they believed in equal rights for women, just not in the Equal Rights Amendment.

Another reporter not long ago interviewed a Mormon woman in Illinois who was involved in the church's coalition there. They had a good talk and became so friendly that the Mormon woman finally confided: "Do you know what we're most afraid of? Do you know what we're all fasting and praying about in the church here? We're praying that Carter won't appoint a female to the Supreme Court!"

She is, of course, for equal rights and for women; she's just not for the Equal Rights Amendment.

What is obvious is that the New Right—the patriarchs and their servant women—do not want equality. The New Right, at the center of which looms the Mormon church, has a colossal investment in inequality. Those who have little experience with the subculture of the New Right may think I am overstating the depth of women's reliance upon male authority for direction in their personal lives. That it is impossible to overstate may be clear from a story told to

* This somnabulance apparently also drove Susan B. Anthony frantic. In 1870 she wrote: "So while I do not pray for anybody or any party to commit outrages, still I do pray, and that earnestly and constantly, for some terrific shock to startle the women of this nation into a self-respect which will compel them to see the abject degradation of their present position; which will force them to break their yoke of bondage, and give them faith in themselves; which will make them proclaim their allegiance to women first; which will enable them to see that man can no more feel, speak or act for woman than could the old slaveholder for his slave. The fact is, women are in chains, and their servitude is all the more debasing *because they do not realize it* [italics added]. O, to compel them to see and feel, and to give them the courage and conscience to speak and act for their own freedom, though they face the scorn and contempt of all the world for doing it."

me recently. A friend of mine, an older Mormon woman who supports the ERA but with ambivalence, called me on the phone. "How are you?" I asked. "Much, much better, thank you," she replied. "I had a talk with the bishop and I feel very relieved and peaceful." "Oh? Was something wrong?" "You know my son, Ed. Well, he was calling me an apostate, and this worried me a lot. Made me feel terrible. So I went to see the bishop and ask him if I was an apostate, and you can imagine my relief when he told me that of course I wasn't. He assured me that I was in good standing in the church. I told him about the problems my family is having, and he told me not to worry, that time would take care of them. I can't tell you how much better he made me feel!"

I can't tell you what despair she made me feel. Her self-righteous son's telling her she was an apostate made her anxious because he is male and holds the priesthood; therefore he has insights into *her* that she is not privy to. But her bishop—thirty-five years her junior, at least—is an even higher authority than her son. His insights into her will be more acute, so she will check out the state of her soul with *him*. She is an intelligent, imaginative woman, but his amateur therapy, his feeble "time heals all wounds"—because he is the bishop and male and *in authority*—satisfied her, whereas if I or any female and therefore lesser mortal had offered her such pap, she would rightfully have scorned it. Not once did it occur to this mature woman that *she* knew—better than her son, better than a young bishop—whether or not she was an apostate; that she was the expert on the state of her soul, that she alone knows what she thinks and feels. Except for God.

Aye, there's the rub. Because who has an in with God? Who is most like him? Who therefore knows more about her than she knows about herself? Men.

This is what patriarchy does to women. Makes them helpless, makes them children and fools.

The fight against women's rights is directed from behind the scenes by men. It is not, in the final and truest sense, a battle of women against women at all. It is men against women, men who use frightened, intimidated women against those of their sex who will no longer be bullied.

Barbara Mikulski (US Rep. Dem. MD) once pointed out astutely that talking about equal rights without the Amendment—the "E. R.

without the A.," a meaningless phrase Reagan popularized—is like talking about independence without the Declaration, protection of individual freedoms without the Bill of Rights, emancipation of the slaves without the Proclamation. The Declaration, the Bill, the Proclamation—all are statements of American philosophy. Before a desired national goal can be reached, it must always be clearly and specifically and officially enunciated. Without a philosophical statement of the belief of the American people in equality for all citizens under the law, such equality will never come about. It is our documented philosophy that governs the content and interpretation of our laws.

Thinking about the church's dishonest and deceptive use of language, I remember what author John Fowles said in the February 19, 1978, *Saturday Review*: ". . . I do believe that almost all human evils in our world come from betrayal of the word at a very humble level." The New Right constantly betrays words at very humble levels. If you say you believe in equality but fight against all bills that would give women real protection under the law—such as men have —what have you done to the meaning of the word "equality"?

The lack of integrity in their use of language turns up again and again. One of the chief concerns of church leaders in the past has been the use of the word "sex" in the amendment, showing their confusion between the sex people *are* and the sex people *do*. Perhaps they have not been confused, but have deliberately sought to confuse others, and to cause others to believe that the courts would be confused. Regardless, acting confused is how they mistakenly construe the amendment to be about legalizing abortion (it is already legal) and homosexual marriages.

"If they had just used the word 'gender' instead," lamented Elaine Cannon, a church spokesman* in Washington, D.C., a year or so ago, implying that the church would have accepted it if they had, "but the word 'sex' leaves everything so wide open!"

On July 24, 1980, National Organization for Women members met in Charleston, West Virginia, to picket a Mormon reception

---

* I use "spokesman" deliberately; she speaks for the men, not herself. No one in the church worries whether or not she speaks for women. They presume that Mormon women think only what the leaders tell them to think and so the men can always speak for them without consulting them. Those of us who demand to speak for ourselves anything the men have not told us to speak are outlaws.

celebrating the opening of a new mission in that state. The church's PR man talked at length to Sondra Lucht, the leader. He was—you guessed it!—*for* equality, just not for the Equal Rights Amendment. The wording in particular worried him. He didn't like the word "sex." "It should be 'gender,'" he told Sondra.

When she related this to me, I advised her to call that man up and confront him with the fact that Mormons in Iowa mobilized before the November 4 election to defeat a proposed state equal rights clause on the ballot which stated:

"All men and women are, by nature, free and equal and have certain inalienable rights—among which are those of enjoying and defending life and liberty, acquiring property, and pursuing and obtaining safety and happiness. Neither the state nor any of its political subdivisions shall, on the basis of *gender* [italics mine], deny or restrict the equality of rights under the law."

Now what is there about this truly beautiful statement to alarm Iowa Mormons, especially since "sex" has so thoughtfully been changed to "gender" to quell their fears?

Equality. That is what is in the clause that alarms the Mormons. And ironically enough, the defeated Iowa equal rights clause sounds very like Utah's, which church leaders would assuredly direct members to defeat if it should come up for a vote in the Utah legislature today.

What is this double-talk about "Equality Yes, ERA No!"

"Family" is another word the New Right is in the process of betraying. To them, it can apply only to a group of people united either by blood or by matrimony, with a man at their head, a definition that does a terrible disservice to the millions of women and children who are not in this situation. The latest census reveals that only about 12 percent of American households are the sort which the New Right would designate as families. What, pray tell, do they call the other 88 percent of us, or don't they even acknowledge that we're here?

Of course, the family is in this condition because women have not been behaving properly—running out to work, and so forth. This is another of the myriads of examples of women's being used as the scapegoats of society, and often, alas, believing themselves guilty, when in fact, so many families are fatherless simply because so many men are abandoning them. It seems to me that my experience is far and away the most common single divorce experience in this country: one day the head of household gets fed up with all the responsibilities and pressures, not to mention his "used" wife, turns her in for a new model and opts out, often abandoning his children at the same time.

I think it is time we stop blaming the demise of the family entirely on women, and look searchingly at the irresponsible way patriarchal society teaches men to behave in human relationships.

In Atlanta in July, 1980, after I had been on the Freeman Reports talk show (the audience packed with Mormons), a Mormon woman came up to me and said, "Surely you don't believe women should work outside the home?" (It turned out that *she* worked for pay, but didn't "believe" in it.) "Millions of women *have* to," I answered. "Like me, they have children to feed, and many have no man to depend on for support." I pointed out to her that nearly two thirds of the 28,000,000 Americans living in poverty are women and children, and that we need the ERA so that those women who must earn livelihoods *can*, which is difficult at present with no way to enforce laws that would give us equal pay.

"Women just have to go out and find a man to support them!" she sniffed. "That's the only solution!"

I was so dumbfounded I could not respond, though I felt like demanding, "Whose man? Yours?"

That that is a woman's only legitimate choice is still a prominent concept in American culture, though now it is promulgated primarily by the conservatives. But the idea of millions of women running wildly about the country looking for a man to marry them so they and their children can eat—when they cannot, under patriarchy, even *ask* him if they do find him—is a ridiculous scenario.

Not long after the excommunication came and Rick left, I asked my twelve-year-old son, Marc, to replace the "Another Mormon for ERA" bumper sticker with one that said, "Another Family for ERA."

"I can't, Mom. We're not a family anymore," he replied sadly.

I took him by the shoulders and turned him around to face me. "Oh yes we are!" I said quietly but fiercely. "We *are* a family, very much a family, as much a family as we've ever been. Families come in all different varieties. We'll always be a family, no matter what!"

"Pro-life" and "right-to-life" are other examples of betrayal of the word at humble levels. As Linda Gordon in her essay "The Struggle for Reproductive Freedom" puts it: ". . . but right-to-life advocates do not usually fight for 'life' in any systematic way. . . . Right-to-life forces have generally opposed the kinds of social programs which would make abortion less frequent: child care, sex education, contraception, etc. Right-to-lifers are not usually pacifists, though pacifism is the only overall philosophy that could make their position on abortion honorable and consistent. They oppose only the specific forms of 'killing' that amount to women's self-defense. They are reacting not merely to a 'loosening of morals' but to the whole feminist struggle of the last century; they are defending male supremacy. . . . The right to life is not the issue of abortion; the issue is women's rights." (In *Capitalist Patriarchy and the Case for Feminist Socialism*, Eisenstein, Ed., Monthly Review Press, NY, 1979.)

But the lovely word "love" has suffered greatest reversal of all in Mormon usage. They who "love" women so, knocked three Mormon women to the ground, kicked one, and had to be physically restrained from attacking the other two with a huge flashlight when we demonstrated in November 1980 at the Bellevue, Washington Mormon Temple. A political cartoon could easily be made from the AP photo taken of that event showing two women lying in the road with their Mormon assailant standing above them about to bash their heads in. All one would have to do is write "Mormon Church" across his chest and label the bodies in the road "American Women." Because figuratively, by attacking our human rights, which is our dignity, which is our life, the Mormon church is assaulting women everywhere. It wants to keep us right where we are today: flat on our backs in the road.

Because I have personally watched my people, the Mormons—who love women—fight tooth and nail against women's rights all across this nation, their protestations of "love," protestations of belief in "equality," "family," and "life" therefore strike me as singularly unconvincing. The real question is, what are they doing *for* women?

If they believe in equality, let them organize in even one state, to get even one law through even one legislature that would give women *real* protection—the kind men have—with the same Salt Lake-directed, single-minded ferocity they display in their fight against all women's issues everywhere. Then perhaps I will begin to believe. If they really love women, let them stop fighting battered women's shelters, day-care centers, planned parenthood, sex education in the schools, rape laws, marital property and divorce laws, ERA—the whole movement for *women's* right to life. Then perhaps I will begin to believe. If they really love women, let them stop insisting that, though *men* have never had to win their civil rights state by state, *women* must. As Barbara Mikulski has said, it's very like Lincoln's advising the slaves to win their freedom plantation by plantation.*

But the time needed to pass a law is only a part of the difficulty we face. The next almost insurmountable hurdle is getting that law enforced. It is notoriously difficult to get male legislators/ judges/lawyers/law enforcement officers/ and citizens in general to do anything about bills that genuinely protect women's rights. Thousands of good laws for women in this country are totally unenforceable and many have been since the day they were passed, which means their being on the books does us no good whatever.

The equal rights clause in the Utah Constitution provides a good example of a purely decorative women's rights statement. I know of no time since it was passed in 1890 that it has been useful to women. When I suggested to some Utah women that they put it to work for them in sex discrimination cases, they were horrified. "If we called too much attention to it," they cried, "the men would take it away from us!" "Then what earthly good is it doing you?" I demanded.

---

* "State by state" is a cruel joke. Trying to equalize laws in this country in this fashion is impossible, which is why the enemies of equality are insisting on it, of course. There are approximately 16,000 laws in this country that discriminate against women. To reach this number, multiply 300 (which is the number of such laws Pennsylvania found on its books when it ratified the federal ERA) by 50 (because Pennsylvania is probably above average in its legal treatment of women and the estimate is thus likely to be low) which gives 15,000, and add the 800+ discriminatory federal laws. Anyone who has ever tried to change even one law to benefit women knows what a monumental labor is involved, and how much time it takes.

Let us say that after five years of trying to get a decent rape law through a state (and we've been trying for nearly twice that long in Virginia), we finally succeed. At that rate, the sun would burn out of the sky before we began to make a dent in the 16,000.

As Eleanor Smeal says in the *National NOW Times*, Oct/Nov 1980: "[Reagan's] letter just underscores how out of touch with the times he is. There are over 800 federal statutes that discriminate against women on the basis of sex, according to the United States Civil Rights Commission. If it takes 8 years to change 14 laws [Reagan brags about having changed 14 laws for women in the state of California during his two terms as governor], according to my arithmetic it would take 457 years to change 800 laws. We may be patient people, but that is ridiculous."

"Better to let the legislature reveal themselves for the bigots they are than to sit and shiver with apprehension that a clause that is worthless to everybody—except as some sort of salve for the church's conscience—might be deleted. Invoke that clause, do it repeatedly, and reveal what a mockery it is."

Another of the many problems of changing laws state by state is that laws which really protect women's rights disappear from the books—are amended or voted out of existence—with regularity. They are at present as ephemeral as sand castles because they have, figuratively, been built on the sand. Women have taken to heart that good, pragmatic piece of ancient scriptural advice that admonishes us to build our house upon a rock. The Constitution of the United States is the rock upon which we have chosen to build: the Equal Rights Amendment to the Constitution is the firm foundation for our house of justice. Any gains we might seem to make without it are built on the sand, and when the winds blow and the rains come they will wash all away. But with the ERA, under the protection of the Constitution of our country, gains women make will be permanent and enforceable. When the winds blow and the rains beat upon them, they will stand.

Why, if the ERA were not able to do what it is designed to do and what we claim it will do, if it would not really give legal equality to women, why is the opposition lavishing millions of dollars and hours toward its defeat? If, as they say, it is "not the answer" to the problem of equality for women, why are they fighting it with all the strength of their multibillion-dollar corporations? The very intensity of their opposition reveals that they recognize it as the rock-solid foundation for equality for American women that it truly is.

Otherwise, why would they bother?

Tired of words and thoroughly undeceived by them, I challenge my brethren in the Mormon church—and all those in the New Right who claim to love women—to prove it by their actions.

If you love us, stop fighting us.

If you love us, help us.

That is what the word "love" meant before you turned it topsy-turvy.

Chapter 7

The Plot Thickens

"COME TELL US what to do about our Mormons!" has become an almost constant refrain as women and men throughout the country realize the mammoth power of the church in its all-out war against
women. The first time I heard this request outside Virginia was
sometime in the early summer of 1979 when I received a frantic call
from the president of the little Kalispell, Montana, NOW chapter.
She outlined how the Mormons had nearly gotten recision through
the last session of the Montana legislature, and begged me to come
to Kalispell and tell them what to do about their Mormons.

I didn't know what to tell them. We hadn't been too successful
with our own Mormons in Virginia; the "fembots"* (as Mary Daly
calls patriarchal women) were still marching at the men's signals.
But I agreed to go, if planes landed in Kalispell, for several reasons.
Mormons for ERA wanted people to know that not all Mormon
women are robots, that many of us refuse to be programmed against
ourselves; we wanted them to know that Mormons are good folk
whom they would like if they met them outside the political arena.
But most of all, I personally wanted to encourage everyone everywhere to confront the Mormon church as they would any legitimate
political opponent. I wanted to put some backbone in women, encourage them not to be intimidated—as the church counts on their
being—by the fact that the Mormon church in its spare time is also a
religious institution.

So I asked Mom to come out to look after the children (Rick had
been in Liberia since March and would not be home until September) and toward the end of August flew to Kalispell, Montana,

* female robots

where I delivered the most innocuous speech of my career, especially considering that the subject was Mormons in politics. Fortuitously (and you can say it's a coincidence if you wish) NOW had that speech videotaped, giving me permanent proof that one of the newspaper quotes contributing to my excommunication was in error.

In the audience that day were several Mormon women. One bolted early in the speech, but four stayed and cheered. Afterward, a pretty, dark young woman came up to where I was hastily finishing my lunch before the waitresses cleared it away, and introduced herself as Arlene Wood, a Mormon. "But not a *good* Mormon," she hastened to add. "I smoke and I don't go to church . . ."

"What *is* a 'good Mormon'?" I asked her. It was beginning to occur to me that those members who thought of themselves as "good" but allowed the leaders of the church to direct the church into anti-human rights paths were not doing the church a service at all, not being really "good" Mormons. I was beginning to understand that to be a "good Mormon" by church leaders' definition meant being less than a good citizen, less than the best human being. It meant abnegating responsibility for one's own moral decisions. It meant not following the example of Jesus Christ, who admonished us all to do unto others as we would have them do unto us—a directive the men of almost all churches in all countries have never interpreted as pertaining to their treatment of women. (And because of which we have not yet entered the Christian era.)

Arlene and I arranged to meet that afternoon, and when we did we liked each other very much. She was with me the next day when I picked up a newspaper in the hotel lobby and read what I was supposed to have said in my speech the day before: "Don't let Mormon missionaries into your home." "Good grief!" she yelped. "That's not what you said! That will get you into trouble!"

Not all prophets are men.

A few days after I returned from Montana, Hazel and I drove to New York City where I was to deliver a speech entitled "Patriarchal Panic: Sexual Politics in the Mormon Church" on a panel—"Some Reflections on Women, Religion, and Mental Health"—at the American Psychological Association's annual meeting. Already this speech had created an ominous stir out in Utah. Church people had been calling my friends there—Jan Tyler, Linda Sillitoe, Doty Williams, and others—trying to get a copy of it. On August 10, I had sent the next-to-final draft of the paper to Linda with this letter:

"Here's the fatal paper, which you'll recognize instantly as not worth all the fuss; a simple, pleasant, warmhearted little discussion. . . . I find myself wishing I'd written a really raging fierce thing so everyone would be satisfied. After all that build up, just *this?*"

All it says is, in short, as you sow, so shall you reap.

September 1, 1979, the day I read my paper in New York, was for the most part uneventful. Some Mormons in the audience were stung to the quick, but most came up afterward and congratulated me. One of the latter was Ralph Payne from Shippensburg State College in Pennsylvania. Later I was to ask him to testify at my trial that the speech had not caused listeners to think harsh thoughts about the church. Most Mormons and others there seemed totally unscathed by my performance.

The church was planning an area conference for about 18,000 Mormons in Washington, D.C.'s, Capital Arena the next weekend. Earlier that summer, Mormons for ERA had helped found a religious coalition named Religious Advocates for Equality, under the guiding hand of Midge Miller, a Wisconsin legislator. At the group's first meeting when we were thinking of ideas for actions, I invited them to come and picket the prophet with us on September 9. Maureen Fiedler, a Sister of Mercy who heads Catholics Act for ERA, immediately extended us a return invitation to help Catholic groups picket the pope a week or so after the prophet-picket. "We'll picket your patriarchs if you'll picket ours!" we agreed, laughing. And that was the beginning of an unusual team: Maureen and I have since been in cahoots in one escapade after another.

In the meantime, KUTV from Salt Lake City arranged to do a short TV special on me and Mormons for ERA the Friday before the church's area conference. Wanting to show Mormons for ERA meeting together to prepare the signs and plan the strategy for the demonstration, they spent several hours at my house that Friday afternoon, and at about 5 P.M. gathered up all the equipment and drove over to the Sterling Park Ward chapel to film me at the organ. Carl Idsvog, the director, had arranged with Bishop Jeff Willis for us to use the building that morning, but since we were eight hours late, we weren't sure about our reception. Carl thought it would be all right, however, and that no one would be upset.

But he was wrong. The cameramen were setting up the lights when suddenly the door swung open and Jeff came stomping up the aisle in a rage.

"What's going on here?" he roared, whereupon he and Carl plunged into a spirited colloquy, which ended with Jeff's huffing back down the aisle and angrily out the door with Carl at his heels, belatedly trying to be diplomatic.

Ten minutes later they both reappeared. Jeff seemed calmer, though still scowling, as he sat in the back and monitored the whole filming process.

Later, on the way home, Carl turned around in the front seat and said, "You're not going to believe this, but do you know what happened out there in the hall? Jeff stormed out the door of the chapel straight into a closet and shut the door. In my face. I was dumbfounded. Surely he must have anticipated, if only momentarily, that he'd eventually have to come out, and how embarrassing that would be. After all, how long can one pretend to be occupied in a dark closet? And of course he did have to come out after a while, and he was—we both were—so embarrassed we couldn't look each other in the face."

(While I was practicing with the choir one Sunday afternoon a couple of weeks later, one of the bishop's counselors came into the chapel to get me to answer a call on the pay phone down the hall. I thought something dire had happened at home, but it was just a Texas Mormon for ERA in town for a day or two wanting to catch up on the news. Just as I began telling him about our demonstration at Capital Arena, and our plans for October conference in Salt Lake, Jeff emerged from his office and strode purposefully down the hall in my direction. When he got to the intersection, he turned right, not left toward the phone, and walked—yes, it's true—into a closet and shut the door. I modulated my voice and said incredulously to Howard, "You're not going to believe this, but the bishop just walked into the closet across the hall!" "Whatever *for?*" Howard gasped. "I think he must be turning into a closet feminist," I chuckled. Jeff's right; I don't have proper respect.)

As it turned out, one of the things Jeff told Carl he was most upset about the day of the filming was that I was wearing my red, white, and blue ERA scarf at the organ; he said he was afraid people would think the church supported the ERA. "I don't think there's any danger of that in Salt Lake," Carl had reassured him dryly.

"He's not afraid of that at all," I guessed. "I think he's afraid that people in Salt Lake will see that he *allowed* me to play the organ wearing an ERA scarf. He's afraid church leaders and Utah Mormons will think he should not have permitted such flagrant dissent. I wear the scarf to church all the time, too; he hasn't said anything about it yet and I'll bet he's been feeling like a weakling for not confronting me about it."

In preparation for picketing the prophet, Religious Advocates for Equality had written requesting an audience with President Kimball. Along with their letter, RAE sent him a statement of concerns:

"*We are concerned* . . . that many of our brothers and sisters at whose side we have stood in other struggles for equality say they are with us, yet are not standing at our side as we seek equal rights for women.
We ask: Where are they?

We are concerned . . . that among many leaders and members of religious bodies there has been a prejudice and premature rejection of the values arising with the women's movement. These values are nurtured by basic faith tenets of our Western religious heritage.
We ask: How can we best speak to your fears?

We are concerned . . . about the fear that women's struggle for equal rights and responsibilities in churches, synagogues, and in civil society is viewed as contrary to religious values.
We ask: Should not all religious women and men be leaders in building a just world for all people?

We are concerned . . . about the distortion of religious values that sanctifies and preserves false idols of sexism and other forms of bigotry and personal negation.
We ask: Where are the love, truth, and justice that are the birthright of all God's children?

We are concerned . . . for our many sisters who are leaving their churches and synagogues because they are not received as equal partners by their religious congregations.

> *We ask*: How can we restore religion to the intended whole-
> ness of creation: "Male and female, God created them.
> And God blessed them."

I had also written personally—again—asking to be allowed to see
President Kimball when he was in the area. Of course, he refused
both RAE's and my requests. So what alternatives for making our
feelings known did that leave us? We have always felt profoundly
guiltless about picketing Mormon meetings because there simply is
no other avenue through which to express dissent in the church. We
would have preferred other ways; we tried to find other ways. But the
whole church system is set up to quash dissent, not to channel it and
use it for growth.

About sixty people of various religious backgrounds met in the
parking lot of a bank just down the street from the arena for a prayer
service and singing before the demonstration. Sister Maureen Fiedler
preached a eulogy about Mormons for ERA:

We are gathered here today . . .
to stand in solidarity with our sisters and brothers, Mormons for
ERA, who cry out for equal rights and human dignity in their
church and in our land . . .
to celebrate their courage and steadfastness in the cause of justice . . .
to let them know—and to let the all-male leadership of the Mormon Church know—that we of other faiths share deeply their
pain and their hurt and their feeling of shame as the resources
of good Mormon people are used by the church hierarchy to
oppose equality—and used to try to defeat the Equal Rights
Amendment to the U.S. Constitution which would guarantee
that equality in law . . .
we are pained because the rights of all of us are trampled and
stepped on by such actions
we are pained because our faith means a great deal to us, and we
grieve to see it used to deny human rights, to keep half the
human race at the level of second-class citizens, to deny our
common God-given call to equality. Women of all faiths—or
women of no faith—identify today with the woman bent over
in Luke's gospel (13:10–17), a scripture we share with the

Mormons. We have been weighed down for centuries by
those who
devalue our minds
abuse and batter our bodies
underpay our work
see us as roles rather than as persons
deny us any right to decision-making
keep us out of sanctuaries and priesthoods
strive to keep us out of our own Constitution and have us maintain our status as second-class citizens under the law. . . .
Those of us in the ecumenical community of faith in the
United States see Mormons for ERA in the role of Jesus the
healer . . .
It is they who—lovingly and courageously—in the face of incredible odds—offer their hands and hearts to women bent over,
so that there might be a healing and a rising of the whole
human race.

Rick had come home from Liberia a few days early to be with me
at the demonstration and Arlene had flown in from Montana. As the
first cars came pouring out of the arena parking lots, we were at the
roadsides—Rick, Arlene, the children, I, and a few friends—at the
exit leading to Virginia, which meant that every person who attended from our stake (diocese) saw us there with our posters. Mine
said, "Honor thy mother, ratify ERA." But the best sign in the
whole group, and one which has since been used again and again,
was held by a black woman and declared, truly: "Bigots make bad
missionaries!" Overhead putted our little plane with "Mother in
Heaven Loves Mormons for ERA" floating merrily along behind.

This was my first picket, and here I was picketing my own church,
my own people. At first I was in an agony of self-consciousness, but
soon saw things which helped me forget myself and even begin enjoying the experience. As a busload of missionaries passed by us, for
example, a couple of them made obscene gestures. We could scarcely
believe it at first, but then it became hugely funny and we laughed
until we nearly cried. When another man, driving alone in his car up
out of the parking lots, repeated the performance, we were quite
overcome with merriment. But there were as many thumbs-up as
fingers-up, and enough of those who shouted out their windows,

"Right on!" "Go to it!" or "Hurray for Mormons for ERA!" that we did not have to rely long on gross demonstrations of hypocrisy to cheer us up. Rick, always the statistician, took the first informal poll of our history and, as the last cars trickled out, announced to our delight that about 20 percent of them had held Mormons who supported the Equal Rights Amendment. Demonstrators at the other exits that day reported similar incidents (both gross and grand) in about the same proportion. We were ecstatic: these were the active members of the church, the "good Mormons!"

About that time I began hearing from Mormons about my American Psychological Association talk, "Patriarchal Panic." Some of my correspondents clearly wished me dead and preferably by their own hands. I remember feeling profound gratitude to the powers that be that one of these men was in Provo, Utah, and not in Virginia, because his letter left the distinct impression that a little rape and murder were all that would relieve his ferocious anger at me. As it was, since he was too far away to get his hands on me, he was reduced to raping and murdering me figuratively by mail:

". . . rather than treating your concerns about these issues in a discreet manner* Mrs. Johnson, you are a whore for the Secular Establishment. The believing women of the church are not toadies; *you* are a toady, a vile toady pandering to a morally bankrupt, anti-Christ world. You are a cheap prostitute for the world—which, by the way, is male-dominated—by immorally exploiting your own accidental membership in the church for personal gain. Your lying soul has fornicated with the vulgar mob-intelligentsia, and like a robot, you obediently spout off all the feminist buzz words, snatching headlines, and getting patted on the back, stupidly. . . . You are a classic case of the born-in-the-faith Mormon gone ratfink—a brainless sycophant to the world, selling your 'true confessions' for a rumor-hungry, anti-religious society, rolling over on your back playing toady to anti-Mor-

---

* This typical patriarchal conviction that women ought to be "discreet" about opposing men whereas men may be as open as they wish in their opposition to women is simply more evidence of the ubiquitous double standard. Politics is a rough game and the church is out there on the field playing rough. In choosing politics, it chose opponents who play for keeps, too. Since the church isn't wearing white gloves in their anti-woman fight, they can hardly expect women to keep theirs on. What in the world do Mormons—and other anti-female religious New Righters—expect women to do? Allow ourselves to be ground into the dust without a whimper? Discreet? I should certainly think not!

mon audiences. . . . You have turned your back on your people and have heaped scorn on the Prophets of God for worldly gain. May your wretched, lying soul find mercy on Judgment Day."

Church leaders at Brigham Young University had my paper reproduced by the thousands and circulated in every conceivable way throughout the student body. I am sure they thought that would harm our cause and serve me right. But I remember as I was writing it how frustrated I felt that only a few scholarly types, mostly non-Mormon, would ever hear or read my paper, and how mightily I wished I could trumpet it throughout the whole church, not to mention the nation. And then to have someone at the most powerful Mormon educational institution oblige me by taking care of that problem as far as the church population is concerned—well, God works in a mysterious way. Now thousands of young Mormon women have a seed planted in their minds, regardless of how shocked and horrified they initially were by my ideas. And seeds, though they may lie dormant for years, need only a little nourishment to grow, nourishment which the men in the church will certainly supply them with abundantly, as I know so well. By defensively taking the offensive, BYU planted a seed of suspicion of the patriarchy in many female students' hearts. The irony is wonderful.

Although I received few positive responses about my APA speech from Mormon men, many Mormon women understood just what I was saying and agreed: "After reading your APA speech for myself, I can put aside the rumors and distortions I'd heard. My heart is clearly with you." "The wording, though strong, was accurate in my opinion. You touched on many of the thoughts that have often crossed my mind." "I felt as if you were talking about me." "Most of my disenchantment with the church has been over issues which you described very clearly in your paper."

On September 16, KUTV showed the "Extra" about Mormons for ERA, the filming of which had driven Jeff into the closet. I wrote to Arlene: "Last night we appeared on TV in Utah. Our reports from there say we looked—as we are—moderate, intelligent, reasonable, pro-Church, and came off much better than poor Barbara Smith who had to cover for the bungling Brethren. I'd be getting pretty fed up with that role, if I were she. I'd be ready to say, 'Okay, fellas, it's your game. You made the rules, you're calling the plays. You take the ball from now on!' I wonder why women allow themselves to be cast in the role of defending policy they have had no hand in making, defending it for the male policy-makers who haven't a clue about the ERA and are just scared to death of losing power. The women end up looking bad on TV because their hearts aren't in it, reinforcing the men's beliefs that women are ineffective. Maybe that's uncharitable, but I don't think so. I hate to see women being made use of against themselves, and such *incompetent* use."

The men finally solved this problem, however, by deciding not to use the two top females in the church but getting a professional public relations puppet in the form of the Chairman (head of the Virginia LDS Citizens' Coalition), and using her instead. Mormons for ERA expect to see the Chairman as the next president of the church's Relief Society. Like Phyllis Schlafly, she has never been a housewife by profession, or at least not for many, many years. For some reason, patriarchy always uses nontraditional women to persuade other women to be traditional. Why Mormon and other women do not eventually catch on to this would be impossible to understand if one did not remember how very deeply asleep the men have lulled them.

Since October 1979, when we flew "Mother in Heaven" again (this time over Tabernacle Square in Salt Lake), we have flown a dozen more banners at Mormon conferences and organized dozens of demonstrations all over the country. Some of our banners are exceedingly cheering: "The South Shall Rise and Ratify" in Mississippi; "Mormons for ERA Love NY for Ratifying Equality" over Rochester; "Show me Equality" over St. Louis; "In Your Hearts You Know Sonia's Right" over the Pioneer Day parade in Salt Lake; "MORE Mormons for ERA are Everywhere" over April 1980 general conference in Salt Lake; and "Mrs. God Hates Sexism; Repent and Ratify" over Salt Lake conference in October.

Through it all, we have enjoyed ourselves immensely. To meet your foe out openly on the battlefield is an exhilarating and freeing experience.

Just after Kalispell NOW called, the Seattle ERA coalition asked if I could come and talk to them around the end of October. They knew Mormon tactics well from International Women's Year days. I agreed to come because I planned already to be two thirds of the way across the continent at the University of Utah's women's conference speaking on a panel called "Mormon Women: Three Perspectives."

There were, as the title suggests, to be three of us on that panel and there had to be ample time left for questions and answers, so each of us had been severely cautioned to take no more than ten minutes. If I have an hour to speak, I can speak without notes. If I have half an hour, I must make a few. If I have only ten minutes, I must write down word for word what I want to say and read it. That's what I did for the Utah women's conference. My paper was entitled, "Off Our Pedestals, or the Chronicles of the Uppity Sisters," and if I read fast, I could just make it to the end in ten minutes.

In it, not wishing to add kindling to the pile I had already stacked at the foot of my stake with the APA speech, I reverted to the approach I had used in my Senate testimony. But instead of quoting early Mormon feminists, I quoted present-day ones, those I had been hearing from by the hundreds all over the church. I quoted their anger at having their roles defined for them by men, at having to ask men's permission for everything they do in the church, for being denied positions they once held in the church, for being forbidden to give one another blessings as our foremothers did, for the power grab called "priesthood correlation" which abolished women's independence in the church altogether, for the ostracism Mormons meet when they do not conform, for being manipulated with guilt and fear by church leaders. I quoted their sadness at waking up to what had happened to us as women and is still happening, and at our unwitting participation in it for so long. I ended with a stanza from a poem one of them sent me from a book entitled *Women in the Pulpit*:

> Sometimes I wish my eyes had not been opened
> but now that they have
> I'm determined to see
> that somehow my sisters and I will one day be
> the free people we were created to be.

As chance would have it, the first day I read my speech at the women's conference, sitting in the audience was a young UPI stringer who had come to cover our panel. I have never met her, but

I know she must have an ear for language, because she picked out the best phrase in my talk. I had borrowed it from somewhere else myself (heaven only knows from where; I couldn't remember, so I didn't footnote it) for its absolute rightness. It is embedded in the second paragraph of my speech:

"I wish there were time to talk at length about why the pedestal as a symbol of women's immobilization and isolation in our male-centered society, more than any other symbol—the gilded cage, the doll's house—reveals our savage misogyny. Briefly, it is physically, intellectually, emotionally, and spiritually cramped. It is precarious, and a fall is dangerous, if not fatal. It maroons women and keeps us emotionally stranded from one another. And by placing us in the position customarily occupied by statues, it reveals society's attempt to render us as conveniently nonhuman, mindless, and will-less as works of art."

Naturally, "savage misogyny" is the phrase she liked, so she wrote it on her pad. Later, when she got ready to write the story, she must have looked at those two most-descriptive-of-patriarchy words and mused, "Now I wonder what she *said* about 'savage misogyny?' Well, since this is Sonia Johnson she must have said that "the Mormon culture, specifically including church leaders, has a savage misogyny." And that's what went out over the UPI wire! The noose of misquotes was tightening around my neck.

I have often thought that misquote a very telling one. Since the material for it wasn't even in my speech, where did it come from? Out of the head and heart of the UPI stringer; out of the church's behavior. If the shoe fits, others will try to get you to wear it.

I was not the only Mormon for ERA the church was watching. The summer before, our embryonic group had sent a letter to all U.S. legislators pleading for the ERA extension; twenty of us signed it, my mother included.

Soon afterward, her bishop called her in (at the request of the stake president who had himself, he said, been called directly by Gordon Hinckley), scolded her severely about her ERA activities, and warned that her church membership was endangered by them. Some months later, when she and my father went in for temple recommend interviews, her bishop asked her if she thought she was worthy to go to the temple. "Of course," she answered unhesitatingly. "Perhaps you'd better think it over awhile," he suggested meaningfully. "I don't need to think it over," she replied, and got her recommend.

Nevertheless, his insinuations distressed her, and when I found out I wanted to shake him until his teeth chattered. I knew him, had known him all my life. The thought of his setting himself up as judge of my mother's righteousness was not to be borne.

I called him on the phone. As soon as he heard who it was, he began shouting at me about how evil I was. I told him I had called to talk about *his* behavior. (In fact, I had to remind him of that several times. Bishops are not accustomed to having to account to mere members for their behavior.) He was having a fit of name-calling on the other end of the line, but finally I was able to get him to understand that if he continued to harass my mother about the ERA—or any other matter—I would take action against him promptly and powerfully.

A few weeks later, Mom wrote to tell me that he had shouted so long, so loudly, and so ignorantly about the ERA in sacrament meeting the next Sunday that she turned off her hearing aid in disgust. That's the spirit, Mom!

But Big Brother kept watching, and one day Mother was called into the bishop's office again. "I called you in to tell you you are in trouble and to warn you," he told her. "You must be more cautious." Gradually, the story came out. Two women from the ward—Mom never learned their names; just anonymous spies, I suppose—had been watching her during a debate between Karen DeCrow and Phyllis Schlafly at Utah State University one evening, and had subsequently reported to the bishop that Mother had *clapped for De-Crow!* "Didn't you know that there were people who would see you applauding?" he demanded. "Why didn't you applaud *both* of them?"

I was horrified and furious. This is the sort of thing one expects to happen in Russia, not America. What does it mean when a person cannot applaud a speaker without being reported to her local bishop, without being reprimanded and threatened?

It means that the church has erected a curtain in "Zion" patterned after the better-known curtain of Iron.

My mother is not the only ERA supporter or supporter of the women's movement whom church leaders in various parts of the country are persecuting. We hear enough from others to know that harassment is a phenomenon occurring churchwide.

If ever I should begin to be persuaded that the tradition of allowing only men to hold the priesthood is beneficial to both men and women (as church leaders would like me to believe), let me remember how judgmental, how haughty, how smug, it has made so many Mormon men, and how it has cowed so many Mormon women, and then let me fight with renewed dedication for the end of male supremacy.

During part of this time I was teaching the gospel doctrine class in the small Mormon Sunday School in Hamilton, Virginia, where my husband and children had fled to escape Jeff Willis and the paranoia and unkindness of Sterling Park Ward. I was still ward organist in Sterling Park and taught a monthly Relief Society lesson there, but Rick and the kids refused to attend church there any longer. The children especially were treated unkindly by their peers.

Linda Sillitoe was also teaching the gospel doctrine class in her ward in Salt Lake City and we often exchanged ideas. In my letter to her of August 10 I said: "Tomorrow I begin work on Sunday's lesson —the educational (so to speak) part of the 88th section [of the Doctrine and Covenants, a book of Mormon scripture]. Fortunately, we're now on turf I really know. We'll have a splendid time ricocheting off the elementary school's walls (that's where we meet). Everyone comes out just to keep me in line. A very united group, eager to outdo each other in showing me the error of my ways—which include despising that all the angels in the 88th section (and there are hordes of them) are male, and that the only female pronoun in the whole chapter refers to the great whore church [referring primarily to the Catholic but including all churches which are not Mormon]. I told them I was certain that women should not provide the symbols for the most evil possible things in the world (as they do in our society) and that we should take great care to refrain from reading those female pronouns to our impressionable children, that from this time out we should instead resolutely refer to that evil old church as 'it.' Did you know that Joseph Smith taught that there were people on the moon and that they dressed like nineteenth-century Americans? Must have been speaking as a man not a prophet there for a moment . . ."

Earlier, I had sent my APA paper to a Mormon woman in Menlo

Park, California. In a letter to her on July 26 I said, "Fantastic as it may seem (maybe even ironic; certainly paradoxical), I have recently been set apart as Gospel Doctrine teacher in the branch where Rick and the kids go. I think however, judging from last Sunday, that I won't last long. I let them in on the secret that women were prophets and judges in ancient Israel—and not minor ones, or powerless ones, as the Brethren would like us to believe. I can't seem to remember how I used to think when I wasn't thinking. I'm preparing to lay some heavy stuff on my Relief Society sisters at my cultural refinement lesson this coming Tuesday night, too, and think my tenure there is about up. Still I find I have to say some things or die.

"Women need to know their history. They need to know things I left out when we were talking about China—1,000 years of Chinese females not being able to walk without support so they could sexually titillate men (the sadistic monsters); cremation alive of widows in India—often very young girls—on the funeral pyres of their husbands, a custom which is still widely observed despite laws against it; and the millions of women who were burned as witches by the men of the church and the scholars of Europe during the fifteenth, sixteenth, and seventeenth centuries, a phenomenon which one male historian says was probably 'therapeutic' for society! Do you suppose he would call the murder of six million Jews by Hitler 'therapeutic?' "

In April of 1979, I sent our newsletter and Linda Sillitoe's *Utah Holiday* articles about the church and politics to the Washington *Post* and *Star* religion editors and to Boston *Globe* columnist Ellen Goodman with this covering letter:

"Revolution is fomenting in the Mormon Church—maybe 'evolution' is a better word (but evolution doesn't foment, and there *is* foment). Whatever it is, it has a sense of destiny about it. It will be slow and difficult, as all change is, but it will *be*. These articles record the beginning of the second act of the drama. The first was blacks and the priesthood. Now all men are equal. It is women's turn.

"Thought you might be interested in the fact that Mormon feminists exist. Not exactly *abound*, of course, but then we are just beginning.

"Wish us well!"

Chapter 8

Writing Him Off

As THE KUTV crew and I were getting ourselves assembled in my kitchen before rushing over to the church the afternoon of September 7, I heard, through the chatter and general confusion, the faint but familiar whistled rendering of Rick's theme song: "My Wife Hates Me," to the tune of "If I Loved You," the mournful whistle with which for nearly twenty years he had announced his arrival home. To everyone's alarm, since none of them had heard anything at all, I began running from one outside door to the other, calling "Rick?" Down the basement steps, out the back over the stone porch, out the other side into the driveway. "Where are you? I know you're there!" Back in the kitchen I am certain they were raising their eyebrows at one another and pointing with circular motions toward their ears. They had come all the way from Utah to do a story about me and Mormons for ERA and they knew, because they had been interviewing me all day, that Rick was in Liberia.

But I was sane and they were wrong. In he walked, looking like an illustration for the old man and the sea, or Robinson Crusoe—a thick hank of nearly white hair from the top of his head to his collar, with two dark blue eyes peering out like searchlights through the fog. He looked so old and so fragile that my heart twisted a little with the awareness of his—and hence my own—mortality.

Although we had not seen each other for six months, and though he had written letters full of love and longing, though I was surprised and very touched by his obviously having made a special effort to get home early to help in picketing the Mormon area conference the next Sunday, we both felt constrained by all the strangers in the house. Instead of embracing, I introduced him all around, then explained to him that we had to get to the church while the sunlight was still strong enough for an outside shot or two. I put him in charge of the Mormons for ERA who would soon be arriving to be in the last part of the film. And later, while Jeff Willis raged at the church and shut himself in the closet, nothing unnerved me. Rick was home, all was right with the world.

While we were at the church he shaved off his great bushy beard, and watching the film in Salt Lake a month later, I thought to myself as I had innumerable times in the past how very beautiful he was. Sitting by me on the floor that night, he looked, despite his gray hair, about thirty years old, and achingly familiar, which is reasonable since he was the backdrop before which I played out my days. Although the preceding six months without him had been easier for me than I had thought possible—even easier, in many ways, than when he was around—ultimately life without Rick in it was unthinkable. Just as life without the church was unthinkable. And yet, I was on the eve of losing them both. I was on the eve of having not only to think the unthinkable but to live it minute by minute.

That night he slipped off to bed about 11 P.M.—which was 3 or 4 A.M. or some such weary hour for him—as the rest of us sat on and talked and planned until it was some such weary hour for us. No chance to say, "Welcome home, Rickin Lu." ("Lu" was our fabricated middle name for everyone in the family—Eric Lu, Kari Lu, Markie Lu, Soni Lu—meaning "Love You.") No chance to hold each other, no chance to talk.

And not much time in the following days, either, what with our picketing the prophet and helping the Catholics picket the pope, working to get pro-ERA candidates elected, and answering the constantly ringing telephone. And certainly not with Rick's doing all his teaching out of town that semester. On Wednesdays at noon he left for Richmond, where he taught that evening. The next morning he headed for Norfolk, where he taught Thursday night. Friday morning, he drove the five hours back to the university again and usually got home that evening around six or seven. So in effect, he was gone three full days every week. Not much time together.

But maybe time wasn't the answer.

The winter before, when he had brought up the possibility of his going to Liberia for six months in March, I had opposed it bitterly. Our children needed the attention of both of us; there were family problems with the potential of turning out to be so serious that I began to suspect his wanting to go was a wish to escape having to deal with them. He, like so many other men of his generation, had not been conditioned to be sensitive to his own and others' emotions, or to deal with them, as females are from the cradle. Since he never understood how to handle personal problems—his, mine, or the kids'—his method of coping was to avoid them, to look the other way as much as possible. He felt out of his element, unskilled, unsure, awkward; and because he felt so helpless, he was always deeply pessimistic, always assuming the worst would happen. This was not useful. Also, never having resolved the acute pains of his own childhood, adolescence, and young manhood, he had to confront specters from his own past when our children had typical childhood and teenage problems.

Though I had been left the usual childhood and family residue, too, as we all have, the difference between us was that I knew I was responsible for those kids. The church and society had told me so often enough. I knew I couldn't fail, because if I did, no one would come in and pick up the pieces. He knew he could fail, because I'd be there, finally responsible, to take care of things. The patriarchal notion of the mother's doing the nurturing and the father's making the rules kept him an adolescent parent. Fathers can't be decent parents until they see themselves—and society supports them—as nurturing, supportive, warm, and loving people first and successful wage earners second. Father as head of the house is not a useful concept in parenting. It allows too much distance, too little final responsibility. It puts an impossibly heavy and unfair burden on women, which prevents even the strongest and best of us from doing the kind of parenting job we'd like to do—and could do, if men took their share of the responsibility.

Before we can solve the ills of society, we must reorganize parenting. Let the patriarchs of the New Right, who are so concerned about the "family," start taking their share of the responsibility as parents, in keeping the family emotionally secure and united and educating other men to do the same instead of blaming women, who are seldom in positions to make policies that would lift pressures from families.

Men own and rule the world. They are the heads of government, the presidents of corporations, the presidents of universities. They are the ones who could, if they cared about families, reorganize society so families could flourish. If they really want someone home when children come home from school, for instance, or someone to take decent care of the little ones during the day, they have the power to institute scheduling flexible enough that at least one parent can be on hand, or see to it that there is good child care available.

To insist that *women*—the powerless, the economically dispossessed of the world—bear total responsibility for child care, and therefore are to blame if families are in trouble, is cruel nonsense. How would men like to be faced with the dilemma of full-time work and full-time parenting *and full blame when things go wrong*? I lay the blame for the disintegration of family life squarely at the feet of *men*. They are the only ones who can do anything about it on any scale that would be helpful to families, *and they are not doing it*.

Naturally any of us would rather avoid situations we do not understand and cannot handle. Naturally any of us would rather avoid difficult and emotionally taxing situations. I always understood this, even while I was feeling—rightfully, I think—put upon, feeling how unfair it was that I was always the one who had to deal with that most difficult of all human areas, the personal and emotional.

But by the winter of 1979, when Rick began talking about going off to Africa, I had become a feminist and was finding that I could not accommodate to his escapist tactics anymore. He was, after all, an adult. He had helped bring these children into the world. Now he could stick around, put *his* personal preferences aside for a while, and work up the courage to tackle the problems parents have to tackle. I so deeply resented the prospect of having to face them alone again that when he told me one night as we lay in bed that he would not go to Liberia if I did not want him to, I answered firmly and at once, surprising us both, "Don't go!" Neither of us expected me to say that, since neither of us had heard me assert myself thus in our twenty years of married life. "I don't want you to go. Stay home. We need you."

He turned over wordlessly and went to sleep, and I knew I had lost. Lying on my side of the bed, rigid with anger, I thought how I had never asked him to forego his footloose and fancy-free travels once in twenty years, how I had never asked him to change his plans for us. It did not seem too much to ask that he stay and help me now during this difficult time. I knew it was a legitimate request.

And I was furious that neither of us had expected me to make it that night anymore than we had ever expected me to do it before, when it was equally legitimate.

I was fairly savage with anger at him and didn't get over it quickly. He left the next day for Liberia, and I wrote him a letter that week that must have scalded his retinas. Later, he justified falling in love with another woman and leaving the family because of that first fierce letter. But even when I thought I would die of the pain of separating my Sonia-self from my Rick-self, I didn't regret having written it. It said just how I felt. I wasn't ashamed of that feeling; it was appropriate. If to keep him I had to continue to cajole and please and pat and soothe all the time, if I never dared tell him exactly how I felt for fear of losing him, if I never dared treat him as adult but had to pretend that his adolescent inability to take responsibility was all right with me and a perfectly understandable and decent thing . . . well, I wasn't interested. Neither was I humanly able to carry on such a relationship any longer. Let someone else be the keeper of his fragile, boyish ego. I refused to be his mother. I had legitimate work to do.

Six months was a very long time to wait for him, but I was used to waiting. I've joked about introducing Rick as "my late husband" on numerous occasions in our married life. There is a biting edge to that which allows one a peep into the hoard of anger that amassed inside me through the years over the matter of waiting. Anger at Rick for making me wait, and anger at myself for not refusing to be further humiliated by waiting. Nothing is only one person's fault, and our waiting game was a game for two.

One night in my kitchen about three years ago, when my mother was in the throes of feminist labor pains, searching back through her life for clues, trying to restructure her experience and see it from another point of view, she emphasized for the hundredth time how very happily married her parents had been. They never quarreled—at least in the presence of anyone else—and neither ever said an unkind word about the other to anyone in their entire lives. She talked about the mutual respect, the partnership, the sharing of values. Suddenly she stopped, a look of surprised recognition on her face.

"Actually," she began hesitantly, "I did once hear Mother complain about Father." (Mom always prided herself that her family, unlike their less educated or cultured neighbors, never called their parents Ma and Pa.) "It was one hot summer Saturday when we had gone to town in the wagon. We had just arrived, parched and dusty, when, seeing an acquaintance he wanted to talk to out in front of the store, Father stopped the wagon, hopped down, and fell into a lengthy conversation, leaving the family broiling in the sun. Finally, even stoical Mother was driven past endurance to murmur at being made to wait—at being *expected* to wait." (Grandma's reaction was eloquent testimony that this was not the first time she had waited for Grandpa.)

Dear Grandma Mary Jane whom I never knew, who died at sixty of cancer of the womb and of exhaustion after bearing thirteen children, and watching several of them die, after helping bring hundreds of babies of neighbor folk over forty years into the stern Idaho valley —dry, rocky, pungent with sagebrush and surreal with tumbleweed. Though I was born ten years after you died, men and women were still as bound and gagged in stereotypical roles as when you were born—tangled and confused about what it means to be male or female, much as Uncle John over on the farm in Woodruff used to say when he was in a mix-up: "I've got the wool pulled over my eyes, my hands tied behind my back, and I'm sittin' astraddle of the fence!"

Waiting is part of the stereotyped role for women—a large part. Waiting to grow, for breasts and hips to fill out, to wear lipstick, perfume, brassieres: waiting to star in the big role—man enticer. Waiting to be asked for a date. Waiting for the phone to ring. Waiting, waiting for the phone to ring. Waiting to be asked to dance. Waiting to be asked to go steady. Waiting to be asked to marry. Always waiting for someone else to act. Passively, miserably waiting.

And if the phone doesn't ring? If no one asks? If you wait, and wait, and wait, and Prince Charming doesn't come riding up? What can you do?

In the fifties, when I was a young woman, there was nothing you could do and still be considered decent. Being able to choose and act on that choice was a privilege reserved for men. That should have told me something. I think it did, but I didn't want—or didn't know how—to deal with it at the time. So I put it away in that deep unconscious filing cabinet reserved for matters which must have frightened me with their too-clear implications of female servitude and subordination. It took me forty-two years of gathering such data unbeknownst to myself before I finally accumulated more than my file could hold and it burst open, forcing me to look.

Waiting is one of the earmarks of subservience. As Milton truly says, "They also serve who only stand and wait." Waiting is a service. The words waitress, lady-in-waiting, waiter are all service titles. Waiting delineates rank. Sergeants don't keep colonels waiting, but generals do. Teachers don't keep principals waiting, but superintendents do. Those in power can make their subordinates wait, can expect them to wait. To keep someone waiting is manipulation, a method of maintaining control; it is a way of announcing and wielding power.

My unconscious servitude to Rick began early in our courtship. I remember sitting on a bench by the service station for several hours while he fixed his car. It was an unspoken assumption in my youth that girls loved to keep boys company during such times, liked to hold things for them, enjoyed watching them clean the points, or change the brake shoes. Having their girl hovering around must have been like having their own private cheerleader. Girls did it because we wanted to be with them more than they wanted to be with us. We were more emotionally dependent upon them, as we had been trained to be. We needed to be around them, and though they liked having us around, they had other interests in their lives. We had been trained to have only one major interest, despite all the other things we might do, and that was *them*. Not because it is any more natural for us females to be dependent and to base our entire lives upon some male's approval and presence, but because patriarchy socialized us thus. It is great for male egos. It is catastrophic for ours.

But I didn't get a real taste of the despotism of waiting until Rick discovered the computer at the University of Minnesota. The next ten years were one long struggle against the humiliation of being constantly rejected for the computer—Rick's "iron mistress," his "three-sexty." Ten years of being completely forgotten for whole days and suddenly remembered apologetically, of my putting the uneaten supper away and going to bed at midnight or one or two A.M., not having heard from Rick since morning when he promised to be home by six.

That he should have thought it natural to keep a human being waiting for six, seven, twelve hours without word made it clear to me again and again how he thought of me, how not completely human I was to him, how much just a part of himself—not a separate or real person to be taken seriously, or about whose esteem he needed to worry. He would never have kept any male friend whose friendship he valued waiting so consistently for years. No peer would have put up with it.

At the time, I thought it was all my fault. If I were more interesting, more sexy, more *something*, he would *want* to come home to me. I blamed myself, when the fault lay in Rick's patriarchal world view.

Part of the unwritten definition of wife is: the one who waits.

I tried to tell Rick over those long years how often I felt rejected and figuratively slapped in the face. I couldn't help but believe he secretly enjoyed the idea of my waiting for him, the constant service of wondering and worrying about him in his absence. Surely there was something more behind his making me wait than mere forgetfulness. He was an extremely intelligent man, but I couldn't get him to understand how deeply he wounded me by showing disdain for the hours of my life I wasted in waiting for him and for the hurt and rage and erosion of love for him this brought about in my heart.

And through it all, I must never make him wait for me. I must never reverse the sadomasochistic game. Yet by calling it that, I admit my own collusion in it. Years ago I should have ceased to care unduly when he came or went, should have planned my life as I wanted without consulting his. Should simply not have allowed him to tyrannize and manipulate me. But I knew that the moment I refused to supply this apparently necessary ego support, I would lose him.

And I did. When I became interested in the ERA, *he* often had to wait for *me*—to get off the phone, to come home from meetings, to come to bed. I ceased to pay much attention to when he came and went. I no longer cared a great deal when he was hours late or rejoiced overmuch when he was early. My life no longer centered around him, as his had never centered around me. I began to live an independent life, such as only men are entitled to. That's when I overstepped my bounds and it was all over.

And I've thought since, with considerable wryness, how for nineteen years I waited for him, and how he couldn't wait for me for one.

It wasn't an easy six months that I waited for Rick to come home from Liberia, but it was a profitable six months. I had not only grown in my confidence to deal with extremely thorny problems on my own, but was rapidly losing my awe of church leaders—as one does if one deals with them often enough, and as is necessary if one intends to bring about change. I learned that they were frightened and unsure when dealing with women who refused to be subservient —which my bishop told several people was why I was excommunicated: I had no respect for the priesthood—meaning, of course, the men.*

While Rick was in Liberia, he had to come to terms with not having been awarded tenure by the state university. He had initially been stunned by the news, and struggled for months with the miseries of rejection and failure. At home I also mourned that he should have to sustain this slap to his already teetering ego just at the time when he most needed confirmation of his worth (we both agreed he was in some kind of mid-life crisis). In one of his letters from Liberia, he told me he hoped I would at least give him tenure, and reminded me that a man who doesn't rock Ferris-wheel seats can't be all bad! (He would soon bring that seat crashing down through the girders, spilling me out into the mangling innards of the machine.)

In our nearly two years of feminism, Rick had often remarked how much he envied me that I had found something so rejuvenating, so absorbing, and so self-worth-producing as the women's movement. "I wish there were such a thing for men," he'd lament. "Just when we men are on the downhill slide of our youthful euphoria of thinking the whole world was before us and we could do anything, you women are just flexing your muscles, beginning to experience that first excitement of going forth into the world to conquer. Somehow our cycles ought to be better coordinated." But, of course, here were sex role stereotypes at their devious, relationship-straining work. Because it does strain relationships for the wife to begin feeling her oats as the children move toward the edge of the nest, just at the time the husband, feeling trapped and powerless—as his wife felt for the first twenty or thirty years—realizes he is fed up with thirty years of

---

* The reasons I was excommunicated increase in number constantly. Officially, the church must by now have seven or eight, taking into account all their press releases, most of which came into being considerably after the excommunication. Unofficially, there are dozens more. The more they think about it, the worse I become.

constant work, but cannot think of anything to do about it except to fall in love with another woman.

Rick tried to fight his ennui by taking flying lessons, but found he so often thought of suicide when he flew that he became frightened. At those times, I would question him anxiously: "Am I the problem? Is it our relationship that's making you unhappy?" And he would always assure me that it was not. Whatever it was, he was near despair a good deal of the time.

And I was having the time of my life. It didn't seem fair.

(I also realize now that he was having a crisis of faith, having watched the church pitting its might against women's rights and behaving in a shockingly un-Christian way. But he seldom spoke of this to me.)

Our cycles were very much out of synchronization. He was accustomed to being the center of my life, but my center had shifted, as is only healthy, to interest in the world around me. He felt abandoned, but he needn't have. I hadn't abandoned him nearly so thoroughly as he'd abandoned me for all our married life while his work consumed so much of his time and interest. At this point in his life he really needed me to be there as I had formerly been—all for him, suffering with him (since my life was his life vicariously lived), giving him my full attention, concentrating on his problems, giving up everything else to be his prop and stay. But I couldn't do this anymore. I should never have done it. By performing motherly duties for nineteen years, I had kept him immature.

So though I gave him, as one adult to another, all the support and comfort I could at this critical time, I had my work to do also and continued to do it.

It would have been a disservice to him if I had re-centered my life around him then, I think. There comes a time when we must face ourselves alone, and nothing is going to forestall that day forever. He needed professional help, but scorned all psychotherapists as incompetents. For a couple of years he had wanted us to move again, but I had put my foot down firmly against it because I had begun to realize how much damage our constant moving had done to the children.

Rick loved to move. It was therapy for him—escape therapy, the kind he had practiced all his life: running away, running away. He became restless if he stayed too long in one place. Moving absorbed him, kept him feverishly engaged in all its myriads of arrangements for six months or so. But when we would finally get settled in comfortably, he would become restless again and begin talking about the next move. I believe it was his way of avoiding coming to grips with the problems in himself.

And patriarchy allows and fosters this kind of avoidist behavior in men. Small wonder that he finally did what society had taught him to do, which is blame the woman in his life for his unhappiness and decide—oh, what relief this must have provoked—that the answer is to shuck off burdensome family responsibility once and for all, and run all unfettered into the arms of the next woman on the list. How easy! All in one step the blame is allocated and the solution emerges. And what a lovely solution—so much more enjoyable than facing up to the demon that keeps you in a cold sweat at night and disturbs your work, the demon that threatens you with extinction at unpredictable times and places, the demon that has haunted you for at least fifteen years and which you would rather suffer than lose your precarious belief that you know more than psychotherapists do anyway, being smarter and a psychologist yourself. Better to feel hopeless and misunderstood, quietly and gently sad. Better to see yourself as something of a hero for having stuck out a marriage as long as you did, having sacrificed yourself for a woman you did not really love but did not wish to hurt.

This is the story Rick devised in order to live with himself. His leaving me, he told the unbelieving children, had nothing whatever to do with his falling in love with another woman; that just happened coincidentally. He hadn't really loved me for a long time, he said, but was waiting until I was strong enough to be able to manage on my own.

Each of us needs a story. The trouble with his is that the facts don't support it. Though he had lost tenure and our future was financially uncertain, by the time he got home from Liberia I felt absolutely safe in his love. By letter he had wrapped me so lovingly and so closely to him again that I felt we could do anything together. We were both intelligent and well educated. We would work something out. Maybe this was a godsend, he hinted several times. Maybe this was our chance to realign role expectations, which were hamstringing us, and let the other sides of ourselves blossom. He didn't want to work anymore. Fine, I said, I'll work, though I can't make the money you do. But uncertain as the future was, knowing he loved me and wanted me "near him always" made me fearless.

The part of his story about waiting until I had become strong enough I find particularly arresting. True, feminism was making me strong, stronger by the day. I was high a lot of the time with the feelings of personal power that suffused me. I had never had such feelings before.

I remember one day going grocery shopping, and as I got out of the car in front of the supermarket, it seemed to me that my body took longer than usual to unfold and reach full height, as if I were several feet taller than my five feet four inches.* As I stood there in the sun and blue air, I laughed aloud at this, it was such a good feeling. Stretching out my left hand, palm up, I smiled at the storefront and boasted aloud: "I could lift you with one hand!"

Powerful and rich and full, wise and competent, that's how I felt. I felt—yes, let me say it—*liberated*, as if I had stepped out of a cramped cell onto an open plain with the wind freshening and the clouds racing, in full vigor of body and mind, ready to change the world.

So what if the wind out here is sharp! There is a warm sun and a clean sky and we are all out here together, all of us, female and male, who care about women, all feeling the same perplexing mixture of joy and loneliness, frustration and hope, all of us having irrevocably left behind the world we grew up in. Having opened ourselves up to growth and its joy, we have also opened ourselves to suffering. But I

---

* The first glimmer I ever got of the politics of size—how easy it has been for men to acquire the habit of looking down upon us figuratively because most of them actually look down upon us in the flesh—was in Malaysia. One day Eric and I were at the local hospital trying to see a dentist. Eric was ten years old, and only an inch or two shorter than I. As we were standing waiting in the hall, a middle-aged Indian woman, who must have been not quite four feet tall, walked past us. Eric looked at her in amazement, then turned to me and gasped, wide-eyed, "I could *kick* her! I could beat her up!"

No feminist then, I interpreted this only as my son's realization that he was bigger than, and therefore not at the mercy of, at least one adult in the world.

Ever since I became a feminist, I have longed to be at least six feet tall. How wonderful it would be to look men—even tall ones—right in the eyes, straight across, like equals, like peers. And to look down on the others for a change. How wonderful not to have to look up to men to whom I do not, in any but a physical sense, really look up at all. And I am certain that the sickening condescension of the Virginia anti-ERA legislators would nearly disappear if so many of us women were not the size of children and therefore obviously addlepated as well. (My twelve-year-old Marc is now taller and heavier than I. Sigh.)

believe we will not only bear everything with dignity, we will triumph.

I just said that feminism made me strong. Perhaps more accurately I should say that feminism taught me my own strength. During one very bad spot in our marriage in 1976, I told Rick I was ready to leave and please to take me and the children to the nearest airport (we were riding along in our motor home doing our Title I business). If he hadn't pleaded with me, I would have gone. I wasn't a feminist then. I only dimly sensed how strong I was. But I could have done without Rick anywhere along the line if I had had to, because I've always been me, underneath all the other pseudo-women I was trying to be. It is so typically patronizing of men, Rick's insistence that he couldn't leave me until I was strong enough. I notice he didn't leave until *he* had another crutch, but that he didn't wait until *I'd* found one. I notice he left me at a time when my need for support was greater than at all other crises in my life put together.

Of course, no one would argue that there was anything noble about Rick's behavior, though patriarchy has given it credence and status. If Rick had said to the kids simply, "I was bored and tired of the same old routine—work, family. After twenty years, there's not great passion in bed anymore," perhaps he would have been closer to the truth. If he had understood himself, he might have gone on to say something like this: "Besides, your mother wasn't paying sole attention to me anymore, and being male, I have been taught that I deserve someone's *undivided attention*. So when this willing younger woman crossed my path and my gonads went into shock, I thought, 'Why Not? It will punish my wife for being happy and strong without me, it will give me what I, as a man, deserve: a new set of warm loving comforting arms when the others have grown stale. It is like moving. It will keep me absorbed and distracted for a few more years.'"

In a society where women are considered merchandise, a man simply discards one and gets himself a new model when situations are less than idyllic. Women are the throwaways of our throwaway society. And almost invariably, the tosser will make it seem as if he were doing the tossee a favor—patriarchal reversal, you know. Rick did it for my own good, he tells the children. And such is the power of patriarchal reversal that he believes his own double-talk.

In fact, I suspect that Rick feels downright *righteous* for having used me for twenty years before he discarded me. He has always been very frugal. "Use it up, wear it out, make it do."

When I told my lawyer some of the inexplicable, puzzling things Rick said to me one night in anger—that he really hadn't wanted to marry me in the first place, that I had forced him to (a shocking exposé of his determination not to take responsibility at all except as a noble, albeit misguided, knight who ultimately saved the day)—my lawyer laughed and said, "Oh Sonia, how perfectly typical! I must have heard that song a thousand times before. So many men sing it to justify their perfidy that it is an almost predictable scenario. Think nothing of it."

What is my story? I've already told it. It does not matter that it is not original. My husband finally succumbed to the younger woman syndrome. He ceased to be the man I knew and loved. Heaven knows, no sign of that good and honorable man has been seen since Halloween 1979. Halloween is the night evil creatures carry off unwary mortals. Perhaps they stole Rick and sold his body to something that now stalks about in it. For a while it was the cruelest mockery that the body was the same but the person inside so changed as to be monstrous.

I miss the man I married, though heaven knows how long ago he really died. I miss his witty little notes in the typewriter or on my pillow, his dancing in his humorous-looking Mormon underwear*— wild, wonderful modern dances for me in our bedroom, so funny and so unguarded that even as I laughed all those years, my heart also clutched a little at how naturally he exposed his awkwardness to me, how he trusted me to love him even while he was looking ridiculous.

As I write he has been gone almost exactly a year. I weep as I write because he is dead in a way I can't grasp since there was no funeral, no formal leave-taking. So dead I won't have him again even in heaven where, when he proposed to me, he told me he wanted to take me: hand in hand through this life and in the next "hand in hand to see God."

And yet, even as I tell myself my story, I know that the other crea-

---

* Mormons who participate in religious rites in the temple are required from that time forward to wear a special undergarment, until recently available only in a one-piece style, like a short-sleeved, calf-length union suit. The purpose of the "garment," as it is called, is to bring to mind often the covenants the wearer has made in the temple.

ture who now inhabits his body must always have been there, crouching in the wings, waiting. I know I have caught the fleetingest glimpses of him thousands of times just at the periphery of Rick's unguarded eyes.

But I am getting ahead of myself. His betrayal was yet to come.

In late October, I went to Utah to speak at the women's conference and to see our son Eric. Rick, who by this time had surely fallen in love with Carolyn, took me to the airport, and instead of simply dropping me off as was his wont, parked and came in with me, solicitously finding me a newspaper to read, sitting and chatting with me until it was time for my plane. Kissing me good-bye with tenderness. Making me feel cherished. A week later I signed the "phony" divorce, after his repeated assurances of its phoniness and repeated assurances that he cared so deeply about our marriage that he was willing to go to extremes to invigorate it. I signed the divorce on Wednesday. On Friday, we went to the play.

I was, I know now, in a state of shock after his announcement, the kind of shock people go into when they discover without warning that a loved one has died. For a while I was mercifully numb. But still, numb with misery. I was profoundly disbelieving on an emotional level, washed by waves of hope that somehow it was not true, that he would change his mind, that there was something I could do. If we could just talk about it, I was sure we could work it out, as we had everything else we had ever been able to talk over.

But underneath everything I must have known the futility of all those feverish plans of mine to help him remember me and feel again the love he had so very recently professed and shown me. Somewhere I could feel anguish of a scope I had never dreamed possible pushing up toward consciousness, welling up like floodwaters in the basement of my spirit's house.

Rick had been noticeably restless in the couple of months he had been home. While he was in Liberia he had been much taken by what seemed to me the jejune poetry of some man who had left his wife and children (what else is new? Yawn.) and gone off to "find himself." This man did lots of sitting around under trees, thinking deeply; his poems romanticize the middle-aged man's dream of being young and unfettered again, starting over, conquering females, finding a whole new world, being *free!*

A few months later, when I was talking to our old friends from

University of Minnesota days, Shirley and Harold Wallace, Harold admitted not being surprised that Rick had followed the stereotypical middle-aged male's pattern. He had seen signs of its coming on a spring or so before when he and Rick had gone camping and motorcycling together in southern Utah. I didn't ask what they were. I suppose my dreams over the six months Rick was in Liberia were trying to tell me that I should wake up to what was happening in our relationship, but as in those dreams, in real life it took cataclysm to wake me up.

Often in the two months since he had been home and teaching in southern Virginia, he had asked me to come with him on his weekly teaching tour, and I had always felt as if I couldn't leave the children on their own for two and a half days. But the week after the announcement I asked to go with him, hoping we could talk on the very long ride, hoping I could somehow understand what had happened, what was in his heart. Needless to say, he didn't particularly want to talk about it; he was, though I did not know it then, in the first euphoric stages of romantic love, feeling great, feeling like a powerful young man with the world before him. He was so abstracted by thoughts of Carolyn, he could hardly get his mind on talk of any kind.

But finally, after touring Williamsburg, with the leaves falling symbolically all around us, after watching with bitterness his eyes fill with tears at the end of the patriotic movie shown there, knowing he had not a single tear for us, after watching him do a very mediocre job of teaching (he was once such a splendid teacher), after the torture of sleeping in the same bed with him for two nights, not touching, not understanding why I couldn't ever touch him again but knowing it was so, we got around to talking on the way home. I told him I needed to understand what had happened. I couldn't catch my breath, it had all been so fast and so final. He assured me that he simply needed space and time, that it was best for me, that someday I would thank him, that he had prayed about it a lot and felt this was the right thing.

I am ashamed to say that habits of trust are not easily broken. How desperately we wish to maintain our trust in those we love! In the face of everything, we try to find reasons to trust. Because losing faith is worse than falling out of love. It pillages and rapes the countryside of the soul. So knowing Rick to have been a prayerful person all his life, I tried to believe he still was, I tried to believe in his answers, tried to understand that he had been vouchsafed some intelligence from heaven that I had not. Since then I have heard Jeff Willis credit heaven with *his* perfidy too, an act as treacherous as Rick's, and understand how little trust women can safely place in men's answers to prayer.

But that day, with Rick holding my hand on the seat between us and soothing me with those anodynes: "answer to prayer," "God's will," "best for you," I wanted to believe as much as he did. So, weeping all the five hours home, I tried to make my adamant heart receive the news that Rick, suddenly, inexplicably, no longer loved me, but would always be, as he put it, my "good friend."

Heaven preserve me from such good friends!

A day or two later, our five-year-old son Noly and I had lunch with Rick in the cafeteria next to the university, and I had my first experience with ESP. Suddenly, I looked at him and said in astonishment, "It's another woman, isn't it?" "Well, yes," he mumbled, embarrassed, but also in delight at the thought of her. "Who is it? Do I know her?" He didn't answer. Then I said, seemingly out of the blue, though I'm sure I must have picked up dozens of subliminal clues as well as perhaps his thoughts, "It's Carolyn Curtis." "Yes," he admitted, amazed. "Yes, it is. How did you know?"

It was then I knew I was beaten. Not because it was Carolyn, but because it was another woman, another harbor, another haven, another support, another mother, another crutch, another pair of arms. He had replaced me, as one does a pair of shoes. I knew patriarchy had won.

Back at his office, he asked me calmly, in a detached sort of way, which two of our four children I wanted to keep, and though I had been mostly successful against tears throughout lunch, at this the floodgates opened again (*where* do all those tears *come* from?) but so did the floodgates of my anger. "For heaven's sake, Rick! Haven't you done enough, ripping yourself out of my heart and life like some dispassionate bystander? I love the children. I bore and reared them. They're mine by rights, and I mean to have them."

Hazel says, and I suspect she is right as usual, that Rick never did really want the children. She advised me to agree to his proposal and see how fast I would have them back again. What in the world would he do with them? she asked. Take them with him to live at

Carolyn's? Leave them alone in a little apartment in Portland while he went around the western states doing his new job?

I think he had to try—weakly—to get them because he didn't want to face what he was really doing, which was abandoning them as well as me. For eight months after he left the house, and while he still lived in Virginia, he seldom saw the children, and then only briefly and superficially. Since he moved to Oregon, he has as little interest in being a parent as he ever did. Children are throwaways, too.

There in his office, his face an expressionless mask, he pointed out coolly that the agreement I had signed (!) divvied up the kids equally between us, and that he wouldn't mind getting me in court (and here his voice got ugly and I saw such astonishing hatred in his face I felt faint) because if he ever did, he would show me a thing or two. He would make me wish I had kept quietly to our "agreement."

He wanted to fight me. He wanted to hurt me. He hated me and was enjoying hating me. When I saw that unreasonable and unprovoked hatred, I was reminded of something I had written to him a few months earlier, talking about the woman in his office who had outwardly befriended him and won his trust, only to turn on him and be the one who effectively prevented his getting tenure. "Yesterday dropped by VPI to see if tests from Larry were there yet and noticed that Marilyn could hardly bring herself to say hello to me. Boy, is her conscience troubled! Funny how much we dislike people we've done the dirties to, more even that we dislike people who have done them to us."

My homespun philosophy for that day, an echo of greater minds, and obviously true. I have resigned myself to the fact that Rick is always going to hate me because he has committed a grave offense against me, for which he will never forgive me.

The same holds true for the Mormon church.

When someone has been your best friend all your adult life, you can't help but grieve at evidence that they are less than together you dreamed they could be. Rick was the dream I dreamed for twenty years.

What do I think he should have done? Dealt honorably with me. Come to me as if I were a grown woman, an adult human being, and said, "Sonia, I've fallen in love with another woman. I no longer wish to be married to you, and I want a divorce."

I'm not saying I would have been sweetly reasonable about it—

heavens, who can be reasonable? But I could have dealt with it. And why should he have come away unscathed? Why should he have escaped so well the unpleasant consequences of his actions? Announcing a *fait accompli* was too easy, a coward's way. He who hated to work things out, who was afraid of emotion, afraid to talk, to argue, to have scenes. But then everyone knows you don't waste effort on worn-out shoes. Once you're through with them, you get rid of them as fast as you can.

One afternoon soon after this we had one of the few serious arguments we had before he left. We were in his room, the room over the garage. "It's all right for you," I cried. "The minute the going gets rough, there are always some woman's warm arms to shelter you. But what about me? What about women, who never have the guarantee of an emotional shelter, who never have a cheerleader, a body servant, an ego protector, and who have the little they have only on one condition: that they agree to uphold male supremacy and not to be whole. You're well taken care of, but what about me? What man in this whole world is going to be willing to give up all those actual and potential cheerleading arms, all those ego protectors, all those body servants, cooks, and house servants, to stand by my side out here on the edge of the world in the wind, coatless and unprotected, looking ahead into a wilderness where only a few faint trails and dim lights signal that someone has gone before us and lived? What man would dare come all the way with me, care about me and the future of love between men and women enough to give up the patriarchal promises of the good life—a surfeit of doting females, the celestial kingdom of female bodies for the taking? What man is going to come with me out onto the frontiers of the known social world to pioneer what it means for men and women to be peers, what it truly means to be partners, colleagues, friends, lovers? Where can *I* turn for comfort, Rick? When it gets cold, when you get frightened at the immensity of the work to be done and the dedication it takes to do it, *you* can turn back with hardly a qualm. You are running back right now into the cozy arms of the patriarchy. But what about me? Where are the arms for me?

"The answer is that there *are* no arms out there for me, even as I look out into the darkness and shudder with loneliness. But for women who have *seen*, there is no turning back. How would you feel if there were no arms out there for you and you could not turn back?

If there were no system that invited you back to its warm, comfortable, safe hearth? I'll tell you how you'd feel: if there were no arms out there for you now, you would not be leaving. You would never choose to be alone. Well, I am going to be alone until the day I die. Think about the system you've chosen when you're lying all warm and snug in Carolyn's arms. Think about a system that holds out this eternal promise of comfort to men but not to women. Think about your slinking back into this slimy, stinking sea of injustice, not being strong enough to resist the siren call of the patriarchy. I need arms around me, too; I need comfort; I need, I need, but I've just got to go on needing, because what I need doesn't exist!"

"Yes, you're right," was all he said to this self-pitying tirade, but I was nearly wild with the injustice of it, wild with the anticipation of loneliness ahead down the long years to the end. If I had been beautiful, I might not have panicked. But I was—I am—a most ordinary-looking middle-aged woman. How, with this inadequate equipment, would I ever attract enough men that among them would be the oh-so-rare, oh-so-to-be-prized one who would be dedicated enough to the same experiment in loving that he would see past my forty-three-year-old visage and choose to step with me over the narrow rim of patriarchy into the wide, unexplored universe of equality?

It took weeks, even months, for this panic to subside; as feminist as I thought I was, I had never really counted on being manless. Now, thank goodness, I am well past the panic phase. I no longer even hope by pretending loudly that I don't hope that I'll ever love and be loved by another man. My life is full and varied and so absorbing that such a likelihood has become increasingly less important. I liked being married, but I have loved my year of singlehood. I feel in control of my life, an exhilarating feeling. I have even loved my year of celibacy, of having my body all to myself, of having no sexual obligations whatever. Marriage is too full of sex as an obligation. It is good to be free of that. It has been good to belong to myself alone.

If it should happen that some feminist man should love me and me him, I will be glad. And I'm sure I could throw celibacy over tomorrow without a backward glance. If it doesn't happen, I have myself, wholly and completely now I have myself, and the wonder and joy of that will see me through this life.

Just before I drove with Rick to Richmond that early November of 1979, hoping we could discuss our "divorce," Jeff Willis had called me into his office to tell me he was in the process of deciding whether or not to call me to trial. So I had that weighing on me during that whole surreal trip—Virginia at its most glorious, trees and sky in some wild red, yellow, and blue romp, Noly in the back seat innocently calling us Mommy and Daddy as if we were still in tandem, my total lack of comprehension of Rick's sudden inexplicable behavior—his casual smile, his calm demeanor as if everything were quite normal, as if he hadn't done anything out of the ordinary, as if this were how life is—while every atom of Sonia was shrieking in pain at his treachery. If I had known he was deliriously in love, I could have understood this extraordinary display of callousness. As it was, I felt as if I were going mad.

When we got to the motel that night, I called a judge I knew in Utah. "Jeff's preparing to call me to trial. What can I do to forestall him?" She didn't know, but had a friend in high church places who would. She would call him and tell me his thoughts on the subject. In retrospect, his advice is humorous, if one finds that sort of thing funny. He told her to tell me to get to know my stake president, quickly. What is funny is that my stake president was treacherous to me from beginning to end.

Hazel and Ron couldn't believe this was happening to Rick and me; they even thought they might be able to "talk some sense" into him. And though I knew how he had sealed himself up tightly in his new love with the glue of total repudiation of all he and I had ever been to one another, my hope could not quite stay dead. So one night they invited us to dinner at a restaurant in the District after a play. This was just after the first trial when Hazel and Ron had watched him behave in such a bizarrely unfeeling way that they couldn't find any place in their knowledge of Rick to store this image of him. "This isn't the Rick we knew," they told me. "Surely he'll come out of this trance and understand what he's doing." "No," I told them. "He won't."

On the way to the play that night, I made him very angry by telling him that he owed me the courtesy of staying with me through the trial, of helping me with the children while I was under such immense stress. "*Owe* you?" he almost shrieked at me. "I don't owe you *anything!*"

That is something women don't realize somehow, that all those hours of waiting and serving and helping and loving and supporting and cheerleading and moving from place to place, giving up one job after another, giving up friends, listening and waiting some more and always being there and not having a life of your own so that he can have a life of his own—all this buys us nothing. After twenty years of that, men owe us nothing. Why? Because they've been paying us off by feeding and clothing us all those years, as if we were faithful family retainers. What about the loyalty, the self-sacrifice, the love and caring and prayer and hope and encouragement—all the intangibles that no one in the world can pay anyone to give, which we gave freely from our hearts—what about that? It is ultimately worth nothing.

As Clare Boothe Luce once said, in every marriage there are two marriages. His and hers. His is always best.

But I took back what I'd said anyway. No sense to argue now. Nothing in our relationship was ever going to change again. Here was where it was, in this murky, dismal swamp, and here was where it was going to stay, time without end. And I was never going to give another minute of my life's time to changing it. So I said, "Just as a favor then, not because you owe me anything. Just as a favor, please stay through the next few weeks." I didn't know how I could face the press about both the divorce and the excommunication at once; I had some vague hope that the furor over the excommunication would die down and then we could separate quietly. But I knew that sooner or later I was going to have to tell the press about Rick. I just needed a couple of weeks to grow strong enough to do it. Either subject separately seemed impossible to absorb into my life; I felt I couldn't face them both at once.

And the truth is I wasn't facing the divorce yet, not really. I was still in shock, though his announcement had been nearly three weeks before, because the bishop's warning had intruded itself between the fact of divorce and the feeling of it. I knew I had to deal with the two problems in my life, as much as possible, one at a time. I had gotten the bishop to hold off as long as I could and it wasn't long enough to mourn Rick and prepare for the trial too, so I chose to prepare for the trial, and then, when it was over, I planned to go out and sit on a log in the woods somewhere and grieve until I was finished. Just mourn and mourn and grieve and grieve. What luxury that seemed to me; how I longed to be able to let go and *howl* against the enormity and the absurdity of it all, howl until the unbearableness softened and gradually ebbed away. But it wasn't time yet. Just a little while, Sonia, I told myself; just a little while and you can get on with the business of saying good-bye to the first half of your life.

At dinner that night after the play, Hazel and Ron tried to broach the subject with Rick, said a few things, and across the table silently acknowledged their defeat to me. Hazel said later, "It's as if he's dropped a thick curtain down behind his eyes. What we said never went past it. He's the most defensive person I've seen in all my life."

Because I could hardly believe it myself, and because I hoped against hope that a miracle would happen—that one day when he looked at me his eyes would clear, a look of recognition would come back into them, and he would lean back against the cupboard with his legs apart and open his arms for me again—I had put off telling my folks. They were both in their seventies, both full of more years of trouble than of joy, and they were already shattered about my conflict with the church and my approaching trial. Oh, how I hated having to add to their suffering by telling them that Rick, whom they loved as much as any of their own children, was divorcing me. That our Rick was dead.

Rick was going out to spend Thanksgiving with them so he could be with Eric, whom he had not seen since he left for Liberia. (Eric had gone out to Utah at the beginning of the summer to work and had been so asthma-free that when he begged to stay to go to school there, I thought it worth a try.) Suddenly one day I thought, "Why should I be the one to have to drop this lead weight on my parents' and my son's hearts? This is Rick's little project; let *him* do the dirty work." While he was out there, Mom called me. "Is anything the matter with Rick?" "Why do you ask?" I countered—apparently he had not told anyone yet. "He looks as if the light has gone out in him," she said. "Both Eric and I noticed it. He doesn't shine any more."

Mom came back on the plane to Virginia with Rick to help me through the trial. As soon as I saw them, I knew Rick had told her. My mother's eyes can hold more tragedy than the stage at the Kennedy Center. I thought her soul was going to flow out through those eyes. I lowered mine so I wouldn't have to look at such naked sorrow. Part of my mourning was for my little mama's hurt. I have wanted so much in my life to give her joy. But the things that give her joy are things I can't do anymore. She will have to be happy just knowing I am happy.

And so the preparation for the trial went on and the children wondered where Daddy was, and why he had even less interest than usual in them. How could I say, "When a man's on his honeymoon he's very single-minded?" That's how you say it. That's how I said it to Kari and Marc; I told them everything, from the beginning. I didn't try to make it worse than it was and I didn't try to make it better.

Rick went into the trial with me and witnessed everything that took place there. When the church press release went out all over the world from Salt Lake City, saying that I had testified that I had said and done things that he knew I had testified I had neither said nor done and could prove I hadn't, he asked to be excommunicated from the church on the grounds that he could no longer be associated with an institution which displayed such "savage misogyny" as they had displayed against me. Rick had a trial sometime in the spring and thus ended twenty-one years of active, temple-going, priesthood-holding Mormonhood. Hazel thinks he knew he might be brought to trial for adultery, and not wanting to be excommunicated for that offense, chose a seemingly noble way out. I don't know. I don't know Richard Johnson anymore and from what I've seen I don't care to. By the time he was tried, I had ceased to think of the Richard Johnson walking about the world as having any connection with "my late husband."

His mother, a good Baptist woman of the non-Southern variety, confided in me a few months ago that she could never understand how he could have joined the Mormon church in the first place. "Did he really believe it, or did he just do it for you?" she asked. "As far as I know, he really believed it," I answered, though I hadn't checked with him for his "story" on that. The reason I think he believed is that he paid a full tithing until he was cut off. And if you know Rick Johnson and his extreme thriftiness—no, why euphemize? —his extreme stinginess, verging on miserliness, you'll understand the commitment that signifies.

On December 12, 1979, one week after the excommunication, Arlene Wood and Hazel and I flew to Chicago where I was to appear on the "Donahue Show" the next morning. Before I left to drive to the airport with Arlene I told Rick, "When I come home, I want you to be gone." It was clear to me by that time that the press was not going to lose interest for a long time—the church constantly underestimated this story's folk hero appeal—and that I would soon have to announce my divorce. It was also clear that I could never tell them the full story, as I have set it down here. Who would ever believe it? Not I, if I hadn't lived it. And besides, it was too complicated to tell to reporters. But the fact, if not the method, of the divorce needed to be known.

In the car on the way to the airport, I asked Arlene, who has also been divorced, whether the pain ever stops. It was hurting me so much right then in the car that I didn't believe it was possible to hurt so much and survive. And on top of it, the total devastation of the excommunication. I was an emotional basket case. The pain was steady and unfluctuating, the control turned up to high hurt, the needle not moving.

"I know you can't imagine this now, Sonia," she answered, "but believe me when I say that it does go away in time. At first it's just like now, an undeviating torment. Then begins the wave syndrome: suddenly one day just before it comes crashing back again, you realize that for a few blessed moments there has been no pain. Perhaps this doesn't happen again for another week, but when it does, you notice that the trough in the wave is wider—your relief lasts a little longer. Before too long, the beautiful pain-free trough is as wide as an hour, then half a day, then two days in a row. And then, the really terrific pain only comes like the trough did at first, once in a while. At first it lasts a day; two days later, when it recurs, it's only the matter of a few wretched hours; and finally, it comes upon you only now and again, rarely, if you're lucky, and is quickly banished."

That night, in the most luxurious hotel I'd ever been in, finding myself wishing I could share the experience with the Rick of the old days and desolated again at the future yawning loveless and churchless before me, I wondered how I could ever get through the show in the morning. I felt dumb with grief, sodden with misery. I could have called and asked Hazel and Arlene to come to my room and talk, but I had never learned how to take comfort from women. I'd been conditioned to understand only how to take it from men, and now I was, I thought, forever comfortless. Since then, thank heaven, women have comforted and strengthened me in spite of myself.

I noticed, when I relaxed a moment on the show the next morning, that the pain—miraculously—was gone for a moment. The wave syndrome has begun, I thought to myself with inexpressible relief. The worst is over.

On the first of April, 1980, Rick's birthday, I remembered him for a while and wrote these two undistinguished poems which I hope will be regarded as journal entries, not judged as poetry:

A PROBLEM OF PHYSICS

Loving has its own inertia.
If when traveling heedless at high speeds
the loved one takes a sudden turn away,
loving hurtles straight ahead
as if the lost one ran alongside still.
But abandoned, unfueled
loving eventually slows,
imperceptibly at first;
gradually the pain, the clarifying
teaching hurt of it all
sighs and ceases, and at last
all is laid to an uneasy rest,
a sort of sad indifference
after the long slowing down,
after the long, unnatural process
of braking a forward-pressing
living thing.
Loving has its own inertia
and its own entropy.

TO RIGID, RITUAL, WRETCHED RICHARD JOHNSON

You'll never be Rickin Chicken again
(I don't suppose you'll grieve over that)
or Rigid, or Ritual, or Wretched Johnson
or Lu
and we won't laugh together about
my wife hates me
or Doris and the loiyer

or anything else
or cry together at the deliberate violence
we must do our 21-year-old memories,
strangling them and half our hearts.
So happy birthday and good-bye to you,
friend of my untaxing youth
enemy and traitor of my
needful sorrowing times.

When I think now about our years together, when they pass across my memory like a dream, ever so faintly—pianissimo, like a dream echo, as if I were at the top of a Ferris wheel—I hear tinkly carnival music, only this time it's some Mozart waltz in a minor key. [I didn't touch him enough, he says. I couldn't, I cry. I was too hurt, too angry. The terrible waiting! It did such damage to my love.]

Kari came in just now to remind me that it is time to leave for Washington to watch Maida's dance troupe perform.

"How are you doing? About done?" she asked. I told her I had come to the end of my marriage, and had just said good-bye to her father.

"You're lucky, Mom, do you know that?" she said. "Not many women get to do what you did. You really got to write him off!"

Chapter 9

Bishops and
Other Sexism

SINCE OUR FIRST meeting over the marvelous Hatch debacle, my
bishop, Jeff Willis, had been calling me in every now and again
throughout the year. On September 20, I wrote to Linda Sillitoe:
"My talk with the bishop on Tuesday went gaggingly. I shouted at
him that he wasn't fit to be the spiritual leader of women since he
didn't understand them, hadn't read any women's history, hadn't a
clue about what was going on in their lives, or about the real meaning of the women's movement. It was his paternal manner that
finally got to me. I remember saying in disgust at one point, 'Oh really, Jeff, cut the unctuous double-talk!' He hasn't seen my APA
paper yet. I have to make a copy for him and wish I didn't have to
face the ordeal of talking to him about it. He won't understand an
idea or emotion in the entire paper and will see it all as hatred, bitterness, and general apostasy, I fear. Well, I guess I knew that when
I wrote it."

That Tuesday, I also cried a little in my confrontation with Jeff
when he told me some awful things a close friend of mine in the
ward had supposedly said about me. (Later, when I called and asked
her, she denied having said any of them.)

But it hadn't been a mistake to cry in Jeff's office. Crying was
something he could understand better than my arguments, better
than my anger. His stereotype of women had no place for intelligence and righteous indignation, but plenty of room for the image of
women as emotional, hysterical, tender—creatures who need to be
protected. My crying immediately reminded him of how powerful he
was, how controlled and mature and wise, and though I hadn't done

it on purpose, it mollified him considerably to see that I was just a weak woman after all who could be hurt by others' opinions. The friend he quoted was one of the few others whose opinion counted to me, and his supposedly recounting her treacherous words did hurt (what was a bishop doing bearing tales from one of his flock to another anyway, I would often wonder as he relayed to me what members of the ward and stake were saying about me. Anyone who says men aren't natural gossips hasn't functioned around Mormon men very long). As I cried for a moment there in Jeff's office, onto the screen of my memory flashed a scene from my student days at Rutgers University.

I was standing before the desk of my doctoral dissertation adviser who was angrily telling me that I was not going about my dissertation in a way that suited him. He shouted at me, from his intimidating height, that my master's thesis adviser had told him I had pressured *him* unmercifully too and hadn't asked *his* advice either all along as I should have. I asked my fuming educator, as calmly as I could, why my master's adviser had never indicated this to me. I suggested that if he hadn't approved of the way I was proceeding, he should have said something to me at the time. And that since he always signed everything I took to him to sign, and since he had not stood in the way of my receiving my master's degree, I had simply assumed he approved.

Even as I asked the question, however, I knew the answer. I hadn't behaved *femininely*. I hadn't asked their advice. I hadn't acted as if I weren't capable of doing all this without their help. Hadn't, in short, acted incompetent, helpless, childish, and infinitely grateful for every little scrap of attention or advice they, as superior beings, had given me. I was twenty-eight years old when I began my master's research. I knew exactly what I wanted to do and how to go about doing it. I proposed it to my adviser. He agreed. I did it. That was that—I thought.

Oh, but not so. I didn't *lean* on him. To me he was just part of the red tape. I cut through him as quickly as possible. And I had no time to linger. Already we had one child and were ready to conceive another. I had to move faster almost than humanly possible, and I did.

Now my doctoral adviser had heard from my previous master that I had not been sufficiently humble and impressed (did not respect the priesthood enough, meaning the men). But this one wasn't going to make the same mistake. *He'd* show me who was boss. I understood this as women understand it, not intellectually, just in the flesh of my face as he scowled at it, just in the resignation of my weary-with-watching-male-ego-signs flesh. And I knew exactly what to do about it, without thinking, without strategizing—cry. So he would know I wasn't trying to show I was as smart as he was and didn't need him to tell me what to do next. Cry—so he would realize I was just another weak little woman and he had no cause for alarm. Cry—so he would feel bigger and more rational, and still, above all else, still blessedly in control.

So I cried on purpose that day, and because I did I became Dr. Johnson a year later, moving with great speed through a system designed to slow doctoral candidates down. Because I cried.

If men hate to be thus manipulated, then they must allow us to be real, they must not force us to manipulate their egos in order to live a full human life. I hate such machinations. I despise them with all my heart. But women are forced to resort to them because men won't otherwise allow us to exist. And we have a right to life.

That day in Jeff's office I not only cried, I also finally provoked him enough that his façade of loving concern cracked and he shouted at me, "I've had enough of this! I've sat here patiently and listened to your tirades and your raking me over the coals long enough. I'm your bishop. You listen to me for a change!"

I was delighted that we were finally getting down to honest feelings, but before we had a chance to take advantage of his dropping his bishop act and become just two human beings trying to understand one another, he caught himself. "I'm sorry," he moaned. "I shouldn't have lost my temper like that."

"Why not?" I asked. Any honest feeling was such a relief in that atmosphere of pretense. I always felt as if I were being forced to participate in a bad drama in which Jeff played the role of morally superior authority, with all the condescension, sententiousness, and fatuity that requires, and I could not be heard if I didn't assume the role of deferential, erring supplicant.

"Because I want you to know that I love and care about you," he answered in his bishop voice. As soon as I heard those words in that voice I knew the patriarchal barrier we had miraculously knocked down for just a moment had been thrown up again between us. We were roles again, not people.

Soon after Mormons for ERA flew our "Mother in Heaven"

banner over the Mormon conference in the fall of 1979, I discovered that three women in my ward were also allowing their fantasies to hover lovingly around the hope of a real "Mother in Heaven," not just the doctrinal shadow the church allows. One of them, Kris Barrett, approached me in Relief Society to show me a poem written by our mutual friend Linda Sillitoe:

SONG OF CREATION

Who made the world, my child?
 Father made the rain
 silver and forever.
  Mother's hand
drew riverbeds and hollowed seas,
drew riverbeds and hollowed seas
 to bring the rain home.

Father bridled winds, my child,
 to keep the world new.
  Mother clashed
 fire free from stones
and breathed it strong and dancing,
and breathed it strong and dancing
 the color of her hair.

He armed the thunderclouds
 rolled out of heaven;
 her fingers flickered
  hummingbirds
weaving the delicate white snow,
weaving the delicate white snow
 a waterfall of flowers.

And if you live long, my child,
 you'll see snow burst
  from thunderclouds
 and lightning in the snow;
listen to Mother and Father laughing,
listen to Mother and Father laughing
 behind the locked door.*

* Published in *Dialogue: A Journal of Mormon Thought.*

"Sonia, we've got to find out more about our Heavenly Mother," Kris insisted, and I replied that women all over the world were saying the same thing. Praying and thinking and talking to one another about her. And getting answers.

A year later in Miami, for instance, I heard one of the many testimonies borne of her. I was staying in the home of Linnea Pearson, a Unitarian minister, after speaking at her church. While I was getting ready for bed, she came into my room to talk. One night a few years before that, she told me, she had addressed Mother God in prayer and had been awakened later by dazzling light above her in the room. From what she saw and experienced then, she knew with a sense of incredible liberation that she was indeed made in the image of God. Several of my Mormon sisters have confided similar experiences to me. I have seen neither Mother nor Father, but I couldn't love them more if I had.

After Kris and I talked at Relief Society, I lent her *The First Sex* by Elizabeth Gould Davis and *When God Was a Woman,* by Merlin Stone, books that had been recommended to me by good Mormon women in Utah and California and that had revolutionized my beliefs about women and deity.

Two other women in my ward, each unaware of the other's spiritual odyssey into the meaning of femaleness, arose and bore their testimonies on the same fast Sunday, one mentioning Mother in Heaven and the other dropping our "Heavenly Parents" into the collective consciousness. Up by the organ I rejoiced silently: "It's happening, Mother. It's happening! And *I* didn't have to be the one to do it!" Perhaps I sensed even then that I was going to have enough *else* to do.

After the meeting they met at the rear of the chapel, those two, embraced, and spoke freely of the oppression of Mormon women as they knew it firsthand. Though admitting and speaking of such things is aberrant behavior in establishment Mormondom, in the Mormon feminist underground it is recognized as the courageous, inspired, and necessary first step forward that it is.

These women, and another whose husband was worried about the books I had lent his unhappy wife, were called by the bishop individually into his office. Were they praying to Mother in Heaven? Was I trying to persuade them to? Was I conducting a Mother in Heaven cult? (Why we should call it a "cult" when it is about Mother seems odd; we do not call it a cult when it is about Father.) All three were emphatic that they, not I or anyone else, decided to whom they prayed, and that I was not holding secret meetings exhorting anyone to pray to a female deity—at least if I were, they had never been invited to attend.

Despite their spunk, in the end all four women were cowed back into their cocoons of orthodoxy by this evidence of the bishop's displeasure. Mormon women, like other women in patriarchal societies, feel deep in their bones that they cannot survive the disapproval of men, perhaps because women so often have not. It is certainly not difficult to get that message.

The patriarchs are threatened again now, just as they were during the witch burnings, by the rising of women and would burn us if they dared.* But since they do not quite dare, they are fighting us in every other way open to them. The New Right, believing that God wills men to rule over women, is as gynecidal in its intent against unruly women as its forerunners, the woman-burners of the Middle Ages. Women's lives are always in danger in a patriarchal society. There *is* cause to fear, which is why we are banding together now against the return of the burning times.

When I heard that my friends had been interrogated by the bishop, I realized that he had begun a serious search for evidence of religious malfeasance with which to justify court proceedings against me. But I felt secure in my knowledge that I had not committed an excommunicable offense—unless they were to judge my political fight against their anti-ERA campaign a doctrinal rebellion, and I felt certain I could convince them it was not. Because it wasn't. Still very naïve about church leaders in those days, I believed they would need evidence to excommunicate me, and that anyone with firm belief in church doctrine would be safe. I had also been taught all my life that, being men of God, they would be able to recognize the truth when they heard it. I was mistaken in that belief; I told the truth and they did not recognize it. Perhaps they chose not to.

Finally it was my turn to be grilled about Mother in Heaven. In his press releases and letter of excommunication, the bishop was to refer to our talks over a year and a half as attempts on his part to

---

* Perhaps one of the reasons my story proved so compelling to the media and to the public is that by excommunicating me for human rights activities, the men of my church symbolically burned me at the stake.

"counsel" me. Even as I read that dreadful letter, I had to smile grimly at that. I had met with him only because it was so clear to me that *he* needed counsel—about fulfilling his obligation as leader to that half of his congregation which is female. He was so profoundly ignorant of even the basic tenets of feminism that I urged him every time we met to read something besides the church's propaganda on the subject, to become informed about women's issues. He never did. But then, neither did the stake president, the regional representative, the twelve apostles, or the first presidency of the church. I suppose I should not be critical of the bishop, bottom man on the totem pole, for following the example of those above him. And actually I did not expect a great deal, even then, from Jeff.

Which is just as well, since we both failed in our "counseling"—he to make me feel guilty for opposing church leaders politically, and I to get him to care enough about women to learn something about their movement, the most widespread and revolutionary awakening in the written history of the world.

"Mother in Heaven is doctrinal, Jeff," I reminded him at the beginning of our session. Appropriately enough, Eliza R. Snow first proclaimed her nearly a century and a half ago, and she was legitimized in the middle of this century by Bruce McConkie, an official of the church who asserts that she is equal in "glory, perfection and holiness to Father."

As we were talking, I was thinking that one of the reasons Mormons have difficulty envisioning or relating to a Mother in Heaven—aside from their complete commitment to male supremacy and the resultant almost total silence about female deity—is that they believe God is polygamous, as all righteous Mormon males will be in the hereafter. Of the billions of mothers up there, which one is ours? It is nearly impossible to imagine any one of those polygamous wives as an individual distinguishable from the others; all of them are as alike as stars in the sky. Polygamy is the ultimate depersonalization of women, even if you are God's wives.

"I know. I know we believe in her," he agreed hastily, and then added in hushed tones, "but we are advised not to speak about her, and we certainly must not *pray* to her!"

"Why not?" I asked loudly (what was all this hush-hush?).

"Because Heavenly Father is trying to protect her."

"From what? From *me*? From my love?"

"Heavenly Father loves her so much," he concluded confidently, as if he were about to say something rational, "that he doesn't want her name sullied by repetition."

Do we sully Father's name when we pray to him?

I thought of the Mormon belief that earthly families are patterned after the heavenly family and puzzled briefly why, if we believe Heavenly Father is trying to protect Mother, Mormons make no effort to emulate heaven and protect earthly mothers from the heart-aches and triumphs and love of their children. It is, in fact, fathers whom society has contrived to protect from the emotional stresses of parenthood. And on earth, the word most common to children's speech, most often called out, most repeated for comfort, is "Mommy." I have never known a mother to feel besmirched by this —harassed, yes; but degraded? Nonsense.

The bishop proceeded to warn me that if I prayed to a Mother in Heaven I would surely end up praying to my earthly mother after her death. Instead of deity, I would think of her when I said, "Dear Mother in Heaven," and that would be idolatry. I asked him if he prayed to his dead father. And why it was any more likely that women would pray to their dead mothers than that men, or any of the rest of us, would pray to our dead fathers when we said, "Our Father in Heaven"?

He had not thought of that; logic was never Jeff's forte.

But he countered with the quintessential male trump card: Jesus taught us how to pray and *he* said, "Our *Father* which art in Heaven."

From an article in *Savvy* (October 1980) by Mormon Chris Arrington (who grew up across the street from me in Logan) comes this Mormon male contribution to obfuscation:

"Though Mormons believe in her, Salt Lake church authority Hugh Pinnock has affirmed that it is against Church doctrine to pray to her publicly, even to add her name to the Father's in a prayer's address.* 'It would be a matter for discipline,' Pinnock said. 'Jesus

* I challenge Hugh Pinnock to find any such restriction in Mormon scripture. When he says it is church doctrine and then refers to the New Testament, he must be reminded that the New Testament *nowhere* mentions Mother in Heaven, and yet her existence is still doctrinal to Mormons. Because she is a unique Latter-day Saint contribution to theology, we must look to latter-day scrip-ture on the subject, and if we do not have specific scripture about her, we should encourage the prophet to ask for some, while each of us individually seeks

taught us the form of a prayer in the New Testament.'"

"That's what men say he said," I agreed with Jeff. "All we know of Jesus has come to us through the sensibilities—rather, *in*sensibilities—of men who thanked God every morning that they were not women, who believed women had neither minds nor souls and treated them accordingly. Hardly objective witnesses."

If he had been interested, I would have explained to him that because of the ruthless censorship in the Bible, feminists find all the more delicious those traces that survive of Jesus's radical feminism. I would have pointed out how the four gospels give us strong reason to believe that he understood and loved women so well that he would never have excluded us from deity, knowing the immense psychological, emotional, and characterological toll this would take of women for ages to come.

Women remember when Jesus reassured Mary that in studying (an acknowledgment that she had a mind!) instead of doing housework, she had chosen the better part. We remember when he demanded equal rights under the law for the woman taken in adultery, in a case where Jewish law absolved men from all responsibility, though everyone surely knew even way back then that it takes two! We remember when, despite the strict blood taboo of the ancient Jews, which forbade a man to touch a woman who was menstruating or to sit where she had sat or eat from a dish she had touched or of food she had prepared, Jesus, in full public view, touched and healed the woman who had been bleeding for years.

No, we do not need to worry about Jesus. Over and over again he defied tradition and broke taboos that crippled women, and I am sure we do not know a hundredth of it. If he were here, he would be working side by side with those who, in his own perpetually new and nonsexist tradition, are still breaking the old traditions of male supremacy.

When fundamentalist believers in the Bible demand to know how I can insist that women should be men's equals when Paul says . . . all the wretchedly sexist things Paul says (I know there are Pauline apologists among feminists, but their arguments strike me as con-

clarification in study and prayer. It was not Mormon doctrine, but tradition that Pinnock enunciated—another arbitrary male decision no more scripturally valid than denying women the right to lead the congregation in prayer in sacrament meetings. Women must stop interpreting men's discomforts and need to dominate as sacred auguries and holy writ.

trived as Mormon women's defense of their present-day Apostles' sexism), I answer that Paul had not known Jesus. He had, in fact, only the briefest exposure to him personally, according to his own account—the middle of the road to Damascus hardly being the appropriate place for Jesus to instruct him in the revolutionary feminist ideology Jesus himself so clearly adhered to. Since Paul was obviously left in the bleakest ignorance, given the choice between following the master or the disciple on the critical topic of women, I choose to go with the Head Man. I am an ardent fan of Jesus. You can have Paul.

I don't believe I said all this to the bishop, but while we were talking about Mother in Heaven I tried to reassure him that, although my private acts of worship—over which he had no jurisdiction—might be somewhat unconventional, I had not and would not advocate publicly that we address Mother as well as Father in our prayers, and when asked to pray in church, I would use strictest self-control in the matter of how many parents got into the salutation.

As we were parting at the door of his office, he told me meaningfully, "I keep *my* wife on a pedestal."

Yes, I thought, you certainly have her safely immobilized. I'm sure he wished my husband would strap me back on my pedestal. Quickly!

After the excommunication Jack Anderson telephoned Alice Pottmyer, a Mormon for ERA, in response to a letter she had written him. As soon as she realized that the reasons for my excommunication which she was hearing from Jack bore no resemblance to those expressed publicly by the church, she began to take notes on the scrap of paper nearest the phone—her grocery list. During that conversation, Jack told her that before Jeff decided to hold a court to excommunicate me, he had called Jack and confided that my offense was teaching the women of my ward to pray to Mother in Heaven,* a

---

* Perhaps the reason he did not admit this to the press is that the concept of Mother in Heaven is doctrinal, albeit controversial, and he hoped to get me on a charge of preaching *false* doctrine. Also, her existence is dangerous to patriarchy, for which reason I should think the whole effort was to keep the issue about her *very* quiet. The less people think about her, the less they will question her position, the church's position about her. The less, in short, they will question male rule. I like to imagine what would happen if Mormons (and others) really began believing in her and her equality with Father: polygamy, the all-male priesthood, all aspects of patriarchy presently so precious to men would be in deepest jeopardy.

blasphemy I had supposedly conducted on two levels: with a small private group of five or six trusted friends—my infamous Mother in Heaven cult, I presume—and the entire Relief Society during my cultural refinement lessons. Jeff told Jack that the women had come to him "very reluctantly" complaining about me.

(I should *say* "reluctantly!" Jeff had to wield his heavily authoritative bishophood to get them to converse with him on the subject at all. The women in my Relief Society class cannot have complained about my Mother in Heaven heresy because I never once mentioned her to them. But I know Jeff told me his wife had been terribly upset about my foot-binding, wife- and witch-burning lesson, and had told him others in the class had been upset also. I should certainly hope so! Any woman who is not upset at the atrocities perpetrated against women in this world, past and present, and will not even bother to find out what they are, is not worth a pin. And any woman who is afraid of the truth and refuses to look at her history participates in and bears responsibility for its repetition.)

Alice Pottmyer's letter to Anderson on December 12, 1979—about which he called her—said: "As a teenager, I was a member of the Chevy Chase Ward and still have many friends there. They told me that in your Sunday school class on December 9, you said Sonia Johnson was claiming more inspiration than Paul or Moses, and that she was telling people to pray to Mother in Heaven. I have known Sonia for two years. We have had many conversations, and though we have not always agreed, I know that if what you said was reported to me correctly, you are spreading false accusations. If you want to know what Sonia has been saying, here is her phone number."

Of course he never called. It doesn't matter if you malign women. They haven't the power to do anything about it if you do.

What is both impressing and depressing to me about the Anderson episode is its dramatization of the nature of the Old Boys' Club. Here is Jack Anderson, nationally known investigative journalist, supposed champion of truth, checker of facts, a man who can presumably be relied upon to get the story straight and whose reputation depends upon his doing so; Jack Anderson, who never once talked to me or checked with any of the women in my ward, yet two Sundays in a row he solemnly told his Sunday school class total absurdities about me on the strength of Jeff's word (which even I, non-journalist that I am, would have recognized as not highly objective or reliable at that moment) because Jeff, being a bishop, is not just a member but a *titled* member of the Club.

Funny how prizes and fame and prominence impress me less and less as I observe them at close hand. The Project Director, Anderson, Hatch—to a man, they are illiterate about women: just plain bone-ignorant.

It has been nothing short of amazing, as well as enlightening, to watch presumably astute men so threatened by women that they completely abandon their reason and professionalism and go berserk. At first I wondered why they chose to believe the worst about me without checking their facts, when in any other situation they would insist on verification. I believe the answer is that they wish to believe the worst in order to justify their fear and contempt of women.

Perhaps women must simply face the sad truth: men are ruled by their emotions—totally at the mercy of them (especially when it comes to women)—and we have to discount a good deal of what they say.

The main reason Jeff Willis had called Jack Anderson, though, was to ask him what impact excommunicating me would be likely to have on the press. While Anderson agreed that excommunication was clearly deserved, he advised Jeff against it. The press, he warned, would be ruinous to the church.

But it seems that Mother in Heaven finally became such a threat to them that church leaders disregarded his warning and put into action their desperate plan to regain control of heaven and earth. As long as Mother remained a shadowy appendage of the *real*—i.e., *male*—God, as long as she knew her place and kept it, she was tolerated. But when she began to get uppity, drastic steps had to be taken to return her to anonymity and powerlessness. The church's battle was, from this point on, as much against her as against me.

Howard and Zella Forsyth, who had first contacted me after reading of my tussle with Orrin Hatch, were visiting me from San Antonio in August of 1979. Howard is Mormon by birth, but has been inactive for years. I showed them our press release announcing the "Mother in Heaven" banner.

"One morning in the mid-fifties as I was carpooling into the District," Howard mused when he finished reading it, "the news came over the radio that in Montgomery, Alabama, a black woman named Rosa Parks had refused to move to the back of the bus when a white man demanded her seat. I'm not a psychic or a visionary, but a great sense of destiny came over me then, and I said to my companion, 'This is an historic event. It's the beginning of something momentous, something that will change history.'

"I have the same feeling as I look at this press release. The proclamation of Mother in Heaven is an historic act, the beginning of something momentous. It will permanently change the course not just of churches, but of religion."

Neither of us knew enough about the women's movement to know that this was not a prediction, but a statement of fact. The concept of female deity was revolutionizing world religion right under our very noses at that moment.

Jeff Willis had been calling me in for interviews every couple of months for a year. I initiated only two of these, one of which followed the Hatch incident in the fall of 1978. That day in his home, he told me that at general conference the week before in Salt Lake City, Gordon Hinckley of the twelve apostles had advised him to warn me about my activities. (Jeff's middle name is Hinckley—his mother's family.) As Rick and I were leaving, he looked at me somberly and said, "If they tell me to excommunicate you, Sonia, you know I'll have to do it."

The other time I requested a meeting was on a subject about which I had to lobby him heavily before he modified his sexist behavior—temporarily.

When the president of the church had, in August of 1978, publicly revoked the policy disallowing women to lead the congregation in prayer in sacrament meetings on the grounds that it was not scripturally sound, and affirmed that women were henceforth to be allowed to say any prayer in any meeting they attended, I expected to see immediate compliance in my ward. After all, hadn't Jeff been telling me that the anti-ERA policy was to be obeyed *because the prophet had spoken it?* Well, the prophet had spoken again. And so I watched with puzzlement as week followed week and still no women were being asked to offer either opening or closing prayer in sacrament meeting. Could it be that Jeff hadn't heard the news?

I cornered Jeff after sacrament meeting one day and brought the prophet's message to his averted-eyed attention. I told him that now that he knew, I trusted that we would see evidence of his obedience to the prophet in the very next sacrament meeting held in our ward.

We did. A woman gave the opening prayer. I sat back, contented. But when week followed week and I saw that women, when they did pray, always gave the opening prayer, but never the closing, I began to understand that the old chauvinism hadn't changed at all but was sneaking around in disguise.

So I cornered Jeff again. He muttered something about its being more appropriate for the priesthood (meaning the men) to close a meeting. I reminded him that Spencer W. Kimball, the president of the church, whom I knew he regarded as the mouthpiece of God, had incontrovertibly stated that women could say *any* prayer in *any* meeting they attended. Why was it, I inquired, that Jeff seemed to think he knew better than the prophet that women were really only fit to open meetings, not to close them? I told him I trusted that we would see evidence of his complete compliance with the prophet's word in the next sacrament meeting. We did. But I continued to keep careful watch, and one more time had to remind him not to establish a pattern antithetical to the content and intent of the prophet's declaration.

I wonder if now again only the priesthood (meaning the men) are worthy of closing a meeting at the Sterling Park Ward. If so, it is in total disregard of the prophet's counsel, something for which I would have been—perhaps was—excommunicated. If I was excommunicated for not respecting the priesthood enough (meaning the men), then why shouldn't bishops be excommunicated for not respecting "the motherhood" enough (meaning the women)? After all, the Mormons make much of motherhood. Motherhood is supposed to make up for not having anything else. Motherhood and priesthood are supposed somehow to be "equal."* (Whatever happened to fatherhood?)

Oh, the Old Boys' Club! How safely men nestle together therein, sharing a righteous and God-ordained misogyny, and would never

* A question I often wanted to ask the leaders of the Mormon church but never got the chance is, "If motherhood is really so revered and so wonderful and is truly the equivalent of priesthood, why can men who not only do *not* hold the priesthood but are not even *members of the church* stand in the circle when their children or grandchildren or other relatives are blessed, whereas the mother, though she may have been a devout and worthy member of the church all her life, cannot? This speaks eloquently of the divinity of maleness in and of itself, which is the basis of patriarchy. Priesthood is merely a smoke screen to hide this fact.

dream of asking each other to comply with the prophet on the subject of allowing women their full prayer rights in the church. It is just women, and therefore, they presume, as ultimately and basically unimportant to the prophet and God as it is to them. To the prophet, probably. To God, not on your life!

The matter of women and prayer in the church illustrates what happens regarding women and the law in society at large. Even after we struggle to get laws that protect our rights, they are often unenforceable, and we must guard them with hawk-eyed vigilance or they will simply be disregarded and will eventually disappear from knowledge. Jeff had to be constantly policed; men in the church have to be constantly policed, though women have been so trusting for so long that the men have taken away from them nearly all there is to take away. Not enough women care about the effects of injustice on the human family—both on the men's characters, which are deformed by not giving justice and on the women's, whose are by not having it. Not enough women love themselves and their sisters and brothers enough to take the trouble to demand and maintain moral behavior on the part of their institutions.

I think this displeases our Heavenly Parents.

Early on, perhaps in December or January of 1979, Jeff announced that the stake president—the Project Director—wanted to see me after church the next Sunday evening. Sunday morning at Sunday school I met the stake president in the hall and said, "Cliff, I'm bringing a tape recorder to our meeting this afternoon. Mormons for ERA think it is in the best interest of everyone to have a tape recorder present from this time forward during all our discussions with you men about the ERA. You may have a copy of the tape, since this is as much a protection for you as for us. Then you'll know we won't misquote you and we'll know you won't misquote us. It will make our reporting to the press much more accurate. Do you have any objections to this?"

He hadn't looked at me during this whole recital, and didn't now. To the floor, he mumbled something like, "I guess it's all right."

So that afternoon I brought my tape recorder. And though I caught a glimpse of him early on, when it was time to meet he seemed to have disappeared. I began to search for him through the halls and ran into Lou, a member of the bishopric. "Lou, have you seen Cliff?" "Whaa—? Who?" he stammered. "Cliff. Cliff Cummings. I think he must be here someplace. Maybe he's in the lavatory."

Just then Cliff did indeed emerge from the men's lavatory. "Oh there you are, Cliff. I was just telling Lou here that I thought you must be close by." "Well, yes, it's been a long, busy day; I needed a rest," Cliff said hurriedly.

Lou and Cliff were thrown off balance because it is the custom in the church, as it is in any self-respecting patriarchy (and believe me, they all are), that men, and especially those men in high positions, must always be accorded their titles: bishop, president, elder—unless one was personal friends with them before as well as after they achieved this exalted rank. Then it is still most proper to address them formally in public, especially if one is a subordinate, only calling them "Joe" and "George" at PTA meetings, or when you meet them at the garage. Naturally, the higher the rank, the more insubordinate the failure to call them by their titles.

I was not a close friend of Lou's. He was a member of the bishopric. Strictly speaking, protocol demanded that I call him "Brother Hamilton." But it was not a gross affront to call him Lou, just a slight shock, an annoyance, perhaps a minute insult. But to call the stake president "Cliff"—*that* was another matter altogether and could be construed in only one way by the men: serious lack of respect for the priesthood, meaning the men.

A clue to basic inequality is that no woman in the entire church, no matter what her position, is ever accorded a title by which to be addressed. Women are all "sister," up to and including the top female in the structure. There are no titles of respect and deference, for all our "exalted" position. There is no rank. No woman, no matter how learned in the scriptures, no matter how spiritually gifted, can ever rise above "sister."

Not that anybody, male or female, ever *should* rise above "brother" and "sister." It seems to me that Christian philosophy is fiercely egalitarian and unhierarchical, and that all this rank business —which is by nature classist and sexist—is un-Christian, perhaps even anti-Christian. But so long as one segment of a society has rank and title, the segment that does not is oppressed. Either everyone should be accorded titles (the same titles for men and women), or no one should. I prefer the latter.

What women do when they refuse to accept the system's definition of itself is to break taboos, which is what I did that day. It was a small but deliberate philosophical and political decision on my part not to acquiesce any longer in my own subordination, but to act equal to everyone, as indeed I am, and all women—and all men—are, as church leaders insist they believe we are. I was only taking them at their word.

When we were seated with the tape recorder prominently situated between us, Cliff announced that he had changed his mind about it. He complained that having it there made it look as if we did not "trust" one another. Very astute of him, I thought to myself, and aloud asked him whether he had noticed that it was always men asking women to trust. That went over his head. It was not "customary" to tape interviews in the church, he went on as if I had not spoken. I told him it was not customary for us to be discussing politics in interviews in the church either. Disregarding everything I said, he began to interview me. I interrupted and reminded him I had agreed to the interview on the condition that our conversation be recorded and that unless I could turn on the recorder, I would not discuss the ERA with him; it was a political matter, and therefore one in which he had no jurisdiction over me. When he persisted, I rose and left the room.

While all the anti-ERA bustle was turning gatherings of the Latter-day Saints in Virginia and neighboring states into veritable precinct meetings, and when every week brought a new newspaper article exposing this and other less-than-savory facts about Mormons as the political tools of their leaders in Salt Lake, my forays with Jeff into the mazes of doublethink were all too frequent, and were always initiated by him. I felt no need and saw no point, after my first attempts at communicating with him, to try again. He was a man who simply would not—could not—hear what I had to say. But I always assented when he asked me to come in for a talk because I knew I had to placate him to keep my membership in the church, and I was willing to suffer for the right to keep the church I still thought and spoke of as "mine."

At one of these truly indescribable sessions, in an attempt to control my behavior through social pressure Jeff told me that many people in the ward were asking him angrily, "Why is Sonia Johnson still a member of the church? Why is she being allowed to do what she's doing?"

"They wonder about my leadership abilities," he told me, but hastened to add, "but I'm not concerned about *that*. I don't want to excommunicate you, and I'll hold out as long as I can, but the feelings of the people are against you."

He called me in several times to tell me the latest gossip about myself, as if I valued people's opinion as much as he did and would be swayed as easily by it. I remember once he told me, in a fatherly tone that shook its figurative finger at me, that I had been overheard to say that when we got the ERA, the first thing I was going to do was sue the church to get the priesthood.

That shows what the men in the church are really afraid of. Never did he call me in and say that he was afraid women were going to lose protections (I think he knew I would have asked him "which ones?" and he would have been left speechless). Though the ERA threatens only legal privilege, the priesthood is a privilege and the men of the church know it and fear the undermining of any sort of male privilege as a bad omen for the others. On a gut level, men must realize that though religious practices are not legislatable, changes in culture can change them just as effectively as law. And the mere existence of the ERA as a serious contender for constitutional status shows that society is moving away from commitment to male supremacy.

It was always disheartening to see the depth of his fear and ignorance and genuine disinterest in women except as they serve the purposes of the patriarchy. He, like so many others, far prefers to continue to think of women functionally—i.e., in terms of what they are "good for," how they can be *used* to the best advantage of others in this world, like a natural resource, on the preposterous assumption that that coincides with what is best for women. Such people are blind to women as separate from the family, as persons in their own right, persons whose individual rights transcend the rights of the family, as men's do. It was like talking to a zombie. I shouted to try to wake him up.

As my world widened out panoramically, with sound, color, and complexity added, the bishop's world seemed ever more circumscribed, tighter and more rigid, smaller, dimmer, like a silent movie, where everything was either evil or good, where there were two colors, black and white, where everything was either, or.

A large ad in the Minneapolis airport shows a person with his mouth taped shut. Written above him is this message: "There's only one problem with religions that have all the answers. They don't let you ask questions."

My head was teeming with questions. My bishop's answer to all of them was "obey." As I was growing up, I must have heard my mother say a thousand times, "Obedience is the first law of heaven and order is its result," which sounded sensible to my childish ears, but less and less so as I grew older. Sometime during my undergraduate education, I began thinking that there had to be higher potential for the human spirit than obedience; even dogs and ponies obey. I also began to doubt that order is the highest value in either a person's or a society's life. After all, the history department had taught me that democracy is notoriously *dis*orderly, as disorderly as totalitarianism is orderly. I was willing for obedience to be *one* of the laws of heaven, as it is of earth, but not the *first*, not to supersede all others. I haven't seen any reason since to change my mind, and can see many reasons not to, chief among which looms the "obedience" and "order"—the totalitarianism—that have all but overwhelmed my church.

When, on November 17, 1980, a group of us ("The Bellevue 21") were arrested at the Mormon Temple in Bellevue, Washington, for chaining ourselves to the gates in protest against the Mormons' holding all American women in chains, one of the church spokesmen made the oversimplified, dichotomous, and therefore dangerous thinking so prominent in the church, and the whole New Right, very clear. He explained to the press that there are two forces at work on the earth today, God's and Satan's. Because the Mormons are doing God's work, those of us opposing their politics must be in cahoots with Satan.

This kind of self-righteous thinking is the foundation of all bigotry. And history shows us that the idea one's group is the only group God loves and listens to invariably proves deadly.

Even if we had been neighbors from birth, or cousins, and grown up in the same small western town, Jeff Willis and I would never have seen eye to eye. I understand his thinking because I have heard ultraconservatism in my church and community (and home) all my life. But he doesn't understand mine. He can only conceptualize liberals and feminists as the stereotypes the leaders of the religious New Right paint for him. I suspect he has known few of us well and per-

sonally, and am nearly certain he has not associated with liberals as I
have had to associate with conservatives. Because of this, I was always at a disadvantage in our talks, because I knew what he was saying and could follow his rationale, whereas he was not able to divest
himself of stereotypes long enough to understand what *I* was saying.
Consequently talks with Jeff were exhausting, like stumbling in a
miasma of unreality backward through time.

One day, for instance, I was in his office when the phone rang. He
excused himself, answered it, talked for a minute or two before hanging up, then turned to me and said with a fatuous grin, "That was
my bride!"

Oh, for heaven's sake! I thought; how can you talk to a man as
deeply embedded in make-believe as *that*? Evilly, I wanted to inquire, "Did she ask when her groom was coming home?" I managed
to restrain myself, but one thing is certain. It never occurred to his
"bride" of twenty years, who has borne four children and is at least
forty years old, to tell her family or friends as she hung up, "That
was my groom!"

Many Mormon couples I know seem to be conspiring, with encouragement from the church, to keep the wife the patriarchal
dream: childish, dependent, subservient, virginal; not to allow her to
grow up from the girlish bride into the strong adult she was meant
to be. Perhaps Judy didn't like my Relief Society lesson about footbinding because in some recess of her unconscious she understood
too well what those little girls' feet symbolized about her own mind
and soul. My heart aches for any woman who has to be the eternal
bride. Like a bound foot, never to be allowed to change or grow
(Mary Daly calls it "mind-binding").

"Oh Judy," I cried out silently, "your Mother in Heaven is not a
'bride.' She is a strong, capable, honest-to-goodness god just as Father
is, and she is not obedient to him any more than he is to her—not
under his authority, but an authority in her own right, as powerful,
as wise and independent as he, both of them obedient to principles,
not to other beings!"

Luckily for Jeff, the omnipresent double standard guarantees that
no such cruel fate as Judy's eternal bridehood will ever overtake him.
She will certainly not call him her "groom." That would not show
proper respect. That would be laughable, insulting—but no more
laughable or insulting than a man calling his wife his "bride." His

doing so twenty years after the marriage ceremony implies that she hasn't changed a bit in all those years (or if she has, she must never show it), that he and she together have kept her perfectly mummified, perfectly bound; it also implies that they feel just the same about each other as they did on their wedding day. But she would have to have been either an idiot or comatose not to have grown and matured at least a little despite her bindings (though for many women, being alone in a box in the suburbs for years with only small children for company is very like being in a coma), and it is pitiable if their marriage relationship and feelings for one another haven't matured since their honeymoon.

Once, after Judy gave a very thoughtful, well-prepared talk in church, I told her how much I'd enjoyed it (on the whole, the women of the church give better talks than the men because they are humble enough to prepare). "Oh," she smiled self-effacingly, "I'm always so embarrassed when I have to speak. Jeff is *such* a good speaker. Compared to him, I always feel incompetent." Another time she bore her testimony about how grateful she was for Jeff because without him she would not be able to understand the scriptures!

This is an intelligent, competent woman, who has a teaching degree. What on earth has happened to her? Like so many other women in the New Right, she seems so bent on keeping her head below her king's that she's squashing herself flat against the ground. Her talk in church was far better than any I have ever heard Jeff give (I suspect she's a good deal brighter than he, which must be an almost intolerable position for a New Right woman), but if I had told her so, she would have been insulted and frightened. A thoroughgoing patriarchal woman is dedicated to the building up of men's egos upon the earth.* She lives her husband's life and identifies with him

* Mormon women are openly taught, as many of their fundamentalist sisters are, that one of their most important duties in this life is to protect and build the egos of their husbands. In fact, the Brethren are so anxious for women to learn this lesson that it turns up everywhere, often in the most inappropriate places. Take, for example, this section from a Motherhood Education lesson in the Relief Society manual, 1978–79, p. 114: "Question: What can parents do to counteract the influence of harmful television programs? Answer: *Exposure to Improper Attitudes Concerning Male-Female Roles:* The power of genuine and virtuous love can be exemplified for children in the daily habits of consideration and concern between husband and wife. It is especially important for a wife to show loyalty and support to her husband as leader in the family. This patriarchal order is the core of successful life. Elder Boyd K. Packer has suggested ways in which a woman can show this support: 'He needs to know that he is protecting you. He

more than she lives her own and identifies with herself. They are both living his life. Neither of them is living hers. She has become him, or is trying to. But he has not become her. Nobody has become her. I wanted to plead with such women not to make themselves negligible so that their husbands would seem consequential by comparison. That is damaging to men, and in such self-obliteration lies eventual disaster for women.

But such a woman cannot listen. She and her husband are spending too much effort keeping her down in that pit, clinging wearily to that pedestal, while exalting him to demigod status. It may be that they have both been made too afraid of their own natures to let her out.

In doing this, Mormon couples are following powerful examples in the church. In the Brigham Young University paper of December 1980, *BYU Today*, the president of the university and his wife talk about "climbing career ladders together." What one discovers as one reads is that the career ladder they are talking about is *his*. She reports: "We have moved fourteen times in seventeen years of marriage, and these moves have caused psychological havoc, depression and bewilderment. When my husband was in graduate school, I would sometimes struggle with the feeling, 'What about me—he's out there growing, learning and developing, and I'm just sliding backwards.' I had to develop the feeling, 'We are in this together—these are our children and this is our career.' I now shudder at the energy wasted in needless whining and feeling sorry for myself—energy I could have exerted toward furthering our career and destiny."*

---

needs to feel and know that he is the leader in the family. He needs a wife and a sweetheart with whom he can share that love, with whom he can have its full, complete expression. He needs to have a circle, a family circle, with children. This makes all that he must face out in the world seem worthwhile. He needs to feel dominant. He needs to be the protector. When he feels this, he is a better man. He is a better husband. He is a better employee, a better employer. He is better adjusted and happier in life. He can do better work. He can even be more prosperous. . . . Young sisters, if you take that role from him, the one he needs, you reduce his manhood . . .' Thus by being loving, by helping her husband magnify his role and by taking satisfaction in her role, a mother can counteract much of the influence of unwholesome television presentations."

Obviously, in the Brethren's minds, the most harmful thing on television is not violence or sex or the ideas that wealth and fame are the prime goals in life, but the occasional image of a mature woman or a mature man.

* One of the hottest-selling books in Mormondom—published by the church—is

I shudder at the very thinly veiled anger, desperation, and despair behind that recital, and at what this woman must have had to do to her spirit to twist herself into such a muddle. What she is really saying is that her husband's life is *her* life, *he* is her career. Their career —what she calls "our career"—is not hers at all, it is *his* career; she is *not* the university president, though she could very likely have become one as well as he.

Who in this marriage is thinking about *her?* Who is living *her* life? Who is developing *her* talents and potential? No one. When women care about their own lives, they are accused of being "selfish," they are warned that God and men will not love them unless they "sacrifice." Sacrifice their own needs, their own desires, their own talents, their own lives for their husbands and families. The message to them is reduce yourself, squash yourself, make yourself nothing and the man everything, even if your whole being and all heaven cries out against this rape, even if it turns your husband into an immature egomaniac and you into a depressed, unhappy woman. The message to women in the Mormon church and throughout the New Right is *not* the gospel message: be fully

---

an unbelievably masochistic, motivating-by-guilt-and-fear little volume entitled *Woman's Divine Destiny,* in which the author, Mildred Chandler Austin, has this to say about the wifely role:

"I once heard a marriage counselor talk about how one should choose a mate as he chooses a shoe: if it isn't a good fit, it will be painful. If we consider this shoe-to-foot analogy, we can see the husband as being the foot, having to climb the rocky road to exaltation. A bare foot is going to find the path too painful; it needs a comforter, a shoe. When I consider what makes a shoe comfortable, I see more clearly how to be a comforting wife. . . . Those of us playing the role of shoes need to seriously consider what happens to shoes that are painful. They are generally discarded and a more comfortable pair takes their place. Some men are honorable enough to endure the pain of uncomfortable shoes . . ."

But obviously if a woman chooses not to be as comfortable as an old shoe, she risks losing the wonderful privilege of being stomped on day after day, year after year, by that ambitious little foot climbing the rocky road to exaltation.

The implication, too, is that women are *not* climbing that same rocky road and therefore have no need of shoes themselves. Do only men need worry about exaltation? If not, where are women's comforters? How are we going to reach those rocky heights without shoes of our own?

And once again, the analogy for women is a *thing,* a nonhuman thing, unlike the human foot, which represents men. It is, apparently, our "divine destiny" not to be persons but always commodities, and in this case a commodity that is *always* discarded sometime during its owner's life, since no shoe is ever comfortable forever.

human, learn, grow, develop *all* your talents, *use* them, be what you are: a child of God.

The message is sacrifice, sacrifice, *sacrifice*.*

Isn't it odd that we do not hear that heavy, funereal thud echoing in the hearts of the men? If self-denial is as fulfilling and sanctifying as they are telling women it is, why are not the men of the churches eager to try it themselves? If our Heavenly Parents require self-immolation, self-obliteration of women, why don't they—since they are just—require it of men?

The patriarchal answer is, of course, that it is the divine right of men, by virtue of being born with penises, to demand that others subvert all their energies, all their capabilities, into making *them* successful. How very fortunate they must feel not to have to do unto women as they require women to do unto them. How stifled they would feel if they had to make their wives *their* career. How they would "whine." How sorry they would feel for themselves!

And rightly so. This kind of dominion is unspeakably, damnably, unjust, immoral, and unrighteous.

God does not require any more sacrifice from women than from men. It is *men* who require it, and we must stop getting the two confused. Men require sacrifice from women because it makes life so very pleasant for them.

This is not a compelling reason.

It is also becoming impractical. Since millions of America's households are now headed by women, women must make their own careers if they are to support their children and themselves adequately. In the Relief Society manual, one of the twelve apostles says: ". . . in the usual arrangement of things, however, it is the man to whom the Lord has assigned the breadwinner's role." Besides wondering where and when the Lord did this, I also wonder in what realms of unreality this good brother's mind is wandering? The United States

---

* A Mormon woman in Virginia wrote to me describing a Relief Society meeting she attended in the Fall of 1980: "The lesson began with a seemingly routine list of the sacrifices we make in everyday life, then quickly progressed into a frenzy of self-denial that was so thick it covered us like fog. Various sisters, sometimes weeping, related their joy at relinquishing successful and rewarding careers to stay home and raise families, or working at menial jobs to put their husbands through school. In the midst of phrases such as 'You've got to give until it hurts,' one brave sister suggested that sacrifice should be tempered with common sense. Her contribution was met with dismayed silence. . . ."

he grew up in is not the United States as it is now, and we must deal with the pressing problems of today, not waste time pining futilely for the past.

Another time, Jeff called me into his office briefly to tell me that the women in my Relief Society class the week before (who turned out to be mainly his wife) had complained to him about my foot-binding, witch-burning lesson: it was not "uplifting." I told him the lesson had not been intended to be uplifting, but to be educational, and that I believed with my whole being that women need to know their history, about the *real* lives women have lived and are living on this earth. And that those lives are uplifting only insofar as the women who lived them fought against the hideous injustices perpetrated against them by patriarchal society. And only insofar as we carry on their work.

This did nothing to allay his fears, and he reprimanded me sharply for not following the manual. I told him I was following what the manual purported to be doing: teaching about women's lives, about women's history (though of course nothing was further from its true intent). He repeated coldly, "You did not follow the manual."

I have always loved the idea of the Relief Society, of women's getting together to educate and care for one another and see to the needs of the community. I even feel affection for the quaint nineteenth-century name. But I have watched the women's auxiliary of my church come to be used almost exclusively to serve the purposes of the men, as I am certain is true throughout the religious New Right. (I was told by women in South Dakota who had attended them that the Four Square Church there has meetings for the women in which they are told to call their husbands "Master" and are instructed in the gentle art of being his slave. Apparently there are some groups even more patriarchal and determined to subdue women than Mormons!)

One of the first lessons in the 1980 Relief Society manual is entitled "Woman's Role in Today's World." Wherever could you look to find a lesson or an article—*anything*—entitled, "Man's Role in Today's World"? Nowhere, of course. It is patently absurd. Because men, as we all know, are varied creatures. To assert that there is just one role for all of them—basically just one man of which all others are only clones—would be ridiculous.

It is equally ridiculous to insist that there is only one right role for women—that there is just one woman of which all others are merely clones.*

Since I became a feminist and learned the devices by which men keep women enslaved, this sort of thing had become too painful to bear quietly, too blatantly heartless and cruel. In the face of it, the somnambulism of the women drove me wild, even made me feel panicky, as if I were the only person in a burning building who knew the house was on fire and could not wake the others to get them out. I could not keep quiet for the life of me. And I offended my sisters.

But just some of them. Many orthodox Mormon women are also fighting the Stepford Wives' syndrome in their own individual ways. And when you see Mormon women rising—women who are among the most thoroughly programmed in the entire world—you know that the patriarchy's attempt to level all women into one colorless, featureless, homogenized mass called *woman* is bound, ultimately, to fail.

When you see Mormon women rising, you know that revolution is simmering in women's spirits everywhere. Everywhere some of us are already on the boil. And we boil bumpy, different shapes and sizes; we boil variously colored—crimson and gold with slashes of green and purple—defying the patriarchal dye efforts to make us interchangeable.

* The New Right does not, unfortunately, have a corner on sexism, however. The idea that women are clones is the foundation upon which our society is built. In the September 1980 issue of *Ms.* magazine, Gloria Steinem, in a piece entitled "Can Half of America be Single-Issue Politics?", tells of her experience in doing research on the very broad subject of the actual or potential impact of feminism on current political theory. During that time she shared offices with a group of male academics who were working on such projects as "Standards of Mental Health in the Soviet Union," or "Social Marginality in the Villages of Nineteenth-Century Poland"—very narrow topics. She hoped, however, that they as specialists could contribute some insights to her research.

Instead, "what most of these kindly scholars taught me," Steinem writes, "was that the female half of the world was largely irrelevant to their studies. Women played narrow and (almost) negligible roles in a universe run by male human beings who were individualized, interesting, and diverse. At best, we were ghettoized into one chapter, inevitably titled 'Women and Whatever.' [Can you imagine a chapter entitled 'Men and Whatever'?]

"I soon learned that my own work on theories of gender-based power was academically suspect as 'single-factor analysis,' while my neighbor's work on one man's military acts during one decade was thoughtful, scholarly, and basic. More generous colleagues tried to comfort me in my limitation with the assurance that my interest really went beyond 'just women's issues,' but they still seemed bemused when I explained that I thought I had progressed beyond 'just men's.'"

But the enemies of women are the controllers of the wealth of the world. They have powerful ways of seducing us.

Last night Hazel called, beside herself with anger. "Did you see that public service announcement by the Mormon church on TV just now?" she stormed. "You won't believe it. It shows this slim, nice-looking woman wandering around a room while in the background a churchman's voice (tragically, still the voice of authority for females) says something like, 'I'm fat, I'm ugly, I'm no good, I hate myself.' After she wanders forlornly around the room awhile, the woman sits down on a couch and the voice continues, 'But I'm feeling better about myself. I can learn to live with myself. It's not what life does to you, but what you do to life that counts!'"

Oh Hazel, of course I believe it. Of course. The message is absolutely clear and as old as the male ego: women themselves—not male-dominated, female-hating society—are responsible for the fact that they feel worthless and depressed. Women must be made to keep on shouldering the guilt for their own oppression, must continue to be made the perennial scapegoats for all that's wrong with their lives, their families, and the society at large.*

---

* A few months before the 1980 election, Howard Phillips, National Director of the Conservative Caucus—one of the New Right organizations—told a California audience that women's liberation is the root cause of the country's many problems. He said that when we used to have one vote per family and that cast by the man of the house, everything was wonderful. But that from the moment women got the right to vote, the country had gone continually downhill. He also condemned the "evils" of women's right to own property independently of their husbands or fathers, and predicted the complete breakdown of American society if women win the right to choose when, or whether, to bear children.

What he really fears, of course, is the complete breakdown of patriarchy, of male control of women's minds and bodies. And it was a pleasure, in a perverse sort of way, to hear him enunciate the real feelings of the New Right so clearly. We have known all along that they do not believe in equality for women, and it was delightful to have them reveal this so resoundingly themselves.

The New Right belongs in the last century. Howard would feel right at home with the kind of rhetoric against suffrage for women that was common then. Take, for example, this excerpt from the Alexandria *Gazette* of December 10, 1866: "Now, sir, in practice its [universal suffrage's] extension to women would contravene all our notions of the family; 'put asunder' husband and wife, and subvert the fundamental principles of family government in which the husband is, by all usage and law, human and divine, the representative head. Besides it ignores woman, womanhood, and all that is womanly; all those distinctions of sex whose objects are apparent in creation, essential in character, and vital to society, these all disappear in the manly and impressive demonstration of balloting at a

What the men are saying through the ad is: "It's all your own fault. Just pick yourself up and stop pitying yourself. Don't blame us, and don't look to us to change ourselves or anything else to help you." The ad assures women that they are not miserable because they need intellectual and social stimulation, because they need more training and better paying jobs, because they need recognition as competent and worthy persons. Women are not miserable because they are ignored, put down, confused by upside-down rhetoric, and not taken seriously all day every day, or because they are discriminated against at every level of the social structure. Women are not miserable because churches they love and trust are pitting their might against their ever being—and feeling like—complete human beings. Women are miserable, the men scold in this ad, because they are doing something wrong again!

The classic blame-the-victim response from the classic victimizer of women—the patriarchal church.

Over the years, Hazel, who is head of a staff of twelve in the business department of her local high school, has continually volunteered to teach a quick typing course to the women of her Relief Society, many of whom, for one reason or another, need to work but have no marketable skills. The church has never taken her up on her offer. Church leaders do not want women to be economically independent. Economically independent women tend to become emotionally strong and psychologically independent as well. They do not have to do what they are told by men out of fear of being financially or emotionally abandoned. They can stand on their own. They are much less malleable, infinitely less "herdable." Hazel will never be asked to teach the women in her ward basic business skills because in their

---

popular election. Here maids, women, wives, men, and husbands, promiscuously assemble to vindicate the rights of human nature.

"Moreover, it associates the wife and mother with policies of state, with public affairs, with making, interpreting, and executing the laws, with police and war, and necessarily disseverates her from purely domestic affairs, peculiar care for and duties of the family; and worst of all, assigns her duties revolting to her nature and constitution and wholly incompatible with those which spring from womanhood.

"Besides, the ballot is the inseparable concomitant of the bayonet. Those who practice the one must be prepared to exercise the other. To introduce woman at the polls is to enroll her in the militia, to transfer her from the class of non-combatants to the class of combatants."

Men have been speaking for women for a very, very long time. And it has been almost unrelievedly humbug and balderdash.

present condition these women are helplessly dependent upon males and male institutions, and therefore entirely in men's power.

So Hazel goes to the county jail and teaches the women there— almost all of whom would not be there, she says, if they could earn a living wage—how to type and take dictation so they can step onto the economic ladder, if only the first rung.

The Relief Society, which began with a glorious vision of what women could be, has gradually been co-opted by the Brethren as a tool to keep women in their place. As Marilyn Warenski put it in *Patriarchs and Politics*, the Relief Society has become the "sisterhood of the brotherhood." The women who head it and the other auxiliaries of the church today are titular heads only, essentially without influence or power.

Power. An unfeminine word, men tell us; and since we have capitulated and let men define for us what femininity is, we should hardly be surprised to find ourselves defined out of the ranks of power. By assuring women that power is unladylike, men have insinuated that God also frowns upon our wanting or wielding it. (Only when Mormons for ERA discovered how to wield power through the media did we begin to have influence upon the church.) So Mormon women cannot talk about power without being subversive. They talk instead about "influence," as if somehow that were a different word altogether. If it is a different word, it is because they have redefined it, betrayed it. "Influence" is the nearest synonym to power in our language, and in thesauruses almost the first word listed as a synonym of "influence" is "power." These two words, like pomp and circumstance, are often used in conjunction, not because they are meant to convey different meanings, but because using them both is a way of emphasizing a point by repetition. "Force," "authority," "control," "dominance," "prestige," "weight," are synonyms of both "power" and "influence." So when the women heads of auxiliaries in the church insist that women should influence, but should not wield power, what they really mean is that women should manipulate men by deviousness, wiliness, coyness, subterfuge—all of which must be a good deal more repugnant to supreme beings (and to decent mortals) than honest, straightforward power.

In a letter to Marty LaBrosse, a pro-ERA Mormon I had met in Seattle just the week before, I wrote on November 5: "My bishop called this morning and asked me to come in tomorrow night. I hope I'm still a member of the church by this time tomorrow!"

On November 6, 1979, in Jeff's office at the church, I noticed that he was unusually agitated. He could not sit, but stood or paced behind his desk.

"Sonia, I have to decide whether to hold a bishop's court for you. I have to make this decision very soon—before morning—tonight!"

"Why? Who is putting pressure on you to make up your mind so quickly?"

"Oh no one, no one! It's just that there comes a time when the decision must be made and you can't wait until it is, you can't put it off any longer. This is that time."

I implored him not to allow himself to be pressured in this way, but to consider carefully what he was doing. I reminded him, as I had dozens of times before, that as far as I was concerned this was a purely political matter, that I was not in opposition to the church as a religion, and that I believed it was not legitimate to excommunicate members for political dissent (though it has happened on more than one occasion).

At some point before this, he had shown me a file in which he had collected news clippings from Virginia, Montana, Nevada, Utah and perhaps other places. When I watched him turn them over one by one and saw that certain lines had been overlined in yellow, I realized that, having failed to prove the existence of the Mother in Heaven cult, he was searching in other quarters for some excuse to excommunicate me, some evidence, *any* evidence. My heart had done an exclamatory thump at this knowledge of his determination to "get something" on me, and I think I had known then that as soon as he found *anything*, true or not, he would pounce. That he was just waiting. . . .

Because for all Jeff's talk of love, his behavior betrayed his true feelings. After the excommunication, for example, NBC needed a neighbor or friend or acquaintance of mine to talk with them about me on film to give balance to their show. So they asked Jeff to suggest someone. He gave them the names of a couple (who had surely written him a warmly congratulatory letter) who were the only people I knew who really hated me—that is, before I became politically embroiled with the church and the Mormons took over the job en masse. Their son and our children got along infamously at the bus stop, so one day the woman came raging into our house, screaming terrible things about our children at Rick and me at the top of her lungs. Finally, seeing that she would neither listen nor run out of steam for hours, I led her gently to the door and, ever so gently, guided her out. Rick escorted her along the path to the road so she wouldn't fall and sue us. That evening her husband called Rick and challenged him to a fistfight out behind Safeway!

What kind of people reach middle age still thinking that problems can be solved by fighting it out behind Safeway? Those are the people that Jeff, out of his great "love" for me, wanted NBC to put on their show.

That loving act was preceded, however, by several others which confirmed conclusively what the patriarchy means by the word "love."

From the beginning of the struggle of wills between Jeff and me, it was an uneven match. I had the intellectual advantage, but that was outweighed by the institutional power he had behind him. Maybe because of this challenge, I enjoyed holding him at bay for eighteen months. I think if I had not wearied, if Rick had left my heart in one piece instead of several hundred, I would not finally have shouted at Jeff that he was not fit to be a bishop because he did not ultimately like or understand or respect or care about one half his congregation, as proved by his insistence that they stay on those damned pedestals or else! If I had not wearied, I think I could have stood him off, and whoever was behind him, for at least six more months.

But I momentarily lost my enthusiasm for the fight, though as I retreated I knew it meant disaster. I felt for just a moment how pleasant it would be to stop resisting, to just let whatever was going to happen happen, to be passive, submissive, meek—all those traits the patriarchy loves so much in women because they make it so easy for men to push us around.

But I only gave up for a moment (though that was long enough for him to scent the wounded prey and close in!). It was not in me to let some small man rip me out of the heart of my heritage just to assuage his ego—and those of his superiors, for theirs were also suffering, I discovered as I came to know Earl Roueche, the stake president, and Gordon Hinckley and Neal Maxwell of the Special Affairs Committee in Salt Lake.

And so I called Judge Durham in Utah with Rick lying by me but lost to me forever in the motel bed in Norfolk. "What can I do to stop the bishop, Chris? If he does this, it will be a terrible mistake." She agreed entirely, and called back with the truly ironic advice that I get to know my stake president right away.

So that Sunday I met the Project Director's replacement (the Project Director had by this time been excommunicated from the church himself, ironically enough, though certainly not for his politics which were impeccably reactionary), and got to know Earl Roueche better than he thought I did. He was cold-eyed, almost reptilian in his manner, distant and noncommittal, refusing to discuss particulars of the situation, but reminding me silkily that I could appeal Jeff's decision (to him!) and assuring me that I could have a tape recorder in the trial—that is, if Jeff should decide to hold a trial—so that the high council court—that is, if Jeff should excommunicate me and I should appeal his decision—could hear the proceedings, including any witnesses I might call from Utah or elsewhere who would not be able to return for a second court hearing.

Roueche was not open with me then. Nor was he later when he held a secret high council court to hear my case without allowing me to attend and defend myself. But I only knew, that Sunday afternoon as I left that first interview, that I had no friend in him.

Driving home from that interview through Virginia's late autumn goldenness, weighing what Roueche's evident dislike might mean, and praying aloud as I often do when I drive alone, I suddenly knew and said aloud, "They're going to excommunicate me from the church!" Standing back from myself mentally to examine how that made me feel, I noted that I was filled with an inexplicable, deep, and very sweet peace. "They're going to excommunicate me, but I am going to be all right," I said to myself softly, wonderingly.

In the tumult of the approaching days, I forgot that incident, but I had confided it to Arlene the day it happened; later, in the midst of the anguish of the trials, she reminded me of it, emphasizing the "But I'm going to be *all right!*" part to comfort me.

As soon as I got home from the November 6 meeting with Jeff in which he told me he had to make a decision that night, I called Hazel and Maida and Teddie and told all three of them that Jeff was on the verge of succumbing to pressure from Salt Lake, or Roueche, or ego, or all three, and solicited their help in thinking of strategies to keep him from catapulting the church into serious difficulty.

I must not give the impression that we, the founding mothers of Mormons for ERA, were not well aware from the outset of the potential in this situation for publicizing and thus helping our cause. We were well aware. But my close friends also knew just as firmly that I did not want to be excommunicated, and none of us, except perhaps Maida, were convinced that it would cause more than a local media stir. If I had known that my excommunication would be the means of broadcasting nationwide what the Mormon church was doing politically to kill women's rights, would I have conspired in my own cutting off? That is a question I am often asked, but cannot answer. I was never posed that choice. I did *not* know the trial would receive worldwide attention, and I *did* know that I would not relinquish my membership without the fiercest struggle I knew how to put up.

Because the Mormon church was my church, my parents', their parents' church. It was where I had had my center for forty-three years. It had made me what I was. It was where I belonged, whether I was comfortable there or whether Mormons were comfortable with me. I was theirs, they were mine, for better or for worse, like family. I loved them while I was exasperated with them, even while I was angry at them for betraying the best in Mormonism and for making my church so much less than it had in it to be.

My church.

"I am a Mormon." With what love and pride I had said those words all my life. Though I knew it was absurd, I felt somehow as if they *could not* excommunicate me, that as with Abraham, an angel would appear and stay their hands before they sacrificed me—to their politics of oppression. I knew it was absurd, and yet I looked unconsciously for that angel right up to the end.

Maida went into action as soon as I hung up the phone. Though it was late, she called Jeff's home to talk to him. He was not there. Judy explained that he was in a top-secret meeting at the church and could not be interrupted. Guessing right away what that top-secret meeting was all about, Maida, in her indomitable way—she's one of those people I have always been glad is on *my* side—told Judy this was an emergency and she had to have the number. Judy gave it to

her, and Maida broke up the secret session at the church at about
11:15 P.M.

Jeff was vastly annoyed at the interruption (I wonder if Judy
caught it when he got home—down there on her pedestal). After asking him who was pushing him to excommunicate me, Maida told
him in very direct terms what she thought—and she was sure the
public would think—of his doing it on the basis of my ERA activity.
He angrily drew her attention to the lateness of the hour. But before
she finished with him, she left this prophetic question pulsating in
his brain: "Jeff, if you think you are annoyed at my calling you at
eleven-thirty at night, how are you going to feel when it's *Newsweek*,
and the New York *Times*, and *People* magazine calling. . . . *And
what are you going to say?*"

Despite the time, she called me up immediately to report the conversation. When she got to the end, I protested, "Come now,
Maida, really—*Newsweek, People!* That's going a bit far, isn't it?"

As it turned out, though it seemed bizarre, that was a very limited
prophecy. But then, no one could possibly have foreseen how fas-
cinating the story was going to prove to the press and the public. Except God.

Who was in that meeting when Maida called, and what were they
saying? We will never know that about dozens of similar meetings
and of urgent phone calls to and from Salt Lake City during the
whole month-long fiasco. We who watched it all unfold, however,
and who heard whispers from those close to the General Authorities
as well as to the local leaders, witnessed the change that swept over
the beehive from the time the first messenger bee arrived, dropping
into the quiet peaceful humming with the news of trouble, until the
entire rhythm of the hive was disrupted, and all was in a state of crisis from top to bottom, bees scrambling over one another to carry
out the order: Save the hive *at any cost!*

By this time, I had come to know Jeff well. I knew he was basically an authoritarian man, a giver and a follower of orders, obeying
his superiors and in turn expecting to be obeyed by subordinates
(which include every woman on the face of the earth!). I knew he always checked with his superiors rather than risk a mistake—I'd
watched him perform this ritual often enough. It was, and is, inconceivable to me that he could have made the decision to excommu-

nicate me on his own, as the church authorities insist that he did.* It is not in harmony with his character. They may have made him *think* it was his decision (which would not be hard to do), promising tacitly to back him behind the scenes all the way if he would take the public flak for the church—the way the Old Boys' Club works. In the end, however, someone would have to authorize it, someone would have to tell him, in effect, "Yes, that's the right decision, Jeff. It's all right with us. Go ahead and do it."

* The press release that went out over the wires on December 5, 1979, announcing my excommunication was sent out from the church's public relations headquarters in Salt Lake City, Utah. Odd, since it was "a local matter," to watch it being handled out of Salt Lake.

Chapter 10

"It's Four O'clock and I'm Still a Member of the Church!"

ONE EVENING, after a long day of getting the Mormons for ERA newsletter ready to mail, I was reading to Noly on the couch in the library when the doorbell rang. (The beginning of the doorbell as harbinger of calamity. Even now, a year later, the doorbell doesn't ring, it *tolls!*) Rick answered the door and I heard men's voices in the kitchen, but I felt no apprehension. It was November 14, eight days since Jeff had paced behind his desk in near hysteria telling me he had to decide *now* whether or not to bring me to trial. Eight days since he had agreed to let me know the moment *he* knew. Eight days during which my embattled spirit had gradually relaxed; every day that passed without news seemed evidence that he was calm and sensible again, not going to be pushed into doing something unwise, not to mention immoral. But when Rick appeared in the library doorway, the look on his face told it all. I knew.

In the living room stood the bishop's two counselors, brothers Stephen Wilcox and Lorin Jensen (Stephen had replaced Lou Hampton, who had been moved up in the ranks for good behavior), dressed as for church—or a funeral—a quiet exultation on Brother Jensen's face. He had told me, hadn't he, that I was not really a member of the church if I could oppose the holding of anti-ERA precinct meetings in the Sterling Park Ward chapel? Well, now I'd find out! Brother Wilcox held out a letter and said something about having been instructed by the bishop to deliver it to me. I took it and said, "Do you have to wait to be sure I read it?" "No, just that you received it." They filed solemnly out again, men to whom the church belonged no more than it did to me, but who thought they had the right to take it away from me. Never in a million years would I have been supposed to have a similar right over *them*. Nevertheless, men and women are "equal" in the church.

I sat where they left me, on the organ bench (we had bought an organ when I came to love playing it so), and slowly opened the letter:

"Sister Sonia Ann Johnson," it began in a strange, square typeface, "by this letter you are advised of and requested to attend a Bishop's court being convened to formally consider the relationship between your chruch [*sic*] membership and your conduct during the past months. The court will be held at 9:00 A.M. in the Bishop's office of the Sterling Park Ward meeting house on Saturday November 17, 1979.

"The personnel of the court will consist of Bishop Willis, presiding, Stephen C. Wilcox and Richard L. Brown, members, and Robert R. Andros, clerk. If you have any objection to the personnel of the court you may make that objection known in writing and in advance of the court date to the presiding officer who will rule on its validity."

Eight days before, when Jeff and I had talked about the possibility of a trial, I had specifically requested that, if one were to be held, the overtly hostile Lorin Jensen *not* be involved. President Roueche told me in our subsequent conversation that Lorin had voluntarily withdrawn before anyone had to dismiss him. Bob Andros should have done the same.

Sitting that night on the organ bench, the letter in my lap calling me to trial for behaving the way the church had always taught me to behave, for being the person the church had formed, I thought about Bob Andros. I remembered when, in 1977, Rick and I had taught the family relations course in Sunday school how I had pointed out one Sunday, quite casually—I was not a feminist then—that if we were to list the attributes of our Father in Heaven, we would be surprised to see that his "role" is a very "feminine" one, as men have defined feminine. Who is home all day, always there day and night to listen to our woes, to comfort, to support and help? Whose primary goal is it to bring to pass his children's eternal life, not to make a certain quota of money or worlds? Who is tender and understanding, totally approachable, will drop everything and attend to us when we need him? Who is loving and nurturing beyond our ability to comprehend those words?

Our Heavenly Father, of course, and he is *male*. Why then is he doing in heaven what *women* do on earth? Why aren't the men of the earth following his example?

Bob was quietly upset by this—he is quietly everything—so much so that he could not let it stand. "You know, Sonia," he stopped me after class with his put-down churchman's voice (how could it *be* that I did not hear and understand this voice years ago? Rick has always used it with me; and I distinctly remember flushing with anger when Bob addressed me that day, but thought *I* was being absurd), "there is a scripture in which Heavenly Father tells us he does everything through his son, Jesus Christ." So? So that was supposed to negate all I had said, whereas in fact it only proved it. I wanted to say, "So what if it is Jesus who is 'feminine'? Jesus told his disciples that if they had seen him, they had seen the Father. If Jesus is primarily loving and nurturing and tender and nonambitious for money or position or prestige, but cares only about his Father's children, then we must assume that God is like this also—if we believe Jesus."

I only thought this to myself because I hadn't the courage to stand up to Bob. So I let him think he had set me straight—how many times do women do this with men in our lives! But because his response was irrational, I knew something lay behind it other than his concern for my doctrinal education. I was perplexed and intrigued by his response—obviously I had struck a nerve. He was feeling very defensive and uncomfortable. But why? Those were my pre-feminist days, and though I could see that by convincing me of something, he was really trying to convince himself, I did not understand further than that. Now I believe I have some light on the subject.

The Androses have many children—nine now, about six then. Bob, by being the head of his family and going forth every day to battle in the great economic world, was doing what the church fathers taught him God wanted him to do; this was his "role," and in filling it, he was like God.

Now what if you introduce to such a man the idea that the God we *really* pray to is not the "masculine" Old Testament God, but the power-through-gentleness-and-love Jesus-type God who is performing in heaven not as men are on this world, but has as his role the role of mother, as we understand it in earthly terms. That means that to be like God, Bob must have to devote his full time—as his Heavenly Father does—to caring for all those children day and night thirty or more years of this life, and myriads of children all of the next. It means he would have to be willing to trade places with Linda forever, and send her forth, perhaps (women cannot be Heavenly Fathers so why should they train for the job?) to do the considerably less Godlike work of making money. (Nowhere in scripture is moneymaking a Godlike attribute.) Would he want to do this? Not on your life, and heaven forbid! So he had to convince himself that God, his model, *didn't do it either.*

But Mormon doctrine teaches a personal God who hears and answers prayers. To assert that God neither personally listens to prayers nor personally answers them, as Bob was arguing, is heresy.

So way back in 1977, Bob Andros thought I was becoming uppity because I could challenge men's role with the suggestion that they emulate God by being more "feminine." I believe I said some very alarming things in class that day: "The church and society are training millions of women to be Heavenly Fathers; women are doing what He does: nurture. But the church and society are training precious few, if any, male Heavenly Fathers. Well, the first shall be last and the last shall be first!"

No wonder he had to put me in my place! Role theory is ultimately based on the most gratuitous nonsense.

Later that same year, our friends the Wallaces came to visit us. After we had heard their four delightful and talented children perform in their family string quartet, I wanted my ward members to share our pride in this exemplary Mormon family. I knew it would make them proud, as it had me, and I knew it would lift their spirits, as it had mine. So I decided to have them play the prelude music in sacrament meeting instead of my playing it so much less professionally on the organ. I called Jeff to ask permission, and he referred me to Bob Andros who apparently was in charge of that sort of thing. Bob said he would talk to Jeff and let me know the decision. I waited. Sunday drew near, and no word, so I called Bob again. He had called Jeff. Jeff was thinking it over. Tell him to think faster, I urged. Bob said he would be back in touch soon. When I had heard nothing from either Bob or Jeff by Sunday afternoon, I seated the four performers at the front of the chapel, and promptly at twenty minutes to five, told them to begin playing.

Their performance was stunning. Proof is that people tiptoed into the chapel as they had never before, and sat in total silence, letting the music flood their souls. Sterling Park Ward has always had trouble with reverence in meetings. Architecturally, it is not a building that produces a feeling of sacredness, and in addition, it is a ward with many small children, a ward in which grown-ups take advantage of the uproar to talk to one another in stage whispers. There is general hum and confusion during the prelude music, and the bishop often has to stand and request that members listen to the music and keep the noise level down.

Not that evening. If ever there was a testimony to the spiritual value of excellent music performed excellently, it was borne that night. It has always grieved me that, except for the Tabernacle Choir (and that is not nearly so fine as I once thought it was, subverted as it is to proselytizing, not artistic, purposes), music in the Mormon church is generally of such a mediocre quality that I have been ashamed—and ashamed of being ashamed—when I have brought non-Mormon friends to church.

Jeff strode into the chapel at ten minutes to five, looking mildly baffled; he walked up to the front and sat down by my family and friends on the first row to make a note of the performers' names so he could thank them in his opening remarks.

At about five minutes to five, I went up to the organ to prepare for the first song. The quartet was still creating the most spiritual feeling in that room I have ever felt there. I had just got seated on the choir seat next to the organ when Bob Andros walked in. He may not say much but his face speaks volumes. Just then, his face said that he had not expected to see this, that he did not like my having gone ahead without his okay.

I felt that, despite my being older, better educated in musical matters, and specifically chosen to provide the prelude music for the ward, the men considered me presumptuous and insubordinate because I had gone ahead without their permission. To authoritarian, patriarchal men, I suppose it made perfect sense that because I was a woman, without authority, my judgment, no matter how superior to theirs, could not be trusted.

In the audience, Rick had been waiting for Bob, too, and, catching and assessing the look on Bob's face when he came in, threw me a sardonic glance. Afterward he told me, "You threatened old Bob, Sonia. He must be used to being obeyed by women."

Personally, I thought it was good for old Bob; I know that experience was good for me. On the spot, as I saw the annoyance flit across his face, I vowed never to ask permission again. Never to demean and belittle myself again. That experience helped water the feminist seed the church had planted and so assiduously nourished over the years.

Not long after the excommunication, I was in Boston talking to the group associated with *Exponent II*, a publication for Mormon women. After I had briefly related the Hatch incident, one woman, in obvious distress, asked, "Sonia, when Senator Bayh's staff asked you to testify before the subcommittee, why didn't you call your bishop or your stake president and say, 'I've had this request. What do you think I should do about it?'" And I said to her, "By that time I had ceased to be a permission-asking woman." At my side, a Boston bishop softly said, "Bravo!"

Bob's name was put forward as scribe in the bishop's invitation to trial. I resolved to ask Jeff to remove him from that duty. I knew Jeff was deeply prejudiced against me and I suspected that Bob was; Dick Brown I regarded as a man of integrity, the sort of person who might do what I had done if he had been a woman. A man, I thought, of courage. I was glad he had been chosen to take Lorin's place.

I read the letter again. This was Wednesday night—late by now. The trial was set for early Saturday morning. Slowly I began to understand the strategy behind it all. They were giving me only two days! Two days to prepare my defense, to prepare myself spiritually, psychologically, two days to find witnesses. *Only two days!* The cruelty of that and the already clear judgment it revealed that had been made about my guilt struck me like a heavy fist in the face. They did not intend to give me a real trial at all! They were not even going to give me a real chance to defend myself. I had been found guilty and now they were only going through the formalities. I felt certain that

Jeff's deciding whether or not to hold the trial had come only *after* he had already pronounced me guilty in his heart.

Thinking all this—Rick had long since finished Noly's story and put him to bed—I was disturbed by the ringing of the telephone. It was the son of a good friend of mine in Nevada, a young man who was a student at Princeton and who had become a friend in his own right. I had met him the October before when he was newly returned from the Japanese mission. Between his mother and me, and because of a natural disposition to love justice, he was converted to feminism in no time. Just the week before, he had been at our house on his way back to Princeton and had helped Mormons for ERA walk a candidate's district.

I will never know why he called, what he wanted to say to me. Perhaps he said it. I only remember that the letter was still in my hand and I said, "Shel, you're not going to believe this, but the bishop's counselors have just left the house. I'm standing here with an invitation to a bishop's court in my hand."

After he had hung up, I called Hazel. We arranged that the four of us—Hazel, Maida, Teddie, and I—would meet the following evening at six for dinner at a restaurant in Vienna, Virginia, to discuss what to do.

I sat for a long time in the chair at the desk after I finished talking to Hazel, refusing to listen for clues that would tell me where Rick was in the house. I could no longer turn to him, and that knowledge, which I had been trying to put off facing, suddenly dug its razor-sharp nails again into the soft tissue of my mind and heart. I jammed my hand over my mouth to keep from crying out. I would not let him know I suffered. He had no right to my feelings or thoughts anymore. He had lost me, too. I would always have the memory of that best friend that he had been, dying an ugly ignoble death, but I would not think of him now. Later, I told myself, the self who wanted to mourn that friend, who needed to grieve. Later, I said firmly. You cannot have that luxury yet. Wait. I bit my hand hard to keep from making any sound, though my whole body was heaving with sobs. I envied Rick his honeymoon with Carolyn. I needed some arms, not to bury the past in as he was doing, but to comfort me when the feet of the men I had loved and honored were turning to clay before my eyes.

I slept little that night. First thing next morning, Peter Gillins,

UPI chief in Salt Lake City, called. "What's this I hear about a trial?" he asked. Startled, I inquired how he had found out. Apparently Shel had called his mother in Las Vegas, who had called her mother in Salt Lake City, who had called her son in that same city, who had called Peter.

Press coverage of the trial had begun.

Thursday, November 15. I tried all day to reach Jeff. Judy told me he was on jury duty (ironies never ceased) and could not be reached all day. Frantically, I explained to her that I had only two days before the trial and that I did not even know what the charges were. Would she please help me get in touch with Jeff. Finally, she made an appointment for me with him at 8 P.M. that night at the Sterling Park Ward chapel. One whole precious day wasted.

During that day, I went numbly about my usual housewifely and motherly tasks. At one point these took me to the little town of Leesburg, Virginia. As I was driving down the main street, who should pass and spy me but Jeff Willis, looking immediately as if he had seen a ghost. The encounter startled me, too, mostly because he looked so very caught in the act—his eyes fairly goggling and his mouth agape. I said aloud to my car's ever-responsive and appreciative interior: "That's the starkest picture of bad conscience I've ever seen!"

That evening, with a weary head full of reporters' questions—word gets around in medialand—I met with the three other founding mothers to discuss strategy. Teddie thought I should not even go to the trial; or that I should hold a court and excommunicate *them!* Surely, she thought, I should not give them the satisfaction of being able to command my presence. None of her suggestions was a viable alternative to me, however. We toyed with the idea of all of us going and demanding to be brought to trial together since we were all equally implicated. In the end, I drove out to Sterling Park Ward alone, and at 8 P.M. sat for the last time alone with Jeff Willis in that office.

As I recall, the first question I asked him was, "Who is my accuser?" "I am," he answered. "Who is my judge, then?" "I am," he said again. "But how can you be both my accuser and my judge? For heaven's sake, Jeff, I've been an American too long to feel comfortable with that. I'm accustomed to at least the appearance of due process. If you've decided I'm guilty—and you must have, since you're willing to accuse me—how can you bring an impartial decision?" "Don't worry, Sonia," he assured me. "I will receive the correct decision through inspiration from our Heavenly Father. The courts of the church are courts of love." Ignoring the love nonsense, I asked, "How do you expect to be able to hear God's will over the roar of your own conviction that I'm guilty? What exactly do you expect him to do, Jeff? Hit you over the head with a lightning bolt? Knock you down on the road to Langley?"

I was not mollified. I was as prayerful a person as I had ever known (except for my mother), and I knew how hard it is to get answers. I had heard mission presidents say they could not tell whether or not someone had negroid ancestry no matter how hard they prayed. I very much suspected that Jeff was more influenced by what his superiors told him *they* had heard from God than he was from what he had personally managed to glean. "Wait just a second, God. I have to check it out with the Big Boys." But I was determined not to view the situation as hopeless—though I know now that it was from the beginning.

"What are the charges against me, Jeff? Please write them down so we will each know this is what you said, and so I won't make a mistake when I tell my witnesses what they need to respond to."

He refused to write anything down. That's what comes of working for the CIA—deep distrust as a first response. So I asked him if he would dictate the charges to me. He agreed to do that. Perhaps because they were not in his handwriting, he could forever deny that they had come from him. I cannot imagine why else he refused to write them himself. These are his exact words as I took them down on the night of November 15, 1979:

"You have broken the covenants you made in the temple, specifically:
1. evil speaking of the Lord's anointed;
2. the law of consecration;
3. your general attitude and expression."

I protested. Where have I spoken evil of the Lord's anointed, I asked? In your APA speech, he answered. Show me the place, I demanded. "You call them chauvinistic," he shot back. "That's not evil; that's true!" I replied. "And what's this about the law of consecration?" "You promised in the temple to give your time, your talents, all the Lord has blessed you with and all he may yet bless you with to the upbuilding of the church and to the establishment of Zion."

"Jeff, I pay a full tithing and have all my life. I'm the ward organist and spend many extra hours practicing alone and with the choir. I teach the cultural refinement lesson in Relief Society, I am a visiting teacher [in the Relief Society], I attend church, we hold family home evenings, I attend the temple. If you're going to excommunicate everybody in the ward who is doing this much or less, you won't have anybody left in the congregation when you're through!

"And tell me how I'm going to defend myself against your annoyance at my 'general attitude and expression.' What does that even mean? Just because men in the church don't like uppity women, does that mean we should all be *excommunicated*?" I thought but held my tongue: "Do we have to have an attitude of hero worship and awe even when our male leaders do little or nothing to deserve it? Why should we be in awe? Because you're *male*?"

By this time it was 9:30 and we were both tired. But I had the most important work still to do. "Why," I asked him, "if this is going to be a fair trial, as you have assured me, was I given only two days to prepare for it? It looks as if you're trying to railroad me out of the church. If you are honest about all this, give me more time to prepare for it, to get witnesses, simply to prepare myself emotionally. You've told me you've spent days in the temple while making your decision. I haven't had a chance to do that. I need to go to the temple, too, to find the spiritual strength I'm going to need."

He steadfastly refused to change the date. I bore down upon him, pointing out that because I couldn't find him all day, I now had only one day to prepare. Would Jesus Christ, whose servant he claimed to be, have refused to give me time to fight the most serious battle of my life? "As his disciple you are obliged, I should think, to consider how he would react to my pleas for more just treatment if he were here himself," I admonished him. "It isn't kind or loving to give me so little time, and Jesus was, above all else, kind and loving." In fact, I thought to myself, very unlikely to "try" anyone. As far as I know, he never turned anyone away. And wasn't it Jesus who said it was not the well who need a physician, but the sick? He said he came for the sinners. Would he then have turned people away because he regarded them as sinners, and only have kept the absolutely well in his entourage? It seems to me that none of the leaders of the church understand Jesus Christ as well as women and little children do. Certainly they give little evidence of it in their actions. Peter denied Jesus three times. What could any of us do today that would equal that for disloyalty? But Peter was not only not excommunicated; Jesus' love never wavered and *he did not punish.* Jesus had no ego problems.

Finally I said flatly, "I can't move from this office until you tell me I can have reasonable time to prepare for this trial." He saw I was serious, and reluctantly agreed to extend the time. I suggested two weeks from the original date, not for any subversive reason, but because it gave me enough time and seemed like a good solid date: December 1, 1979 (I've since learned that December 1 was the day Rosa Parks was arrested the first time; I am honored to have come to trial on her anniversary). He told me he would let me know about the date, but—and I pushed him to say it again—I could trust that the trial was postponed. Only after he had assured me of this several times did I agree to leave his office that night. At home, I phoned Hazel to share my victory. I had, I thought, successfully kept the men from holding an unjust court and dishonorably pushing me out of the church.

Friday I spent calling my witnesses—Ralph Payne from Pennsylvania, who had been present during my APA speech in New York; Jan Tyler, who had heard my "Uppity Sisters" talk at the University of Utah's women's conference; John Bailey, Maida Withers and Teddie Wood who had known me through it all; Esther Peterson, President Carter's adviser on consumer affairs, who thought the whole Mormon church's anti-female stance was shocking and the trial a violation of the spirit of freedom which pervades the Constitution; my mother because she wanted so much to help me and because she believed in my integrity. All Mormons, because only Mormons can be involved in church courts.

Mom had been out to Virginia earlier that year and had stood in testimony meeting to tell the members of my congregation how proud she was of me, how I had always been a person of extraordinary faith and courage, and how much she loved and admired me. On the stand, I gasped when she stood up, knowing she was well aware of the feelings about me in that room. If it is true that I have faith and courage, it was apparent that day where I had learned them. God bless my beautiful mother. After the meeting, some woman in the ward came up and said, "I'm so glad you said those things!" But the bishop greeted her coolly. To him, I'm sure she sounded like another uppity woman, the kind he hates and fears.

As I sat with Rick and the children at the supper table Friday evening, I felt I had the situation as much under control as possible. Everyone had agreed to testify, and I liked the feeling of knowing I would not be alone with those men the whole time. I had asked Linda Sillitoe to come out and be the Boswell of the trial, to bear back to Utah the truth as seen through her clear eyes. And just under the surface all the sorrow about Rick lay uneasily, biding its time.

At 7:30 the doorbell rang and Jeff appeared at our supper table. "How about the evening of November twenty-seventh?" he asked. "That sounds good to me," I agreed. "But it's a week night and may be hard for my witnesses, some of whom are coming from Utah. Still, I'm grateful for the extra time, and I'll find some way to do it." With that agreement, in front of my entire family, he left.

And left me pondering hard. A bishop friend of mine had earlier advised me to try to get the stake president to preside over the case at a high council court, the kind of court men have access to in the church. Bishop's courts are only for women and children, or men who either don't hold the priesthood or hold the lower order thereof. High council courts, where fifteen men—not fifteen people, fifteen males—hear the case, an equal number speaking for and against the defendant, make at least a nod in the direction of justice and due process. Many of the fifteen men on the high council court, for instance, probably do not know the defendant well, and so there is the added advantage of some objectivity, which heaven knows bishops and their counselors are not blessed with an abundance of, constantly associating and working with the people in their congregations as they do and hearing all the scuttlebutt (often passing it along in their turn). As I watched Jeff's broad back retreat out the door, I decided it was worth a try. Just seeing him again made my heart sink. He was going to bungle things. And, in my haste to escape the molasses of Jeff's thought processes, I leaped into the icy waters of Earl's treachery.

Leaving the table immediately, I phoned Earl Roueche. "I know you have the authority to take this trial under your jurisdiction," I told him. "I now formally request that you do so."

So far so good, but at this point I made a fatal mistake. I would continually forget about the power and unity of the Old Boys' Club, how disloyalty toward one is disloyalty toward all, how they therefore all stand behind one another. (I was about to learn that loyalty, with men, is amoral.) Men have kept us women divided against ourselves, cut off from one another in dozens of ways. So because we have no corollary of the Old Boys' Club, it is easy for us to forget how the Old Boys' egos are all bound together: if we disparage one, we disparage them all. We—women—are the enemy. Against us, the men will stand united no matter how much they may secretly despise one another.

Unwittingly I said, "I feel certain Jeff is going to bungle things."

Earl's voice went stiff, and I knew I had said something very wrong. "I will speak to *the bishop* and get back to you," he said, the ice fairly crackling along his tongue. He did not get back to me, ever; but then why should he have kept his word? I am only a woman, and an uppity one at that. How can I expect church leaders to act decent under such trying circumstances?

At 10 P.M., the doorbell rang again. *Nobody* rings our doorbell at 10 P.M. I felt suddenly very apprehensive. Again Rick answered the door, again I heard male voices in the kitchen. This time I felt fleetingly like a Jew for whom the SS has come. I was in my pajamas, so I quickly put on my robe and went out into the living room. There stood Jeff again, with Lorin Jensen—two men whose intolerant faces I could scarcely bring myself to look at in the full unthreatening light of Sunday morning, let alone in the frightening, late-night dimness of the living room. Again I sat on the organ bench. Rick sat across the room. Jeff and Lorin sat on the couch between us.

"I'm here under the direction of the stake president," Jeff began tonelessly, "who has taken over the jurisdiction of your case."

"Oh, thank goodness!" I breathed in relief. "Does that mean that I will be able to have a high council trial?"

"No, you will have a bishop's trial, as planned."

"But I thought you said President Roueche—"

"I have two commissions to carry out for President Roueche tonight," he interrupted. "First, I have been directed to take your temple recommend."

"Have you already had a court and found me guilty?" I asked, unbelievingly. But even as I spoke, I realized what must have happened. Jeff had told Earl what I had said about wanting to go to the temple to prepare myself for the ordeal, and they meant to cut me off from that. Perhaps they feared the press might make use of it. I understood immediately, too, that they did not want members of the church to know that I had gone to the temple to prepare to meet them in battle for my membership. Only they are allowed these tokens of worthiness, these symbols of closeness to deity. The situation had to be kept dichotomous: good versus evil. So I must be quickly cut off at the pass.

I refused to give him the recommend. But the men in leadership in the church control the definition of the situation. "If you don't turn it over to me, I'll just tell them at the temple not to honor it," he said icily. At his hate-filled tone, I began to cry.

He went on, his voice like a recording, his eyes staring past me: "My second commission from the stake president is to tell you that the trial will be held as initially set, at my office tomorrow morning."

I was stunned. Wasn't this the same man who the night before had promised me that I could have sufficient time to prepare my defense? Wasn't this the very man I had invited to sit down at my supper table, just three hours earlier, when he had come to tell me I had a reprieve until November 27?

Wasn't this man, who was so blithely breaking his promise and was so gestapo-like in his behavior toward me, wasn't this man a *bishop of the church?*

I was sure I had not understood him correctly.

"But Jeff, you gave me your word that I wouldn't have to go to trial so soon. Isn't your word worth anything?"

"I am acting under directions from the stake president. This has nothing to do with me," he informed me for the fourth time.

"That's what they said at Auschwitz," Rick interjected grimly from across the room. Jeff ignored him.

I was trying to understand. "Is President Roueche going to preside over the trial?"

"No, I will preside."

"But how can this be under his jurisdiction, as you say it now is, and he not preside? What does it mean when you say this is under the jurisdiction of the stake president? Will he even be present at the trial?"

"No."

"Jeff," I searched desperately for a way out, "if this is a bishop's court, and you are the one in authority, it is your decision, not the stake president's, when to hold the trial. You can decide to stand by your promise."

Again, this had nothing to do with *him*. The stake president had so ordered, he intoned with glazed eyes and robotlike inflection.

"You're wrong. Oh, you're wrong! It does have something to do with you!" I cried. "You gave me your word, and you're breaking it, not the stake president. You should have told him, 'I promised Sonia that she could have until November twenty-seventh, and I am an honorable man. I cannot and will not break my word to her. If you wish to change the time, you will have to do it yourself.' You should have said that to him, Jeff."

"I have my orders," he repeated flatly.

"Well, then, I just want you to think a minute or two about Jesus Christ whom you profess to follow. Do you think he would ever have broken his promise to anyone, or hurt anyone, as you have done, because someone else 'ordered' him to? Do you think he wouldn't have had the courage to be honorable in the face of great pressure to be otherwise? Do you think he would have been so unloving, so unkind, so cold, and so cruel as you have been here tonight? Would he have kept me from seeking comfort in the temple? Who is your master, Jeff, that gentle loving man, or an inhuman institution?"

I cried openly and unashamedly through all this. How many betrayals can one endure? First Rick. Now the bishop had shown himself a spineless pawn without a lick of moral gumption, and the stake president had been revealed as a deeply treacherous man. I knew in my bones as I turned, defeated, and walked out of the room, that men are not honest with women. That they do not believe it is necessary, especially when the Old Boys' Club is threatened.

In the library I called President Roueche. It was 10:20 P.M. The phone rang and rang and rang, and I knew it did not ring in an empty house. "All right, Earl," I said to the deaf phone, "remember, you are the one who declared war!"

I sat holding the phone as it rang on and on. I heard Rick seeing the Brethren out. Soon he came into the library and sat down. I looked at him and saw what he was, and wondered how I had ever been so foolish as to trust my heart to him. He seemed all pulsating ego, just as I had seen Jeff be just a few minutes before in the living room. All ego, all hungry ego, like little bird beaks spiking up out of the nest, I thought dreamily, listening to the empty ringing. Someone has to feed them constantly, constantly, constantly, or else . . . they find someone else who will. "I'm tired," I thought. "I'm tired, and sick to death of male ego. Society has created monsters. Let Carolyn take over the care and feeding of this weak baby bird." And I despaired that, irrevocably heterosexual, I could find no comfort now, either in faithless men or kind women. I felt so cut off from loving at that moment that it was an actual physical pain. I only knew how to "love" men and I thought I would never be able to do it again after this night.

"I'm ashamed of men; I'm ashamed of us all," Rick echoed my thought softly. "We're all bastards, Sonia. All of us. Do you know what they tried to do as they were leaving tonight?" he asked incredulously, disgustedly. "Jeff said, 'You know, Rick, we men in the priesthood have to stick together,' the implication being *against* the women. Can you imagine? They tried to buddy-buddy me; they tried to turn me against you!" (If they only knew how unnecessary *that* was, I thought bitterly.)

He went on. "I'm ashamed of what I witnessed in that room tonight. I'm ashamed of what happened in the kitchen on their way out. You're right, you know. Men *do* hate women. They're afraid of women. I saw it."

"Yes," I said. "I know."

The phone rang in Roueche's house for the twenty-fifth time. I hung it up carefully and ponderously as if I were hanging up on the old loyalties and trusts, and called Hazel. "I have one night to get ready, Hazel," I said. "Tell Maida and Teddie. Now I'm going to get to work."

Everything seemed unreal and as if it were passing in slow motion. I sensed that I had pushed off from the shore of my homeland, never to return. For a moment I was flooded with nostalgia for the old lost innocence, for the world that had never really existed except in my myth-benighted mind. "That's the reason, of course!" I thought. "That's the reason we can't go home again. Home is not really ever there; it was always in our perceptions, which change. . . ."

"Sleep by me tonight, Rick. I can't bear to be alone," I said to him. "Hold me this one last time," because by morning I won't even be able to make out the shoreline any longer, I thought to myself.

So we went to bed together, he and I, who had shared the same bed for twenty years. We did not kiss or caress. I turned on my left side. He curled around my back with his arm across my side, and went soon and heavily to sleep. "If you could only be the man I made you in my imagination," I mourned. "Where is a man to match my woman?"

As I lay there with Rick's arm growing heavier and heavier across me, his body performing like the furnace it is, growing warmer and warmer and finally uncomfortably hot, I thought of all I had to do before morning. The day before, Thursday, when the papers had carried the first news of the trial, a young CIA lawyer in my ward had offered me his professional advice. That morning, Friday, I had been so besieged by media people and had needed help so badly just to care for my family, that I had called his wife—my friend Kris Barrett—and asked for help: could she somehow, with her own three little children, find a way to organize dinner for the Johnsons too that night?

As it grew dark and no dinner arrived, I began to feel guilty for laying an obviously too-heavy burden on her. But at about 7 P.M. her lawyer husband, Mike, was at the door with our dinner—our second one, as it turned out. On his way to the car with the first one, a couple of hours before, he had dropped the whole thing, broken every casserole dish and destroyed the food. Kris had simply marched back into the kitchen and prepared a whole new meal for us. (I wonder whether the Barretts got anything to eat that night.) (This second, safely arrived meal was the one I invited Jeff to share with us and which he declined just a few minutes later when he arrived with the good news of the ten-day amnesty.) Setting the food down very, very carefully on the table, Mike repeated his offer of help. "I'm serious," he insisted as I saw him out the door. He knew he needed to insist because Mike endures life by refusing to let anyone see him take it seriously, by laughing at it and everyone in it, including Mike.

After Rick had disgustedly let the Mormon gestapo out later that night, I called Mike and asked him what I should do. "Write down everything that has happened thus far between Jeff and you," he instructed me. "Outline what witnesses you had called and what you think they could have contributed to your defense, insist that you are therefore appearing under duress at this trial, and plead for a stay of execution."

Warmed on the outside by Rick's faithless furnace, I began typing, and spent the entire night in the library preparing a document sparklingly entitled: "Request for Extension of Time." Sometime near morning I crept back to bed to warm up again, wishing, oh, wishing, for some comfort in the yawning comfortlessness. I was learning the lesson I was going to need all my life: I must be enough for myself. Alone, I must, I will, be enough.

I lay on my back watching the curtains become opaque with morning, and prayed, tears running softly to form warm puddles in my ears and from there to sog the pillow at the back of my neck. "Is this my last morning as a Mormon, Mother?" I asked. "Who am I now that I'm not Rick's wife? Who will I be when I'm no longer a Mormon?"

My fierce anti-self-pity self retorted, "You will still be Sonia. Or perhaps, you will finally *be* Sonia."

"Please, God, let that be enough!" prayed my weaker, not-so-sure self.

Who took care of my children all that long, cold Saturday in November? I cannot recall. I moved about in a haze of fatigue, getting ready to face a man about whom I had learned some very disquieting things the night before, a man who had broken his promise to me without a qualm, who had treated me unkindly, and who I knew—as the church had always taught me—could not, therefore, have the spirit of the Lord. I knew he meant to excommunicate me that day without a fair trial, and I knew that when I appealed his decision, the stake president to whom I would have to appeal was also a dishonorable man. All those clay feet, all those sayers of the word only.

But though bone-tired and miserably disillusioned, I was preparing in my spirit for the fight of my life. If they were to strip me so shoddily of my right to membership in the church for which my foreparents and I had sacrificed so much of our time, our talents, and our means, I would make them work as they had never worked before. I knew my heart. I knew God knew it. And I knew the leaders neither knew it nor cared to know it, and because of that would likely make one of the most serious moral errors of their lives and excommunicate me.

Sometime early Saturday morning the doorbell rang again and another letter was handed me, reminding me that the trial would begin at 11 A.M.—the night before, they had generously given me two extra hours. So a little before 11 we arrived at the church, Rick and I, and were met by a wonderful sight.

A hundred feminists were gathered in the parking lot of the church, several of them holding the banner bearing the beautiful words of the proposed Twenty-seventh Amendment to the Constitution of the United States which would set women free. I never loved those words more than I did that gray morning, seeing all those female faces so courageously and lovingly gathered in my behalf. It was my first experience of the enormous network of support among women in the movement. I was touched and even a little shaken by the significance of what I was witnessing. Something in me fairly leaped with joy and hope for humankind as I saw those women, united, standing there. If women will come to the aid of women, we can rescue the whole world, I thought.

Dear sisters, many of you traveled all night to get there for me. You were the comfort I had sought in the night and could not find. When I saw you I knew I was not going to have to do it all alone. I was not going to have to be enough. There *were* arms, and they were yours. And though they will never be *all* the arms I will yearn for, they will be enough. Women are enough for ourselves.

Now, a year later, having met thousands—tens of thousands—of feminists the world over, I marvel that after forty-three years of following men's rules, watching men for clues to how I should be, seeking to please men, having my eyes always fixed on them and hardly being aware at all of other women—I marvel at the miracle of femaleness. I cannot seem to get enough of it, cannot watch women enough, cannot hear them enough. How is it I did not really *see* half the world's population, including myself, for nearly half a century? I cannot begin to express with what pleasure I now watch my sister feminists' lives, delighting in the myriads of evidences of intelligence and wisdom, of good humor, liveliness and playfulness, of loving care for women everywhere, for the children, for the men, for the old and the poor people of the world. I cannot get enough of the words written by women. Every word sounds different in my mind from the way it sounded when men used it. It is a new word, with new meaning (or the original one restored), richer, more provocative, healing, mine. My language, finally.

When I see a woman bend to button her child's coat, or leap to hit a tennis ball, the beauty of it almost hurts. I love to be hugged by women; I love their soft cheeks pressed against mine. I feel as if they have bestowed a blessing on me with their touch, with their marvelous woman's hands and arms. In the presence of women who know they are women, who are strong and unafraid—and therefore in jeopardy—I feel in the presence of priestesses. When I recently met an old woman who had marched with Alice Paul in Washington over fifty years ago, I could hardly speak. I felt like kneeling before her and putting my forehead on her toes. I do not know how to show my reverence for us. I feel like making the sign of something over the heads of the women who come up to talk and to touch and to have me write my silly name. I want to say, blessings on you and on me, wonderful woman. Rich, mysterious, lovely and graceful, the stumpiest of us, the homeliest of us—to me, we are all achingly beautiful. Thank God I have found women, and still have half a life before me in which to watch them with awe and wonder. And in which to be one of them, a woman among women.

The women were there at the church for me. I saw them for the first time and began to understand what it meant that they were there and that they and I were women, all in it together.

So was the press there. Very there.

As soon as I had hung up from telling Hazel that Jeff had just goose-stepped through my house, Hazel and Ron notified other feminists briefly, then spent the rest of the night calling the press. In so doing, they changed forever the history of the Mormon church. Georgia Fuller, head of NOW's Women and Religion Task Force, got busy immediately calling ERA supporters to join a prayer vigil for me outside the church. All night, the phones of the women's network and of the media burned while I sat alone and unsuspecting, writing down the sorry tale of betrayal.

When I walked up to the church, at least forty media people bore down upon me—from the New York *Times*, the Washington *Post*, *People* magazine, CBS, NBC, *Newsweek, Time*. They asked me how I felt. What did I answer, I wonder? They asked me what the charges were. I told them as well as I could. Was I guilty? No, I was not.

It is not hard to talk to the press, even when you are half asleep, when you answer as honestly as you know how. I must have looked simply dreadful, however; all the press people were extraordinarily gentle with me, as if I might break. I did, in fact. At one point, one of them asked me how I would feel if I were excommunicated, and I began to cry. Naturally, that moment became a full-page picture in *People* magazine, and prominently featured Teddie. The woman who should have been in that picture was Hazel. She is the one who, when there was no press around, comforted and sustained me. And has ever since. For loyalty, for love, for good sense, and for absolute reliability, no one in my life has ever outdone Hazel Davis Rigby.

Guarding the door was Brother Hattaway, who, though he is one of the most tediously sexist men in my most sexist ward, has a marvelous wife. He came to be known among us as the Avenging Angel, his crew-cut red hair standing on end like hellfire. As the trial dragged on hour after hour, he finally let some of the media people inside to get warm. They sat on the floor against the wall at the end of the hall. Several trips to McDonald's kept the group from starving to death, and no one left—five hours, and no one left.

Mike Redford-Holmes-Barrett* had arrived early to try to persuade Jeff to let me have a tape recorder, or him, or Rick, or someone in the trial with me. He promised Jeff that I would not request a copy of the tape—that, in fact, I would sign an agreement to that effect—but for the sake of any appeal, and for the purpose of checking among ourselves who said what to whom (fresh in Mike's mind was Jeff's recent broken promise), we needed a verbatim record of the proceedings. Jeff agreed. Mike set up the recorder, and came out to tell me it was all systems go.

Escorted inside by the Avenging Angel, I wondered how such a familiar building could seem so utterly strange, as in a dream when you know you are in your own house but nothing is familiar. The Sterling Park Ward meetinghouse is architecturally what might be most kindly described as "suburban tacky," the tasteless sort of building the church is now erecting everywhere. Except for the spire, it could be a ranch-style office building. Rapidly disappearing are the

---

* I asked Mike how he wanted to be portrayed in this book and he answered, "How about a cross between Robert Redford and Oliver Wendell Holmes?"

church's truly lovely and distinctive buildings, such as the Logan First Ward meetinghouse in which I spent so many hours of my youth:

A building with a sense of its sacred duty built in, and with a real pipe organ, gorgeous, real-wood wainscoting and paneling, a certain quiet dignity. And on the back wall, behind the choir seats and overlooking the whole, a large original oil painting of a pioneer woman in blue standing with a child near a covered wagon. A sense of history, of permanence, of continuity about everything, and a rich odor, which comes perhaps from its being structurally solid and built with fine materials.

There is also something symbolically right about climbing steps to go into a church, and about a balcony, from which one can look out upon it all with a sense of high purpose, of space, and of spiritual ease. A balcony from which, winter following winter, I watched the snow falling silently upon the rooftop. There is a spiritual depth possible in a room of the proportions of the First Ward's meetinghouse. It is a building that commands reverence, makes it natural and easy. I hope it survives the madness of the current meetinghouse and tabernacle destruction that has infected church leaders. They care too little about our spiritual need for beauty and for continuity; they seem to have little sense of history. If I still had any claim to that building in Logan, I would fight to preserve it.

But I would not raise a finger to save the Sterling Park Ward meetinghouse with its cheap panelings of assorted woods, its Masonite walls, its tinny little electronic organ, the whole complex sprawling without dignity like a wounded amoeba. Instead of beauty, serviceableness. No wonder the babies howl all the time they are in there and children fret and adults whisper loudly to one another and walk in and out all during services. That building simply cries out for irreverence.

The bishop's office is also a singularly undistinctive room: dark paneling, red indoor-outdoor carpet (in those days), some heavy chairs around the room, and a giant desk over at the right side as one comes in, with the headman's chair behind it. In that chair on the morning of November 17, 1979, sat Bob Andros, the man I had requested be replaced by some more objective scribe. On Bob's left, in a chair drawn up at the side of the desk, sat Jeff. On Bob's right, against the wall, sat Dick Brown and on his right, Steve Wilcox. The three members of the court rose and shook my hand when I came in, and as we went through the greetings, I scanned the room for the tape recorder. Everyone but me sat down. "Mike told me you had agreed to tape this meeting," I said to Jeff. "But I can't see the recorder. Where is it?"

"Let's begin with a word of prayer," Jeff intoned, ignoring me.

"I'd like to get everything on the tape, including the prayer," I persisted. "Let's turn the recorder on first."

Silence.

I began to understand. "You *are* going to tape this, aren't you, Jeff?" I asked. "The stake president told me I should tell you he said it was all right to tape it, and Mike said you had agreed. Are you going to allow these proceedings to be taped?"

Silence. I waited, and while I waited for him to answer, I took the first of many micro-naps. For a few seconds, I fell sound asleep standing up with my eyes open. It was a remarkable sensation.

Continued silence. I was in no hurry. I could wait. *They* were the ones in a hurry about everything.

Finally he spoke to propose again an opening prayer, which I believe we then had. Sometime toward the beginning of events, at least, someone offered a prayer. I do not remember who did it or what he said. Immediately afterward, I took up the question of taping again. "*Are* you going to allow this meeting to be taped, Jeff?" I persisted.

Another long silence. CIA men must be accustomed to asking, not answering, questions. I think, too, it must be one of their tactics to use silence as a wedge to pry open the mouths of others. I also suspect his mind was skittering about, trying to think of some reason that would satisfy me without telling me the truth. It seems that men in positions of authority in the church and other patriarchal institutions have an unwritten imperative never to level with women even if it may seem harmless to do so.

I waited patiently.

Finally he said into the waiting, "No."

"Why not?" I asked.

Silence. Another long wait during which I availed myself of another micro-nap. If this goes on much longer, I thought to myself, I'll be perfectly rested in no time.

Finally, "If we come to something I think needs to be recorded,

I'll turn on the recorder," he announced, and tried to begin the interview.

"Why not, Jeff?" If he wasn't going to be honest, at least let him squirm on the hook.

At this point, Dick Brown could not restrain himself any longer.

"You're not very trusting, Sonia," he smiled. I noticed again how it is always the men asking women to trust them.

"You men have not shown yourselves worthy of trust," I answered. What have you got to hide, I wondered silently, that you are afraid to record this meeting?

I repeated all that Mike had probably told them earlier about my signing over all rights to the tape. Dick muttered something about the freedom of information act. I told him Mike had assured me that that only applied to data that were government-connected. He was still doubtful. Perhaps he was thinking that such a tape could be subpoenaed, though he did not say this, and I did not think of it then. Whatever they were thinking and worrying about, I could not move them.

Jeff interrupted here and began to open the trial. I interrupted in my turn and gave each of the men a copy of my "Request for Extension of Time," asking them to read it before we continued. The men read it quietly. Dick finished first, then Steve, and then we all sat for five or six minutes while Jeff finished. When he finally looked up, the first thing he said was designed to dismiss the document and get back to beginning the trial. Dick, however, looking very troubled, said, "Bishop, I think we ought to consider this request seriously, if what it says is true."

"I never promised her I would give her more time," Jeff said quickly.

I leaped to my feet. "I won't go on with the trial another second without a tape recorder or someone in this room with me! Jeff is not telling you the truth. He *did* promise me more time, here in this office night before last, and again last night in my kitchen in front of my entire family. But who is going to believe what *I* say? Without a tape, without a witness, it will always be my word against his. Jeff is a man, and an important man, a man in authority, the *bishop*. And who am I? I am just a woman, without importance, without any authority. Who will ever believe my word against his? If someone in this room doesn't think about protecting *my* rights, I must refuse to stand trial!"

I was wide awake now, trembling with rage, and feeling physically as if I had been kicked in the stomach, hard. Jeff had lied—shockingly, unequivocally, egregiously lied, knowing I knew but not caring a damn about me, only caring about the *men's* opinions, knowing they would believe him before they would believe me. I was learning more about the Old Boys' Club than I wanted to know; it makes me feel ill even now to think about men's unity against women, and their assumption that God backs them in it, believing that God understands and approves since he knows how you have to treat women.

If the bishop could lie with such ease, what was to keep all these men from lying about me and about what happened among us there at that "trial"? Nothing, and I knew it; the knowledge dropped on my heart like a stone. So when they eventually did publish lies to the world about the trial, I was not surprised. By then, I knew them and how they rationalized their dishonesty. I knew they had lost the spirit of truth and were unworthy to call themselves disciples of the woman-respecting, gentle, honest, and courageous Jesus of Nazareth. By then I felt nothing but the sorrow of having said farewell to my fondest illusions. When Jeff lied that morning, something in me died finally and forever. We cannot pretend not to know what we know; we cannot will ourselves to trust in the face of treachery. Trust has to be earned.

Dick, at this point still fairer and less frightened than the others, suggested to Jeff, who sat dumbly and heavily as if his mind had been caught in a tar pit, that they excuse me from the room for a few minutes while they discussed my request, which to him seemed worthy. Jeff assented, and I left the room.

Out in the cold, unlit hall, the Avenging Angel was guarding the reporters sitting against the wall trying to get warm. They jumped up when I emerged and began calling questions to me over the flaming head of the Angel. He hastily ushered us all outside where the barrage of questions struck almost with physical force. "Is it over?" "What's going on in there?" "Have they decided?" I told them what had been happening, emphasizing the lack of due process for me, the fact that I was not allowed a tape recorder as Jeff had promised my lawyer, and that I was in there all alone with no one to verify my side of the story. I told them about the "Request" and how the men were now studying whether or not to give me a real trial. I did not tell them about Jeff's perfidy. I was ashamed of what that would say about my church. For the same reason, I did not tell them about the stake president's treachery. And also, I had not yet come fully to grips in my own soul with the implications of their spiritual pygmyhood.

When I was called back inside, I could see at once that my brethren were not happy, but I did not understand why until much later. They had decided, they told me, to give me an extension of time for my trial, time to get witnesses and to prepare my defense. I believe I have Dick Brown to thank for that decision. Again, I suggested December 1 as a good date. Jeff said he would have to make a decision on that later. Dick suggested that we have recorded in the minutes that this gathering had not been a trial,* but a "pretrial planning session." I laughed that we were instituting a whole new procedure in the church, we were making history. No one seemed greatly amused. I was so relieved, I could have laughed at anything.

"But," I pointed out, "I'm going to need to know specific charges against myself before I leave here, so my witnesses will know what they need to deal with. What matters worry you most?"

And so I organized us to get some charges pounded out. Jeff was worried that I had said in my APA speech that patriarchy had to go. "Jeff," I said, "that paper was a tangent; it is not the sort of thing I have said anywhere else or need to say again. I believe that what I said there is true, but I can promise never to say it again. [I had no idea then how basic this issue is and how totally unskirtable.] I repent of saying it. The only things I cannot repent of are what I say and do about the Equal Rights Amendment. Those, as far as I am concerned, are political matters and have nothing to do with my doctrinal beliefs or attitudes. And I stand firm in my belief that the church leaders must allow me the same constitutional right as they have to pursue my politics with freedom, even to the extent of opposing theirs."

He still seemed worried that I did not believe in patriarchy. I was

---

* Later, however, to make the real trial appear legitimate, Jeff wrote in his letter of excommunication, which the church picked up for the press release: "During two court sessions lasting over seven hours . . ." I had only one court session, and it lasted less than two.

surprised that he considered it a doctrine of the church; I could think of no place in scripture that said so. "But what does it matter what I believe if I don't say anything about it?" I demanded. "What if I just sit quiet and harmless not believing in it?" He was still unconvinced. In exasperation I said, "Jeff, as you sit up there on the stand Sunday after Sunday, if you could see into the heads of all the members of the congregation, if you could see what they *really* think, you would drop dead of shock. They just don't *say* it. And I don't have to again either."

But he did not want me to repent of that paper. He did not want to hear me promise not to berate patriarchy again. That was really the only ammunition he had. That, and that I prayed *in private*, in my own home, to Mother as well as Father in Heaven.

When the excommunication letter was published, one of the charges was that I did not believe that God has set up his work upon the earth in the way the church teaches. This obviously means that I do not believe in patriarchy. It means also that my repentance was not acceptable because they needed evidence to oust me before more Mormon women started thinking they could oppose the Brethren openly with impunity. Why didn't the men who wrote the press release have the courage to come right out and say, "You are excommunicated because you do not believe in the divinity of male supremacy"? Because, I think, none of the leaders of the church want widely understood either outside or inside the church that it is necessary to believe in the rule of men in order to be a member of the Mormon church. To the extent that the church begins to come down hard about patriarchy, members are going to begin waking up to what patriarchy really means, and realize that a belief in patriarchy is antithetical to a belief in equality, that one cannot rationally hold both beliefs simultaneously. The church, while beating its PR drums across the land in support of equality, might find it awkward to explain why, if they believe in equality, they are excommunicating people who will not accept males as God's only divinely chosen rulers.

For a similar reason, they made no fuss about my Mother in Heaven proclivities. It would not do to get members of the church thinking too hard about the anti-patriarchal implications of a Mother in Heaven, a god who rules in her own right, not through her husband, who is god first and wife second, and *is not a polyga-*

mous wife. To make the problems of patriarchy and Mother in Heaven worship overt in the church was to open several dozen cans of wildly writhing worms. So the men had to retreat into vagueness.

We talked in that "pretrial planning session" about my having supposedly told women in Kalispell, Montana, not to let the missionaries into their homes. Because I knew a videotape of that section of the talk had just been speeded on its way by Arlene, and because I knew I had neither said nor meant what they presumed, *and could prove it*, I agreed right away to that as one of the charges. My "Uppity Sisters" talk at the Utah women's conference distressed them, at least the UPI report of what I had said did, but this was easily disproved since I had read the speech word for word and also had tape recordings to prove I had not said that Mormon culture and especially church leaders were savagely misogynist (but even if I had, that hardly seems serious enough to cut a person off from eternal life, which is what the men believe they are doing when they excommunicate). The last charge was that I had caused people not to take the council of the president of the church seriously. I agreed to accept that as a charge because it seemed to me impossible for them to prove. In the first place, I did not and do not believe it is true, and in the second place, what evidence could they possibly produce to prove it?

But I still had not understood. They do not need evidence, they do not need proof; they would and could say anything they pleased without a single scrap of evidence, and the members of the church would believe it implicitly. I still did not comprehend that the sort of totalitarianism and utter disrespect for individual human rights and processes of justice I associated with countries like the Soviet Union was the system upon which the courts of the church—at least in my case—were working. I was too American to believe it could happen to me. I was too Mormon to believe it could happen in the very institution I had always trusted most to be fair and just and honest. I still thought that somehow my church would come through on the side of these principles, although it was clear that Jeff and Earl had failed their integrity courses along the way somewhere. I still thought that even though the men might eventually excommunicate me, they would give me a fair trial, they would be honest about why they had ousted me. I still had much to learn.

And all through the discussion of charges, because I had done everything I had done in the process of working for ratification of the ERA, all our talk centered around the Equal Rights Amendment. I told them repeatedly the central truth about me: that my entire effort was political in nature; that I was not in doctrinal opposition and had no interest in reforming the church except in its political outlook, and that I was willing to repent of anything that did not infringe on my political and constitutional rights to fight for the ERA.

I also made an effort throughout to help them realize that their problem, the church's problem, was not one little Virginia housewife. That getting rid of me would not solve anything. That I was a symptom of a very deep, very ancient, and increasingly painful disease in society and religion, and that unless they became aware of it and dealt with it in some sensitive, realistic ways, the problem of women in the church was going to intensify until it made the issue of black men's holding the priesthood look like a tea party. I tried to give them warning. But since none of them anywhere along the hierarchical line knew anything about the women's movement, except the stereotypes pumped out by the right wing, they did not understand what I was saying.

They will before very long.

At some point in that long, gray afternoon, I asked Jeff if the court were going to hear witnesses against me at the trial. Jeff and Dick exchanged a meaningful look and muttered something to each other like, "We probably won't be able to get any of them to appear."

What kind of people had my ward family become that they would vilify me behind my back but were too cowardly to face me? Perhaps it is because they had little to say. Is it excommunicable that at the end of a lesson about Ibsen, I kissed the book of his plays because he had seen women's condition so clearly and sympathized so deeply exactly one hundred years before I gave the lesson? Is it excommunicable that I wore an ERA scarf when I played the organ? That I wore my "Another Mormon for the ERA" button to church to counter their "Equality Yes, ERA No" hypocrisies? Is it excommunicable, in short, that my presence constantly reminded them that all was not well in Zion?

It took us four hours to establish the charges; four hours of talk about my ERA activities, in which context I had said and done all I had said and done that offended them. When we had finished, Jeff asked us to leave the room while he prayed to know what date we should hold the "real" trial. So we all filed solemnly out together and stood in the foyer of the church, making small talk while I would have given a good deal to have had my ear against the door. If I had, would I have heard him ring up heaven and say, "President Roueche, what shall I do now?"

After a dignified interval, he solemnly let us back in and announced that he had received an answer to his prayer. December 1 was apparently all right with God, the same place and the same time. I had not sat during this, and now prepared to leave.

"Uh . . . Sonia," Jeff began, "we think it is inappropriate for you to speak to the press about this. It is, after all, a private, sacred matter, which should remain between us and the Lord." (It was then that I realized they had been angry at me earlier because I had spoken to the press while they conferred about my "Request.")

"Jeff," I answered patiently as to a child (When would he realize that I would no longer allow him to define the situation for me?), "this may be a private, sacred matter to you, but it is *my* trial and to me it is neither private nor sacred. It is about the Equal Rights Amendment, which belongs to every American citizen. To me it is a public, political matter."

Dick, looking distressed, interjected, "But they won't understand. They'll make us look ridiculous."

"Why—are you doing something ridiculous?" I asked. "Dick, you can see that the media coverage on the trial thus far does not make *me* look ridiculous, and I am a Mormon. Reporters will probably also take my word for what happens in these meetings because so far I have been honest with them. If you deal honorably with me, I will tell them so. If you do not deal with me honorably, I will tell them so. It's entirely up to you. You can choose whether or not you look ridiculous."

They squirmed miserably at my having this kind of power over them, the power women should not have to make men behave decently toward them. Men should continue to be allowed, apparently, to do what they wish to women with impunity. But men are, in fact, going to have to learn in difficult ways that they have seriously underestimated us.

I knew by this time that the press was my only protection, my only leverage for a fair trial. The men's fear that I would reveal the kangaroo nature of the court remained my only protection against total villainy. Under heaven knows what immense pressures from above, Jeff was losing whatever grip he had had on morality. Even Dick was beginning to crumble at the thought of the Old Boys' Club having to take the unpleasant consequences of its actions. I silently thanked Hazel for the forty reporters outside the door in the cold, who would force the church at least to go through the motions of justice.

Outside, I faced the cameras, the poised pencils, the microphones with the joyful news: "It's four o'clock and I'm still a member of the church!"

Chapter 11

Interlude

I HAD WON a reprieve and I had not won it easily. (When someone at work asked a member of my ward what had happened in that first session to make it possible for me to emerge with the promise of a real trial, he is reported to have said simply, "She outfaced them.")

That bleak Saturday afternoon at the church, after the reporters asked their last questions and began packing up their equipment, Jeff suddenly appeared at the microphones. Without introducing himself, he made a thirty-second statement and disappeared as quickly as he had come.

"Who was that masked man?" quipped a woman from one of the networks. Reporters began shouting to one another, "Was that the bishop? What did he say? Did anyone catch what he said?" Very few had, and only a couple had reacted fast enough to snap a picture, which all the less-than-lightning-quick subsequently had to borrow. "Ask him to come out again," they begged the Avenging Angel in vain.

Standing over in the prayer service Georgia was so skillfully conducting, I saw Jeff flash out and back in and suddenly felt very tired. Rick, in a honeymoon trance, stood by my side, but was so thoroughly disconnected from my emotional life that it was as if we had never met. The group of ERA—and Sonia—supporters were singing, "Sonia is our hero," which made me feel silly, in a warm sort of way. Hazel and Ron and Alice, who had stood by valiantly all day long, were near and singing to me loudly. Everything was real—the people, the songs, the prayers. But I felt as if I were not a part of it, as if I were watching all this subsequent business from a great distance. Perhaps that is how people feel after fighting an intense and prolonged battle. Perhaps that's what battle fatigue is.

Afterward, Hazel and Ron stopped by the house briefly to offer whatever comfort they could, but they had their own family to worry about and soon had to go. My kids needed supper and talk and comfort and I could hardly move for weariness. I needed Rick to be a responsible parent, to get supper for the children, to explain things to them, to reassure them, get them settled for the night, and only then get his own needs met in Carolyn's arms. But he was rebelling not only against husbandhood but against parenthood as well—against all responsibility; a free, footloose teenager again, he leaped almost at once on his motor scooter and made for her house.

Well, boys will be boys, the patriarchy croons.

So will men.

And where was the Relief Society that terrible night? The women's organization whose motto is "Charity Never Faileth," and to which I had donated thousands of hours of my life? The Relief Society had been specifically organized to come to the aid of members. Like other Mormon women, I could not count the meals I had prepared over the years for others in need. And I was still a member of the church, had given a Relief Society lesson within the last month, had played the organ the week before in church. Where were my sisters? Not a single loving call, not a loaf of bread, not a card to say I'm sorry. There was a good deal of syrupy love talk in my ward in those days. Everybody, from the bishop on down, "loved" me. But no one said, "What can I do for you, Sister Johnson?" One of the most depressing discoveries of that whole miserable time was to find out what Jesus's gospel of love meant to my people. I was ashamed.

Even that night, when I was tired enough to die, and needing to find the emotional and physical wherewithal to care for my children, reporters never stopped calling. Finally I unplugged the phones, but before I did I had heard a dozen complaints about the bishop. "He wouldn't talk to me when I called," they all said, baffled. "And I can't figure out why not. How can I write a balanced story if I don't have his side of it?"

How could they be expected to understand the paranoia of Mormons, the absolute dead certainty in Mormon hearts that no one will ever understand us, that we will be misquoted, misunderstood, ridiculed—in short, that we will be persecuted. After all, don't the scriptures tell Mormons that in the last days—which these are—the Saints will be persecuted again as they were in their early history in this country? Yes. But the scriptures do not say why. They do not say that perhaps we Mormons will bring it upon ourselves by taking the wrong side on every human rights issue that arises; that by being anti-black civil rights, anti-female civil rights, anti-minimum wage, and so on, we cause justice-loving people everywhere to regard us with suspicion and disgust. No, we must believe it is because we alone are righteous. In denying blacks the priesthood for so long, in denying women a place in the Constitution, we alone are on God's side. We must expect to be misunderstood and must endure being persecuted for righteousness' sake.

I did not try to help reporters understand this and so much more that explains Mormon defensiveness. I just said, "I'm sorry the bishop won't talk to you. I'm sorry he won't tell you his side of the story, because when his side isn't represented, he is going to think you aren't being objective. It won't occur to him that you don't tell his story because he won't tell it to you."

That turned out to be a prophetic judgment. The next day, as Rick and Mike and I were talking in the library, the doorbell rang. My heart gave a mighty stroke against my ribs. The ominous doorbell again. And sure enough, in strode Jeff with dark and stormy brow, trailed morosely by Dick Brown. A very different Dick Brown from the warm and urbane man of the day before. We enthroned Jeff in the big recliner, Rick sat by the desk, and I sat between Dick and Mike on the couch.

They were horrified and infuriated about the press. The whole nation was full of it, and the church came off looking bad everywhere. They could not understand that a sorry state of affairs is bound to look like a sorry state of affairs. They did not understand that you cannot manipulate the media. Reporters are not stupid. They have eyes and ears and brains to register what they see and hear, and what they were seeing and hearing was an all-male body throwing out a female who refused to kowtow to their political commands. A patriarchy divesting itself of an uppity female. Regardless of all their attempts to convince the media otherwise, still to this day no one but Mormons, and only those Mormons who accept unthinkingly all statements made by church leaders, believe I was excommunicated for any reason other than my political opposition to the church.*

What struck the three of us most ominously about Jeff that day in the library was his almost total incoherence, his air of being about to fall apart. He was a man caught in a true dilemma, being pulled fiercely in two opposite directions at once. He and Dick had come in the hope that they could get me to stop talking to the press. Now that the Old Boys' Club was under fire, Dick had become a staunch member overnight. "How can you care about the church and at the same time talk to the press?" he asked me uncomprehendingly. In other words, how can you tell the truth about the shoddy business going on in the church when you have been trained from birth to protect the reputation of the church above all else? I told him I figured it was the church leaders' responsibility to look out for the church's reputation, and that if church leaders did not want sleazy things known about the organization, they should stop doing them, not try to shut up those of us who were reporting them. I reminded him that I had told nothing but the truth—and not all of that— about the pretrial planning session, and nothing but provable facts about the church's nationwide involvement in anti-ERA politics, and that being quiet in order to protect the church's reputation was as diminishing to my integrity as being unethical was to the integrity of the church.

He could not understand. As a staunch believer, he probably could not imagine the church leaders' ever going too far for him. Men have such an enormous stake in the Old Boys' Club. Which is the reason that the crack in the "protect-the-church-no-matter-what" system had to come from women. And explains why women will continue to be in the vanguard, not just in the Mormon church about civil politics, but in all churches' internal patriarchal politics. Not that there are not Mormon men out there who are livid about the church's anti-human rights stands and practices. But that women, being outside the system whether they know it or not, have so much less to lose. Nothing to lose, in fact, and everything to gain.

* In a way that I did not understand clearly at the time of my trial, but that the men obviously did on some level, anti-patriarchy and pro-equality are synonymous. Although I was sincerely willing to repent of my anti-patriarchal statements and promise not to make them again if that would pacify the leaders, eventually I would have had to break that promise. But when I offered to make it, I had not yet made that realization; I have come a long way in my excommunicated year.

Sitting in my study that day, Jeff began talking about the date of the coming trial as if it had not yet been set. "Just a minute, Jeff," I interrupted. "You have already set the date for the first of December."

"I never agreed on December first," he said.

I felt as if I were in the midst of a recurring nightmare. Frantically I turned to Dick, "You know he did, Dick," I pleaded with him to verify. "I went right out to the press and told them what had just happened inside, and what had just happened was that Jeff had agreed to postpone the trial until December first."

Dick sat stubbornly glum and mute. In desperation, I turned to Mike on my other side. He was obviously alarmed at this morally and emotionally disintegrating Jeff. "Jeff," he said, keeping his voice calm and reasonable. "Now that the eyes of the country are upon the church, you must act honorably. If you decide to have a quiet private little kangaroo court, you will do the church infinite harm. If you want to protect the church, act with honor and decency before the press. Stick to your word. Do what you say you'll do."

Then Jeff, in a rambling, disconnected way, began talking about how it was the bishop's prerogative to decide whether witnesses would be allowed at a trial, and that he was not sure he was going to allow any. Mike jumped into the breech quickly. "You *must* allow witnesses. You *must*—for the sake of the church's reputation—appear to give Sonia a fair trial. And besides, you have promised her that she could have witnesses. The press must not learn that you have broken another promise."

And then in his extremity Mike, who was serving as a local missionary at the time, had an inspiration. "Look, you guys," he argued, "you're making a mistake by not talking to the reporters who are calling you. This is a once-in-a-lifetime missionary opportunity. Be nice to them; they're only human, you know. When you treat them curtly and even rudely, as I've heard you have done, you can't expect them to give you sympathetic treatment. When they call, be genial; be warm; ask them what they know about the Mormon church. Offer to send them a Book of Mormon. You are being contacted by the major media persons in this country, an opportunity you won't ever have again. Do some good public relations work for the church. You can change the tone of the reportage about the church if you'll change your defensive attitude and treat reporters like friends, not enemies."

Rick and I seconded this proposal eagerly (both of us realizing it was a stroke of genius; Mormons have been urged by the prophet to work hard at bringing other people into the church). We urged Jeff to get his side of the story into the press coverage, to do his PR best for the church, assuring him that this could make a difference,* and testifying to him that one of the reasons the press was so sympathetic to me was that I assumed they knew their business and were trying to get as objective and as true a view of things as possible. That is all I ever hoped for: objectivity. Obviously, Jeff and other church leaders and members did not want objectivity. They wanted the press on their side, or silent. But this is not the way it goes. Not when you are not buying your publicity.

When they finally left, the three of us stared at one another in dismay for a few seconds. "Whew!" Mike finally whistled. "We're in trouble!" We discussed the very real possibility that a letter would soon arrive, late at night probably, ordering me to attend a trial immediately at some obscure place, and that whether or not I attended, I would be excommunicated on the spot. We had all been impressed that Jeff viewed his having allowed me off the hook again as a terrible misjudgment, and we supposed that his superiors were making that clear to him in no uncertain terms. And we were not at all certain that he had been deterred by our pleading with him to be honorable for the sake of the church and to become more skillful in handling reporters.

Mike figured I needed some kind of legal protection against being

* Reporters soon began telling me how dramatically the bishop's tone on the phone had changed. "He's downright jovial!" one of them whom Jeff had all but hung up on in earlier times related to me in amazement. Several others told me he had offered to send them Books of Mormon. Grateful as they were, they were all still disappointed, however, that he would not answer any of their questions. But apparently Mike had at least helped Jeff to stop viewing the church as a victim and himself as impotent. Jeff's new image of himself as chief Mormon evangelist *pro tem* to the media of America may have given him a feeling of control again. Perhaps he even thought—and if he did, it is merely because it is a typical Mormon way of thinking—that this situation may have developed just so the most important formers of public opinion could come to know about the only true church of God upon the earth. Whatever occurred in Jeff's psyche, he got a new grip on himself. I thanked Mike silently a dozen times a day as I hung up the phone from speaking to one reporter or another who had just been proselytized by Jeff.

hauled off in the middle of the night to face a secret tribunal, so he devised a document for me to hand to the bearer of the possible kangaroo court summons which required the stake president's signature, thus guaranteeing me a reprieve from instant ousting. I tacked it to the edge of my bulletin board and began waiting for the doorbell to toll. Mike called a couple of times a day to see whether I was still unsummonsed, and one night for some reason he came to the house himself and rang the doorbell. I was so tense from listening for that dread sound that I very nearly fainted. He left with firm instructions to call me on the phone before he ever decided to drop in again at night.

In a less direct way, Mike is probably also responsible that Jeff did not lose grip and try to get rid of me in the dark of night. If Mike had not been in the library with Rick and me when Jeff came to threaten me with a secret, soon, and witnessless trial unless I stopped talking to the press, I believe Jeff might have done it. But he cannot have been certain he could trust Mike to protect the Old Boys' Club no matter how low it stooped, as he knew he could trust Dick Brown. Mike has a streak of real love for justice and fairness in him, and I think Jeff sensed that. Mike had heard him mutter about media injustice, trial dates, and witnesses, and might go so far as to corroborate my story. I think Mike would have corroborated my story, and I believe he would have done so to the press if he had had to, though he would not have wanted to. Although he has a great stake in the Old Boys' Club, being an Old Boy, he has an even greater stake in his own integrity and in his opinion of Mike. Thank goodness for Mike. For many reasons.

On November 27 the arrival of another letter from Jeff, announcing that the trial would be held as agreed on Saturday, December 1, allowed me to breathe freely for the first time since the Sunday he seemed about to shatter in my library. Instead of being held at his office, however, as we had agreed, and during the day, the trial would be held in the Oakton stake center, beginning at 8:30 P.M. in the high council room, and would be "strictly held to one hour and thirty minutes."

When I read that last line, I knew conclusively that church leaders were only going through the formalities, the motions, of a trial for the sake of their media image. Such a strict time limit for a trial, which I had never heard of before, reaffirmed what I had suspected all along: the decision had been made and the leaders did not want to be confused by facts.

The second paragraph of the November 27 letter was especially interesting, in a grim sort of way. "During the last court session there was a good faith understanding that you would be sincere in prusuing [*sic*] in further court sessions those specific issues agreed upon. Your actions since that time and your statement to me that you are not on trial but that your cause is on trial violates [*sic*] that understanding. Your breach of this understanding prompts me to remind you that the purpose of this court is to consider your actions of the past several months and whether or not they have placed you in a state of apostasy."

I was genuinely puzzled by the accusation that I had not been sincere in prusuing [*sic*] the specific issues agreed upon. To every single reporter who asked me what the charges were, I recounted those we had agreed upon together in the pretrial planning session. I had no idea what "actions since that time" he was thinking of. I had never said or given any "good faith understanding" (and who was *he* to speak of "good faith understandings"!) that I would not say how I felt about my own situation to every reporter in the entire world and I certainly never told anyone—except perhaps Jeff, since he asserts that I did—that my *cause* was on trial, not me. I always knew I was on trial, but I also knew, and I never intimated in the pretrial planning session or anywhere else that I thought differently, that all I had done I had done in the context of the struggle with the church over the issue of ratification of the Equal Rights Amendment. If we had had a tape recorder in that first session, no one could have found anywhere that I agreed that I would not vigorously assert that this was the case. I believed it absolutely then, and I believe it now, though I understand the ramifications of what I was doing much more clearly now than I did then.

And then, after accusing *me* of changing the charges, which I had not, Jeff himself proceeds to change them, substituting a new all-inclusive charge I had not even heard mentioned before: apostasy.

The entire letter is an attempt to intimidate me, to cause me to doubt what really happened in that first session, to cause members and leaders of the church to think I had somehow violated a promise, an overt trust, which I had not. I understood immediately how it was intended to manipulate me and the opinion of anyone who read it, and I saw how Jeff, in fact, was doing precisely what he was accusing me of doing, while making it look as if I were the unethical one. It is a very typical patriarchal letter, a bullying, lying, blame-the-victim performance, turning everything topsy-turvy. If I had had any respect for Jeff or Earl Roueche or whoever else was involved by that time, it would not have survived that letter. But the most morally appalling letter was yet to come, and it would be the one the church distributed to thousands of media people, sent with missionaries door to door, and sprinkled like unholy water over the stiffening body of the church.

Rick left for Logan to be with Eric at Thanksgiving, to break the news of the divorce to Mom, and to bring her back with him to help me during the trial. Mike and Kris invited the children and me to their house for Thanksgiving dinner, along with another couple from the ward and the missionaries. When we arrived, none of the others had. I asked, "Where are the Thornleys? Where are the missionaries?" They both looked awkward and embarrassed. "They're not coming," I answered for them, "because of me." "Sister Thornley felt she just couldn't be here with you," they confessed.

I was sorry to have spoiled their Thanksgiving. But they were kind about it, and tried to take my mind off the missing celebrants. It was hard to stop thinking of Sister Thornley, though. She had been my visiting teacher. She had also been the cultural refinement teacher for the morning Relief Society, as I was for the evening, and we had often exchanged ideas and materials and taught for each other. I did not know then what I was told later, that one of my former best friends in the ward was encouraging my sisters to have nothing to do with me. Her father had once told her to shun all "enemies of the church." She was spreading the rumor that Kris, because of her association with me, was possessed of the devil, and that that was a definite likelihood for anyone who got too near me. Linda Andros, my visiting teaching partner, was very close to this friend and had called me a week or two earlier to tell me she could not go visiting teaching with me anymore because she had been "reassigned." At the time, I thought it was her husband who had persuaded her to shun me (and it is likely he did as well), but I think most of it was my "friend," my good "Christian" friend, who studies the scriptures constantly. (What has she learned from them?)

So my very conventional, very obedient, very anti-ERA, very role-oriented visiting teacher, Sister Thornley, would not join me and my innocent children for Thanksgiving dinner. But a few months later, I discovered that we were bound by more than held us apart: her husband also left her and her four children for a younger woman. I wanted to say to her, it happens to women on all sides of all issues. It has nothing to do with being anti- or pro-ERA, being a feminist or a traditional woman. It is the patriarchy at work, and it works against all women. It works even harder against you who are so loyal to it because it leaves so many of you unable to fend for yourselves economically, because it leaves you blaming yourselves, not knowing that men are just cashing in on the sweet promise of unending female arms outstretched to comfort them. Patriarchy says *all* women are commodities—not just feminists.

In this way, all women are bound to one another: we are all the objects of the same outrageous mockery of real love. But I am sure Sister Thornley still feels more loyalty to men than to any living woman, including herself, and is searching for another man to make it legitimate for her to live upon the earth. Because she thinks that not to be approved of by men means that she cannot survive in this world. The taboo is very deep and very powerful, and a cause of immeasurable suffering.

We had a glorious autumn that year; the weather was still beautiful deep into November. One afternoon while Rick was away in Utah, my five-year-old Noly and I took a walk down Hickory Lane and around on Youngscliff Road. The outer world could not have been less like my inner world that day. The sun was warm on the soft, lustrous pearl-gray branches, the sky was as blue as it gets here, a few hardy insects were making a last, harmonious foray into the shrubbery, and in my heart it was deepest winter. The blessed numbness that followed Rick's announcement barely a month before had long since worn off, and the reality of what I had experienced from the hands of my brethren in the gospel was like a gaping, throbbing wound in my chest. I was in constant physical pain, a pain-spill from my mangled emotions. Sometimes I felt that if I could not moan aloud, I would burst and die. But reporters were around much of the time, and when they were not at the house or on the phone, my children with their big hurt eyes wandered like lost souls around the house. So I did not moan, I did not cry. Day after day. Somehow I endured. The thought of Rick's laying the divorce on top of my mother's sorrow over the trial made me bite my lips to keep from groaning aloud, and I sometimes caught myself wishing she had died before she had to see any of this.

We met a couple of neighbor women, Noly and I on our walk, and all stood in the road in the sun and chatted. They commiserated with me about the trial, and asked whether there was anything they could do. I told them I would let them know if there was, and wondered what they would do if I suddenly started screaming and running amok, as I felt like doing. They did not know about Rick. Where was he, they asked politely. I told them, the skin around my mouth stretching taut as I tried to speak normally. A lovely walk on which I thought I might bleed to death. When we got home, I knew I had to begin dealing with the dammed-up emotions or they would burst through and drown me.

So late that starry, wind- and moon-swept night, I let myself out of the house and, with the wind whipping my coat against my legs, walked along the deserted roads and howled my anguish to the churning clouds and the crashing branches. Just wordlessly opened my mouth and howled. The immensity of the pain frightened me as it rose up and filled me again and again, as if I could never empty it all out no matter how loud or long I ladled it to the wind. I thought of King Lear howling his misery to the cold, rain-blasted heath. Betrayal, treachery from those we loved and trusted—we all have to howl about that, good king, or go mad.

Before the final notice of the excommunication, I got one other rare chance to grieve. On the evening of December 4 I had been on Tom Snyder's "Tomorrow Show" in New York and Connie Kaplan, an NBC employee, offered to walk me back to my hotel. Lonely and heartsick, I accepted with gratitude. The fifty-foot Christmas tree glowed outside the RCA building, so lovely there against the black sky that tears threatened to come to my eyes as I remembered my twenty Christmases with Rick. Of course, it took very little to bring tears in those days. It was a serious problem to keep from crying all the time. I wanted to cry unceasingly, until I was as bleached dry as a bone on the desert sand and my heart was as empty, cleaned out so it could rest.

Talking quietly and pleasantly, Connie took me across the street to watch the skaters down in the rink, and I began to relax the steely grip on myself I had had to achieve in order to do the show, and even slowed my steps so we would not get back to the hotel too quickly. Then I noticed with delight how the great lighted cathedral of St. Patrick's appeared suddenly to be leaning backward against the sky, preparing to leap into the air with a mighty whoosh, almost as if it were lifting off already and if you just watched a moment longer you would see it soar away into the night. Must be those flying buttresses, I thought, smiling inwardly. "Would you like to go inside?" Connie asked, noticing that I lingered near the steps. I hesitated for a moment—what had a Catholic church to say to me?—then, "Yes, I would like that very much."

Inside, it was dim and warm, with flickering candles, and the quiet, reverent rustling of two dozen or so worshippers. As we walked slowly up the aisle, I drank in the richness of the carved, arching ceiling, the colors and textures of the altar cloths, of the windows, of the images, the rich, civilized, intelligent complexity of it all. A compulsion to notice every detail came over me, as if I were seeing everything for the last time, like a person who knows that in a few hours she will be blind, with a deep and inexplicable sorrow saying goodbye. An odd impression, I thought at the time, not comprehending the power of that building as a symbol of the civilization into which I was born.

But that power soon overwhelmed me and to my alarm, I did begin to cry—hard—muddling matters by feeling as if I had to explain why right then to myself as much as to Connie. "None of this has ever really belonged to me," I wept, embarrassed but determined to express if I could the enormity of what I was just realizing. "None of this has ever really belonged to women. All the great church architecture, the religious art, music, poetry—Michelangelo, Mozart, Gerard Manley Hopkins—none of this has ever really belonged to us. As far back as we can see clearly into the past, the church has belonged to men. The worship, the music, the art, the poetry, the architecture—it was all *by* men *for* men. I thought it was for me, mine, this heritage, this precious thing we call "Western civilization." I thought I had a part in it, that it represented me. I have loved it so and been so proud.

"But the fact is that I have always been excluded from it, always outside it, always, as all women have. I have no history, I have no heritage, no civilization. Women have not left our mark on this at all; we have never really participated in it, been a part of it. It is as if we have never lived, millions of us, for thousands of years. Where are women's buildings, women's books, paintings, poetry, government? Where is our past? Where are our roots?

"It has all been deceit and illusion."

But though it has never been mine, says nothing about me, I felt unaccountably bereft saying good-bye to it that night. Who would have thought that saying good-bye to an illusion would make one feel so desolate? I grieved as I relinquished allegiance to the male world, which was the only world I had ever known, and stepped out forever onto the uncharted frontier beyond the definition of patriarchy.

Back in Virginia, my old friends in the ward would not come to my aid, so Arlene, who hadn't two pennies in her pocket, left her three kids and husband to their own devices and flew to my side from Kalispell, Montana, to answer the phone, sort out whom I should talk to, give directions for finding the house, help feed the children and read them bedtime stories, be with me in as much love and sisterhood as she knew how to give. Which is much. Having her here was pure heaven. She knew instinctively how to talk to reporters— friendly, sane, down-to-earth. Her instincts proved invaluable, especially the day the excommunication letter arrived. Arlene is one of the blessings of my life. In fact, so many people rose up to bless me in my travail that I could not help seeing, in the old Mormon way, the hand of God in all of it. As, in fact, I still do.

Rick brought Mother home with her huge, tortured eyes and quivering lips. And her consuming need for reassurance, for explanation, for understanding. The talks she needed drained the little energy I had left at the end of each day, and I felt I could not bear the weight of her grief and my own. She could not find comfort and would not take what comfort I could offer her.

Like many Mormons, my mother has a compartmentalized mind, and never the contents shall meet. In one compartment, Mom knew I had done nothing wrong; that in fact perhaps I had done a difficult and necessary thing for which God would bless me. In another compartment, even though she knew that the leaders of the church were doing precisely what I said they were doing and excommunicating me for saying so, she thought I should not reveal their political secrets. God would not like it, because God was president of the Old Boys' Club. No matter that I was telling the truth; no matter that my life was as free from sin as my mother could possibly wish, no matter that I had been prayerful all my life and even more so than usual through the entire business. I had to be wrong, because if I weren't, the leaders were, and not only wrong, but wicked on top of it for excommunicating me, and she could not face that—that they could be wicked. That they could make a mistake, okay—she was wise enough to know that, in one compartment. But that they could be unrighteous—no, she could not accept that.

Like many other Mormons, she could insist on a belief in equality as being a correct, God-ordained principle, and in the neighboring compartment believe that patriarchy is the only social organization acceptable to God. As long as she held these contradictory ideas in perfect balance, never letting herself see into them both at the same time, she was all right. It was only when something jarred her—like my trial—and she had to face the contradictions that she could not cope.

Orwell, in 1984, called it doublethink.

So night after night Mother wrestled with my soul and her compartments. I had no wish to hurt her belief in the church. I believed its doctrines myself. I simply wanted her to understand what I had been about so she could find some comfort. I wanted her to see that I was not trying to tear down her beloved church, that if it would stop fighting women, I would instantly stop fighting its politics. I tried to help her understand that I had done much that I had done, especially in my first innocence and trust, out of my deep love for the church and in an attempt to help it avert what I later recognized as its inevitable crisis over women's rights within and without the church. She could not believe me, because she had heard the church's anti-Sonia propaganda. Hurt and needing her comfort, not her constant condemnation, I finally asked her who knew my heart best, the church's PR department or me? The church's PR department or God? Did God take his directions from the PR department?

She could not understand that one can have a relationship directly with God without the leaders of the church as intermediaries. She could not understand that when the church leaders are angry, God is not necessarily so. She exhausted and depleted me. I needed, I *needed*, and for the first few days she could only take, and demand more.

But then the letters, which were pouring into the house at the rate of around 250 a day, began to do for her what I never could. When the greatest influence in your life has been public opinion ("what the neighbors think" as we always heard our folks refer to it at home), public opinion is all that can change your perceptions. And what my American neighbors thought, all over the nation, was that I was a heroine. It was not lost on her that the pro letters came from a generally more intellectual and professional group of people than the anti letters, and outnumbered them 95 to 1—until the "Donahue Show," that is, when the Mormon anti letters began pouring in; the "Donahue Show" deeply upset Mormons of a certain ultraconservative, anti-intellectual stripe.

So Mother opened as many as three hundred letters a day, writing me cryptic little notes on them—"bishop's wife"; "calls you Joan of Arc"—or underlining certain pithy passages. She began to feel much better, calmed and reassured. The rest of America did not think I was in a pact with Satan. It admired me. Mom basked in the praise, and our nightly, fruitless, exhausting conversations ended.

All the while, Arlene deftly fielded hundreds of phone calls daily, with warmth and good humor, and sat up most of the night writing everything down in her journal.

I have reason to remember one of those calls in particular. "This is Ben Franklin," the voice announced when I picked up the phone. "Sure it is!" I laughed, wanting to retort, "and this is Betsy Ross!" but restraining myself. "No, really. This *is* Ben Franklin, from the New York *Times*," he insisted, and then went right to the heart of the matter: "I think you *want* to be excommunicated." "Well, you're wrong," I told him honestly, and by the time he finished the interview, he knew he had been.

Michael Weiss, in his interview for *People* magazine, asked me the typical questions, and I answered them truthfully. "How would you feel if you were exonerated?" I answered (this is taken from his transcription of the recorded interview): "Very pleased. It would heal a serious breach in the church. And there really is one. I think that if I were exonerated, it would mean that it's all right to do what we're doing, to go out there and work for the ERA. It would mean the church leaders were tolerant of divergent political beliefs. It would be very healthy. I think it would be the best thing that could happen."

"What would you do if you were excommunicated?"

"I'd mourn a lot—" (I broke down sobbing at this point). "But I'd keep on doing what I'm doing. And I'd just have to accept that they made a mistake. It would be a grievous thing. I've told Jeff that if he excommunicates me, I cannot repent because I haven't done anything wrong. I'll be out forever." I didn't understand then, though I understand it very well now, why I should have to make a choice between my politics and my religion. "It's like trying to decide which child to save from the fire."

I mention these two typical interviews because after the excommunication, the church's PR department shipped tons of anti-Sonia propaganda to the wards and stakes of Zion. Foremost among the evidence of their moral rectitude and my vileness was a syndicated article by some man named Buchanan. The titles of this article varied from place to place: "Sonia, World Class Phony" I remember, but the one I am sure Jeff loved and which most church people saw was "Bishop Willis Is the Hero!" Buchanan asserts that I am lying, that I do not believe a word I'm saying, but that I'm such a good actress I have deceived every reporter in the country—not to mention all the media producers and talk-show hosts—but *him* (a trace of arrogance there). To the question of why was I taking such enormous trouble to do this, he provides this pseudopsychoanalytic answer: out of some deep-seated neurosis and misery, I have developed a positively voracious appetite for attention. And so I have aggrandized myself, made myself appear to be a martyr, while all the time I am chuckling inside, fairly lapping up and rolling around in the publicity.

Speaking of motives, I am puzzled in my turn about this Buchanan person's, not to mention the motives of the church's PR department. So far as I am aware, Buchanan is the only reporter who wrote about me without speaking to me—or anyone close to me—at all. Neither did he assign anyone else to do so. It must be much easier to pursue an ego- and Old Boys' Club-enhancing thesis at an uppity woman's expense unhampered by fact.

In all of America's media, his was the only voice that vilified me.* And his is the story the church's PR department broadcast like seed all over the church. His is the only non-Utah story in the files on my case in the Brigham Young University library at this writing. This is

---

* Alice has since informed me that Buchanan's sister—whom Reagan appointed U. S. Treasurer—joined the church a few years before my excommunication. Which perhaps explains Buchanan's extraordinary bias.

the church whose leaders "love" me, the church which preaches that "the glory of God is intelligence; that is, light and truth."

I am ashamed of the lack of charity among the leaders of my church.

The two weeks between trials passed very quickly.

Linda Sillitoe and Kathryn MacKay (who took Jan Tyler's place at the last minute because Jan was being harassed by her doctoral committee at the University of Utah for her political outspokenness) arrived from Salt Lake City, and the night before the trial they and Arlene and Mother and I sat in the library, at the end of the interlude. Back in Salt Lake, Linda wrote this about it:

NOVEMBER'S END, 1979

Five women talking
church and politics
(religious politics)
in a room lit yellow
in a Virginia woods.

We laughed at the disaster
that hadn't happened
yet and held our breaths.
Suddenly through the window
a vast current of dark

swept in on us, a flood
of event dry as dark air.
I floated out on that tide
and peered back from miles out.
I saw us there, all of us,

women in a yellow room,
and me seeing not the future
but us where we were,
like dew on a slick leaf
in the murmurous night.

Chapter 12

Trial in a "Court of Love"

"I MAY NEVER feel warm or be able to sleep soundly again. It's the wee hours of December 2, 1979; I huddled in a waterbed in the spare room of the Johnson home feeling outraged. Wide-eyed and trembling, I have come to the living room to sit and write out my desperation to find some sense in this night."

Thus wrote Arlene in her journal.

"December 1st was what is called a 'media event.' Translate: chaos. I plugged in the phones at 7 A.M. and they never stopped ringing until I unplugged them before *attempting* to go to bed. Press all over the nation wanted 'comment.' The only words I could think of were 'rotten' and 'un-Christian.' Sonia, however, stuck to politics and took call after call, often speaking live over radio broadcasts from coast to coast. Once again I was struck by her dignity and strength. She did weep, but only when friends were able to cut through the clog of press calls to offer her their love . . . or when her mother wrapped concerned arms around tired little shoulders.

"There were TV cameras and microphones dragged in and out all day long. Noel looked tiny, somehow smaller than his five years, as he stepped through a maze of cables and tripods to stand waiting for a word with his mom. A 'Can I go to Kevin's house?' could mean a half hour's wait to Noly. 'Shhhhh, your mom's on a live news broadcast, Noel. Can I help you, dear?' He'd shake his head no and wait. Kari and Marc were less resolved, Marc running through the day in hyperactive petulance, Kari . . . that girl is furious, wounded! Her pain seeps out sullen, the fury sarcastic. It is this lovely young woman who worries me more than anyone else in this home, and as I watched her all day my eyes welled with tears and my throat tightened. To think *religious* leaders—*my* religious leaders—have brought all this agony down on the heads of a family makes me feel murderous.

"CBS was the last news team to interview before time to leave. They decided to follow us all to the stake center for the . . . (I *refuse* to call it a 'trial'! It was a kangaroo court, pure and simple; a ridiculous charade by nasty men hoping to convince the public they are *loving*, caring 'men of God.'). I suggested Kari and I ride in the CBS camera van, with the two cameramen. Partly I knew it would be easier than all of us (Sonia, Rick, Mrs. Harris, Marc, Kari, and I) cramming into one car, but also I hoped to give Kari my ears and undivided attention, ease her tension—maybe even make her smile—in the remaining hour before her mother was drummed out of the religious community that has been so large a part of this family's life. And Kari and I did laugh as we rode in back of that van . . . about me in a tiny pair of Noel's mittens because I hadn't brought mine from Montana, about the cameramen's conversation, about a lovely (if spooky!) young woman from Atlanta who had somehow located Rt. 1, Box 233 and was *following* the CBS van.

"The men in front were talking about how that Atlanta beauty could follow *them* anytime and then suddenly ended up in a bizarre debate over brands of doggie treats! I said to Kari, 'Isn't this a letdown? I mean, here we are, riding around with network news and the only inside scoop we get is one guy's dog likes Bonz while the other guy's pooch prefers Milk Bones!' Kari laughed, but she also said, 'Well, those two are stupid men. News is stupid. This trial is stupid. The whole Mormon church is stupid. And Noel's mittens look stupid on you!' I thought she was about to cry, hoped she'd cry. She didn't. Without tears I didn't feel I could hold her. . . .

"I wasn't prepared for the eerie atmosphere at the stake center. We knew beforehand that the Mormon structure, so like every other Mormon structure from coast to coast, would not be open to the crowd that was congregating outside. But I hadn't expected darkness, the black windows. The Unitarian church next door had thrown its doors open as a place all of us could warm ourselves during the waiting, the hoping. And the bright Unitarian lights only served to dramatize the blackout at the Mormon church."

How did I get dressed that day? What did I wear? Did I fix my hair, wash my face, brush my teeth? Who fed the children? Did I eat? I don't remember.

I *do* remember that the night of December 1, 1979, was moonless and bitterly cold. When our car pulled into the drive of the Oakton, Virginia, stake center at about 7:30 P.M., a great shout went up from the hundreds of people—mostly non-Mormon feminists, female and male—gathered on the front lawn, their flickering candles making the whole scene shadowy and Halloween-like. Media people separated themselves from the throng and swarmed down upon us. By the time I stepped from the car, they were waiting expectantly with their microphones poised, so I read the statement Mike had prepared for me, which expressed his total belief that in the end President Kimball would come to my rescue:

"It has been my constant prayer these past weeks that Bishop Willis and President Roueche will be inspired to decide this matter in accordance with God's will, and exonerate me of these charges. I am, however, confident that the Prophet will—if necessary—step forward at the proper time to vindicate me, and to vindicate the constitutional rights of *all* citizens to exercise their political rights as conscience dictates, without fear of religious repression."

What does it mean to Mike that President Kimball did not step forward? That he never deigned to see me or speak to me personally or even to write to me?

I remember little clearly about the next half hour, except that I answered dozens of questions from reporters who arranged themselves in a semicircle before me, their lights blinding me, the whole scene surrealistic and haunting. The singing of those keeping vigil sounded far away, like an echo, and ERA banners, seemingly unattached to the earth, swayed behind reporters' heads like ghosts.

At eight o'clock I left the group and walked up to the shadowy front door. It was locked. Pressing my face against the dark glass, I peered in. All was pitch black inside. I was nonplussed, and stood uncertainly, wondering whether I was expected to knock. Arlene cherishes that picture of me not being able to get into my own trial.

In the meantime, however, Rick and Ron had been checking entrances to find a way to take the video equipment in. They found Lorin Jensen blocking an open side door, and when he refused to let

them in after they stated their purpose and asked permission to
enter, they simply ignored him and pushed past. As I stood in-
decisively at the front door, someone came running around the
building to tell me the side door was open. Rick and I were both
summoned to enter, and I realized that they were going to allow him
to be in the trial with me. With the press of the nation standing at
their door, they did not dare totally refuse me due process.

We were led to the high council room. I shall never forget the
effect that room had upon me as I entered.

Three high-backed armchairs arranged side by side in front of a
huge desk. Behind the desk, Jeff sat with Dick and Steve at either
side and Bob at a table appropriately on Jeff's far right. At the back
of the room, by the window to the courtyard where the watchers had
assembled to hold a prayer vigil for me, sat Marvin Poulton, a member of the stake presidency.* ("What is he doing here?" I wondered.
"This is procedurally incorrect.")

The men in front rose in slow motion as Rick and I entered the
room. In the century before anyone spoke, all my senses were registering the intimidating components of that room. The layout alone
said everything. If it had been a stage set, the audience would have
known as the curtain opened that there was no hope for me. And the
feeling in the room smote my heart with despair, the feeling of men
about to assert their divine right to supremacy. It hung in the air like
a bad odor, as palpable as smog. They meant this time not to let me
slip through their fingers.

In that century as we all faced one another wordlessly—which
must have been only five seconds—I felt the fight go out of me; I felt
stupid with fatigue. It was no use struggling—I had lost long ago. I
had lost when I decided to be a human being and not a role. I knew
as we stood there that those hopeful witnesses had come long distances in vain, that their words would not be heard, that nothing

---

* Mormon males have taken very much to heart Joseph Smith's pronouncement
that "the glory of God is intelligence." The CIA, FBI, and MI are full of them.
Intelligence of the latter sort was well represented in the courtroom that night,
though there was precious little evidence of that sort Joseph Smith had in mind.
The Avenging Angel, who escorted us into the room, was an FBI agent; Jeff, presiding, worked for the CIA (in personnel then; he was reassigned when after
the trial numerous complaints were sent to the Director about a chauvinist of
his stripe working in personnel), and Marvin guarded our dangerous backs as be-
fitted a brave officer in the Military Intelligence.

anyone could say or do would stop the patriarchal wheels from grinding me to dust.

I shook hands grimly all around. The men met my eyes with a quiet confidence bordering on exultation. It seemed obvious that they had been receiving strong bolstering and guidance from above—and I do not mean heaven. They felt very secure and certain sitting there. They knew their duty, and they were going to do it. "My church—my club—right or wrong!" might as well have been branded in neon on their foreheads.

"I will see the patriarchy in full regalia tonight," I sighed to myself. As soon as we sat down, I scribbled a note to Rick: "It's thumbs down, isn't it." Not a question; a statement. Rick agreed with a nod. I tried not to resign myself, not to give up, tried to think how to turn them from their purpose. But I was so tired. There were no reserves left. I was totally drained, numb. From the great distance of acknowledged defeat, I watched the men go through their performance.

Jeff began by asking someone to give the prayer. Again I do not remember who, or what he said. I do remember thinking that I was the one who should be offering the prayer there that night, as I had—ostensibly, at least—the most to lose. (All along, however, I had had moments of clarity when I knew that though I might lose this battle, I would win the war, because the church's taking up arms so openly against women was a mistake of incalculable proportions.)

After the "amens," Jeff stood to read the charges against me. In my appeal to the stake president several weeks later, I wrote:

"The agreement made at the hearing of November 17th was breached when additional, previously unstated charges were introduced at the hearing on December first. These charges included subjects as diverse as family preparedness and something about a new gospel which makes women incredibly happy. Never having heard them before or since, and never having seen a copy of them, I can only say that I recall that there were many and that I was very surprised to have them appear suddenly at that time when I could not prepare a defense against them, or even understand them fully. They served only to confuse the witnesses and myself, and to divert our testimony away from the real issues. This error was particularly egregious in light of the time restraints placed on the hearing."

Linda Sillitoe interviewed the witnesses afterward. In her report for the January 1980 *Utah Holiday* she wrote:

"Each witness was read the charges from a single, typed sheet, prefaced by an all-caps heading: any mention of the Equal Rights Amendment was prohibited, and witnesses would be excused [asked to leave] if they spoke about it. The charges seemed unfamiliar to most of the witnesses . . . 'There were several questions included in each charge,' recalls MacKay, 'many adjectives, many qualifying phrases.'

"Johnson was informed that she was charged not only with hampering the church's worldwide missionary effort, but with damaging other church programs, including temple work, the welfare program, family home evening, genealogy, and family preparedness (food storage). Witnesses were unprepared to assess Johnson's impact on this panoply of church programs."

Maida told Linda she tried to find out specifically what the false doctrine charges were, and (now I quote from the *Utah Holiday* article again) "guessed that there might be some reference to the APA speech, 'Patriarchal Panic.'

" 'She's not on trial for her speeches,' Withers quoted Willis as responding.

" 'Well, then,' Withers returned, 'is she on trial for her activities in the Sterling Park Ward?'

" 'No.'

"Withers tried again. 'Sonia, have you ever addressed any gospel issue in your speeches?'

" 'Not to my knowledge,' Johnson said.

"Witnesses said the charges were difficult to address according to the rules of the court. Witnesses may testify only from firsthand experience and information. Each had come prepared to deal with her or his own experience in hearing Johnson speak, observing the audience, and analyzing their own impressions. They could not speak to influence on members and nonmembers nationwide, assess hindrance to worldwide programs, or address the charge of false doctrine when, in their experience, she had not been speaking in a religious context. In every case, the context was the Equal Rights Amendment, and that they could not mention.

"Each left feeling frustrated and ineffectual."

Maida had asked to be my first witness, to establish the background against which I had done all I had done. She had just begun to read her statement when Jeff interrupted to remind her of his instructions not to mention the ERA. "I'm trying to explain the context in which Sonia acted," she argued. "How can I not refer to the ERA?" And she went ahead with what she had written for a few sentences until Jeff interrupted her again, very annoyed and imperious this time, and told her that he would have to tell her to leave the room if she persisted in talking about the ERA. "I am not talking about the ERA," she insisted, "I am talking about Sonia. It is impossible to talk about any of her actions as they pertain to the church without mentioning the ERA."

"You are forbidden to mention that word again before this court," he said with great finality.

I thought of John Bailey's statement, of Teddie's, of Esther Peterson's, of Mother's, and I knew none of them had a chance before this court, that they would not be allowed to say what they wanted to say and what needed to be said. Besides, time was passing very quickly. Maida's struggle of wills with Jeff had taken up much of it. So, mentally and with sadness, I crossed four witnesses off my list.

Months later, when my appeal of the excommunication was before Earl Roueche, Maida wrote him a long letter, listing eight ways in which she considered the trial faulty in procedure and intent. Numbers 6 and 7 of these were:

"No formal written charges were given to Sister Johnson or any of her witnesses until the trial was actually in session, even though there had been an extended pretrial meeting where these charges were solidified. Understanding of the complexity of the charges and of the eventual examples cited by the bishop was essential for a meaningful trial to take place. This lack of clearly defined charges demonstrated to me, as a witness, a clear lack of integrity and sincerity on the part of the court in addressing these charges. Consequently, as a witness, hearing a one-page list of charges read to me for the first time as I sat before the judges made serious and thoughtful treatment of the issues totally impossible. Serious dialogue between the judges and the witnesses did not occur.

"The charges read to the witnesses at the trial were not those published by Bp. Willis in his public statement regarding the excommunication of Ms. Johnson. Also, the examples listed in Bp. Willis' excommunication letter were not cited in the charges during the trial.

Therefore, the witnesses were overwhelmed and quite unable to respond effectively since we did not really know what the bishop was looking for. There was a definite 'hidden agenda' at the trial. For example, the first charge (negative effect on church programs) did not spell out the missionary program specifically as it did in the excommunication letter. The charge at the trial listed missionary work along with genealogy, temple work, family preparedness, etc. It was like looking for a needle in a haystack. How were we to know they were only looking for her comments on 'missionary work' in her strategy session on lobbying in Montana?

"As witnesses, we felt as if we were testifying on her behalf hoping to land, if only by accident, on a concern of the court. I feel witnesses were allowed to testify only because Ms. Johnson insisted. There was no indication during my testimony of sincere interest in finding out the truth of the matter. This has been the motivation for some to say it was a kangaroo court and was the reason Ms. Johnson felt defeated and the calling of further witnesses to be futile."

When I appealed Jeff's decision to him, Earl Roueche held a secret high council court for me, to which I was not invited and about which I had no knowledge at the time, a procedure that openly flouts Mormon scripture (Doctrine and Covenants 102:13 and 18): "Whenever this council convenes to act upon *any* case, . . . in *all* cases the accuser and the accused shall have a privilege of speaking for themselves before the council. . . . After the evidences are heard, the councilors, accuser and accused have spoken, the president shall give a decision. . . ." The beauty of being a reigning member of the Old Boys' Club is that you can change the rules of the Club at will.

After Maida, Ralph Payne, a psychologist I first met at the APA convention, testified. He told the court that "non-church members present at the speech felt that her reactions were not strong enough. In fact, during the question-answer session, after the papers, one person in the audience asked why these women did not 'cast a vote with their feet' and walk out of or leave their churches. Their reply (including Dr. Johnson's) was that their churches and beliefs meant too much to them to abandon. . . . While some non-church members present seemed to feel the actions of Dr. Johnson and others in Mormons for ERA were at best mild reactions, the response of the members present at the symposium was unanimously positive. The church provides no forum for such open discussion. The issues needed to be raised and discussed without the suppressing effects of heresy accusations. After the paper session, several church members spontaneously gathered to continue the dialogue on the issues she raised."

Then he said what hundreds of others would later write: "Damage has been done to the Church's reputation, but it certainly has not been done by Sonia Johnson; it has been done by the convening of this trial."

A day or two later, he wrote me this letter:

"I must admit that the trial experience was a surprisingly harrowing one. Prior to coming in to your stake center, my anxiety level was quite low (maybe .5 on a scale of 0–10). It hit 2–3 while waiting, then shot up to 10+ when I actually entered the trial room. I am sure I did not realize the seriousness of the situation until then. The feelings of responsibility to say whatever would be helpful for you were intense. Your suggestion to write something in advance was probably the only thing that kept me from being mute with anxiety. (Even doctoral orals were not as frightening.) You have my deepest sympathies over what you have been through recently. Having only experienced five minutes' worth, I can't imagine how you have managed it for such a long time!"

The next witness was a woman from Utah who wanted to be among the witnesses because she had heard me speak both in Provo and Salt Lake. But she wished her identity to remain secret because she feared losing her job. Knowing just exactly the correctly humble and deferential tone to take with Mormon males, she was the perfect witness. I watched her in stunned amazement get those egos in the palm of her self-deprecatory little hand, and was grateful that she was willing to do what I could no longer do for any reason: play the male–female, master–servant game which so many Mormon men so much need for their egos, and without which they do not know how to relate to women at all.

The content of her statement was also unerring. She told them she taught young Mormon women in a special program for the intellectually gifted at a church-owned institution. Many of these young women, she said sadly, feel as if there is no place in the church for them, as if the church wants only women who are willing to sacrifice their talents and intellectual capacities to full-time wife- and motherhood, which they were not willing to do, and that this made them unacceptable as "real women" in the church. "These young women are not dispensable," she cautioned.

"But," she continued, coming to the point, "for the past year and a half, I have been able to say to these troubled young women, 'If there's a place in the church for Sonia Johnson, there's a place for you.'" Here she paused for effect and got it. "Bishop Willis," she asked, "what am I going to say to them if you excommunicate Sonia?"

If she had stopped then, she would have left the prosecutor-judge very unsettled and impressed against his will. But sensing her advantage, she pressed it too far by pleading, "Please don't turn this into a witch-hunt!"

The conciliatory mood she had established in the room disappeared on the instant. Although I could sense that something had gone amiss, Rick had to explain to me later what it was. "She shouldn't have reminded those men of witches," he told me, and went on to explain. "Men are basically very much afraid of the spiritual powers of women; that's why they try to keep them from discovering them, from using and developing them—cut them off from the priesthood, set themselves up as women's spiritual leaders. When she said 'witch-hunt,' out of the slime of womanfear in their unconscious slithered the specter of *women in power over men,* and they instantly united against their age-old enemy, woman; woman as mysterious, woman as witch, woman as powerful, woman as god. I know," he concluded softly, "because I felt it in myself when she said that word, and I looked up quickly and saw what I was feeling pass simultaneously over the faces of the four men seated before us."

Even without the "witch-hunt" she could not have saved me, of course, but she might have left those who had set themselves up as my judges longer in nagging uncertainty about the wisdom of their verdict. Still, she was wonderful, and her act—for I hope it *was* an act—a grim reminder of all that lies ahead of women in establishing ourselves as adult human beings who do not need to fawn and grovel and coax and coo in order to be allowed to function in the world.

My last witness was Kathryn MacKay, niece of the regional representative, Julian Lowe. Earlier that evening, at dinner with her aunt and uncle, she had asked her Uncle Julian whether it was true that Gordon Hinckley had come out to Virginia the year before, and whether the Virginia LDS Citizens' Coalition had been organized under his very direct supervision. "Uncle Julian," she asked, "is Sonia telling the truth about that?"

"Yes," he answered.

Kathryn was calm, soft-spoken, and direct, refusing to play the Mormon male-female power game—or perhaps, like me, she has forgotten how. I felt more comfortable with her, though I knew that by refusing to be obsequious, she was not influencing the men much. They do not know how to hear female human voices (womanly), just female "role" voices (feminine—which is a male definition of women and not truly female or womanly at all). With Kathryn, they could not hear any of the voices they understand in women: coy, meek, hesitant and uncertain, blame-taking, self-depreciatory, reassurance-and-approval-seeking voices.

Linda wrote in *Utah Holiday:* "MacKay explained the association with Johnson that brought her to the trial to testify and cited her as 'an inspiration.' 'She gives me hope that I can work through issues within the structure of the LDS Church, because she has managed to do that so effectively herself.' "

Kathryn finished at 10 P.M., the time I had been preemptorily informed the trial must end. So I was surprised when Jeff asked if I wanted to call any more of my witnesses. When I saw the excommunication letter, however, I understood the strategy: "During two court sessions lasting over seven hours," Jeff wrote, modifying the truth as he went along, "your witnesses were heard and your evidence presented to your acknowledged satisfaction."

Very misleading, that sentence. In the first place, as I have pointed out, I had only one trial session, and it lasted less than two hours. In the first meeting with the bishop and his counselors on November 17, I had no witnesses and presented no evidence whatever, because there were no charges. In fact, I refused to be on trial *because* I had no witness in the room with me, no witnesses to testify for me, and had had no time to prepare any evidence.

In the second place, neither my witnesses nor my evidence was heard to my satisfaction in the one short trial I had. I decided against calling the other witnesses because the court was refusing to hear testimony, not because I felt all had been satisfactorily heard. Refusing to allow even the few witnesses we managed to squeeze into the very limited time to talk about my beliefs, my motives, my behavior, is evidence to me that no one in that court wished justice to be done.

Because I knew further discussion was futile—my witnesses were not being allowed to speak about anything relevant to the case, and the atmosphere in the room was oppressive enough to discourage human life—I told Jeff no, I did not want to call any more witnesses.

He reminded me of the videotape and equipment I had brought. I told him that in the interest of time (and life—how long can one survive such hatred?) I would simply tell them what was on it. And so I explained how I had come to be speaking to a group of sixty NOW members in Kalispell, Montana, the August before. Feminists in Montana had fought a desperate but ultimately successful battle against the Mormon-led recision attempt in their state, and though they had won, they were frightened about future attempts. "What can we do about our Mormons?" they wailed. I reminded them that the church had chosen politics and could not now expect to be without opposition in that arena, that it could not expect to hide behind its ecclesiastical skirts and say, "Don't touch us; we're a church. And if you *do* touch us, we'll yell 'persecution!'" I told them that I knew positively that the church had organized political action lobbying groups in many states, and that they should therefore not feel nervous at all about confronting the church politically in any way they ordinarily confronted other political opponents. "The church needs some reality therapy. They need to get feedback from you," I said. I reminded them how important the church's image is to Mormons, how much money the church spends yearly in looking wholesome— as if they had invented the family and are the only people in the world who value it (which of course is total nonsense). "They care about your opinion."

Here is the direct quote from the transcript of the videotape: "The leaders of the Mormon Church are somewhat isolated in Utah. Those who are directing this anti-ERA activity need a taste of the consequences of their behavior, and one of the things everyone can do is write and call church headquarters and say, 'I am outraged that the Mormons are working against my equal civil rights, and if your missionaries ever come to my door, I wouldn't consider letting them in.'

"That's political lobbying, pure and simple," I pleaded vainly with my prosecutor-judge and his cohorts. "Lobbying is deal-making: you have something I want, I have something you want. Let's make a deal. The church wants women to join the church, women want the church to unhand the ERA. Women should therefore say, 'If you'll listen to us, we'll listen to you.' That's political. That's lobbying. And the church is training members to lobby all over the country. How can it not expect to receive the same treatment?

"This is not an attack on missionary work. I wasn't talking religion. I was telling women who want legal reform one of the very few ways I believed they could put pressure on a powerful political opponent to get it to sense the enormous amount of negative public opinion it was creating with its anti-human rights activities. I wanted them to let the church know it could not fight against justice for women with impunity—just as they would let STOP ERA know. Women have a right to share political information and strategies about political enemies; it is not our fault that the church has chosen to be our political enemy, but it has, and it must take the consequences of having done so."

But Jeff and the Club leaders were not to be deflected from their goal by facts. Who was stronger, they or this one little woman? They simply could not lose face to the world even if it meant losing thousands of potential converts and members—which it has. Face, as I have learned to my disgust, is the highest value in the Club.

And so, after testifying emphatically, as Rick can affirm, that I did *not* believe missionaries should not be allowed into people's houses, that I had no desire to hurt missionary work and could not if I wished—how much power their fear credits me with!—that I was talking about political strategy *only*, that I had not done it since and if they asked me not to, never would again, Jeff wrote in his version of the trial, the excommunication letter: "You testified that you believe and have taught that missionaries should not be allowed into people's homes."

The second offense I was charged with from the pretrial planning session was supposedly saying, in my "Uppity Sisters" speech in Salt Lake, that "Mormon culture, specifically including church leaders, has a savage misogyny," which was the quote the UPI stringer mistakenly credited me with. Again I referred them to my speech, which they had a copy of, in which I say instead that "the pedestal, more than any other symbol, reveals our savage misogyny . . . It reveals society's attempt to render [women] nonhuman . . ." I pointed out that I had read this straight from the paper, that it had been taped by several people, and that it was inexplicable to me why they persisted in believing their misquote of the UPI misquote over evidence that proved without doubt that I had never attributed "savage misogyny" to either church leaders or Mormon culture.

At this point one of the other two, Steve or Dick, leaned forward intently, looked sternly at me, and asked, "But *do* you believe church leaders have a savage misogyny?" I wondered, "Am I here on trial because of what I *think* or because of a public statement I am supposed to have made?" And hadn't Jeff told Maida that I wasn't being tried on my speeches? It was all too confusing. But I answered, something about sexism being like polluted air. Everyone breathes it; no one is exempt. "Are you saying, then," he insisted, "that church leaders have a savage misogyny?" "No more than any of the rest of us," I answered, "but in a sexist society—in a sexist world—they are not immune." "Then you are saying that the leaders of the church are misogynists?" "I did not single them out publicly; that phrase was meant to indict society in general. I did not even imply that it was directed at them, because it was not." "*Are* they misogynists?" he persisted fiercely, and I could feel the teeth of his will tearing into mine. Why is he doing this, I wondered, unable to believe that information extracted from me like this could become another and new charge. "*Are they?*" "Yes," I said quietly. And the look of triumph on their faces was a wonder to behold.

Entrapment is bullying, and bullies are cowards.

And so it should not be hard to extrapolate what Jeff wrote in the excommunication letter: "You testified that you believe and have *publicly* stated [italics mine] that our society, specifically including church leaders, has a savage misogyny; when, in fact, it is church doctrine that exaltation can be gained only through the love that results in the eternal bonding of man and woman."

The illogic and double-talk of that statement is exceeded only by its total lack of truth.

(Later, when I appealed the bishop's decision of excommunication to President Roueche, I wrote: "During the bishop's court proceedings, I was asked if I believed church leaders shared in society's misogyny; that is, if they were influenced by our cultural bias against women. I answered that I thought they were not immune to such influences. I do not, however, believe that that constitutes either a public statement or an attack on church doctrine, and I believe our church leaders would be the first to acknowledge that we are all, themselves included, able to improve ourselves in this respect. I reiterate: I never publicly stated or implied that church leaders specifically have a savage misogyny. I believe my actual statements were historically accurate, and are in no way intended as an attack on church doctrine.")

The court was concerned that I was leading people astray. I protested that I was not leading anyone, that I had no following and did not wish to have one. Just as I was finishing this protestation of innocence, the group outside began to sing, as if cued: "Sonia is our leader, we will not be moved!" Rick and I looked at each other and smiled for the first time that night. The five threatened gentlemen in the room would not have believed me anyway. They only understood power in terms of constituents or backers. I think they have little understanding of personal power, which is not power over others, but power to act.

By now it was about 10:15 P.M., and Jeff, Dick, and Steve retired to the stake president's office from which they emerged twenty minutes or so later with a typed statement saying that they would have to think over what they had heard, read the new documents that had accompanied my witnesses from Utah,* pray, and wait for inspiration from God.

When Jeff said the decision would not be announced that night, I smiled grimly to myself. "So you're still trying to foil the press, are you, gentlemen?" I believed I recognized this strategy for what it was, but I was surprised that they had chosen it.† I had mentally

---

* From all over the country affidavits had been arriving at the Willis residence from people who had heard me speak and hoped their testimony would help the bishop realize that I had not caused them 1) if they were members, to take the council of the first presidency lightly, or 2) if they were nonmembers, to think harshly of the church as a religious body. Some of those who wrote sent me carbon copies. The Utah witnesses also gave me copies of the affidavits they had brought from Utah to present to the bishop.

† Since the trial, I have gained a perspective I was too close to have at the time. I believe now that we did not understand the hierarchy's real fears, which may not have been of my alienating potential converts, but of providing a model of loyal opposition and dissent to *members*. I believe now that the prime objective of the whole trial was to keep control of the membership. So to the degree that the letters told about my strength, my obvious love for the church, my intelligence—all my virtues—to that extent they confirmed the Brethren's worst fear

assessed the effectiveness of their possible media alternatives and I had discarded this one on the hunch that, rather than discouraging the press, it would serve to raise the already considerable suspense surrounding the trial to hysteria pitch. "You've chosen incorrectly," I told them in my mind. "You would have been better off simply to have given the verdict and gotten the whole thing over with." Even though that would have been less dramatic for the media, and given less national attention to the Equal Rights Amendment, I would have preferred it. I selfishly wanted the weight of not-knowing lifted from my spirit. But I acquiesced to it as a strategy without inner resistance because I knew it would be good for the ERA. It would keep that vital issue before the public for another few days. So I sighed, and went out to be totally inarticulate for the first few moments before the microphone, feeling stultified from breathing the miasma of male supremacy that clouded that high council room and the minds of the court.

I was constantly amazed at the church's PR people during the whole wretched business. All of them are professionals, and all of them together were not a match for the good common sense of three or four women who had not had a single course and had little experience in dealing with the media. Judging from this one experience, I

—that I was a leader and might provide a model for other members—and very likely hardened rather than softened their resolve against me.

All this regard for me must have proved me as dangerous as they suspected. They must not allow Mormon women to have as a role model a woman who does not ask permission of the men. If they had believed that others found me "kooky," or not basically sound or credible, and discounted a good deal of what I said, they might have relented. But people were taking me seriously; they respected and admired me. That could not be tolerated.

The Mormon church had made me what I was, and now, like the Frankenstein monster, I could not be controlled by ordinary means. I had slipped beyond their customary methods of control. Not being able to manipulate me by guilt or fear anymore, the church fathers would have to use their biggest guns against me.

Mother took her undelivered testimony home that night. Later she had it hand-delivered to Jeff:

". . . The number of spontaneous calls and letters Sonia has received expressing outrage at this action and offering support and sympathy, is incredible. Many from active LDS members who say, 'Bless you, Sonia, for saying what I didn't dare to say.' Judge Reva Beck Bosone called expressing admiration and encouragement, and said, 'My mother always taught us to do right and fear not. We need people like you in Congress.'

". . . Sonia is willing to take risks necessary to bring social justice. She is fighting a desperate political battle, using political methods . . . If you excommunicate her, it will be a blot on your own name forever."

would advise the church to drop all the men—who invariably did and said the wrong things—and hire women only from now on. A gift for public relations must be part of "women's intuition"!

In fact, from a public relations point of view—as well as a moral one—I wondered at the time why church leaders went on with my trial at all. It would have been so wise of them to drop it. I could only conclude that in their arrogance they could not conceive of the world's believing a little woman's quiet voice over their big powerful male authoritative ones. It must have stunned them. And still haunt them. As must the question of what this bodes for the future. I can answer that question. What it bodes is that churchmen cannot ultimately win over women. In the end, they will have to relent.

The witnesses had been sequestered in a special room with Lorin Jensen as guard. They were instructed not to communicate with people outside, not to leave the room unaccompanied, and not to talk to one another about matters concerning the trial. (John Bailey says that Lorin's not letting them mention the ERA in that room was an admission that the trial *was* about the ERA.)

Hazel could see my children through the window. "Poor Marc, not knowing what was happening to you in there. He was freezing. We'd keep asking this man [Lorin] why they couldn't come inside or we couldn't go out and tell them how much longer they'd have to wait. Ron came to the door. I walked over and said, 'They've told us it won't be very long now.' The Avenging Angel had just told Ron it would be at least a half hour longer. While I was at the door, one of the men from the hall came quickly, shut it, and told me to go back in. Then he bawled Lorin out for letting me talk to Ronald. Lorin protested that he hadn't let me—I had just done it."

Hazel doesn't ask permission either.

"One of the female witnesses needed to take some pills," Hazel continued, "so one of the guards went with her to the drinking fountain. The halls were pitch dark because all the lights were out. I said I had to go to the bathroom. Lorin said he would help me. I said I would do it myself, thanks. He called to somebody out in the hall, which infuriated me, so I just went. The hall was very, very dark. They had told me where the bathroom was, and I sort of knew anyway because our stake center is about the same as yours. I went out there and couldn't believe it. At every window a man stood in total blackness. I felt surrounded by ghouls.* I could see down to the left where the man was guarding the people who had already been in with you."

"Esther's children kept pushing themselves through the door to see if everything was all right with her. At one point, she went to the door to speak to them. She wasn't impolite about it. But she wasn't intimidated one bit, either.

My lovely quiet mother was working on her testimony in the corner as hard as if it would save me.

Meanwhile, outside in the cold, many small dramas were taking place. The Avenging Angel was demonstrating to the press and those others who watched with me the depth of the sexism of some Mormon men. He occasionally had to make an announcement or a request, and every time, he skirted the women who were conducting the prayer service and who were clearly in charge, and found some man. Tom Hart, a tall, imposing lawyer friend of mine, had to keep saying, "The women are in charge. I'm not in charge here." But the Avenging Angel was not going to talk to a woman because he simply could not believe that when there were men present the women were not *really* under their direction, no matter what everyone said. He had seen the women of the church acting as if they were—and saying they were—in charge of things, just like the women there that night, but everyone knew that Mormon women are always under the direction of men. So he could not credit what he was seeing; it probably seemed so "unnatural" to him that he dismissed it as impossible.

So the Avenging Angel would skirt the women again and find Ron

---

* Arlene recorded in her journal: "When Sonia, Richard, and Mrs. Harris came out of the stake center, followed closely by the witnesses, the lights of the press conference glared and I could clearly see that all of those people who had been inside were *ashen*. I caught sight of Ron Rigby speaking to his wife, Hazel, as the press conference ensued. And when I worked my way through the clot of bodies crowded as close to Sonia as possible, Ron told me that Hazel had told him that when witnesses were led by the guard through pitch-black hallways to the rest rooms, those hallways were lined with men—guards—who all wore small, white triangle badges on their lapels. They glowed their identification through the darkness. In other words, if one walked those black church paths without an escort and without a glowing triangle, one would be . . . what? Arrested? *Bludgeoned?* Shot? My God, what's happening inside this, this *cult*, to which I was born?

"During the press conference, after he read his pre-prepared statement, the bishop was booed. Not loud enough nor long enough, either. I wanted to slap his pious face and demand to know what CIA tactics were doing inside a religion—*my* religion!"

Rigby out on the fringes of the group and tell him, "These people are making too much noise. You're singing too loudly, and it is working to Sonia's disadvantage." Ron told him he was not in charge but that he would tell Georgia who could decide whether or not to dampen the group's enthusiasm. "We wanted you to know you had supporters out there, Sonia," Ron told me, "and we wanted the men in there to know, too."

The AA appeared again very shortly to tell Ron that the trial looked as if it would last at least another half hour, and suggested that Ron advise the demonstrators and media people to wait down the hill at the Unitarian church where they could keep warm.

Ron talked to the women, who asked, "Do you trust that man, Ron?" "It hadn't occurred to me not to, you know," he confessed to me later. "I couldn't think why he would lie to me. But Georgia said, 'It wouldn't be the first time we've been lied to.'" Ron decided to announce to the group what he had been told, but Georgia and many others said, "We're going to stay here. We don't trust him."

Not fifteen minutes later, the trial was over and we came out of the church. When the Avenging Angel appeared, Ron said to him angrily, "You lied to me. You just flat-out lied to me!" "I accused him of trying to get the crowd dispersed before everyone came out," Ron told me. "He quickly denied it, but by this time none of us believed him. I had to send runners to get people back."

Ron and other Mormons were shamed before nonmember eyes by the Avenging Angel. He had "an obnoxious manner," they reported; "very proprietary, very bossy." "Puffed up with his own importance," Ron described him. They were all humiliated that he dealt as he did with nonmembers. In addition, Ron had suggested to him, "Think what you could do for the image of the church if you were to let these people, who are behaving in a dignified and reasonable fashion, into the cultural hall to get warm!" "I have my orders," said the Avenging Angel, the FBI agent.

I asked Linda Sillitoe for her impressions of what was going on outside the church. She replied thoughtfully: "It took a certain amount of devotion to stay out there all that time. Everyone was very serious. Even the press. They stayed, and were orderly and polite." Though she felt they held the church in contempt, they were sympathetic to me and to the questions of First Amendment freedoms and separation of church and state that the trial inspired.

"It was a different experience for the Mormons than for the non-Mormons," she continued. "People were operating on many different levels. There was real turmoil going on inside the Mormons. When the trial went late, the Mormons considered it a good omen. Maybe someone was getting through. The non-Mormons were angry. 'Why are they delaying in there?' they demanded. 'We think they are trying to foul up press deadlines.'

"To the Mormons, who had attended our own churches thousands of times, being locked out of a Mormon meetinghouse in the freezing cold and pitch dark—except for a few drizzling little candles—was a shocking experience. It seemed so hostile and hateful, such a slap in the face. We Mormons were also troubled by our double perception. When the Mormon guards were hostile and nasty to everyone, we knew why they were responding that way; they were just like the people in our own wards. We understood their fear and confusion. But we could also understand the impression they were leaving with the onlooking non-Mormons, and were ashamed. When we sang, 'She's got the whole world in Her hands,' and 'Sonia is our leader,' we Mormons knew how these songs were sounding to Jeff, while the non-Mormons were blissfully unaware, and therefore able to enjoy the singing with a single mind. The Mormons were in double minds all night, an uncomfortable condition. But there was at the same time a sense of validation because now others could see what we were up against, being liberal Mormons in a reactionary church. We did not feel so alone and non-understood in our experience.

"The non-Mormons were more political about it all, and many of the non-religious people did not understand the religious seriousness of it nearly as well as they did the political significance. But all the speeches were serious, even emotional, trying for your sake, Sonia, for the sake of other Mormons there, and just out of plain decency, to show respect for the church. But the respect obviously did not go very deep, and was seriously if not fatally eroded by all they saw there that night.

"And not least of all," Linda concluded, "the non-Mormons were warmer; they were full of hot Unitarian coffee, and sips from flasks which were circulating from one frozen hand to another.

"The Mormons were cold. Somehow this is very significant, though it sounds obvious and insipid. It was a critical factor, as symbolic as it was actual. And the Mormons were afraid. For you, Sonia, as for ourselves. If you were excommunicated, what did that mean about our relationship and future with the church? That was the question in all our minds as we waited out there in the cold."

Because I felt nothing and therefore remember painfully little about what happened afterward, I have relied on Arlene's late-night-nervy, very feeling and vivid journal account:

"After the press loaded into vans and cars and drove away, the stake house was hauntingly abandoned. For the hundredth time I thanked God for a free press, that this atrocity would not slide past Americans unnoticed. Those of us who yet remained walked to the Unitarian church to congregate, warm ourselves in each other. Several stood to speak, including the eerie beauty who had materialized in Virginia from Georgia and who had followed the CBS van so adeptly. Georgia Fuller of NOW added a note of humor to an otherwise sobering night by telling of a woman who owned and operated a 'Rent-a-Potty' business. Georgia had been making arrangements for rest-room facilities—before the Unitarians offered their building. She had, after years of ERA rallies, foreseen the crowd and the long wait during Sonia's trial. 'I knew we would all have to pee at some point during this night and knew the Mormons wouldn't let us in to use their johns,' she quipped. 'So I called this person who makes her living renting port-a-potties out to groups holding rallies, concerts, fairs, etc. When I told her the potties were for the night of Sonia Johnson's excommunication trial, what did she tell me? She said we should rent a couple of motor homes because they would be cheaper and besides, people could get warm inside them! Now, I'll tell you, it is a little difficult to get choked up over rest rooms, but I was touched that a woman would pass up money for her business to try to help us find the cheapest and most convenient way to pee! She did so because she cares about what we stand for and what Sonia is going through in the name of us all!'

"I was touched, too. Rather ridiculous to be choked up over port-a-potties. But I was on the verge of weeping anyway and would likely have cried at a rodeo. But as we all crammed into the car to ride back to Sonia's home, Mrs. Harris suddenly said, 'I don't think women should talk like that.' 'Like what, Mom?' 'Well, that woman said "pee."' Sonia's voice took on a heavy tone, 'Mother, everyone pees. Every human and animal on earth must pee at various times during any given day.' Kari chimed in from the back seat, 'How about piss? People piss. Is that better, Grandma?' Mrs. Harris was sitting stiff, rigid. 'I think such words are distasteful, and . . .' 'Mother, you amaze me! It seems what you have done is totally discount those wonderful dedicated people who sat in that room this night, all because one person said one little word, pee. Did you hear anything else, Mother? Besides pee, did you hear the caring, the hope, the strength and the idealism? I can't believe it, Mother; I really cannot believe it! At your age, surely you know the whole world pees!' And we rode the remaining miles in nerve-raw silence.

"Sonia's face was so terribly drawn and her eyes so flat as she hugged me good-night, spoke our favorite nighttime parody of an old Mormon prayer phrase: 'Let us all go to our various beds in peace and safety.' I feel so helpless. I wish I could carry some of the horror for a woman who seems even tinier tonight than she did this morning. All I can do is answer her telephones and pray she gets a decent night's sleep for once in weeks! So many times I have heard her up wandering in the darkness. Sometimes she opens the door to the spare bedroom and whispers, 'Are you asleep, Arlene?' Of course, I never am . . . And one of the fondest memories I shall carry will be of when she came in the room and we stretched across the gurgling water bed and shared secret fears, hopes, and dreams. Two worried adults slumber-partying.

"I hope I can stencil this room, this house, this night, forever on my mind. I want all my life to be able to conjure it up, be able to place my mind and heart right back here, at this moment in time—this night when I have had to personally question everything I have known, felt, or believed in all my thirty-five years. I want to be able to re-feel this rage and this betrayal. Oh, I could possibly learn to forgive the church its ratty politics—that's nothing new with them anyway. I could even let bygones be bygones where my own brainwashing about the One True Church and the infallibility of the Prophet and the lie of free agency is concerned. But I'll not forgive or forget watching so closely while the One True Church that spouts its love and concern for families gnawed on the guts of one of the most devout Mormon families I have ever known. I question the God Mormonism taught me, but pray whatever it is will continue to bless Sonia with the strength she has had to this point. And I pray it has not forgotten the youth caught in this ugly, sacrilegious arena.

The Johnson children will pay a high price for something not one in their midst deserved in the first place. There's Mrs. Harris, too . . . So caught in pride in her daughter laced with fears for her soul. May she be blessed, too; may she be able to span the generations between 'bodily functions,' to 'pee' and right along to 'piss.' I will require no blessing, for I have always called it, 'whizz!' "

Chapter 13

My Last Days as a Mormon

DECEMBER 2, 1979. Fast Sunday. The church was packed when Arlene and Linda, Mom, Rick, the kids and I came in. The press had converged upon us outside, and I recognized several media people in the audience. The only seats were near the front on the right side of the chapel, and my entourage took their places there. Still so hurt, crushed numb, I walked up to the organ and began playing the prelude music: "Sweet Hour of Prayer."

Down in the congregation, Arlene was scribbling busily away in her journal: "It was an ordeal to walk inside the church this morning. Press all over the lawn, ward members visibly shaken. I'm on the verge of tears, filled with admiration as Sonia walks to the front of the congregation to take her place at the organ. Someone else was prepared to play that organ today. . . . The crowd is buzzing. This religious community expected, rather hoped, Sonia Johnson would never more be amongst them, that after her trial she would slink away in shame. They want to forget, but she won't allow it. The shame is not Sonia's; it belongs to every person here today *but* Sonia."

That's a loyal friend thinking. Still, she was right about one thing: the crowd was buzzing. It was an extraordinarily noisy Sunday, and even at its best, Sterling Park Ward is chaotic. Jeff walked to the microphone: "If you would like to talk, please do so outside." The decibel level hardly dipped. Again he took the microphone: "Brothers and Sisters, may I remind you that it is not the youth causing this disturbance?"

Linda wrote about that Sunday morning in *Utah Holiday*:

"All who played roles in the trial the night before were dramatically before the congregation, as if characters in a morality play. Lorin Jensen, the counselor who had disqualified himself (and who had guarded the witnesses at the stake center), officiated. Seated next to him on the stand was Bp. Willis and his other counselor, Steve Wilcox, a young man of about 25. The high councilman who had filled in for Jensen [Dick Brown] at the trial now officiated at the sacrament table. The stake president's counselor who had observed from the rear of the trial room gave an announcement about temple statistics. The young ward clerk [Bob Andros] was seated on the front row, and began the series of testimonies. Sonia was not seated in a pew, but in full view—at the organ, or when not playing, facing the congregation."

We sang "Far, Far Away on Judea's Plain" to open the meeting, and the Avenging Angel's wife gave the opening prayer:

"Strengthen our dear bishop," she prayed with a trembling voice—at which point Arlene records that I moved my hand from in front of my face and stole a peek at the praying woman—"and cause the restless spirit to subside."

A baby was blessed by its father as its mother sat quietly by. We sang "God Our Father, Hear Us Pray," one of my favorite hymns, while the sacrament was being prepared. I loved playing it, especially knowing it was probably the last time I would ever accompany a Mormon congregation. My whole life of music in the church flooded upon me as I played the last sacrament hymn of my life as a Mormon. When the sacrament was passed to me, I took it. I knew God was not offended with me; I knew I had done no evil in the sight of heaven.

Arlene was thinking other things entirely: "I'd forgotten the *din* in a Mormon gathering!" she was writing in her journal. "Every mother here seems to have at least four youngsters squawking. I'll bet the press are amazed. A woman walks out carrying a screeching infant, tugging a toddler with her other hand; the father, of course, remains seated. Sonia watches that young mother leave this testimony meeting with the most incredibly sad expression on her face. I'll bet she's remembering all the times she herself left such meetings to quiet her babies . . ."

Bob Andros set the tone of the ensuing testimonies by assuring us all that the bishop and stake president were directed by the Lord. The next person was duly "grateful for the sincerity, integrity, devotion, of our bishopric . . ."; the fourth told three "features" of a good testimony, and testified to the truthfulness of church leaders. Again.

And then Kris Barrett came up to the stand, with one infant on her hip. Arlene writes: "I could *kiss* her, though Sonia has cringed, bowed her head and covered her eyes with one hand—likely afraid for the consequences Kris may have to face." Tearfully, Kris told how much she loved me and how grateful she was for me, how "thankful for the parts of me Sonia helped me discover." She told the congregation that she had had a long association with me and hoped it would continue—*in* the gospel. Then she said, "The bishop and his counselors are hearing a lot of voices right now; when you're hearing a lot of voices, it's hard to hear the right one. I pray that they will."

Several children came forward to bear their testimonies and the bishop helped them. In the audience, Arlene, who wrote mercilessly about Jeff, scribbled: "I am overcome by nausea. Jeff gazes *grandly* around the room as the child speaks. He smiles unctuously to his flock."

Then a teenaged girl came to the pulpit with a five-and-a-half-page written testimony full of "I always have and I always will's." She was the twelfth person to bear her testimony. It was about ten minutes after the hour, and meetings end on the half hour.

As I sat there, trying to realize that this was undoubtedly my last Sunday in the church I had loved with all my being for so many years, I felt a great desire to speak one last time as a Mormon to other Mormons. I wanted to tell them how much the church had meant to me, how much they had meant to me, how precious the memories of my Mormon years would always be, and how precious the teachings of Jesus Christ.

Also, as Linda recorded in her *Utah Holiday* article, "I wanted to defuse the anger and tension in that chapel. I've done it before and I thought I could again. I wanted to acknowledge the bad feelings many of them had toward me, and let them know I understood. And I wanted to see if I could protect Kris Barrett somehow."

I was filled with a sense of history. It was the end of one era, the

beginning of another. I wanted to say good-bye—God be with you—
and Godspeed.

But the moment I left the organ to take my place in line for the
microphone, a man stood up at the rear of the church and walked to
the front. When Kari saw him, she whispered to Rick, "That man's
going to filibuster!" Rick scoffed, "Oh Kari!" "He is," she insisted.
"You wait and see. They've got it all planned out!" He came up to
the stand and sat down ahead of me in line. That's all right, I
thought; when it's my turn, I will just walk up ahead of him.

But when it was my turn and I started to rise, *he* stood up quickly
and began his long, rambling testimony—which violated every fea-
ture of a good testimony we had been instructed about earlier in the
meeting. He began with a description of the Pennsylvania countryside, something about his grandfather, how amazing the church is
that it can be run by amateurs. Then he settled down to business,
bearing his testimony to our "tremendous" bishop, speaking on and
on.

Down in the audience, Kari looked triumphantly at Rick. The
congregation sat in nervous suspense, waiting to see if I would get a
chance to speak. But we all should have known I wouldn't. In the
belief that truth has its own power and hardly needs eloquence, I
speak what I believe is true. What would the men do if I bore testimony to the truthfulness of the gospel, which I was about to do?
The men could not risk it, because they had to make members everywhere believe that I had not been excommunicated for political
reasons, but was an apostate.

At about twenty-five after the hour, Lorin tugged mightily and obviously on the speaker's jacket, and told him in a loud voice to finish
up. I prepared to rise when he finished. But he had not completely
left the pulpit when Lorin leaped and captured it, saying hastily,
"Brethren,* this meeting is at a close!"

Everyone was stunned. I looked down at my family; their mouths
were agape. The media people looked incredulous. Everyone in that
room knew I had been deprived of my last chance to speak in the
Mormon church—calculatedly deprived.

Arlene wrote: "My God, Kari called it! A filibuster in *church!*
Sonia looks stricken as she steps back to the organ. Mrs. Harris's

---

* Under stress, men reveal themselves. By addressing only the men, Lorin showed
us that to him women are too insignificant to be acknowledged.

shoulders sag. Sonia's last opportunity to bear her testimony and these *Christian* bastards won't allow her to!"

Jeff told the press that I was fifth in line when the meeting ended. Not so. It had been my turn when the blond fellow stepped in before me to filibuster, making it most certainly my turn next. And the men on that stand knew it.

Anne Cole wrote in the Loudoun (Virginia) *Times-Mirror:*

"One member of the church who attended Sunday's service said, "It is within the tradition of the Mormon church that we all have the right to speak, and it gave the appearance that she was not given that right. . . . The unfortunate thing is . . . that many of those people will have a chance to speak again. . . . We did Sister Johnson a gross injustice by not letting her speak. We'll never know what she had on her mind to say . . . and I think we're all the worse for that."

After we sang "It Came Upon a Midnight Clear," the Avenging Angel closed with prayer (notice that his wife gave the opening and he the closing prayer: Jeff's insistence that members of the priesthood must authoritatively have the last word). Mom told Arlene she was going to "go have a few words with the bishop." She walked resolutely up, got Jeff's attention, and told him she had just witnessed one of the most unkind and disgraceful actions of her seventy-three years. "I am ashamed of this church!" she concluded. Some others in the audience were also furious. One man asked Jeff if he could swear before God that he had not done it intentionally. Jeff hung his head and said, no, he could not. Judy told reporters that Jeff hasn't a vindictive bone in his body. Perhaps, in being submissive, subservient, self-effacing and self-erasing, she has never given him cause to fear that she will become as powerful as he, or more so. If she does—which she easily could—she may see a vindictive bone. We do not really know the men we're married to until we become ourselves and human. They love us for what they think we are, what we nearly destroy ourselves to be for them; and when we get tired enough and angry enough and physically ill enough to say finally, "I've had it!" suddenly the strangers inside their skins leap out at us.

While Mom and my friends were cornering the bishop, one of the men in the ward came angrily up to Kris Barrett and snarled, "You make me want to puke!" Because she had said something loving about me in a church of "love."

That meeting at the Sterling Park Ward that morning, as Linda Sillitoe puts it, "squats in the mind."

In a speech entitled "Don't Use My Name," Linda describes what happened next. "After the meeting, Kris was besieged by reporters. NBC filmed her outside the meetinghouse. The NBC reporter was present throughout the meeting and recognized well the impact her questions would have on Kris's future in that ward and community which was so polarized. Finally she asked her, with the camera rolling, 'Do you agree with Sonia?'

"Kris paused and looked down at her little boy who was pulling at her dress. The cold Virginia wind blew her hair back. I was standing behind the reporter, listening, and I held my breath. Then Kris looked back at the reporter. 'I don't think that's an important question,' she said. 'Our church teaches us that we have to figure things out for ourselves. I don't have to agree with Sonia, or the prophet, or anyone else. I just have to think it out for myself and find out how I feel and what I will do. I know that Sonia has done that for herself. And it's not important whether or not I agree.'

"The reporter nodded, the camera stopped, and the reporter, her face tight, stepped forward and shook Kris's hand. She knew courage when she saw it, and had tears in her eyes. That is only one—though one of the best—of the moments of courage, compassion, and clear thinking that I have witnessed. I am grateful to have seen it."

Four days excommunicated, I was sitting the next Sunday with Mom and Hazel and Arlene on the back row in sacrament meeting, mute with grief, when Jeff read the press release about my excommunication to the congregation. (I understand that it was read in many Mormon churches that day.) I listened with dull dismay as he read words I knew were not true to those people who trusted him as a servant of God. I had not testified to those things. I knew it. He knew it. And God knew it. And that's when he made that most telling of statements: "I want all of you to stop speculating and judging, and to know that in the end there is only one judge, one final judge, and that is . . . *me*, your bishop!" Arlene and Hazel and Mom turned to me in shock. I shrugged my shoulders. "As long as God is male, men are God."

Several months later, one of my friends in the ward told me that many members there were congratulating themselves on their behavior during the entire experience. "I can't understand it," she puzzled.

"Are they pleased that they had the self-control not to stone you or something? I wonder what they have to be proud of. What did they *do?*"

But a few, a very few, do have cause to be proud. When Brother David Homer brought over the excommunication letter on the afternoon of December 5, he stood in the doorway to the kitchen, holding out the dreaded sealed envelope, and said, "We've been sent by the bishop to give you this letter. We don't know what's in it, and we've been instructed not to stay around to find out." He paused. Then his kind old eyes started to fill and he said, "Sister Johnson, if there's anything I can do, if you need anything, just let me know."

Then one afternoon a week or so later, the doorbell rang and there was Sister Louise Wynn, whom I knew only slightly, with her primary class of eleven-year-old boys. They had brought us some food— I remember the cheese ball. Louise put her arms around me, held me close, and murmured something dear and comforting in my ear. One of the kids interrupted loudly, "I hope the church will take you back." "I hope so too," I said.

In the mail one letter arrived. It was from Tim Anderson, a bass in the choir: "I understand you were at Sacrament meeting last Sunday [December 15] . . . Candy and I are both so happy you came. Please keep attending. We consider you a choice person, as do a great number of the rest of the ward. You have a lot of friends here praying for you. We want you to know this—that you are among friends whenever you attend a church function."

I am afraid that was just wishful thinking, Tim.

How wishful was demonstrated at the next month's fast and testimony meeting, when Judy Willis stood and thanked everyone profusely for all the telephone calls, all the visits, the food, the cards, the letters, the gifts and assurances they had given the Willis family during "their ordeal." I was sitting in the midst of the congregation, knowing she was speaking at least partly, if not entirely, for my benefit. It seemed to the Willises to have been a contest between Jeff and me. I must be made to understand now that he had won, that the ward loved *Jeff*, that they had sustained *him* and supported *him* and *his* family through *his* difficult time. I must understand that righteous church opinion was on *his* side and against me. She told how close to Jesus Christ Jeff had been, closer than she had known anyone could possibly be, so close she had been in awe of him (she works hard at deifying him). And their marriage had been beautiful. It was all almost, she said, as if they were already in the celestial kingdom.

I was not surprised. I believe Mother and Father in Heaven comfort and bless all their children and do not take sides against any of us. I was receiving the same kind of comfort and assurances of love from heaven that Judy was describing. And surely this is as it should be. Surely this is how we strive to be with our own children. We let them work out their own problems with one another, all the time loving them all with all our hearts, hoping for the very best for each of them but never at the expense of the others.

Recently, at a stake function of some sort, Elaine Hatch (Orrin's wife) walked up to Kris Barrett and said, "Is it true that Sonia goes off all the time and leaves her children alone?" "No," Kris answered, having helped me make my child-care arrangements. "It is not true."

All Mormondom bristled with rumors. People called me from afar and asked, "Is it true that you are making millions of dollars from this whole thing?" "That you drive an enormous car and have every luxury you want?" "Is it true that you're on tranquilizers and are deeply depressed, despite all the fame and glory?" "Is it true what your visiting teacher says, that you don't care about or love your children, that you had given up on family *before* the church excommunicated you?"

In three widely separated states, it was believed by Mormons that my supporters put on black armbands, broke into the church with hatchets, and chopped up the pews, the sacrament table, the organ, the pulpit. People swore they had heard me say Spencer Kimball was not a prophet; they had heard it with their own ears. Was it true that I had said I felt bad because the Utah women had not given me enough support? I had been seen in a half-dozen states personally going door-to-door telling people not to let the missionaries into their homes. I had gained sixty pounds—had gone completely to pot —and tons of makeup had to be used to cover the ravages of my degeneracy whenever I appeared on television. I had been heard to say that I thought Jesus Christ was the Devil.

I have learned a good deal about myth and folklore in this excommunicated year. But this sort of thing is to be expected. Orthodox members must explain me in ways that keep church leaders perfect and infallible. In addition, I have a difficult message which is hard to express, and I don't always express it well. Even expressed well, it is not easy to understand. Sometimes, when I am speaking to a group that includes many hostile Mormons, I try too hard to make them understand, and consequently come across as far more intense and frightening than I actually am. The fact that justification and total exoneration of church leaders in this case is absolutely mandatory for most members, coupled with how hard it is for me to say with exactness what I want to say, means that most church members will never be able to understand my side of the story to any appreciable degree. I do not expect ever to be exonerated by my own people. But that can be borne, because I exonerate myself.

And so, as a mythical character, I began my life outside the Mormon church.

Chapter 14

"Dear Sonia, . . ."

"Wow, ARE YOU stupid!"

"You have joined the ranks of the great—Martin Luther, Joan of Arc, Galileo . . ."

"You overbearing little biddy!"

"You have inspired us, uplifted us. You have our everlasting gratitude."

"I am sick of your whining, sniveling, lying face . . ."

"Cheer up, Sister Johnson. God loves the brave.* Don't feel lost. You're still His kid!"

"Silly Sonia, you are a disgrace to your family and the Mormon church."

"As a Mormon woman whose forebears crossed the plains to Zion, I salute you."

"Do us a favor, please. Forget the Mormons. There are a lot of freak groups who would welcome you. Go join them!"

So wrote the Mormons. But they accounted for only about a fifth of the total mail which snowed down around me thickly as soon as the story of the trial became known throughout the country: over 5,000 letters, cards, and telegrams. Of these, at least 85 percent are supportive of both the Equal Rights Amendment and of me, and more than half the Mormon mail is positive.

The negative letters, even those that were deliberately insulting or outright hostile attacks, were in a way as beside the point by the time of the trial as the positive ones: all too late to influence me one way or another. I had already chosen my path. I had set my life

* Many people wrote commending my courage. This embarrassed me because I knew something they didn't: I haven't even enough courage to stop shaving my legs!

firmly on course. So though the Mormon hate mail did not convince me that I had offended God, neither did the sympathetic letters convince me that I was a hero. I always felt like what I was—a Virginia housewife.

The Mormon hate mail was, of course, depressing, particularly the sameness of it—like the paper dolls Mom cut out of folded paper for me when I was a child. I came to refer to it as "clone mail"—the party line all the way, without a trace of genuine, honest, individual free thought. All alike. Interchangeable. I was cheered, on the other hand, by the kindness and understanding of the sympathetic mail, and though I am immensely grateful for it—it helped me heal—I could and would have continued my work without it. Women work for justice for women because it satisfies the deepest hungers of our hearts, not to spite or to please anyone else. That is true, anyway, for this woman.

Most of the Mormon anti letters portrayed what I call the "Jim Jones syndrome," the idea that Mormons should follow their leaders —since they are prophets of God—no matter what.* As one Mormon woman wrote:

"If you believed he were a prophet in the very same way that Moses, Elijah, Abraham, etc. were prophets, then you could not go against his mandate; even if it were to never buy a Toyota car, wear red shoes on Tuesday, or use Gold Medal flour!"

Or drink the purple Kool-Aid?

Another major theme of outraged Mormons is that I am a liar— about the church's political organization, and about why I was excommunicated: "You *know* the church's 'political organization' as you call it simply does not exist," "You *know* why you were excommunicated. Why don't you tell the world the truth? You *know* you are unworthy!"

At first I was perplexed by such letters. What did they know that I did not? Then someone sent me a letter she had received from Bar-

* In August 1978 at the Alice Paul march in Washington, D.C., a couple of returned missionaries from BYU tried to tear down our "Mormons for ERA" banner. In the ensuing argument, they took great pride in assuring us that they would follow the prophet no matter what. Maida, hoping to demonstrate how frightening this mindset was, and attempting to prove that even for them there must certainly be limits to this kind of obedience, asked them if they would go out and shoot all black people if President Kimball so directed. Without hesitation, they both answered, "Yes."

bara Smith, President of the Relief Society of the church, which Barbara had apparently sent to those members who were troubled enough to question her about my excommunication. Her letter gives a partial answer to why members think I am guilty of something quite different from anything mentioned in the press or the church's press release or my own statements, and also provides the most insidious example of the accusation that I am lying:

"Your compassionate concern for Sonia Johnson is shared by many people," Mrs. Smith writes, "including the local and general church leaders. *They have an insight and information beyond that released by the bishop or by Sonia Johnson* [italics mine]."

Sister Smith was not the only culprit, or even the most influential one, sending out this message, however. From a letter written by Elder Marion G. Hanks, one of the General Authorities of the church, to a Mormon woman in Alabama, come these contributions to the genre of insinuation and character assassination:

"May I give you my own assurance, and express it in sorrow, that Sister Johnson was not 'tried' because she 'believed in free agency or in ERA.' *Having had nothing at all to do with the detail of the proceedings, watching it about as most members of the church have,* I must confess my own feeling that Sister Johnson was not put upon by anyone but in fact impaled herself *for reasons that a lengthier observation of it all may reveal.*" (Italics mine.)

Having just admitted not knowing any more about this matter than she, and certainly never having met or spoken to me, he then goes on to speak of my "*apparently irresistible need to destroy others,*" and compares me with men in the book of Mormon who "*deliberately misled and harmed others.*"

These excerpts make quite clear that in Smith's and Hanks's judgment, which they do not hesitate a moment to pass along to members (though Smith is head of an organization whose motto is "Charity Never Faileth," and Hanks certainly considers himself a disciple of the loving Jesus of Nazareth), I am hiding something very dark indeed and the Brethren, in their great love, are gallantly protecting me in it. Here are leaders who in one breath talk about sorrow and compassion, and in the next insinuate something which is devastating to my reputation: the Brethren have information—very mysterious but *very damaging* information—that, if known, would tarnish my name sufficiently that *everyone* would condone the ex-communication.

Hanks, of course, does more than insinuate. Speaking out of total ignorance, he states as fact two opinions that show neither love nor compassion, neither a desire to understand nor sorrow, but the anger and vengefulness of a threatened male.

(I once, not long ago, admired him more than any of the leaders of the church. He was the only one who seemed to be listening—really listening—to women. As I have said, loyalty among men is amoral.)

I suspect this was the tenor of most letters emanating from church headquarters, and that they have had the desired effect within the church. Surely these rumors have flown to nearly every ward and stake in the country.

On the phone one day, a friend was hemming and hawing around. "Go ahead, say it," I urged her. "Well," she said, "the manager of one of the Deseret book stores [church-owned] in Utah took me aside when I was out there and whispered, 'We all know she committed adultery.'" And later at church on the East Coast, a good brother told her angrily, "Sonia had better stop doing what's she's doing or they're going to tell what they know about her!"

Believe me, if the Brethren knew anything, everyone in the country would also know it—immediately. I cannot express with what joy they would have welcomed *any* irregularity in my life and conduct at the time of the trial. Their every act shouted from the rooftops how badly they wanted to discredit me. Sending the Buchanan article all over the church with the bishop's fictionalized version of the trial, and sending the Virginia Chairman scurrying around after me for six months telling media people in every state where I appeared that I was lying are only two blatant examples. Not having evidence, they did most of their discrediting by insinuation and rumor, as the Smith and Hanks letters so damagingly demonstrate. I began to hear echoes from all over the church:

". . . because of the extent to which you have allowed yourself to be deceived, I am persuaded that you have been involved in a serious moral transgression for which you have never repented through the proper Priesthood authority," writes one woman hopefully.

Much of the furious Mormon mail was generated by my appearance on the "Donahue Show" on December 13, 1979. The Mormon antis were angry, it seems to me from their letters, for two reasons: I appeared to good advantage, and I did not appear with a spokesperson from the church. They had so hoped I would look and act like an apostate; they had hoped that when they saw me they would immediately understand why the church had excommunicated me. What they saw instead was a woman they instantly recognized as having come out of the core of the church: my voice, my speech patterns, my gestures, even my physical appearance are very, very Mormon; they are the voice, the gestures, the appearance of a Relief Society president, which I have been, a Mutual president, which I have been, a Relief Society teacher, which I have been, a Primary teacher. And it frightened them deeply. Somewhere in their unconscious, a voice of doubt whispered the terrible question, "Could the church have made a mistake? Could she be telling the truth?" I sounded honest, though they *knew* I must be lying. That I caused them to doubt even for a moment made them very angry at me. I did not look and act like an apostate. I was not loud or shrill or horrid.

It was all very confusing.

So confusing that they were compelled to drown out those nagging questions by writing to me. Many of the letters I received after the "Donahue Show" began like this:

"I watched you today on the Phil Donahue Show, and was brought to such strong emotions inside of me I felt impressed to write to you."

"I watched your interview and woke up in the early hours of dawn thinking about you—so here goes."

"For weeks I have wanted to write you."

"I was so disturbed by your comments on the Phil Donahue Show that against my better judgment I must write you."

"For several weeks I have felt impressed to write to you . . . tonight *for my own welfare* [italics mine] to share some feelings I have about you."

The need to reestablish their certainty, their momentarily shaken conviction that I was really an apostate, their great need to reaffirm *for themselves* their own orthodoxy, these were what forced them to write to me. Many of the letters are very long. By the end, each writer feels noticeably relieved, because each has demonstrated to her or his satisfaction the error of my ways. They have borne their testimony and said all the sacred phrases again, have reconvinced themselves that *they* are in good standing with God, accused me of lying, warned me of personal ruin and disaster if I continue "living a lie," and promised—with relish—that I will certainly be punished.

That I refused to participate with a Mormon woman on the show infuriated them.

When Donahue's staff asked me to be on his show, they requested names of representatives from the church with whom I would agree to meet. They had already tried Barbara Smith and told me the Brethren would not allow her to do it. So I gave them three other names: Gordon B. Hinckley, Boyd Packer, and Neal Maxwell, or any member of the Special Affairs Committee, though I preferred Gordon who heads it. "None of them will appear," I assured Donahue's assistant. "But they should be given the chance." The church's PR department in Salt Lake handled her call. No, the men would not appear, but he (Heber Woolsey) would find someone. Donahue's assistant called me back. "They have a spokesperson," she said. "Who is it?" I asked. They had not told her. "Find out, please," I urged, and was not surprised to learn that it was the Chairman of the Virginia LDS Citizens' Coalition. I agreed to meet with her, but as soon as I hung up the phone, I knew I had made a mistake, though I did not know why. Something was wrong and kept nagging me. So I cornered Arlene and made her listen to me think it through aloud from the uneasy feeling clear out to the conclusion.

I concluded that I must make it policy—and adhere to it from that time forward—never to appear with Mormon *women* on such programs, as the men in Salt Lake so very obviously and fervently wished me to do. I recognized the same syndrome I had watched, aghast, in Virginia: the men *behind* the women, the women fronting for them; the men never having to be accountable, never having to take responsibility, never having to be put on the spot, to face the consequences squarely, or to be made personally uncomfortable. The men manipulating the women, telling them what to do and say; the women, like "fembots," going about saying and doing it, serving as unwitting tools of their own oppression.

I reasoned that since women in the Mormon church do not make policy, they should not be put in the untenable position of defending it. Let those who make the policy defend it, I decided, and vowed that I would never consciously be a party to allowing the men to hide behind the women's skirts while making all the decisions and directing the whole unsavory business from that protected vantage point. The Chairman had no idea of the extent of the political organization going on under Hinckley's direction. Why should I, who *did*, be pitted against her ignorance? I could see, of course, how the men capitalized on her ignorance. When she subsequently trailed along behind me all over the United States trying to pick up the pieces, no matter which of the states she was in she could say, "The church isn't doing this, or that, in this state," without *exactly* lying. She did not know, and the men did not tell her because her ignorance suited their purposes. I was ashamed for her, and for them.

(In February, two months to a day after the excommunication, I asked Gordon Hinckley in his office, "If you think what you're doing is honorable, if you think it's decent, why don't you own it? Why don't you tell the members of the church what you're doing, how the church is politically organized all over the country?" He said members of the church *did* know. I told him it was clear that he didn't receive my mail.)

Why, I asked myself as I pondered the problem before the "Donahue Show," should I let the men decide how I was going to handle my business? I would not. I would either speak on the media with the men in the church who *knew* I was telling the truth and who, if they chose to deny it, chose to perjure themselves, or I would speak with no one. The media was interested in *me*. If the church wanted to ride along on my coattails, it would ride *my* way.

I thought I perceived another strategy in the church's selecting the Chairman. The public relations office of the church had been insisting vainly for weeks that the excommunication was a totally "local affair"—though they sent the excommunication press release out from their Salt Lake City headquarters. If I were to appear on national television with the Chairman of the Mormon lobbying group in Virginia, it would give credence to the idea that the problem only concerned Virginia, was very localized and small. Church leaders wanted to contain it, encapsulate it, make it out to be a benign tumor instead of the rampaging cancer it is.

But most important, it became apparent to me that by making women confront women, the leaders of the church were able to say, "It's just the ladies quarreling again!" They wanted in this way to trivialize it, to imply that it was not an important enough matter to warrant the concern of the very busy, very important, very holy men of the church. They did not even send a man of lesser position, making it quite clear that "this is just a women's issue, and, ho-hum, we men cannot be bothered." Gordon tried this on Jan and me in February when we sat in his office. I asked him about a memo that had gone out of his office to ERA coalition leaders in Missouri and Illinois about a meeting in which he had detailed the guidelines for organizing state and local church political action groups.

"I don't remember any such meeting, do you, Neal?" he asked ingenuously of Neal Maxwell, who was also there. "No, I don't recall any such meeting, either," Neal answered in wide-eyed innocence. "Then why," I demanded, "did you send out a memo about it, if there was no such meeting?" (I could produce that memo in court.) "Oh, perhaps someone in my office did it." Gordon waved vaguely, stifling a yawn. "I'm so busy in my capacity as one of the twelve apostles that I really don't have time to run the Special Affairs Committee; I spend less time with that than with any of my duties."

"Well, then, I would suggest that you get someone in here to get your business in order, because it is obviously a shambles—people sending out memos with your signature on them which you never read about meetings you never held outlining guidelines you know nothing about."

Trivialize the issue. "It's the least important thing I do." Right now, killing the Equal Rights Amendment is number one on the church's list of things to do, tying for first place with getting more missionaries into the field. That is how "trivial" it is, and Gordon Hinckley, because he is the one who has been chosen to head this effort, is in a position of great power in the church.

And so I called the Donahue people back. "I have just made a policy to which I intend to stick. I am never going to meet publicly against another Mormon woman. I have no quarrel with Mormon women or any other women, and I am not going to let the men make it appear as if I do. The women are merely obeying the men. If the men changed their minds about the ERA tonight, the women would change theirs by morning. No, my quarrel is not with my sisters, who are only following orders; it is with the policy makers of the church, those who are issuing the orders the women are obeying."

"We have to have someone on with you," she insisted.

"Well, I will meet with any of the leaders of the Mormon church (and all the leaders are men) or all of them together if they wish, but since they won't come, if you want me you will have to take me alone. I will not make this look like a fight among the women—it would please the men too much. The ERA battle is a battle of men against women and I will not be a party to further deception."

I did not care very much which way she decided. I had never watched Donahue, so I had little knowledge about the show. At the time of my excommunication, we had had television for less than six months in our family (I wanted to instill the habit of reading in my children, and I did). I did not know any of the shows, any of the celebrities. I lived in quite another world. And even if I had known how delightful Phil Donahue is, and how vast an audience he so deservedly has, I would not have protested if they had taken me off the show; they had a perfect right to do so.

But they didn't. "We want you, but what can we *say?*" she wailed.

"Tell the audience that the church would not send an official spokesperson," I answered, anticipating that this would encourage questions and allow me to explain why I refused to meet with the Chairman from Virginia. Because at that time, the Chairman was not "official"; she became official very shortly thereafter, however, you may be sure!

Perhaps Phil didn't get the message right. He said instead that the Mormon church hadn't sent any representative, or something like that, and the Mormons stormed his citadel with thousands of letters, as only Mormons can (many of them solicited by church officials here and there across the country). And so the Chairman and Barbara Smith had their turn, which was just fine with me, and for the next six months the Chairman was sent by the Special Affairs Committee along behind me into the media offices and studios of this nation to try to undo the damage I was doing by telling what I knew was the truth of the church's anti-ERA campaign. And what I knew —since I had been there and since I knew my heart—was the truth about the excommunication. Her following me about was also all right with me.

Very all right. The church, by reacting so violently as to send the Chairman darting desperately about after me, gave me immense credibility and power, made me appear dangerous, intriguing, and, not least, persecuted. As usual, the church's PR department had participated with the Special Affairs Committee in convincing the nation's media folk—and hence the nation's citizens—that the Mormon church oppresses and persecutes women.

Many Mormon letters criticized me "for bringing the church into this by calling yourselves Mormons for ERA." I pointed out to these folks that they had it backward: the church chose politics first and forced us out there into that arena by doing so. They asked me, "Why do you have to knock the church?" and I answered that the church started the fight by knocking women's rights.

To these troubled brothers and sisters who wish I would not include the church in my fight for the Equal Rights Amendment and women's rights in general, I make this solemn promise: "The instant the Mormon church decides to be only a church again, and as the greatest living enemy of women's rights in America marches off the battlefield, I promise I will never mention it again."

Though some of the issues were idiosyncratically Mormon, many were universally sexist techniques of dismissing women. Many warned me that I was being "used": "The ERA is using you and your former association with the church for its own gain." "Apparently you are advised by your organizers to exploit the Mormon relationship as long as it serves your purpose."

Writing me off as a tool of the enemies of the church (though there is no organization in this country named "ERA") is as convenient a way of disposing of me, and as often used against women, as labeling me "emotionally disturbed." It is highly unlikely that a man in my situation would be dismissed as merely being used by others without his understanding, without his volition. Patriarchal persons are so bogged down in stereotypes of women that they refuse to believe we can act on our own initiative out of our own integrity, as men do. That would be too admirable. Men act, men use. Women by nature are passive, meant by God to be used. Hence, I am being used, and instantly cease to be a threat. Just another Anita Bryant (in her former life), another Patty Hearst (in hers); somebody is obviously pulling my strings, doing my thinking. Poor Sonia.

Mormons are especially prone to this kind of thinking because it describes precisely and unfortunately the reality of so many Mormon women's lives.

With infinite variations, this view of women as passive, not-very-bright vessels dogs women from the cradle to the grave. I remember lying on the cold, papered examination table at the University of

Minnesota clinic, twenty-seven years old, in my fourth year of gradu-ate school, six months pregnant with my first child, and being asked incredulously by the young intern whether my husband had not told me how to avoid developing a calcium deficiency. I was dumbfounded by the implications of that statement: that some-one superior, such as a husband, had to teach me everything, or I would be bone ignorant. And of course the repairman, the insurance salesman, the movers—all wanted to talk to my husband, and if they had to talk to me punctuated their every sentence with "Now, when your husband gets home, ask him . . ."; "Your husband will want me to explain this to him, so have him call me"; "When you've both thought it over, have your husband let me know . . ."; "Where does your husband want me to put this?" and so on ad nauseam.

As for being used, I long to be. Any group in this country that sup-ports the ERA and other women's issues can easily enlist my services. More than anything in the world, I want to be useful to women.

Another New Right explanation for my behavior which effectively stifles the voice in the mind's back room that nags, "What if she is telling the truth?" is that I am a money-mad egomaniac doing all I do for publicity and pelf:

"Sonia 'Cry Baby to Press' J., What's the matter? Is the coming election, Iran, and the Russian invasion taking headlines from you?" . . . "Drop everything! Leave for Hollywood this minute. I'm sure they can use an actress of your caliber." . . . "Your name made the front page. So did Jim Jones." . . . "It is really a low point when you have to feed your ego on the cheap shot Donahue Show. Thank heaven everyone isn't blind to your stunts."

Women of the New Right also disassociate themselves from me in their minds by accusing me of being unfeminine, the peculiar as-sumption being that to be content to be treated unjustly under more than 16,000 laws in this country (which state of affairs men would not tolerate for two minutes!) is somehow "feminine."

When I was doing a TV show in Atlanta, a Mormon woman in the audience asked, "Why are you wearing a dress? You know you want to be a man!" (Sigh. Yet another good soul who knows me bet-ter than I know myself.)

I told her that on the contrary, I am glad to be a woman and have never wished to be a man, but I would certainly like some of the benefits men enjoy. I would like my work in the home—which society so hypocritically tells me is all-important and then never compensates me for—to be considered of some economic value when my husband dies or leaves me, or when I am old and need social security. When I work outside the home, I would like to make as much money as men make for doing the same work or work of equal value. And I cannot imagine anything more rewarding than to have people presume before I even open my mouth that what I am about to say has some value, and when I do say it, to presume that I know what I'm talking about, as people presume about men. For women to be taken seriously would be novel indeed. I would like to help make that a reality.

One Mormon woman tells me she "would prefer to do things that are more femine [*sic*]." The night my "file" burst open in direct response to the bigotry of the Project Director, one of the truths I knew by epiphany is that men are the ones who decide what is "feminine." And—what else is new?—they do it without consulting us. I for one resent that, and refuse to accept their definition. It does not apply to me or to any woman I admire and respect. We are not weak —physically or mentally, emotionally or spiritually. We do not need to be protected by others, only by the law. We are not incompetent, we are not by nature any more dependent, submissive, unsure, clinging, fearful, manipulative, seductive, childish, than the men we know. We do not need or desire to live vicariously through men and children. None of this describes me or those of my models who are most womanly. The womanly women I know stand up straight and strong on their own feet, on their own merits, and on their own terms. Men no longer define us for ourselves, and therefore we are not—thank goodness—"feminine." We are womanly. Let those women who are afraid to grow up, afraid to be human beings, be "feminine" for the men.

New Rightists dismiss me as a tool of Satan "to destroy the home," "to thwart the work of the Lord." But I am associated with less illustrious villains, too: "It appears you were chosen to act as a "modern-day Judas." By whom, I wonder? One of the most difficult experiences Mother had to face, she said, was going to church in those early months after the excommunication and facing the lugubrious commiseration of the members of her ward. "They take my hand in both of theirs," she reported, "and with pity spilling out of their eyes, murmur their condolences and sympathy as if I were the mother of Judas Iscariot."

But the most vicious strategy for discrediting and dismissing me—one that even the champion of truth, Jack Anderson, indulges in occasionally about me—is to pronounce me "demented," "mentally disturbed." Label me away. I've often heard sophisticated people say that Washington, D.C., is a small town. I finally understood what they meant when a man who worked in the same office as a member of my ward called and told me the explanation he received of the excommunication: "Sonia's seriously emotionally ill. In fact, she's having a nervous breakdown."

That accounts for it, then! What a relief! Now we won't have to pay any attention to what she is saying!

I assured the office mate of my ward "friend" that on the contrary, I was in excellent emotional health, and reminded him that mental illness is a time-honored method of explaining away ideas, especially women's ideas, of trivializing and negating them. Many women have ended up in mental institutions just so that their families—or governments—would not have to deal with their "nonconformity," their "non-femininity." It is simply another of the hundreds of strategies for minimizing the importance of women: we can't possibly have real courage, or real commitment, or serious thought; we cannot possibly understand philosophy or religion or politics or care about those things in any "real" (meaning male) sense. So if some woman *seems* to, it must be some peculiar individual quirk caused by emotional instability, by the basic unsoundness of being female, which means being uncredible, which means being written off. Which means being insane.

When news of my arrest in Bellevue, Washington, at the Mormon temple in November of 1980 reached a town in Pennsylvania, Mormon church leaders there called a special meeting to inform and warn members. "Sonia Johnson is deranged. We don't know how far she will go. We must stick together as a religious community." A woman working with the young women in the ward there said she has heard them say on several occasions that the reason I do what I do is that I am mentally unbalanced.

Thus am I categorized, labeled away, that I may be negated.

The truth is, I was not *sane* until I was a feminist.

They all want me to repent: "Please, Sonia, repent of your lies.

You know yourself in your heart that this is the only way. Tell the truth about your excommunication."

When Mike Barrett and I went to see the stake president to receive from him the word that the first presidency had refused my appeal, Earl Roueche read portions of their letter to me. (I was not allowed a copy of it.) The last sentence tells how much the Brethren love me, and that they hope I will do all I can to get back into the church.

"What *can* I do to come back into the church, Earl?" I asked. And for the next hour and a half, we discussed the Equal Rights Amendment. Earl said he knew the church's anti-ERA campaign was God's will and announced in solemn churchman tones, "You have offended God." "No, Earl," I corrected him. "I have offended *you!*" I told him I thought God might very well be offended by him and other leaders for not telling the truth about why I was excommunicated. "We have sat here for an hour and a half, talking about my actions in relation to the Equal Rights Amendment and the church. We have not talked about a single one of the official charges. When we are in private, we always talk about the ERA. Why don't you tell that to the press?"

Marvin Poulton, he of military intelligence who was in the back of the room at my trial, had been sitting in this meeting becoming more and more enraged. Finally he burst out, "You really wish we would do that, don't you?"

"Yes," I answered quietly. "I wish you would tell the truth."

Tellingly enough, President Roueche could not even remember the formal charges against me, though he had held a high council court on the basis of them, after supposedly studying the appeal which discusses them at length. I don't blame him. They are so absurd, I can't remember them myself. Not to mention the fact that they are continually in a process of evolution, being reinterpreted and changed every time the church restates them.

Almost all the anti letters display a phenomenon Bonaro Overstreet described nearly thirty years ago in an article entitled "The Unloving Personality and the Religion of Love." She says there are certain persons who "conceal their unlovingness from themselves and rarely suspect that what motivates their daily actions is by no means an outgoing love but rather a consuming desire *to take in from their world*—to take in love, comfort, approval, protection, reassurance, adulation." Such people, she says, are attracted to churches because there they feel safe from difficult and complicated human relationships.

Surely Mormonism has its quota of these people; I have heard from many of them. The "love-feigned" syndrome, the serious conflict between what they know they ought to be feeling and what they *really* feel is very clear:

"Every day more and more observant people join the other side because they are sickened by your behavior and wish you would come to your senses and put an end to such obnoxiousness. Signed, A True Friend. P.S. We pray for you."

Equally ambivalent are these confused souls:

"I feel so deeply for you and understand why you say the terrible things you do. I hope you pay attention to this letter because it is written with the deepest sincerity and because I care about you as a person. Signed, A Lady, AND PROUD OF IT! P.S. I am not telling you who I am for I want no part of ERA or you!"

"In all the 'fun' you are having with your campaign, I sincerely hope you will think through statements and impressions you are leaving with others. You express such 'pain and agony', poor me, self-pity image . . . May you find strength and comfort and peace, I sincerely hope for you and your family."

"I hope you are enjoying the feeling of power you have at the moment. Your moment will not last long compared to eternity. By then I hope I have perfected myself to the point where I will be able to resist the temptation of saying I told you so. This letter is sent with love . . . one child of God to another."

And from one loving Mormon brother, following in the gentle, loving footsteps of Jesus Christ:

"Dear ERA QUEEN Sonia: You provoke one to sorrow and laughter. Your hypocrisy is so blatant and your rhetoric so confused and lacking in truth one can only think, 'what prize is that woman striving for? She who so tastelessly puts on the martyr façade, while claiming such ecclesiastical understanding and knowledge.' Obviously your doctorial [*sic*] degree did not increase very much understanding of truth. The laughter comes in the ridiculous things you profess to believe. . . . Well, Lady 'Queenie,' enjoy your reign. You have some following I would suspect, but I hear many have written you off. Satan too had a following. Are you his advocate? There are those who recognize you as such. He must be really holding his sides with laughter. Signed, With love and sorrow for you."

Because so many of my loving-hating brothers and sisters in the gospel are so angry at my breaking the taboos of the patriarchy, they want desperately to see me punished, and the quicker and harder the better. They fervently hope I am unhappy *right now*, and will become progressively more so:*

"You must live a very unhappy life," writes a Mormon man who "cares about me." "Maybe you can wake up and realize what you have done to your life by being the Devil's Advocate. Woman, when are you going to wake up and understand your own problems come from your selfish greed for *power?* May Lucifer continue to enrich you with the curses he has so cunningly entrapped you in."

"History will bear this out," writes another, "and history proves that people who fight against things that are Sacred go down in infamy and broken in spirit as well as other ways, and you don't need to think you are different."

One "loving" Mormon woman who is working toward her Ph.D. in family counseling at BYU warns me hopefully that if I don't repent fully for that terrible sin she *knows* I've committed(!), "Finally, behavior becomes so bizarre and unreasonable that you will no longer have control of yourself. The final stop is the State Mental Hospital or Prison for murder. I have seen no other alternatives for those who blind themselves to the truth."

Regardless of what happens to me in the future, my enemies cannot lose. Life is not always easy for any of us and I will certainly have my difficulties just as everyone else will. The difference obviously is that when *I* have troubles in the future, my enemies will pounce on them with glee as proof that God is punishing me, whereas the troubles of others will be interpreted as evidences that God is testing them, and even that God loves them, since God tries those he loves most.

I am written off by a good many who choose to believe that I lost

* And regardless of the truth, the myth in the church will *always* be that I am unhappy. Excommunication supposedly turns me over to "the buffetings of Satan." From now until the end of time, stories about me in the Mormon church will have me weeping and wailing and gnashing my teeth. Otherwise, there is no justice. Otherwise, I might not have been wrong. And I *must* be believed to be wrong, or the leaders of the church are not infallible. And where does that leave Mormons?

my husband because of my ERA work, as another evidence that the ERA breaks up families and that therefore I am wrong. (We do not even have the ERA yet. What's breaking up all the families?) The assumption is that all women who want justice under the law hate men, and therefore cannot have happy marriages. They love my divorce and jump to all kinds of untrue conclusions from it which say more about them and their fears than about me and the ERA:

"I am sorry you have apparently not had a happy relationship with men in your life . . ."*

"Will women have to suffer marital estrangement as Sonia has in order to attain their rights?"

The issue was a difficult one to deal with back then, not because the ERA had broken up my marriage, but because I found the divorce so difficult to discuss. My heart was broken by it; I missed Rick terribly, and the thought of him gone forever to other arms and never mine again, and the dishonorable, hurtful way he had dealt with me made me weak with misery. No one would want to talk about a fresh grief the way I had to talk about mine, day after day, to strangers, knowing that the ERA opposition—and all my "loving" Mormon brothers and sisters—were gloating. But it was easy to deal with the divorce philosophically, if not emotionally. Rick had always been an ardent supporter of the ERA and of my activities. That was not the problem. I always told reporters what I think smug Mormons need to remember: the divorce rate in Utah, which is about 70 percent Mormon, is as high as the national average, and occasionally higher. At the time Rick left me, at least three other women in the Sterling Park Ward were getting divorces, all of them wildly anti-ERA and very traditional women determined to be only wives and

* Even supposedly sympathetic Mormons sometimes say this without realizing how quintessentially sexist the assumption behind it is: that women cannot transcend the personal, the private, the petty. We cannot really care about issues the way men supposedly do: disinterestedly, altruistically, intellectually. We are bound to our own small personal, emotional worlds. This is one of the most common ways of dismissing women and of not giving credence to our ideas: "It's only because she has had some bad experiences with men." Would the same people ever maintain that President Reagan or President Kimball oppose the ERA because they have had some bad personal experiences with women? Of course not! But that is far more likely, it seems to me, than that women the world over want justice under law because of some bad experiences in their personal lives with men. I certainly didn't think of myself as having had bad experiences with men when I became pro-ERA.

mothers forever—roles, not people. And two of the other husbands had left the wives for other women. So of the four of us in the ward I knew were getting divorces—and there may have been others—three were anti-ERA. That's three quarters of us! That's 75 percent. Should I therefore categorically state that 75 percent of divorces in the Mormon church—or anywhere—are caused by women's being anti-equality? Of course not. That is as clearly nonsensical as it is to say that ERA is the cause of divorce. Marriage on all sides of all issues, in all churches, among all races, is precarious today and very fragile—because (and I believe this as much as I believe any other one thing) *because* men and women are not considered equal.

Feminism and divorce do not have a cause-and-effect relationship; that is, feminism does not *cause* divorce. Instead, both are effects of the same cause. A prime cause of both is mistreatment of women in their marriages and in society.

At the time our great suffragist foremothers were struggling for ratification of the Nineteenth Amendment, giving women the right to vote, the antis were saying exactly what they are saying today against legal equality. And so should we, as Howard Phillips of the Conservative Caucus did in California in the 1980 campaign, lay the moral decay and all problems of society at the feet of voting women? *We* may laugh. But in fact, patriarchy does just that: lays the blame on women for all evil. And women must stop accepting that blame. It is not evil for women to have justice under the law any more than it is for them to vote. It is evil for them *not* to be protected in this greatest of all democracies. Like our foremothers, we should carry banners every day at the White House declaring, "America is not a democracy. Women do not have liberty here. How long must women wait for liberty?"

Church people of every denomination wanted to know whether I was part of a movement for priesthood for women in the Mormon church. I had to laugh a little when I read those letters. When Marc was about four years old and we were living again in Palo Alto (having just returned from two years in Africa), I was asked to participate on a panel to raise money for a struggling journal produced by liberal Mormons to help other liberal Mormons survive the ever increasing anti-intellectualism of the church. (Ironically but not surprisingly, the man whose project this originally was has now been totally co-opted by the church.)

The three-member panel agreed to meet one evening before the event to get to know one another and to figure out what we could say or do that would be provocative. The moderator, Sam Taylor, had been chosen for his colorful, forthright ways, Connie Bennion had been chosen as the ideal Mormon woman, and I had been chosen to represent—what? the untraditional woman? I can't think why, if this is the case, since I was merely being a wife and mother at the time, and having babies and teaching Relief Society like everyone else. It must have been something about me, some attitude, that caused others to divine the dangerous beginnings of humanness in me before I did. Anyway, none of the three of us knew the others, so we met at Connie's one evening. She left Sam and me alone in the living room for a few minutes while she went out to get us some brownies, and while she was gone Sam, whom I had just met, and who awed me because he was a "famous writer," turned to me and said, "Do you think women ought to have the priesthood?"

I responded just as many Mormon women do when asked this question nowadays: with shock and horror (see how emancipated I was?). "Oh no!" I answered quickly in alarm. "I should say not!" To my surprise, he looked disappointed. It was hard for me to imagine any Mormon male looking disappointed at such an obviously correct disclaimer offered in such correct tones of dismay. Years later, I guessed with amusement that he probably was looking for a way to show some difference between Connie and me, and sighed as he thought of the difficulty of trying to make me look radical.

Several months ago I called Sam when I was in town. "Remember when you asked me if I thought women should have the priesthood? Well, Sam, if you and I were to do that panel again tonight, we'd really give that group their money's worth!"

In August 1979, the month before we flew the Mother in Heaven banners, I sounded my private war cry against the totally male godhead—the root of patriarchy—and male priesthood by writing a poem called "Initiatories." In it I described my feelings in the washing and anointing rooms of the Mormon temple where women hold the priesthood; where, as ordained priests, they pronounce cleansing blessings upon parts of the body and make promises in the name of God.

Here in these quiet rooms among my beloved mint-scented sisters, I first thought seriously about Mother in Heaven. I became so intent

upon her one day that I had to restrain myself from calling aloud.
That day I wrote the poem:

INITIATORIES

Daughters of prehistory's Mariners—
Shining women who governed all Eve's earth—
I meet them in the patriarchs' temples,
tamed, diminished,
priestesses to men.
But not vested there with Father's power alone;
Mother, thy glorious gifts,
like vast subterranean springs
flow with potent secrecy through womankind
to lift and heal and cleanse every whit.

(The air quivers with possibility.
Will they recognize thee? Will they
call out?
At last begin to sing,
who for so long have had no song?

Mother, teach thy daughters to sing women's songs.)

Lips that they will never speak guile,
loins, legs,
all blessed by women's hands,
wonderful and womanly, those hands
that bear me female and whole
through homelessness to thee.

Fearless Queen of Heaven,
here among thy burning daughters,
consumed with longing for their hands to be
thy hands,
their voices, thy voice,
like Deborah, I would lead armies
against the ancient enemy,
I would fight to the death daily
those who daily try to obliterate thee
from my heart.

Mother, teach thy daughters to win women's wars!

Someday soon, the women of the church are going to understand fully and act upon the implications of those initiatory rooms in the temples. Women hold the priesthood there; hold it in and of themselves, as Mother in Heaven does, not "through" men. They lay their hands on our heads and forgive us our sins. No greater priesthood power than that is claimed by men anywhere in the world.

But I do not have to worry about the problem of women and the priesthood now. Other good, active, dedicated Mormon women, with husbands in high positions and in high positions themselves (for women) are thinking about it with a great deal of seriousness and frequency. I would like to have been the first in that arena, but one can only pioneer one front at a time.

Mormons on both sides of the ERA issue wrote to me about Mother in Heaven: "We are active church members (I teach gospel doctrine class; my husband recently called to be stake patriarch). Sometimes I can't pray because Father in Heaven is a man and how can a woman relate her problems to a man? Even an exalted one. Why is Mother in Heaven so silent? We need her advice and need her as a role model."

Another writes: "I am 70 years old and the great-great-granddaughter of Hyrum Smith, brother of the Prophet. My grandfather was Hyrum Smith Walker . . . How often we sang 'Father-Mother may I greet you in your royal courts on high,' without fully comprehending what we were saying. He-She are two halves meant to become one whole."

As I read these letters—and there were many of them—I smiled at the irony that because of my rebellion against male domination of heaven and earth, six months after the excommunication I was giving sermons in male-dominated churches around the country. I remember one in particular: Mother's Day, in a large midwestern Methodist church. (The minister did not realize that he was taking his life in his hands when he asked a feminist to speak on Mother's Day!) The sermon was scheduled near the end of the service, and by the time I stood up to speak I felt beaten half to death by male references: father, son, lord, master, king, prince, sons of God, son of man; he, him, his, whack, crack, slap!*

* In my feminist-blossoming months before I was excommunicated, women were always assailing me about my concern with male pronouns in the scriptures and elsewhere. "Hairsplitting!" they snorted. "Purest nitpicking. The words 'man' and

"Every Sunday is Father's Day in this world!" I stormed at the congregation, but gently, in my Mormon woman's voice. "Every Sunday is redolent with praise of maleness. Even today, a day ostensibly mother's, we have had father's day *again*, have sung 'This is My Father's World,' have praised 'Father, Son, and Holy Ghost.' Mother has been tacked onto this service—and onto most services in this land today—as an afterthought. She is never central to our worship, on this or any other day. Mother's Day is the aberrant day on which we strain unsuccessfully again to believe the nonsense that femaleness is really valued in our culture and in our churches. Despite glowing rhetoric to the contrary, the actions of churchmen continue to make excruciatingly clear that to be female is to be despised, rejected, and excluded."

I went on to read to them this paragraph from a letter written by a Mormon woman in southern Virginia: "Recently a class of first graders was being shown pictures of many different birds. The teacher asked if anyone could tell her why the male of each species

---

'men' and all male pronouns are generic," they assured me patiently as if I were not very bright. "They refer to *all* people. *I* have never felt excluded. *I* have always felt as if the scriptures were speaking directly to me. So what's the matter with *you?*"

But I knew about language; I knew that words are symbols, and I knew how profoundly and unconsciously symbols affect us all. I knew these women were deceiving themselves. The fact that only male pronouns and words are used to signify humankind is of monumental and deadly significance to women, underscoring and reinforcing as it does that not being male, we are therefore not human.

Then I began to run across studies showing that when people were given statements such as "early man discovered fire," and "When man invented the wheel . . ." they always without exception, male and female, envisioned *male* persons. Of course. That's what it means to live in a patriarchy: the underlying assumption of our entire world view is that everything of any importance is done by men.

When the scriptures say "he" they *mean* "he," just like most textbooks and other books in the world. Men are the real people. Women, like children, are not full persons, have not yet entered as peers into male consciousness. Church leaders, by insisting, as President Kimball of the Mormon church does, that women are *made* to be mothers and wives, tell us how inconsequential everything nonsexual about us is, how inconsequential is everything but our wombs, breasts, and vaginas (except maybe our hands which allow us to serve our husbands and sons). With men like this at our ecclesiastical head, women hardly need scriptural evidence to prove how invisible we are as full, complete, individual, real, adult human beings.

My acting as if I were a *person* is what finally drove church leaders beyond the boundaries of good sense.

was so much prettier and fancier than the female. A little boy immediately answered, 'Because God is a man.'

" 'I believe,' my correspondent concluded, 'that this small, innocent child has explained why some people are against ERA. Women aren't worthy of full human participation because *God is a man.*'"

I told the Methodists how, when I first instructed my children to begin all prayers with "Dear Mother and Father in Heaven" or "Dear Father and Mother in Heaven"—stressing that they reverse the order often so that in their minds one parent did not always and automatically precede the other—my son Eric, then fifteen, balked.

"Why are you asking us to do this?" he asked. "It doesn't feel right."

"It doesn't feel right because you aren't accustomed to it, that's all. But someday it will seem as peculiar to leave her out as it does now to include her.* Praying in this way should help us imagine and accept deity as also female, should help us see the potential in women as well as in men. When we can visualize a female God with all the power, all the strength, all the glory and wisdom we now attribute to a male God, we are well on our way to being able to value and love women.

"And Kari and I need her for a model: strong and fearless, her head high, her hand mighty. We need her so we can understand that independence, strength, power, and intelligence are as much women's heritage and as much a part of their nature as kindness and gentleness.

"You boys need Mother in Heaven so you will realize that to be gentle, loving, and sensitive is as much your birthright and your nature and as basically an aspect of God as to have power and to be in control. You need Mother so you can begin to respect your sister and me, your girl friends, and eventually so you can respect your wives as much as you respect your father, your uncles, and the guys at school, seeing in women also literally the image of God. When you come to understand her you will know that there is no divine sanction for you to rule over women, because your Heavenly Father does not rule over Mother. Neither does she rule over him.

"And," I neared the end of my lecture, "all of us, male and fe-

* Just recently he confessed that every time someone prays in church now, to the ritual opening—Our Father in Heaven—he adds silently, "and Mother." I was very pleased and encouraged. Habits of sexism *can* be broken!

male, for the sake of the survival of planet earth, need to view our Heavenly Parents as lovers of peace, of mercy, of freedom, and of human life. The Old Testament God—that savage old warmonger—needs to be driven out of our hearts forever." (As I drove him out of the Methodist church that Mother's Day. Mentally watching him exit in a flurry of white robes and beard, I thought, "Good-bye and good riddance, you old barbarian!")

"Let us teach our children," I begged the Mother's Day Methodist congregation, "to pray to their Father and Mother in Heaven, so they have a chance to grow up balanced and whole. And let us teach our daughters to sing those words from the play *For Colored Girls Who Have Considered Suicide When the Rainbow Is Enuf*: 'I have found God in myself and I love her fiercely.'"

In short, let us ratify the ERA in heaven so we can ratify it on earth.

New scholarship, much of it by women, is now revealing that matriarchy and female deity worship were probably the first real religions, later systematically wiped out—and then written out—of history by men.

I have been all over this country in the past year, and everywhere women are talking about the Goddess. Whether or not they are interested in worshipping a deity of any sex, they are saying to one another in a spirit of sisterhood and in the effort to make one another whole, "May the Goddess bless you," or ". . . be with you," and they assure me with smiles that if I ask her help, God will surely respond. Many, of course, are in religious earnest about her, and I understand very well how heady it is to realize that God is one of you instead of one of the Old Boys; how heady the unaccustomed feeling of power and worth when you comprehend that deity is on your side too, not exclusively a member of the Old Boys' Club and church.

But personally I am not willing to replace the patriarchal Old Testament God with the matriarchal one that preceded him, the Old Boys' with the Old Girls' Club. What is the use of exchanging one brand of sexism for another? Many women who are sensitive to the phenomenon of god-discovery going on are also concerned lest we women, in our turn, exclude men from deity as men have so devastatingly excluded us.

And now that we are undertaking the long overdue reorganization of heaven,* we must make sure there is a model there, and a representative there, for every human being. Everyone must be empowered, because we have sons and husbands and brothers and fathers as well as sisters, mothers, and daughters. Surely we must hate disenfranchisement so much that we will never inflict it on anyone else. None of us is free so long as anyone is oppressed.

I haven't much interest in establishing a uniform view of deity as one being equally female and male—androgynous—or as truly sexless, or as two separate beings—female and male—or as a host of beings of both sexes: the great cloud of witnesses Luke speaks of. It does not finally matter a great deal to me whether we all agree that we are children of God (which makes God parents) or creations of God (which makes us artifacts) or whether we simply view whatever is there that loves us as our friend. I have had quite enough of institutional methods of enforcing uniformity of belief.

What *is* important to me is that we refuse to use our particular view of God as justification for treating other people basely, as Jesus has been used against non-Christians and as his and God the father's maleness has been used against women throughout Christian history.

One thing I am certain of: whatever God is, is not hurtful to any

---

* Remembering the arduous, occasionally excruciating, process of my own reorganization of heaven, and how much even one other person's perspective and support helped, I sometimes suggest in my speeches that people get together and hold Reorganization of Heaven parties where everyone makes her or his own particular contribution to untying the knot of male supremacy that binds deity to their thrones and us to ignorance and oppression.

Individually and in small informal groups, there is a religious revolution of such immense proportions flourishing today that it will eventually make the Reformation look like a Boy Scout picnic. We do not know what this period will be called in years to come—after all, those living during the Reformation did not go about exclaiming, "Isn't it wonderful to be alive during the Reformation!"—and we may not even see clearly that we are in the midst of the greatest religious revolution since patriarchy took over the world millennia ago. We are too close to it to have perspective. But men and women all over the country have been talking to me about religion this past year, and I predict that religion will never look the same after women—feminists—have done with it. It may take no longer than fifty years for us so to change the face of it that if we were suddenly able to step ahead into that time, we would not—thank goodness!—find much that was familiar. Most especially, we would find missing the basic hypocrisy of lip service to the Golden Rule. Women are going to make religion deliver on its teaching that everyone, including men, should do unto others, including women, as they would be done by. Women are demanding that religious institutions and people be ethical and honorable, not just mystical and powerful. Women are demanding—and we will get—equal rights in church as well as state.

living thing. The Mormon concept of God as the ultimate Old Testament patriarch has been hurtful to me. God does not exist to be used as evidence that some human beings should be denied the fullness others have.

But I do believe in God and my belief is very much influenced by my Mormon background. So are my prayers. Sometimes I pray to my Heavenly Parents, sometimes simply to Mother, less often nowadays only to Father (after all, I dealt exclusively with him for forty-two years! I'm sure he understands); and sometimes, when I am feeling very good about myself, very strong, very blessed, and very happy— which is more and more of the time—I feel profoundly non-hierarchical. At such times, I address whoever is listening as "my dear, good friend."

Kris tried to tell me recently why the prophet does not have a revelation from God telling him what so many of us already know, that the time has come to acknowledge and worship Mother in Heaven as well as Father in Heaven so that the equality in heaven can be translated into equality on earth.

"The people aren't ready for it yet, Sonia," she explained. "They couldn't accept it. God cannot give us truth until we are ready for it." (Were they ready for the Sermon on the Mount, Kris?)

I wish she could have been with me that Mother's Day in Wisconsin when I chased the patriarchal Old Testament God out the door of that church. People swarmed up at the end of the service to embrace and thank me, many of them in tears. One older woman held my hands until she could stop crying and then said, "I've been sitting in church for sixty-eight years waiting for something. I know now that what I've been waiting for is what you said today. I've been longing all this time for word from Mother and I didn't even know it." A gruff old fellow took me by the shoulders and barked, "I wish there were ten thousand of you!" "There are!" I barked back— "millions." There was anger and pain, too. "They stole her from us. They had no right to do that!" Indeed.

Not ready, Kris?

Everywhere people hear about her, Mother in Heaven is like a drink of cool water in the desert. If religious authorities would "authorize" her, every woman on earth and a good many men would fall on their knees with such joy and relief that all heaven would overflow. You know who is not ready, Kris? It is the religious authorities, the men with the biggest stakes in male supremacy; they are who is not ready.

To instate Mother in Heaven on her throne with equal power would destroy patriarchy. And they believe patriarchy is God's plan, mostly because it suits them so well. Patriarchy means the rule of the men. Rulers always have privilege; that's the number-one fringe benefit of ruling. They make the rules and they enforce them; they give the orders; they decide what the money will be spent for, including how much of it they'll keep themselves and how to keep it away from others—predominantly women. Controlling much of what happens to them and others around them makes them feel powerful, invulnerable, godlike. This is a good feeling, much to be desired, and to be preserved at all costs.

So the privileges that guarantee men these comfortable feelings are codified in the law, which is why women receive little justice under patriarchy. Any system that holds that men have inside information from God about what's best for everybody, but most especially what's best for women, translated means what's economically best for men. And what's economically best for men has almost always been disastrous for women.

But even Mormons, as profoundly patriarchal and hence sexist as they are, believing the earthly family reflects the pattern of the heavenly family, will agree that no earthly parents in their right minds would communicate with their daughters primarily through their sons, especially on matters having to do with being female. It is difficult to imagine parents who, when their daughters are suffering deep distress about their journey as women through the world, would speak to them, comfort them, and counsel them by sending messages to them through their brothers.

Think for a moment of those brothers: persons who have not spent a single second of their lives being female, never had one menstrual cycle, without a clue about how it feels to be female—in short, the world's ultimate *non*-experts on the subject. Can anyone imagine parents trusting them even to understand the message in the first place, let alone to pass it along accurately?

Of course not. Such a system doesn't make sense. What it does make is a farce of the notion of loving, caring deity.

Our Heavenly Parents—or whatever nonsexist configuration God is —speak directly to their daughters all the time, on all kinds of mat-

ters, not just those related to home and family. All things that affect
our planet are matters that concern us. We are involved in the life of
humankind, in the life of the universe. We are the offspring of
heaven, and bigger than we dream.

Since we are women, though, our Heavenly Parents speak most
particularly to us about woman-ness. Any female who has lived a day
on the earth is already an expert on what it means to be female. She
already knows more about who she is, how she feels, what she wants
and needs than all the men who ever lived put together could ever
know about her. No man on earth, no matter how good or well-
meaning, has the answer for any woman, let alone for *all* women.

We women know we are not clones, though society has tried to
convince us otherwise for a very long time.

We know the same answer will not do for all of us, or even for
most of us, any more than one answer will do for all men. Most
women do not feel any more fulfilled being housewives than most
men would feel being farmers. We are as individual and as different
from one another in all respects as men are from one another, and as
able to direct our lives, given a decent chance. Each of us hears her
own answer—from her own heart, from each other, from heaven—
and for most of us it is the same as Jesus's to Lazarus at the tomb:
"Come forth."

In our own individual, peculiar, idiosyncratic, unique, and personal ways, each of us is coming forth, not asking permission anymore, not waiting to be "authorized" by men. *We* are the authorities
on ourselves. If the men in the churches and the legislatures want to
know what to do about us, they must ask *us*. This is our business, to
be about women's business, to be about our Heavenly Mother's business, which is the business of re-creating us in her image and of
healing the deepest wound ever inflicted upon the human family:
the dehumanization of women—and thus of men—through patriarchy.

The letters that cascaded down upon me after the excommunication told of the coming forth of Mormon women. All across this
country they are waking up to their oppression, and when Mormon
women wake up, we know patriarchy is doomed. A woman who held
"about every position open to women in the Church" but who can
no longer "choke it all down" wrote:

"My heart goes out to those women who are suffering; I have been there and I am appalled that I allowed them to put me through some of the things I went through as a younger woman in the church. . . . I never knew so many lonely, isolated women in my life as when I was active in Relief Society. So many go through the whirl but inwardly they are hurting. The Lord help us all!"

". . . There is not one vestige of actual authority that a Mormon woman can hold in her home or elsewhere," writes another longtime member, "that is not subject to Priesthood authority and 'leadership.' I do not agree with this situation and can see nothing Christlike in one sex 'leading' the other, and in one sex being the 'head' of the home. It is hard to furnish myself with any real definite teachings of the Savior which give a plausible reason for this doctrine to be so zealously perpetuated in the Mormon Church. It always leaves me with the feeling that women are regarded as semi-children, in need of being 'led' through this life by the men, and thus are not regarded as full-fledged adults. I can't get it through my head why there must be a 'head of the house,' and why a married couple can't function as a united pair of people, both working for the common good. It appears to be the male subjugating the female. It makes these men who promote this doctrine seem like little boys who must feel superior to little girls at all cost. . . ."

An Arizona woman very eloquently sets forth some of the common problems among Mormon women (and women in general): "It became a case of 'following' my husband where his work took him. And to complicate the situation, three months after we arrived he was made bishop over a large ward of 800 people. Nine years later, with four children, hundreds of ward dinners and meetings behind us, we moved to Phoenix. Three months after we arrived, my husband was made a member of the stake presidency. I remember so vividly that day. One of the apostles was here to interview both of us and set my husband apart. When he asked how I felt about the new calling, I started to cry. I was very pregnant with my fifth child and all I could think of was that I wouldn't have my husband at home anymore. He would always be in a meeting somewhere. I said to the apostle, 'I don't want to lose my husband again.' But, of course, I was assured that all would be well. We were doing the Lord's work and blessings would be 'poured out' upon us. Well, I don't think the apostle realized what I was saying or trying to say. And I'm sure he didn't realize that I would lose my husband, emotionally and spiritually. Now, as I look back, I should have said in that interview, 'I think you are making a mistake in asking my husband to take this calling. He has a more important calling—his children and his wife.' I should have told my husband, 'Look, I can't support you in this. I need you, the children need you. I can't raise five children all by myself. It is physically impossible.' But I didn't say any of these things. I just sat there blubbering. I could see how much it meant to my husband to receive this call. He loved the recognition, the adulation of the people, the feeling that he was loved and needed by God to do His work here. I couldn't fight that. And I thought it was wrong for me to have such thoughts and so I tried to do what was 'right' and accept the calling.

"Now, years later, it isn't any easier to talk to my husband about my feelings toward church authorities and even the church itself. Our children are all married, my husband now holds an even higher church position. And I, though not a typical Mormon matron—fat and harried-looking—am not-quite-thin, and have chronic back trouble. We (the Mormon wives, whose children are raised) are all suffering physical problems. We are battling boredom, fatigue, and depression,* and trying to figure out why we are so unhappy."

Another writes: "I know there are hundreds like me, all with a story to tell. Stories of how we try to cope in our male-dominated society. I have heard many of these stories from friends. There are lovely friends of mine and others also who are leaving the church behind in their search for a better way for women . . . The day a woman admits to herself that she has been sold a 'bill of goods' will be happening more and more frequently. It is an agonizing process, but it brings personal growth and development and progress—that favorite Mormon word."

"All four of my grandparents were converted and encouraged to immigrate from Denmark and Sweden by young thoughtless Mormon missionaries who preached the gathering to Zion," writes a seventy-three-year-old Mormon woman. "What they accomplished, my grandparents, by the move was to lock their children and grandchildren into a system of absolute male authority. Half, at least, of the people in the LDS church are women. But this half is pushed

---

* Recent studies reveal that three quarters of psychotherapists' or family counselors' patients in Utah are Mormon women, and that the problem afflicting nearly all of them is severe and chronic depression.

aside as nonentities, authorityless, to live their lives as slaves to the men. The usual way in the past was for the authoritarian brethren to harass the husband of any wife who showed a spark of intelligence and ability to make her own decisions, insisting that he, the husband, put her down and keep her there. The place delegated to women by the authorities was in the kitchen and the bedroom. My father was an LDS bishop and two of my uncles were bishops. Another uncle was president of the Manti temple, as was my brother. My mother, grandmother and aunts bore children and worked in the house, garden, raising chickens, etc. They eventually became physically exhausted and laid down and died to get some rest. . . . I personally know how hard it is to throw off the chains of complete submission to absolute male authority, and my sympathy and love are with you."

An Idaho woman requests, "I would like to be in touch with the nearest Mormons for ERA organization. Grandma always said Mormon men didn't treat women right and Grandfather agreed. I understand now what she was talking about. Stand on your convictions."

Another champion writes: "You had the guts to do it! And it had to happen someday. The women are so brainwashed by the constant hammering at all meetings that they really believe no heaven for them unless men take their hands and 'let' them pass in. How could we, they, have accepted this all these years?"

Many Mormon women view themselves and their sisters as "brainwashed." Writes one fifth-generation woman: "I am always amazed at the cowlike acceptance so many women in our church have of the chauvinistic policies so blatantly and consistently spouted. There are some of us too gutless to act on our beliefs, so I do take my hat off to you!"

An old woman from a very royal Mormon house writes: "My grandmother came with Brigham Young's wagon train. My father was a pioneer. I have a mother who was brought to Utah on the second through train from New York to San Francisco. She was solo contralto of the choir when the Temple was dedicated. I too once was an organist and had my curls lovingly touched by our bishop, David O. MacKay. 'Uncle David' as we called him then. That's my background. Believe me, you are not out of order or wrong in your beliefs. . . . Standing on your own two feet in your belief is all that

God can ask of you and He will bless you and see you through this. Keep your chin high!"

"I do admire your spunk and courage in standing up to the leaders of the church and hope you never give in," a relative of Spencer Kimball writes. "Women have been second-class, abused people long enough and no Christian church should try to keep them from becoming equal to any male in any office of the church. . . . Any church that calls itself the Church of Jesus Christ should remember that women were last at the cross and first at the tomb. Our faith alone entitles us to equal rights."

So from the sidelines, I am watching Mormon women come forth —in my lifetime!—unwinding their mind-bindings as they come, taking their place in living action—not in dead rhetoric—at men's sides. There is a splendid performance previewing in the churches of the world in which Mormon women will not be just stars, but meteors. I wouldn't miss it for the world, and I'm sure our Heavenly Mother wouldn't either.

The letters did me good, all of them. They helped me get perspective on my journey—where I had been, where I was going. They convinced me, if I had needed convincing, that I did not want to be like the "true believers"—intolerant, narrow, ignorant, unloving, hateful, punitive. I saw clearly which portion of humanity I stood with.

And my already zinging sense of urgency shot up. There was so very much to do and so little time!

Chapter 15

Invincible Summer

"If you had it to do over again, would you do it differently?" This is the question I am asked most frequently these days. People are curious to know if I lie awake nights, regretting, "Oh, if only I had not done this, not said that . . ." I answer that I have no regrets. I sleep well at night.

It was worth everything, and more.

As I look back upon this incredible year, I see that it was, like a long-ago time Dickens describes, the best of times as well as the worst of times. What made it best is what it taught me about myself and hence about all women.

I learned that I could, all alone, support myself and my children—no inconsequential realization for a hitherto very dependent woman. Though I thought I could not possibly write a book and begged Doubleday—futilely—to give me someone to do it for me or with me, I have, all alone, written this book. I learned that I can move audiences to action as well as to laughter and tears. And I have discovered in myself untapped sources of energy and strength.

Though all this has given me much-needed confidence, best of all is that doing these things has been fiercely satisfying, unbelievably pleasurable. If I could have my wish, it would be that I could spend my life working as I am now for women's rights.

Like a bystander, I observed myself through this turbulent year and was reassured and heartened by what I saw. Even when my heart was breaking, in the center of myself where I am most truly Sonia I was calm, unafraid, always at peace with myself, never despairing. At every turn I somehow felt certain how I should proceed. I did not agonize about what to do next, what to say, how to appear. I turned myself over to my instincts and found them trustworthy.

And I never felt abandoned by God, never felt helpless, out of control, never feared I would crack under the strain, never resorted to drugs or alcohol or worried about losing either my mind or my immortal soul.

Through it all I felt borne up on wings of angels.

While on one level I was devastated, going about the wretched business of burying my dead—a marriage, a faith, a large portion of a past—on another I was moving eagerly and confidently ahead about the business of living more fully than I had ever done, using all my senses, all my powers. Never for one second would I have chosen to return to life as it had been before. Because however much I hurt— and I *hurt!*—I was aware the whole time that I was involved in some personally momentous, infinitely desirable, even miraculous process of growing up—and up. Human beings are so complex. Inexplicably, I felt marvelous the whole time I felt miserable.

Camus understood and said it for me: "In the depth of winter, I finally learned that within me there lay an invincible summer."

My children, too, shattered at first by their father's abandonment and the church's cruelty, have completed the greater part of their course in grief. Even through the most trying times, I felt they were with me, loving me, though for about six months my own need was so great I had little of myself to spare them in theirs. I tried to surround them with my friends, with counselors who had the emotional wherewithal to hear and bear their heartache. I knew I had to get myself through mine as quickly as I could for all our sakes, so I fought the guilt that hammered on me from all sides about being away from home so often speaking (which is how I was putting the peanut butter in the cupboard) and healed myself with the love and support of thousands of feminists all over the country. When those times come that, mother or no, woman or no, we need all our strength for ourselves, we must rely on whatever support systems are out there, and I did.

But that desperate time is long past, and to my way of thinking, my relationship with my children is in good repair. We have had to work together as never before. And it has not been bad for them to have a mother who is also a real person, imperfections and all.

My beautiful Kari is no longer so sullen—though being a fifteen-year-old feminist in our macho neck of the Virginia woods would make even Susan B. sullen. An exceptionally insightful young woman, she will someday be a better feminist than I. I long to leave her a legacy of justice, to be able to say before I die, as I did in a poem I wrote to her:

> *Come daughter come*
> *full and spilling, come*
> *to the feast and sit down*
> *at the table*
> *heaped with honey and hollyhocks*
> *squashes and pomegranates,*
> *small furry animals tumbling*
> *through the apples.*
>
> *After all the work and waiting*
> *after all the fear and sorrow*
> *come dear hurry*
> *come full and spilling*
> *run laughing*
> *to the feast.*

One day last winter my son Eric put his arm around me and said, "Mom, you're my hero." It is no small thing to be hero to a seventeen-year-old male, especially one who until now has regarded you, when at all, as the supplier of food and clean socks—a sort of life-support vending machine. I am touched by the loyalty of my twelve-year-old Marc, who protested when I asked him to go to church with me one Sunday, "Why should I be interested in a church that doesn't think *you're* worthy to be a member of it?" He is also, like the older two, learning to take responsibility for his own life. Facing and defeating his devils, as Hazel says.

When I was arrested with twenty others in Bellevue, Washington, in November 1980 for chaining myself to the gates of the Mormon temple, I called my children to tell them I wouldn't be home that night as I had planned. Kari answered the phone. "I won't be home tonight, honey, because, well . . . I'm in jail," I confessed. "Congratulations!" she cheered. Marc grabbed the phone and demanded, "Are you *really* in jail, Mom?" "Yes, I really am." "Oh, Mom," he chortled. "I'm so proud of you!" And the next day, my irrepressible six-year-old, Malaysian-born Noly, with the corkscrew curl at the nape of his neck, proudly announced to his first-grade class when given a chance to say a couple of sentences about his family, "I belong to an ERA family, and my mom's in jail!" No other kid in the class topped that.

My children. My friends.

If I have taught them to cherish individual liberty, then I have taught them a great deal. If I have taught them to risk everything if necessary in its defense, I have taught them an even greater lesson. But if I have taught my daughter to bow to no man, and my sons that to exploit women is to weaken themselves, if I have taught them all, male and female, to love and honor women's liberty, I have laid the foundation for a new world.

From its earliest beginnings, my transformation from housewife to heretic appalled my father, being as he is so thoroughly a man of the New Right. Also being as he is so thoroughly indoctrinated in the patriarchal nonsense that God will do with me whatever the Old Boys tell him to, Dad firmly believes I have forfeited my eternal salvation, and mourns that I will not be with the family in heaven.*

But there was a time when Dad mellowed. It was when he found that he had cancer, and death appeared imminent. One day during this time, when I was on the phone with Mother, he picked up the extension and my heart sank. I did not feel like listening to another of his fear-and-guilt diatribes just then. But he surprised me. Feeling strong intimations of mortality, he had for a moment seen everything clearly and gotten his values straight. "I don't care what you did, Sonia," he said. "None of that matters. The only thing that matters is that we love each other."

Dad's equivalent of the road to Damascus.

Soon, however, the doctors could find no more trace of cancer, and realizing that he was not dying after all, Dad appeared to revert to caring most what the neighbors think (which also includes his younger brother, though he lives far away), which is why he was be-

---

* Mormons believe that those who go to the best place in heaven do so as families. Don't ask me whose, your father's or your husband's; I have never been able to get that straight and neither has anyone else. Especially when combined with the hedonistic belief that in That Place men will be polygamous, which hopelessly muddles the family-togetherness picture. Believe me, as one who knows from long experience of burying my head in the sand, it does not bear thinking about.

side himself with fury when I was arrested. "Now you've made an ass of yourself before the whole nation!" he fumed.

I liked his attitude better when he was dying.

To be fair, a little of the mellowness of the cancer-scare days has clung to Dad. Perhaps merely a sign of the passage of time or, more hopefully, a sign that no vision is entirely wasted on us mortals.

Not the least of the pleasant discoveries I have made this year is that I am enjoying being free of Rick. And I have begun to think that the arrival on the scene of the blond chick was as providential as it was predictable. If she had not appeared, I may have had to invent her. When I confessed to a friend that I was puzzled at never having been very angry at Rick about the divorce, just hurt and sad, she suggested, "Maybe unconsciously you were relieved." Yes, I think that is the truth of it. What I felt for him, and had for many years, was mostly dependence, fear of being on my own. Women often confuse dependence and love.

But though I have "written him off," and am glad to shift the burden of him to other shoulders, I knew him as a boy; he knew me as a girl. We are the repositories of each other's youth. I will always love that thin, shy, dark, intense, troubled Easterner that he was, as I will that troubled, sleep-walking, brown-haired, soft-cheeked Mormon girl that I was.

How many different me's there have been between that girl and the present Sonia! But we are still friends, she and I. I can never despise her or patronize her. I am so proud of once having been that girl, as proud as I am now of being quite someone else.

For nearly a year after my excommunication, I attended church in the Sterling Park Ward whenever I was home on the weekends. This surprises lots of people. "Why in the world would you want to do that?" they ask incredulously.

I went because I am in some ineradicable ways Mormon, and that's where Mormons go. I went because I wanted to remind everyone that I had not wanted or chosen to be excommunicated, that I had been excommunicated unjustly. I went because I was appealing the excommunication and wanted my Mormon family to remember that if I had my way, I would again be an official member of the church. The Mormons are my people and I am theirs, whether we like it or not, whether we are comfortable with one another or not. Though they can disown me—like a family—like a family, they shouldn't. That is not a loving way. There are too many Sonia Johnsons—potential and full-fledged—in the church, and we are not dispensable. The church loses when it loses us, far more than we lose when we are evicted. They cannot take from us whatever good we have gained from the church. We can continue to benefit from that all our lives. But they can no longer benefit from us. And they are gravely shortsighted to minimize our contribution.

By attending church, I hoped to give the Mormons some notion of the "loyal opposition," a concept quite lacking in the ordinary Mormon mind. James Chapman, an excommunicated Mormon from California, in a speech entitled "The Legitimacy of Responsible Dissent," explains it well. When Jeff excommunicated me, I was a "real Mormon" as Chapman defines it here:

"It is said that open dissent implies contempt for the church and that if a person doesn't agree with the way the church is operated they should get out and go someplace else . . .

"I would say that for those who take this position it is as if they had no real understanding of the place of their church in the world. Mormonism to real Mormons is not just another church, another voluntary organization . . . it is the Kingdom of God. It is the mortal system, the Earth, the Universe, and the world beyond. It encompasses all that exists. To tell a Mormon dissident to love the church as it is or leave it is like saying that if you disagree with the way the world is today, you should commit suicide. . . . Those who stay with the church, but are in a dissident position, may be the most loyal to the church. Those who stay and fight for change in the church just may be those who love her the most."

In my response to the National Women's Party welcome to Mormons for ERA in January 1979, I said, "But make no mistake. As Mormons for ERA, we care for our Mormon culture and heritage. We care very much. It may seem paradoxical, but we do what we do *because* we care."

I attended church because I thought members of my ward should not be allowed to forget, and should be forced to reevaluate, what they had seen happen before their eyes that November and December of 1979. They needed to have their unconscious knowledge that the church is fighting vigorously against women's rights stirred up into consciousness again periodically for a few moments. They needed to realize that the problem of women in the church and world is still very much with them, that it will never go away, and that they have certainly not rid themselves of it by ousting me. They needed to be reminded that there is growing unhappiness among members about the church's virulent anti-female stance. I sat there to remind them of the immense pain and anger of good members everywhere.

I attended church to alert Mormons that the church is sitting on a time bomb labeled *women.*

"Okay, but then why did you stop going?" I am inevitably asked next.

That is a more difficult question. One reason is that I did not like to leave my children every Sunday morning. Sunday feels like the day we most need to be together. I felt uncomfortable sitting in church without them—and they refused to go with me.

But though that is a true answer, it is only a very partial one, the easy part. The major and difficult part is that I came to the end of my tolerance of a number of things. The stifling, power-hungry maleness of the Mormon establishment, for one. I had grown too caring, too proud and protective of women to sit quietly as they were systematically belittled in large and small, overt and covert ways week after week. For another, I came to the end of my tolerance for grieving, and to go to church was to grieve again for something which I slowly began to understand had never really existed except in my own mind, but which nevertheless was inexpressibly dear. I grieved because when I opened my eyes I did not find what I valued about my mind's church in the real institution at all. What was there was not the church I had thought it was when I was a child and a young woman. That beloved idea—that what the institution said it valued and what it *really* valued were the same—that idea was dead. Sitting in church after this realization was like attending its funeral week after week. It was like a continual wake for a grand illusion, a continual viewing of the corpse of my idealism. The form was the same— we prayed, we sang (we sang my songs but it was like hearing history), someone spoke and said what we knew they would say, we took the sacrament—but the life had gone out of it because the life that it had had I had given it with my love. Every Sunday I mourned again for the loving, free place my mind had made of my church, but about the absence of both love and freedom I could no longer deceive myself.

To continue to view a corpse is not wholesome. So I do not go

anymore. I have said good-bye to Mormonism as a viable religion,
though I am in many ways—by heritage, in much of my world view
—irrevocably Mormon and would not change that even if I could.
Though I didn't actually stop attending until October 1980, sitting
in church on the evening of December 23, 1979, I wrote my formal
farewell:

> *The church of my childhood*
> *was red brick, too.*
> *Smug and warm inside, I'd*
> *watch the snow battling the windows*
> *or one cold star low in the cold sky*
> *and rejoice at being inside with Mama*
> *and the choir*
> *hymning the wintry day to its close.*
>
> *In blue by the covered wagon,*
> *the pioneer woman poised above us*
> *on choir breath*
> *whispered, "Fear not."*
> *God-wrapped in that singing room,*
> *what was there to fear?*
>
> *Tonight in maturity's church*
> *good-bye, good-bye who I was in the*
> *warm silent service with snow fighting*
> *to break through the windows of my youth*
> *and ghost voices forever echoing*
> *down the dusk and farewell of the wintry day.*
>
> *Hello at last, cold star and blowing snow,*
> *and you, my pioneer sister*
> *with your grave and steady eyes*
> *who knew so well what there was to fear*
> *and feared not.*

A reporter for the Atlanta *Constitution* recently asked me if, now
that I was no longer theologically Mormon, I had acquired any non-
Mormon habits (alluding, I'm sure, to smoking and drinking). "Yes,"
I replied, "in fact I have. I have acquired the habit of free thought."

In my deepest winter, before I felt the stirrings of the summer in myself, I turned again to Hazel. "Wouldn't it have been wonderful if I could have been divorced *this* year and excommunicated *next?*" I wailed. "Together they're too big, too overwhelming!"

"Sonia, you're going to be glad someday that it happened like this," she prophesied. "Just think. You'll only have one hard year instead of two!"

Wise Hazel, right as usual. Mourning two deaths does not take twice as long as mourning one, and the pain, though intensified, is not doubled. I grieved the combined griefs in one heavy-duty mourning, and now the pain of the two betrayals has settled, as heavy things do, to the bottom of the stream of my life, carrying with it many of my vague fears and discontents. There on the bottom they form a rich, dark bed of experience over which I am flowing clear from the springs of myself, sparkling in the sun, rejoicing. I once told a Washington *Post* reporter, when she asked if I regret, that I had stepped into a stream and it was taking me.

The stream was myself, and it swept me away.

Knowing that I am an ordinary woman, and having discovered what I am capable of, I feel a degree of optimism about women in general that I have never felt before. Since I have not only survived but triumphed, I have learned that triumph, not just survival, is possible for women like me, ordinary women, everywhere. We are all more than we dream. All stronger and more courageous, all better and wiser. From uncovering my hoard of personal riches, I extrapolate the secret hoards in all women, and know, because I am Everywoman, replicated by the millions everywhere, that because of us, the women's movement cannot fail. Our yeasty richness will leaven and change the world.

Now, tonight, hearing the menacing anti-woman murmur rising to an open-throated roar in this country, I think of a poem I call "Daughter of Eve":

> *Listening to the sinister wind*
> *I am perversely*
> *opulently serene*
>
> . . . .
>
> *Afire with an inextinguishable hope,*
> *I launch my bright kites*
> *into America's future.*

Chapter 16

All on Fire

"And so how do you feel now about the Equal Rights Amendment? What are you proposing?" This is the next most frequent question I am asked after "Do you regret anything?"; "How is your family taking it?"; and "What about the church?"

As I speak now all over the country, crossing state lines to incite people to riot for human rights, a frequent response from the audience goes something like this: "You seem to be, well, not . . . *balanced*. Would you say you're *obsessed* by the Equal Rights Amendment?"

And I answer, "If by obsessed, you mean would I give my life to see it ratified, the answer is yes, I'm obsessed. I'm obsessed by the desire for justice for women. I burn with it. It consumes my life."

The first time I gave that answer, the faces in the first few rows—which were all I could see—registered acute embarrassment, and I could almost hear the thoughts behind them: "Oh, now, *that's* going too far!" "Just as I thought—a kook!" "Unladylike!" "Immoderate!" "Extreme!" As I saw these thoughts pass across those faces, I became very angry, as I do in the presence of sexism, knowing that no one would be embarrassed if I were a man talking about justice for men. So I let them have it.

I reminded them that, in every country of the world in all ages, men who have been willing to take enormous personal risks that other men might be free are called heroes. When we remember Patrick Henry's fervent "Give me liberty or give me death," we think, "Right on, Patrick! Quite right!" It gives us the delicious shivers precisely because it is *not* a balanced, moderate statement. All our founding fathers were immoderate men, obsessed with the idea of justice and willing to risk everything for it. The reason we do not

think of these men as kooks is because we never doubt that *man*kind
is worth laying down life for.

But *woman*kind? Let us not be absurd. We all know that *women*
are not worth that kind of sacrifice, that if those patriots who went
to the tyrants and said, "Let my people go!" had looked out the window and seen that their people were all female, they would have
yawned and said, "Oh, well. Never mind," and gone home to bed.

Women are the ones who *do* the sacrificing, not the ones others
sacrifice *for*. We do not believe our human rights are worth anyone's
giving their lives for. We are embarrassed that anyone should think
so, or suggest such a bizarre thing. "Me? Oh, goodness no, don't pay
any attention to me! And please, nobody give their lives for my civil
rights. I'm not worth it! I'd feel too guilty. Wait until the economy
is healthy, until the energy crisis is resolved, until there is no threat
of war anywhere in the world, and no hunger—in short, wait until
the sun burns out of the sky. Then I'll press for my rights!"

Everything takes precedence over women's problems. Everything.
And because we have always relied for acceptance upon putting our
own needs and desires last, if at all, we are frightened that men
won't love us anymore if we begin to demand justice for ourselves.
We are afraid of appropriate feeling and appropriate action, because
the only appropriate feeling for women in the United States today is
fury and the only appropriate action is immoderation.

If we are not furious, we are not well.

The founding fathers were outraged enough—by only a tiny fraction of the number of unjust laws that oppress women in this country today—to lay down their lives in battle if necessary. If men were
in our place—if they had no protection under the Constitution and
were at the mercy of at least 16,000 unjust laws—they would be rampaging in the streets. But they would never have let things come to
such a preposterous pass in the first place. They consider themselves
too valuable to be so scorned.

If we women do not soon begin to think we are worthy of the
many and immense personal sacrifices it is going to take to get our
civil rights, if we do not love ourselves and other women—and men—
enough to make those sacrifices and expect and accept them from
others, we are simply not going to get justice.* We must learn from

* It is time for us to ask and expect our husbands, our fathers and brothers, our
male friends, the public figures and famous men who say they care about justice

the men that to gain anything, we must be willing to risk everything. A time comes in every human rights movement when unless its proponents are willing to do this—to risk their reputations, their careers, their human relationships, their lives—the movement dies. We have come to that place in the women's movement.

As Susan B. Anthony so clearly understood more than a hundred years ago, "Cautious, careful people always casting about to preserve their reputation or social standards never can bring about reform. Those who are really in earnest are willing to be anything or nothing in the world's estimation, and publicly and privately, in season and out, avow their sympathies with despised ideas and their advocates, and bear the consequences."

We should understand and act upon the knowledge that every woman in this country has infinitely more to lose than to gain by "moderation," by being "ladylike" and "credible." Women have never been credible; we are kidding ourselves if we think we have or are. We will become credible only when we show forcefully that we will no longer be walked on, when we no longer lick boots and cower. When we love ourselves and men enough and are proud and angry enough to come forth and refuse to be oppressed one moment longer, only then will we be credible. Doormats—or old shoes—inspire no respect in anyone, including and most especially and most

---

for women to make sacrifices for us, to take risks, professionally, economically, emotionally—in all ways. How many of our influential husbands, our doctor, lawyer, corporate president or vice-president husbands, will put anything on the line for us? How many of our just ordinary man-on-the-street friends will lobby, write letters, give money, stamp and address envelopes, chauffeur, tend children, picket, go door to door for candidates? If we ask our men, will they prove they love us by doing for us now what we so desperately need? Or are we, by the hundreds of thousands, going to discover that the men we have trusted and respected have feet of clay? I wonder.

Will Alan Alda, will Phil Donahue, will Ed Asner—will these famous and very credible men who have so often said they support us take some serious risks for us in this most critical time? I have a favorite fantasy in which these men put together a road show which they take to all the unratified state legislatures and which is so powerful and moving that the Old Boys realize they must do the decent, honorable thing. Even in realistic moments, I believe men like these could win a state or two for us. Will they?

We will soon see who of all the men who say they love us and care about the quality of our lives *really* do. I hope against hope that men will justify our having loved them and will give us reason to continue to do so by responding in time to this crisis in women's—and human—history. It will be terrible if we lose the ERA. It will be a cataclysm if we learn that the best men do not care.

seriously themselves. When we do not value ourselves, no one else does either. So we must make it difficult—make it wretched and miserable—for men in power to fight us. We must stop allowing them to walk across our faces with their cleated boots while we apologize for being in their way. Only then will they—and we—respect us. It is time to desegregate the Old Boys' Club.

We do it, this work of justice, for the whole human race, men as much as women. I am often accused of hating men. I do not hate men. I hate the male-devised and -imposed system of supremacy called patriarchy. I hate it because it is lethal to both men and women. All persons born into and reared in a patriarchal society participate in the oppression of women and the aggrandizement of men. Most of us participate unwittingly, but participate nevertheless. Not to participate is a perpetual act of conscious will, behind which lie months and years of the most grueling and agonizing reeducation, and the most intense love of other human beings. Not many men understand well enough to take the trouble to reeducate themselves about the long-term advantages—to themselves as well as to women —of true equality. It is difficult to understand—or at least, too few men seem willing to try to understand how feeling superior and exerting power over others gnaws away at their own integrity, leaving their souls barren.

I do not hate men, but neither do I automatically respect and trust them anymore. And neither do I accept any longer the role of guardian of their egos. Many women, even in the women's movement, are still playing that role, afraid of hurting and alienating men by coming right out and defining the fundamental social evil, which is that men have oppressed women for thousands of years. My feeling is that ultimately we cannot be too concerned about whether we hurt and alienate. Our prime objective is not to win men's love and support by pillowing their egos, and we can do the work of justice ourselves without men's help, if necessary. I hope it will not be necessary. But by ourselves, we are enough to change the world.

It is an extremely difficult habit to break, this softening of blows for men, which women have been so well trained for so long to do, one of the implications of it being—besides that they will not love us if we don't—that men are not capable of handling difficult truths. I don't believe this for a moment. I have confidence in men. I am not afraid that they will shatter if I say that men have been and are our enemies—beloved enemies, perhaps, often unwitting enemies, but enemies nevertheless. I expect them to understand that I do not believe all men set out consciously to hurt and stunt and thwart and destroy us. I also expect them to be decent and mature and secure enough to examine the evidence that this is the case without having tantrums or psychotic breaks, and to begin to help put a stop to it. I believe that the majority of men are capable of this and more, as is evidenced by the fact that more men than women support the Equal Rights Amendment.

When we fear to be honest and open with men, when we fear they won't be able to take it, we patronize them; we underestimate their emotional maturity and belittle their love of justice. Men don't need coddling, which is fortunate since we haven't time for it. Our time must be spent on the bonebreaking work of equality, and men must find their own strength to come along with us. We haven't enough energy or time to proselytize them, only enough—and barely that—for the immense and lifelong struggle before us. We are happy when they join us, but we cannot beg them to, or cajole, or spend our precious time helping them gently along. They are grown-ups. They are intelligent. They can read as well as we. They can figure it out. And to the extent that they are mature, and if they love us, they will join us, and we will be glad.

The cries of "man hater!" hurled at feminists are, it seems to me, a classic example of patriarchal reversal—of the "pedestals-are-the-pits" syndrome. This accusation is an attempt to disguise and to cover up men's own hatred and fear of women; it is a projection of their own unacceptable feelings, an attempt to drown out the fact that matters are just the other way around. When we begin to point out the misogyny of society, men and women whose total allegiance is to men attempt to distract us from the truth by turning it upside down, by pinning the blame on us. Women, most of whom don't, have every reason to hate men, and men precious little reason to hate women, except that they have abused us unconscionably for ages—and people always hate most those they have treated worst.

I cannot hate men. I have three sons whom I love as much as if they were daughters. But I mourn for them a thousand times more than I do for my daughter. She knows and loathes the inequities of the system and is fighting mad—a healthy, appropriate, and constructive response. My sons do not understand what is happening to them; the insidiousness of it defeats me, defeats them. It is everywhere—in the very air they breathe—that they must be tyrants to be real. Benevolent, gentle tyrants, perhaps—if they are lucky, they get that message, though many men do not—but still tyrants. And always at the mercy of their egos. I mourn for them that they have no models to follow out of the morass, that they see so few men horrified enough at what sexual bigotry is doing to the men as well as to the women of the human family that they have dedicated their lives to establishing equality. They only see their mother, which makes sexual equality look like another trivial women's issue, when it is, in fact, the most crucial issue on the face of the earth. If it is not dealt with effectively and globally and *soon*, the patriarchs hurtling headlong toward nuclear war will destroy the human race.

And women must do most of this work of equality, because men are lulled into an even deeper sleep than we are struggling to wake from. Women must rise up and be the saviors of the world.

Many scoff, "What makes you think women would do things any differently from men?" I am as aware as anyone of how women are co-opted by the male system of insensitivity and brutality. But still, the fact remains that, for the most part, women, in whose bodies life begins, do the nurturing and the protecting of the human family. Not because they are more nurturant by nature, but because this extraordinarily difficult role has been assigned them by men who want to do easier things. Women are the ones whose lives are poured into others' lives to make them possible and, sometimes and ideally, full and rich. Women therefore have a tremendous stake in human life, as a man has in the business he has owned and operated for twenty years. Life has been our career, almost our total responsibility. When a son or daughter falls in some obscene, casual, and useless patriarchal battle (women do not make military policy; we simply suffer men's wars), our life's work, our very existence, is negated. What have all those hours of careful tending and teaching, feeding the right foods, taking to the doctor and dentist, helping with homework, hearing the heartaches, insisting on decency, on baths, and vitamins—what has come of all that? That it—our lifework—should be totally wasted cannot be borne. Women are less and less willing to bear it, and will not if they have any say about it. That is why we must soon sit in the positions to say *no* to war and death—and have that *no* become policy, in the same way men's sole *no* to life has been policy for so long.

For the sake of the preservation of the human race, women must establish equality on this planet. This is why women are rising and coming forth in every nation under the sun.

One thing anguish has taught women is that we are incredibly strong. We can endure and survive anything. Every living woman has, after all, somehow survived so far in a world hostile to female-ness, to her very being. We are survivors of an offensive to enslave and destroy us which we each fight off every minute of our lives. But though it is a real feat, it is not enough merely to survive. We must see to it that neither women nor men yet unborn have to come into a world as dangerous, as gynecidal, as the one into which we were born. Standing as we are on the bowed shoulders and backs of the millions of caring, dedicated women who preceded us in our struggle for life, we must not now be dead weights, burdens. Recognizing that we are where we are because we stand on those shoulders, we must bow our own necks so the next generation of women can stand even higher, improving the quality of existence for every living soul, civilizing as we climb. Any woman who thinks she has made it on her own and owes no one anything is an ignoramus, a fool, and an embarrassment to womankind. We are who we are because of the courage of great women. We are deeply in debt.

We must pay as they did, by lifting in our turn. Lifting is risky; therefore, an immoderate act.

Men have always understood that they had to risk, to fight, per-haps to die for their human rights. They have always understood that justice is never bestowed, but that it is always wrested by intelli-gence and courage out of the hands of fate. What makes us think women's rights are going to be won with less travail than men's? Surely we understand that to win human rights for women, upon whose oppression the entire economy of the world rests, will require far greater immoderation, far greater sacrifice than has ever been nec-essary before in human history.

And we also know that immoderation—radicalism, if you will—is in the mainstream of the most hallowed American tradition. When we disobey laws to demonstrate that the laws of this country do not protect or include us, we are among the historic American patriots—the Boston Tea Partiers, the suffragists, the marchers in Selma,

Montgomery. Let us not forget that we are in the company of the great when we risk everything, immoderately, for justice and liberty. And we must not let the opposition define us otherwise. They, not us, stand outside these most honored themes of American history. Let us remember, as we picket, as we chain ourselves, as we have our pray-ins, as we go on hunger strikes, as we put our lives on the line for women—let us remember in whose footsteps we follow and take courage.

Who remembers the names of those in whose footsteps our opposition is treading? Their faces do not appear on our currency or in our textbooks. Or in our hearts.

Having before us powerful models, we can in our turn leave our children a legacy of courageous action. They can—and should—read about *us* in their history books. What greater lesson can we teach them than that justice is worth all they can give, and that if the few who guard it cease to believe this, life ceases to have meaning for the many?

We must not be deceived or defeated by the hypocrisy and condescension of those men who suggest that we seek equal rights state by state. When did men ever have to win their rights state by state? We must demand *now*, and if necessary at the peril of our lives, that we be granted civil rights in the same way white men in this country were granted them: by constitutional decree.

Women are locked in a life-and-death struggle with patriarchy. But while *it* is showing signs of senility, *we* are fresh and new to the world, as if we were just being born—because many of us are, young and old alike. Young and old women alike, we represent a new world of youth and vigor, and we cannot—if we *choose* not—be gainsaid. We are half the population of the world, more than half the population of this country, and our time has come. But it can pass us by if we sink into despair, into another "season of silence." It can pass us by if we are afraid of doing what other fighters for human rights have had to do to win them.

Women's time has come, but it can pass us by if we are afraid of civil disobedience, the kind of immoderate action which Thoreau named a duty. As Frederick Douglass said, "The limits of tyrants are prescribed by the endurance of those whom they oppress."

We stand at a crossroads in human history where for the first time equality under law is possible on more than a limited scale. We have no guarantee that this time will ever come again, that the circumstances which conspired to bring this precious fragile little chance into being now will ever conspire to do so again in the next ten thousand years. All we can know for certain is that it is here right now. And that, fortunately, so are we. And I like to think that we are here in this country at this time, the hundreds of thousands of strong women, and the men who genuinely love us, because we are the ones who can take this tiny chance hugely enough to fulfill its destiny. Right now, for just this one moment, justice is possible.

Just barely, I grant you. But possible nevertheless. A circumstance never before given this world. And we will never have a better time, a stronger chance. The possibility for justice is always fragile, always fleeting. And if we do not succeed, it will be because we were not willing to do what it takes. It will be upon our heads forever that we did not care enough. We must not spend the rest of our lives mourning to one another: Oh, if only we had recognized our place in history, if we had only understood our mission, if we had only risen to our potential, if we had only not been so afraid.

I do not believe in the progressive view of history, that things get better and better—with a few brief setbacks such as Hitler and Hiroshima—and that if we only wait long enough and live good lives, right will somehow prevail. I remember that millions of us were burned alive, nearly dead from torture and sexual abuse, *after* what men call the Dark Ages, in the rational days of Shakespeare and Bacon, of Descartes and Locke!

A better time for women to win legal justice will never come. This is the best we are going to get.

I often hear people say, "It will take a miracle to pass the ERA." "So?" I ask them. "So don't you believe in miracles? *I* believe in them. I have to. I have seen them with my own eyes. I saw us win an extension of time for the ERA in the fall of 1978. That was such a slim little hope, none of us really dared believe it was possible, that we could really do it (grossly underestimating ourselves, as usual). And then we saw the Red Sea open before us. A true miracle, and those of us who witnessed it should never doubt again. It happened once, it can happen again—if, that is, we rise as we rose then.

I have faith in American women. I believe that when it begins to be apparent that our only chance for justice, for full humanity, is about to be lost—perhaps forever—we will rise as we have never risen before. If we do, nothing can withstand us. And we will win.

Susan B. Anthony—that most immoderate, extreme, unladylike of women (arrested for civil disobedience when voting before voting was legal for women)—was speaking once to a group of young women, and feeling very frustrated. She had spent seventy years of her life working for women's rights and could not get some women to care enough to spend seventy seconds. "I really believe I shall explode if some of you young women don't wake up and raise your voices in protest," she cried. "I wonder if when I'm under the sod—or cremated and floating in the air—I shall have to stir you and others up. How can you not be all on fire?"

I often invoke the great women of our past, because I think it is legitimate to invoke any good and caring souls in this work, and also because I remember something Susan B. Anthony wrote shortly before her death: "I don't know much about the other life . . . but this I do believe, that if anyone there can help or influence those who are left behind in this life, I will come to you." And so I pray, "Susan, Elizabeth, Sojourner, Alice—all you great liberty-loving women whose atoms float over our land—come back to us now and stir us up. Right now, when there is still time to win the struggle you so courageously began. Come back and ignite us again. Make us burn as you burned. Dear sisters, help us be all on fire!"

Sonia Johnson

SONIA JOHNSON was born in 1936 in Malad, Idaho, and grew up in Logan, Utah. She graduated from Utah State University and was married a year later. She moved many times in the course of her husband's career, but managed to earn an M.A. degree from Rutgers University while caring for her first child, and finished her dissertation for her Ed.D. degree only hours before delivering her second. She was a part-time teacher when her other children arrived, the third being born in California and the youngest in Malaysia. Ms. Johnson lives with her four children in Sterling, Virginia.